Adobe® GoLive™ 5.0

Classroom in a Book

Adobe® GoLive™ 5.0 Classroom in a Book® for Windows® and Macintosh

ISBN: 0-201-71017-X

10 9 8 7 6 5 4 3 2 First Printing: June 1999

Any references to company names in sample templates are for demonstration purposes only and are not intended to refer to any actual organization. The names of guitars and amplifiers listed herein are real, however the vintage guitar company is fictitious and no offer of sale is being made for the listed guitars and amplifiers.

The Princess and the Frog Prince by William Baeck.

Three Little Hermit Crabs by Judy Walters von Alten.

Forever Four by Tanya Wendling.

Adobe Systems Incorporated, 345 Park Avenue, San Jose, California 95110, USA.

Contents

Creating Rollovers

Creating Animations

Using Actions and JavaScript

Creating Forms

Using Cascading Style Sheets

Getting Started

Welcome to Adobe® GoLive™ 5.0—the future of Web site management and page creation. GoLive is an extremely flexible design and production tool that offers unparalleled precision, control, and seamless Smart Object integration with Adobe's professional Web applications, including Adobe Photoshop®, Adobe Illustrator®, and Adobe LiveMotion™. Easily create rollovers and animations, and add Macromedia® Flash™ (SWF) files and QuickTime movies to your Web pages. Then model your site with the new management tools, and publish it on the Web.

About Classroom in a Book

Adobe GoLive 5.0 Classroom in a Book® is part of the official training series for Adobe graphics, Web, and publishing tools developed by experts at Adobe Systems. The lessons are designed to let you learn at your own pace. If you're new to Adobe GoLive, you'll learn the fundamental concepts and features that you'll need to master the program. If you've been using Adobe GoLive for a while, you'll find Classroom in a Book teaches many advanced features, including tips and techniques for using this exciting Web design tool.

Although each lesson provides step-by-step instructions for creating a specific project, there's room for exploration and experimentation. You can follow the book from start to finish, or do only the lessons that correspond to your interests and needs.

Prerequisites

Before using the *Adobe GoLive 5.0 Classroom in a Book*, you should have a working knowledge of your computer and its operating system. Make sure that you know how to use the mouse and standard menus and commands, and also how to open, save, and close files. If you need to review these techniques, see the printed or online documentation included with your Windows® or Mac OS documentation.

Installing the program

You must purchase the Adobe GoLive software separately. For complete instructions on installing the software, see the Introduction to the *Adobe GoLive 5.0 User Guide*.

Navigation Services

The Navigation Services feature changes the appearance and behavior of the Open and Save dialog boxes. This feature is always available at the system level, and can be controlled on an individual application basis.

Due to conflicts between Navigation Services and Mac OS 8.6 and earlier, the lessons in this book do not use Navigation Services. Adobe strongly recommends deactivating the Use Navigation Services option. By default, Adobe GoLive does not use Navigation Services. However, if you need to deactivate this option, choose > Edit > Preferences > User Interface> Display, and deselect it.

Installing the Classroom in a Book fonts

To ensure that the lesson files appear on your system with the correct fonts, you may need to install the Classroom in a Book font files. The fonts for the lessons are located in the Fonts folder on the *Adobe GoLive 5.0 Classroom in a Book* CD. If you already have these on your system, you do not need to install them. If you have ATM® (Adobe Type Manager®), see its documentation on how to install fonts. If you do not have ATM, installing it from the Classroom in a Book CD will automatically install the necessary fonts.

Copying the Classroom in a Book files

The Classroom in a Book CD includes folders containing all the electronic files for the lessons. Each lesson has its own folder, and you must copy the folders to your hard drive to do the lessons. To save room on your drive, you can install only the necessary folder for each lesson as you need it, and remove it when you're done.

To install the Classroom in a Book files:

1 Insert the *Adobe GoLive 5.0 Classroom in a Book* CD into your CD-ROM drive.

2 Create a folder named GL_CIB on your hard drive.

3 Copy the lessons that you want to the hard drive:

• To copy all of the lessons, drag the Lessons folder from the CD into the GL_CIB folder.

• To copy a single lesson, drag the individual lesson folder from the CD into the GL_CIB folder.

If you are installing the files in Windows, you need to unlock them before using them. You don't need to unlock the files if you are installing them in Mac OS.

4 In Windows, unlock the files that you copied:

• If you copied all of the lessons, double-click the Unlock.bat file in the GL_CIB/Lessons folder.

• If you copied a single lesson, drag the Unlock.bat file from the Lessons folder on the CD into the GL_CIB folder. Then double-click the Unlock.bat file in the GL_CIB folder.

Additional resources

The *Adobe GoLive 5.0 Classroom in a Book* is not meant to replace documentation that comes with the program. Only the commands and options used in the lessons are explained in this book. For comprehensive information about program features, refer to these resources:

• The *Adobe GoLive 5.0 User Guide*, included with the Adobe GoLive software. This guide contains a complete description of all features.

• Online Help, an online version of the User Guide. You can view the online Help by choosing Help > GoLive Help. (For more information, see Lesson 1, "Getting to Know the Work Area.")

• The Adobe Web site (www.adobe.com). You can view the Adobe Web site by choosing Help > Adobe Online, if you have a connection to the World Wide Web.

color:maroon;
STYLE>
-- Begin main table -->
BLE BORDER="4" CELLPADD
<TR>
<TD><A
//www.adobe.com/">Adobe</A>
<TD>GoLive</TD>
<TD><IMG BORDER="0" HEI
gif" ALT="Title"></TD>
</TR>
<TR>
<TD><SPAN CLASS=
</TD>
</TR>
<TR>
<TD><B>DHTML
</TR>
TABLE>
EQUIV="content-type
charset=iso-8859-
n table
="4" CELLPADD
e.com/">Adobe
GoLive</TD>
<IMG BORDER="0" HEI
Title"></TD>
<SPAN CLASS=
<B>DHTML

Lesson 1

```
<TITLE>Wel
<STYLE TYPE=

e{color:maroon;

</STYLE>
AD>
Y>
<!-- Begin main table -->
<TABLE BORDER="4" CELLPADDI
06">
    <TR>
        <TD><A
tp://www.adobe.com/">Adobe</A>
        <TD>GoLive</TD>
        <TD><IMG BORDER="0" HEI
le.gif" ALT="Title"></TD>
    </TR>
    <TR>
        <TD><SPAN CLASS="headli
AN></TD>
    </TR>
    <TR>
        <TD><B>DHTML ani
    </TR>
</TABLE>
DY>

  P-EQUIV="content-typ
  charset=iso-8859
  come to Adobe GoLi

main table -->
DER="4" CELLPAD

D><A
dobe.com/">Adobe</A
D>GoLive</TD>
D><IMG BORDER="0" HE
="Title"></TD>

D><SPAN CLASS="head

D><B>DHTML
```

1 Getting to Know the Work Area

In this lesson, you'll learn how to use the basic features of Adobe GoLive by exploring and modifying an existing Web site. You'll practice using site windows, document windows, the context-sensitive toolbar, the most commonly used palettes, and online Help. When you've finished modifying the site, you'll preview your work in both Adobe GoLive and a Web browser.

About this lesson

In this lesson, you'll learn how to do the following:

- Open a Web site and page in Adobe GoLive, and customize your work area.
- Display a graphical view of a site in a secondary site window.
- Use the View Controller to see what files haven't been used yet in a site.
- Use the toolbar to both format text and locate a file in the Files tab of the site window.
- Display, hide, collapse, move, and resize palettes.
- Use the Objects palette to add an image placeholder to a page.
- Use the Inspector to link an image placeholder to an image file.
- Use the Color palette to color text.
- Add keywords to a page.
- Display context menus and use online Help.
- Preview a site using Adobe GoLive and a Web browser.

This lesson takes approximately 30 minutes to complete.

If needed, copy the Lesson01 folder onto your hard drive. As you work on this lesson, you'll overwrite the start files. If you need to restore the start files, copy them from the *Adobe GoLive 5.0 Classroom in a Book* CD.

Note: *Windows users need to unlock the lesson files before using them. For more information, see "Copying the Classroom in a Book files" on page 2.*

Getting started

In this lesson, you'll open, view, and modify a Web site for a fictional company called First Strike Matches. As a result, you'll learn about the Adobe GoLive work area, including its site windows, document windows, context-sensitive toolbar, most commonly used palettes, context menus, and online Help.

First you'll view the finished site in your Web browser.

1 Start your browser.

2 Open the Index.html file, the home page for the site. The path to the file is Lesson01/01End/Matchbox Folder/Matchbox/Index.html.

The home page welcomes viewers to First Strike Matches and contains links to other pages in the site: a page that describes product features and a page that provides answers to common questions.

3 Explore the site by clicking links on the home page and the other pages of the site.

4 When you have finished viewing the site, close it and quit your browser.

Setting up your work area

We recommend that you set up your work area as shown in the following illustration. Place the document window at the top, the primary site window at the bottom, and the palettes on the right side of the desktop. (To move a window, drag its title bar.)

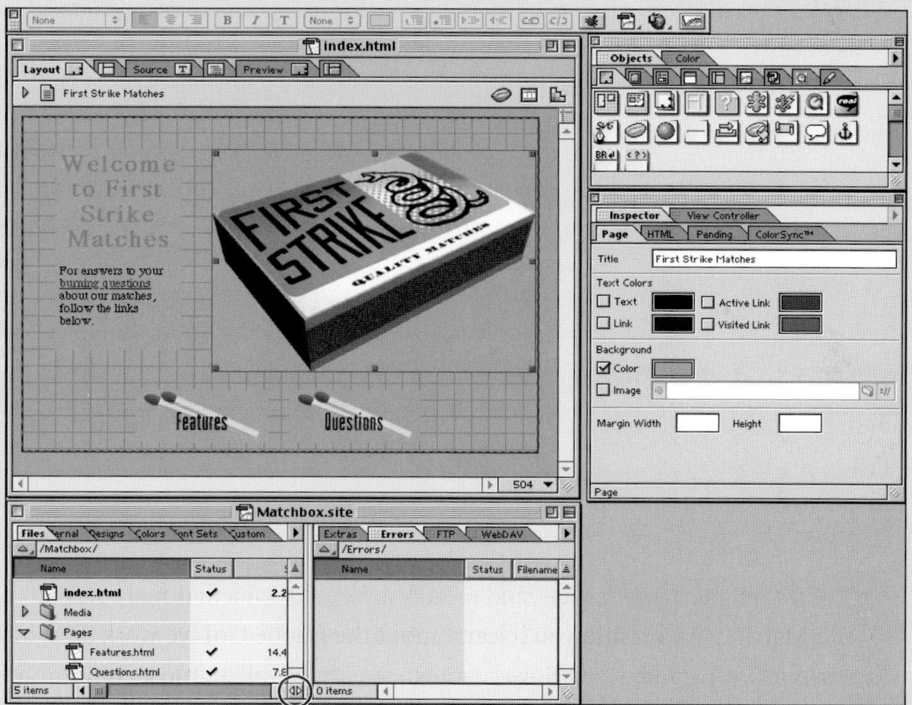

To display or hide the expanded pane of the primary site window, click the double-headed arrow in the lower right area of the window.

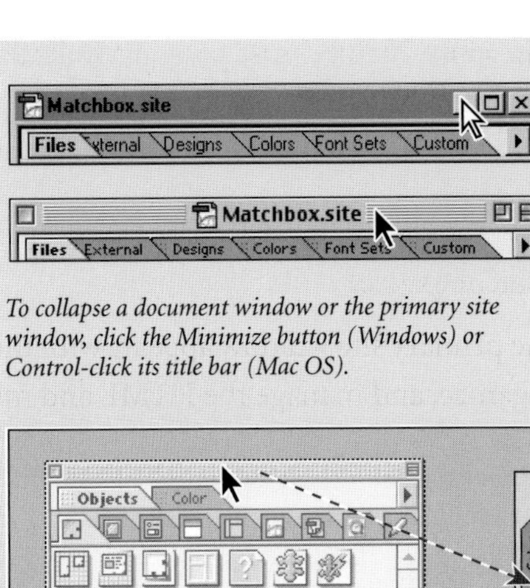

To collapse a document window or the primary site window, click the Minimize button (Windows) or Control-click its title bar (Mac OS).

To expand one of these windows, click the Maximize button (Windows) or click the tab at the bottom of the screen (Mac OS).

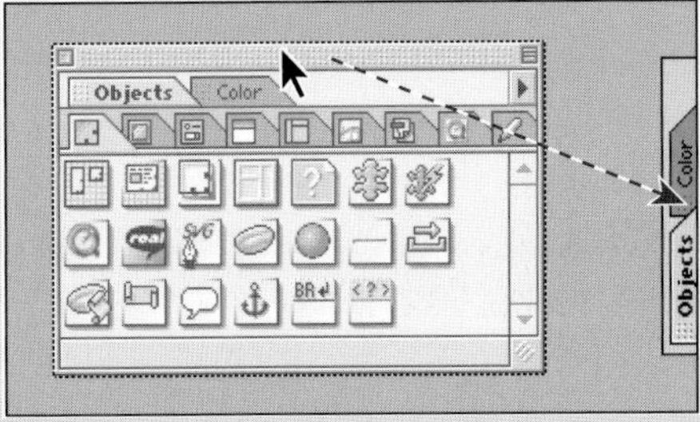

To collapse a group of palettes to a tab at the right of the screen, Ctrl-click the title bar of the group window. To expand the group window, click the tab at the right of the screen.

If your workspace is limited, you can keep the primary site window collapsed and still connect files to placeholders on the page using the Point and Shoot button in the Inspector. Drag from the Point and Shoot button to the primary site window, and continue to hold down the mouse button. The primary site window expands, and you can drag to the desired file in the window.

Using site windows

You'll begin this lesson by opening the First Strike Matches Web site in Adobe GoLive. First, you'll view the site in its primary site window and then you'll view the site in a secondary site window.

Using the primary site window

You use the primary site window to manage the resources for your site, including files, e-mail addresses, URLs, a custom color palette, and custom font sets.

1 Start Adobe GoLive. A new document named Untitled.html opens, and several palettes are displayed in several groups by default.

Because you don't need a new document or palettes at this point in the lesson, you'll close Untitled.html and hide any displayed palettes.

2 Choose File > Close to close Untitled.html.

3 To hide each group of palettes, click the close box in the upper right (Windows) or upper left (Mac OS) corner of the group window.

Now you're ready to open the site.

4 Choose File > Open, select the Matchbox.site file, and click Open. The path to the file is Lesson01/01Start/Matchbox Folder/Matchbox.site.

When you open the Matchbox.site file, the primary site window appears with the Files tab selected. You use the Files tab to view, organize, and manage the HTML and media files that are used to create your site.

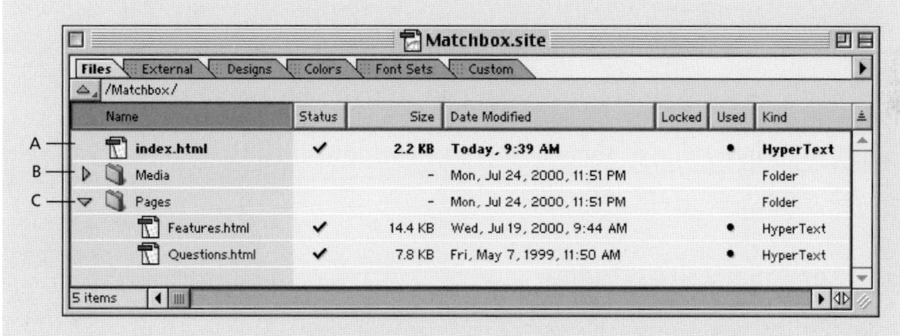

***A.** Index.html, home page for site* ***B.** Media folder where you store images and other media files*
***C.** Pages folder where you store HTML files for additional pages*

To make room for other windows and palettes that you'll display during this lesson, we recommend that you position the primary site window at the bottom of your work area.

5 If needed, reposition the primary site window by dragging its title bar, and resize the window by dragging its lower right corner.

Now you'll select another tab in the primary site window.

6 Click the Colors tab to select it.

The Colors tab contains a list of colors that are used in the site. You can use the Colors tab as a custom color palette to easily color text and objects throughout your site.

Now you'll display the right pane of the primary site window.

7 To display the right pane of the primary site window, click the double-headed arrow () in the lower right area of the window.

The right pane appears with the Extras tab selected. You use the Extras tab to view, organize, and manage additional files for your site, including HTML files that are used as components and stationery.

You can easily hide the right pane when you aren't using it.

8 To hide the right pane of the primary site window, click the double-headed arrow below the scroll bar for the left pane.

Using a secondary site window

Now you'll display a graphical view of the site in a secondary site window.

1 To display a graphical view of the site, click the Navigation View button ( ) on the toolbar, or choose Design > Navigation View.

Clicking Navigation View button on toolbar

A secondary site window appears with the Navigation tab selected. You use the Navigation tab to view how your site is structured from a navigational point of view. The home page appears at the top of the tab with a plus sign. When you click the plus sign and any additional plus signs that appear in the tab, you can expand the view, so that the pages that are linked to the home page appear below it.

2 In the Navigation tab, click the plus sign to expand the view.

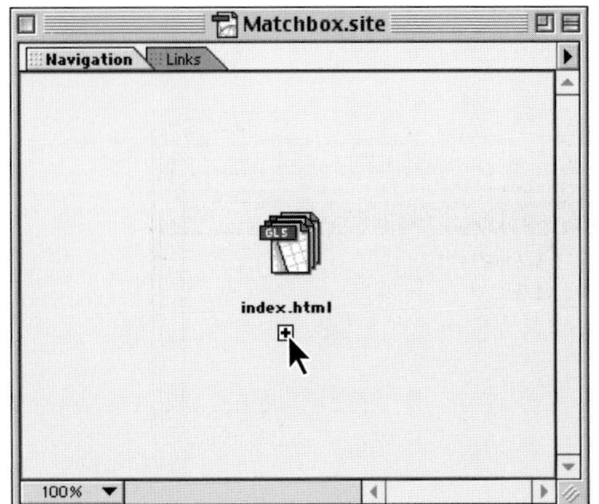

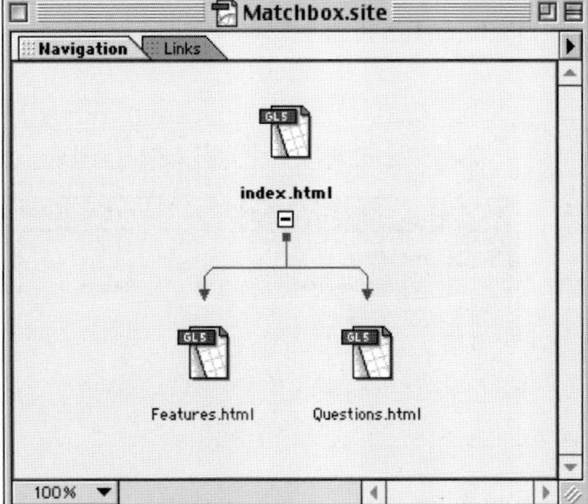

Clicking plus sign *Expanded view*

If desired, you can change the orientation of the view using the View Controller.

3 Choose Window > View Controller to display the View Controller.

We recommend that you position the View Controller and any other palettes on the right side of your work area.

4 If needed, reposition the View Controller by dragging the title bar of its group window, and resize the View Controller by dragging its lower right corner.

5 In the View Controller, click the Navigation tab. Under Orientation, select Tall. The pages that are linked to the home page now appear to the right of it.

Now you'll use the View Controller to see what files in your site haven't been used yet.

6 In the View Controller, under Show Panes, select Scratch.

The Matchbox.gif file appears in the Scratch pane, indicating that it hasn't been used on any pages of the site. Later in this lesson, you'll use this file to add an image of a matchbox to the home page.

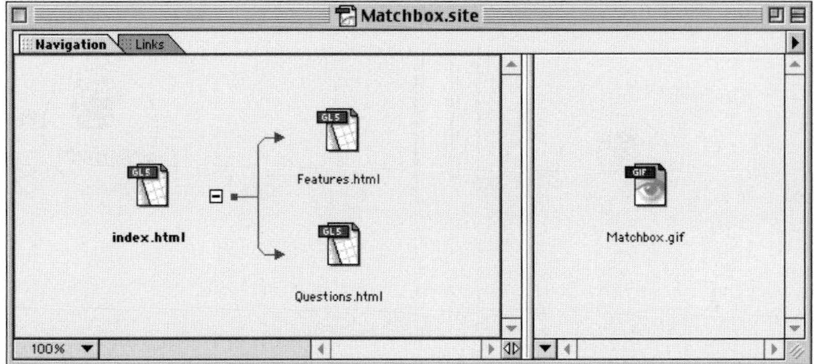

Navigation tab with Scratch pane shown

Because you have finished using the View Controller, you can hide it.

7 Choose Window > View Controller to hide it and any palettes in its group.

You can easily move a tab between site windows to customize your work area.

8 If needed, reposition the secondary site window so that it doesn't overlap the primary site window.

9 Drag the Navigation tab from the secondary site window to the primary site window.

Now you can select and view the Navigation tab from within the primary site window.

10 Click the Navigation tab to select it.

You can also move a tab outside of a site window so that it appears on its own in a new site window.

11 Drag the Navigation tab from the primary site window to an empty space in your work area.

When you move two tabs to two separate windows, you can sometimes use them in conjunction. For example, if the Navigation and Links tabs are in separate windows, you can select a page in the Navigation tab as a way of locating the page in the Links tab.

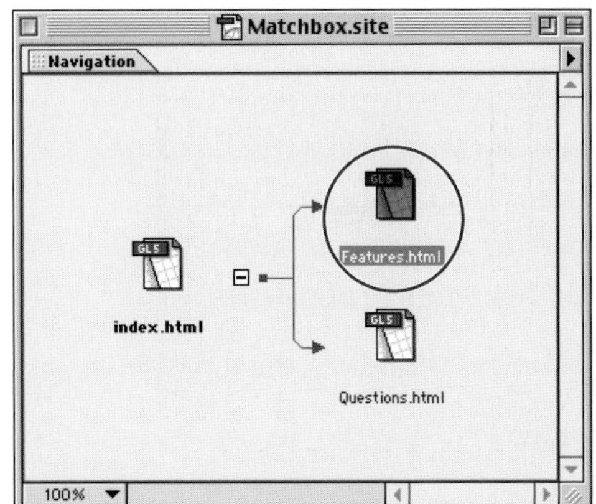

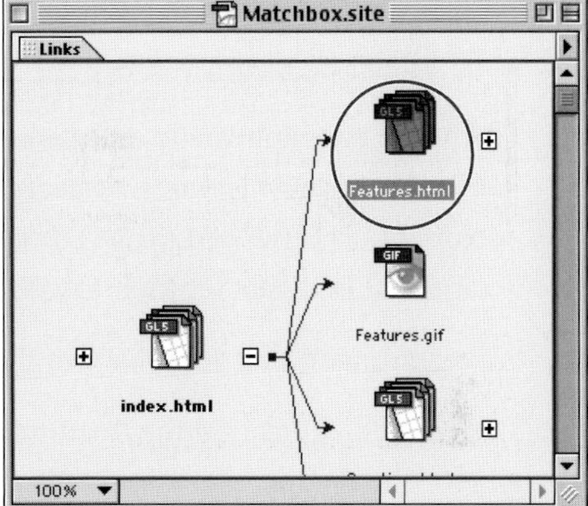

Once you've customized your work area by moving tabs between and outside of site windows, you can easily return the tabs to their default configuration.

12 Click the triangle in the upper right corner of the primary site window to display a menu, and choose Default Configuration.

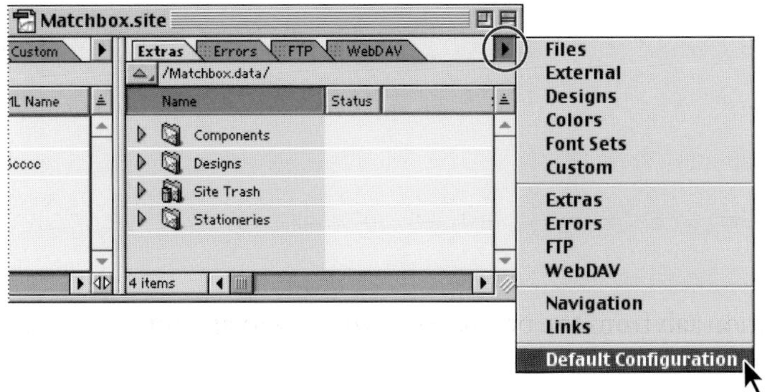

Choosing Default Configuration from pop-up menu

Using the document window

Now you'll open the home page for the First Strike Matches Web site in Adobe GoLive. You can open the home page directly from the Files tab of the primary site window.

1 Click the Files tab of the primary site window to select it.

2 In the Files tab, double-click the Index.html file.

The home page appears in a document window with the Layout Editor tab selected. The document window features a variety of tabs, which you use to either edit or preview your document. You use the Layout Editor tab, or Layout view, to add text and objects to your document, as well as set their attributes, using a variety of palettes.

We recommend that you position the document window at the top of your work area.

3 If needed, reposition the document window by dragging its title bar, and resize the window by dragging its lower right corner.

The document window contains a variety of objects as shown in the following illustration. You'll learn how to add these objects and other objects to your pages as you work on the lessons in this book.

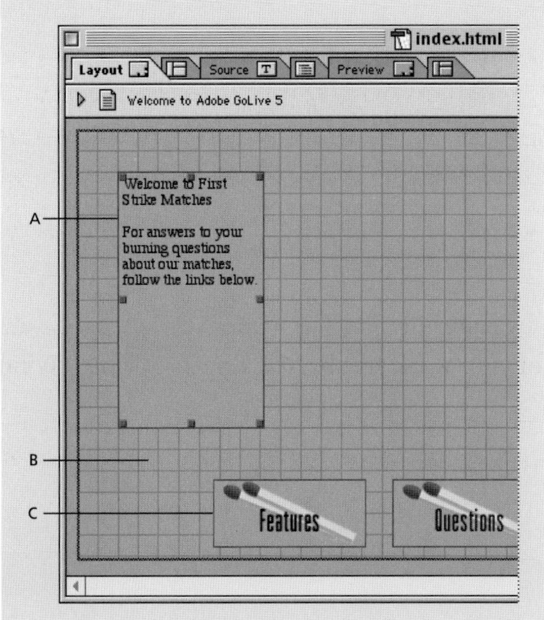

***A.** Layout text box* ***B.** Layout grid* ***C.** Image*

You can easily change the document view by selecting another tab in the document window.

4 Click the HTML Source Editor tab (T) to view the document in Source view.

You use the Source view to design your document using an HTML text editor.

5 Click the Layout Editor tab to return to Layout view.

Now you'll change the title of the page. When viewed in a Web browser, the title of the page appears in the title bar of the browser.

6 Select the page title, "Welcome to Adobe GoLive 5."

7 Type **First Strike Matches** as the new title, and press Enter or Return.

Using the toolbar

In Adobe GoLive, the toolbar is context-sensitive, which means that its contents change depending on what you have selected in the work area. When you edit a document in Layout view, you can use the toolbar to modify selected text and objects. When you work in the site window, you can use the toolbar to perform general site-management tasks.

Now you'll use the toolbar to format text on the home page of the First Strike Matches Web site.

1 If needed, display the toolbar by choosing Window > Toolbar, and reposition the toolbar in the upper left corner of your work area by dragging its title bar (Windows) or lower left corner (Mac OS).

2 In the document window, select the "Welcome to First Strike Matches" heading.

3 Click the Bold button (B) on the toolbar to make the selected text bold.

4 Click the Align Center button on the toolbar to align the selected text in the center of the layout text box.

5 Choose 6 from the Font Size menu on the toolbar to apply a custom font size that overrides the browser's preferences.

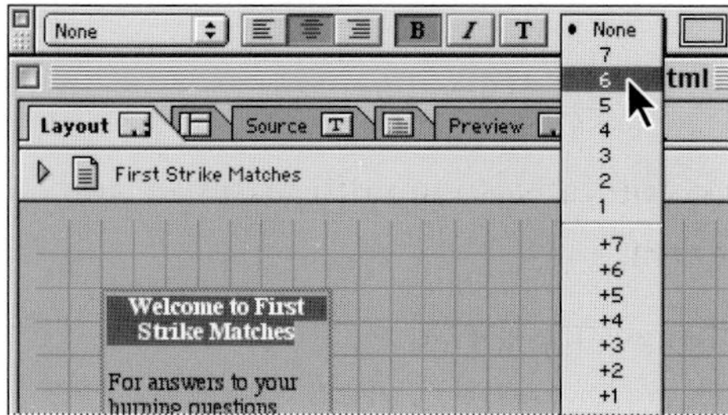

Choosing 6 from Font Size menu

6 Click in the blank space outside the selected text to deselect it.

7 Choose File > Save to save the Index.html file.

Now you'll use the toolbar to locate a file in the Files tab of the primary site window. Using the toolbar to locate files within a site can save you time when working with unfamiliar or larger sites. You'll locate the Matchbox.gif file, which you'll use later in this lesson to add an image of a matchbox to the home page.

First you'll switch to the primary site window, so that the contents of the toolbar change to provide you with site management tools.

8 To switch to the primary site window, click its title bar or click the Select Window button ( ) on the toolbar.

9 Make sure that the Files tab of the primary site window is selected.

10 Click the Find Files in Site button ( ) on the toolbar.

11 In the Find dialog box, make sure that "Name" and "begins with" are chosen from the menus. Then enter **Matchbox** in the text box, and click Find.

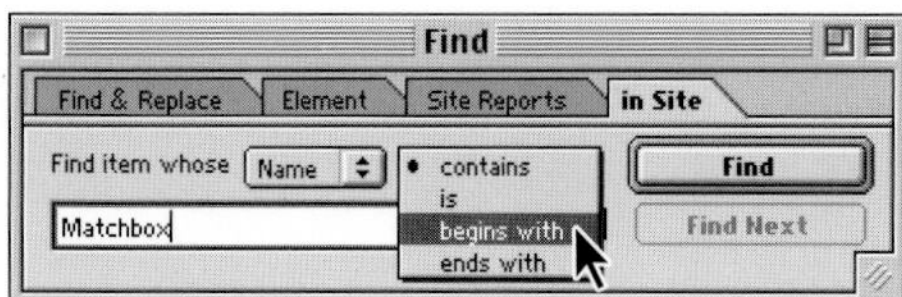

Setting options in Find dialog box

In the Files tab of the primary site window, Adobe GoLive automatically opens the Media folder and selects the Matchbox.gif file.

Using palettes

Adobe GoLive features several palettes that you can use to perform a variety of tasks. You can display and hide palettes as you work. You can also reposition, resize, and collapse palettes to make better use of your work area.

1 Choose Window > Reset Palettes to display all palettes.

Because you need only the Objects palette, Inspector, and Color palette to complete the rest of this lesson, you'll hide the groups of palettes that don't contain these specific palettes.

2 To hide each unneeded group of palettes, click the close box in the upper right (Windows) or upper left (Mac OS) corner of the group window.

If you aren't using a group of palettes right away, you can also collapse the group to a tab at the right of the screen, rather than hide it. When you need the group of palettes later, you can expand it for your use.

3 Ctrl-click the title bar of the group window that contains the Inspector and View Controller to collapse the group.

4 If needed, reposition the group window containing the Objects palette and Color palette by dragging its title bar, and resize the window by dragging its lower right corner.

Using the Objects palette

The Objects palette contains several tabs. Each tab contains a group of related icons, which represent HTML tags, structural page elements, or generic site objects. You use these icons to add objects to your pages, including layout grids, layout text boxes, floating boxes, tables, images, and more.

To display the Objects palette, you can choose Window > Objects. By default, the Objects palette appears with the Basic tab selected.

1 If needed, click Objects to bring the Objects palette to the front of its group, and then click the Basic tab ( ) of the Objects palette.

Now you'll view the name of the icons in the Basic tab of the Objects palette.

2 To view the name of an icon, position the pointer on top of the icon. The name of the icon appears at the bottom of the Objects palette.

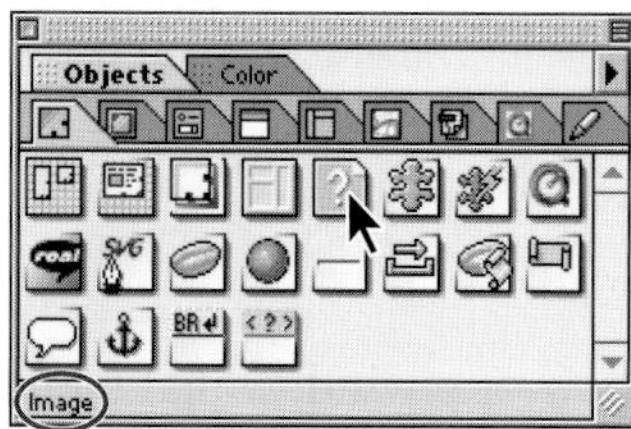

Viewing name of icon

Now you'll use the Objects palette to add an image placeholder to the home page. You'll use this placeholder to add an image of a matchbox to the page.

3 Drag the Image icon from the Objects palette to the blank space to the right of the welcome text on the home page. (You can also double-click the Image icon in the Objects palette.)

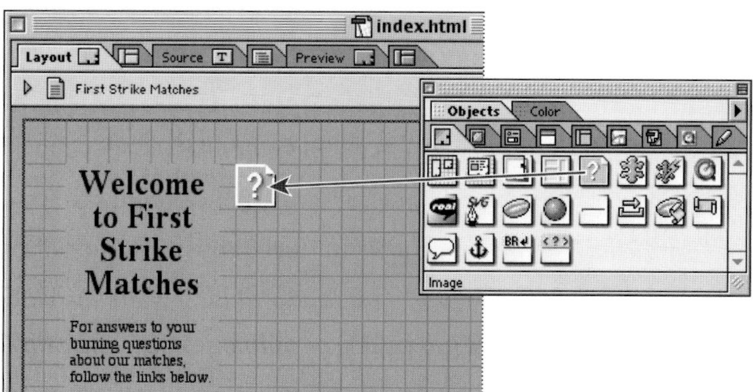

Dragging Image icon to document window

Now you'll use the toolbar to precisely position the image placeholder on the page.

4 Make sure that the image placeholder is selected. On the toolbar, enter **170** in the Horizontal Position text box and **32** in the Vertical Position text box.

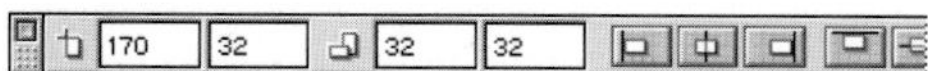

Using the Inspector

The context-sensitive Inspector lets you set attributes for what you have selected in the work area, such as text and objects in the document window, or files and other elements in the site window. To display the Inspector, you can choose Window > Inspector.

Now you'll use the Inspector to link the image placeholder on the page to the Matchbox.gif file in the Files tab of the primary site window.

1 Click the tab at the right of the screen to expand the group window that contains the Inspector and View Controller.

2 If needed, click the Inspector to bring the Inspector to the front of its group.

Because you have the image placeholder selected in the document window, the Inspector changes to the Image Inspector. Notice that the word Image appears at the bottom of the Inspector, indicating the name of the Inspector.

3 Drag from the Point and Shoot button (◎) in the Inspector to the Matchbox.gif file in the Files tab of the primary site window.

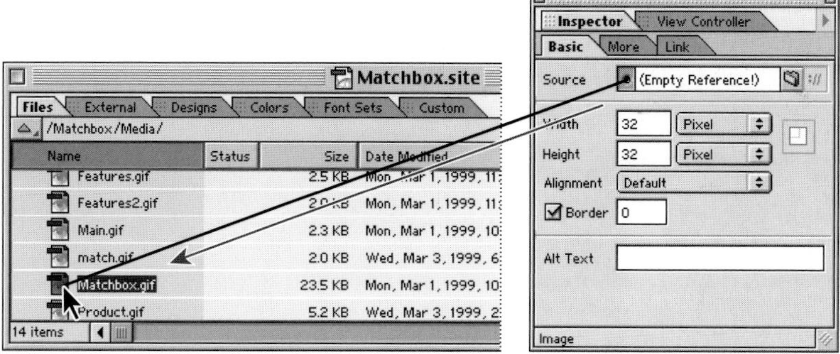

Dragging from Point and Shoot button to image file in site window

When the link has been successfully created, the path to the file appears in the Source text box in the Image Inspector.

Using the Color palette

The Color palette lets you color text and objects on your page. After making a selection in the document window, you can choose a color from the Color palette to have the color automatically applied to your selection. To display the Color palette, you can choose Window > Color.

Now you'll color the heading on the home page orange, so that it stands out even further on the page and attracts viewers.

1 In the document window, select the "Welcome to First Strike Matches" heading.

Notice that the word Text now appears at the bottom of the Inspector, indicating that the Inspector has changed to the Text Inspector. You can use the Text Inspector to set attributes for the selected text, such as creating a hypertext link or applying a style.

2 Click the Text Color field on the toolbar to select it and display the Color palette.

Notice that the Color palette contains several buttons. By clicking these buttons, you can display several individual palettes from which you can choose when selecting a color. In this lesson, you'll use the Web Color List button of the Color palette, which contains 216 colors that don't dither and are safe for use on the Web across platforms.

3 In the Color palette, click the Web Color List button (). Then select #FF6633 from the list, or type **FF6633** in the Value text box and press Enter or Return.

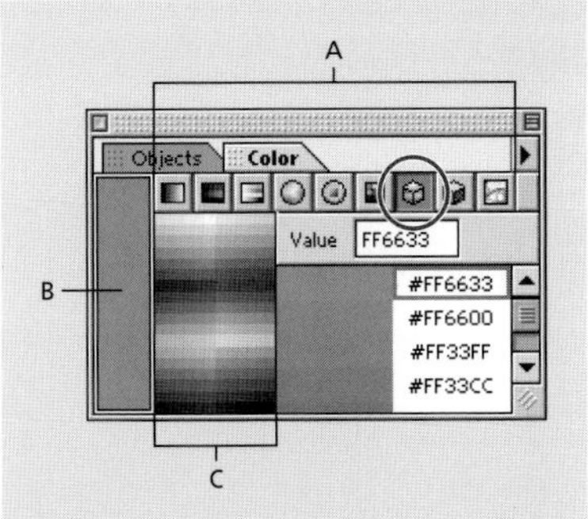

A. Buttons that display individual palettes
B. Preview pane C. Swatches

Adobe GoLive automatically applies the color to the selected text in the document window.

4 Choose File > Save.

Adding keywords

Now you'll add keywords to the page. Keywords are used by search engines to identify the topics on your page.

1 Click the triangle (▷) next to the Page icon in the upper left corner of the document window to open the head section pane.

You can use the head section pane to store information about your page, including the page title and keywords.

2 In the Objects palette, click the Head tab (⊟). Then drag the Keywords icon from the Objects palette to the head section pane in the document window.

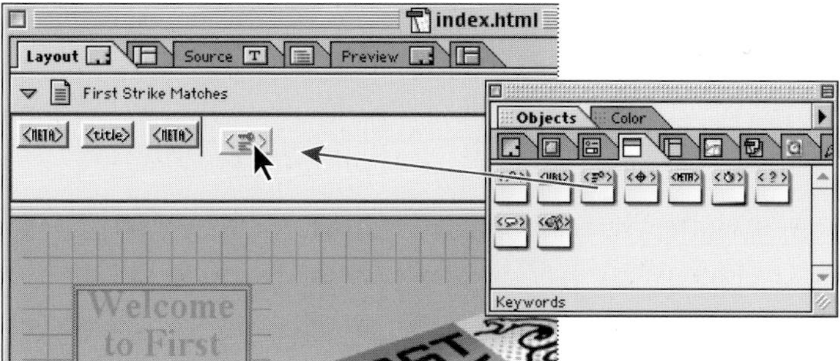

The Inspector changes to the Keywords Inspector.

3 In the Keywords Inspector, enter a word or phrase that you want to use as a keyword in the text box below the scrolling text box. (We used the phrase "First Strike Matches.") Then click Add, or press Enter or Return.

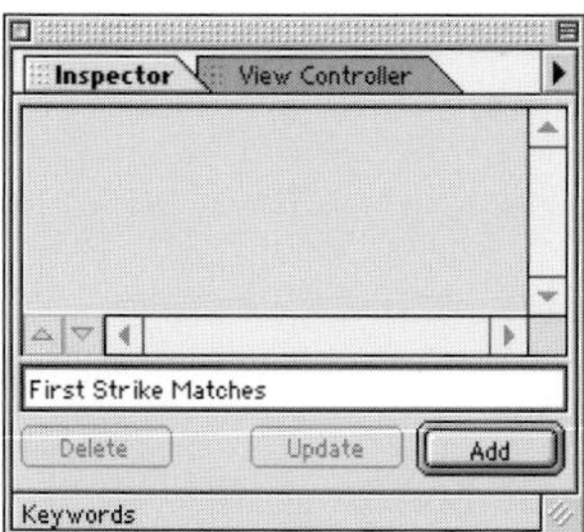

4 Click the triangle next to the Page icon to close the head section pane.

5 Choose File > Save.

Using context menus

You can use context menus as a quick way to choose commonly used commands. To display context menus, position the pointer over the active window or selection. Then do one of the following:

- In Windows, click with the right mouse button.
- In Mac OS, press Control and hold down the mouse button.

Previewing in Adobe GoLive

Now that you've finished modifying the home page of the First Strike Matches Web site, you'll preview the page in Adobe GoLive. To do so, you first need to make sure that the Preview Mode is activated in the Modules Preferences.

1 Choose Edit > Preferences, click Modules in the left pane of the Preferences dialog box, select Preview Mode, and click OK.

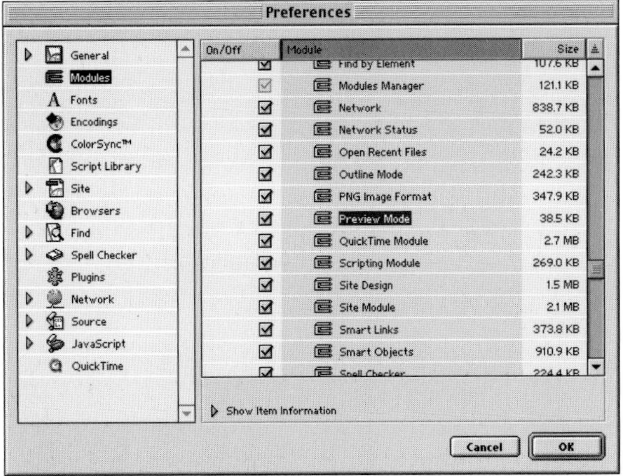

2 In the document window, click the Layout Preview tab (▣) to view the document in Preview.

The Preview displays an approximation of what your page looks like when it's finally published on the Web. You can test links, preview animated GIFs, and preview QuickTime movies in the Preview.

If you are using Adobe GoLive for Mac OS, you can use the View Controller in conjunction with the Preview to see an approximation of what your page looks like in a variety of browsers.

3 In Mac OS, click View Controller to bring the View Controller to the front of its group, or choose Window > View Controller to display the View Controller. In the View Controller, choose "Explorer 5 (Windows)" from the Root CSS menu to see how your page appears in Microsoft Internet Explorer 5 on a Windows platform. Try the different menu options and observe how your page changes in the preview. Notice that the text increases in size whenever you switch to a Windows-based browser.

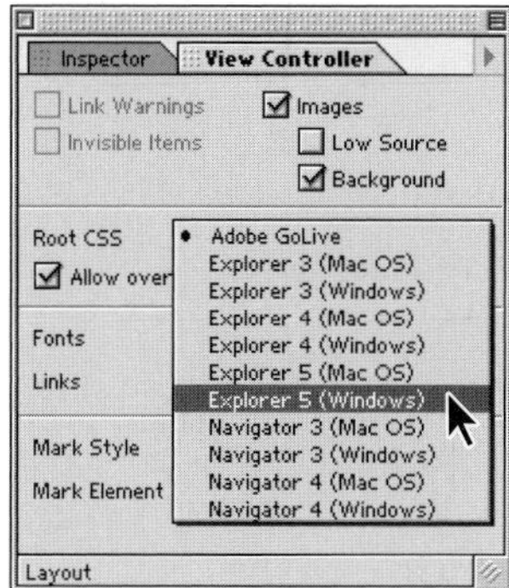

Choosing option from Root CSS menu (Mac OS)

4 Test the links on the home page and the other pages of the site.

Previewing in a Web browser

In addition to previewing your page in Adobe GoLive, you should always preview it using a variety of browsers, browser versions, and platforms. You'll need to use browsers to determine potential browser differences and to preview items for which Adobe GoLive doesn't provide native support.

To preview your page in a browser, you first need to install one or more browsers on your hard disk.

1 Make sure that each browser is installed on your hard disk and that all plug-ins for previewing are placed in the browser's Plug-ins folder (or any other location that your browser uses for multimedia extensions).

Next, you need to set preferences for browsers in Adobe GoLive.

2 Choose Edit > Preferences, and click the Browsers icon in the left pane of the Preferences dialog box.

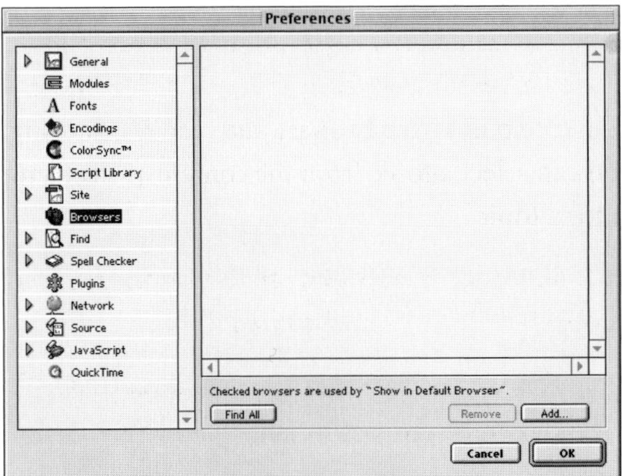

3 Do one of the following:

• To add all browsers on your hard disk to the browser list, click Find All.

• To add a single browser, click Add. Then select the browser, and click Open (Windows), or click Add and then click Done (Mac OS).

4 Select one or more browsers in the scrolling window that you want to be launched when you either click the Show in Browser button ( ) on the toolbar or choose Special > Show in Default Browser.

5 Click OK.

Now you're ready to preview the page in a browser.

6 Click the triangle in the lower right corner of the Show in Browser button on the toolbar, and then choose the desired browser from the pop-up menu.

Choosing browser from pop-up menu

7 When you have finished viewing the site, close it and quit your browser.

Using online Help

Adobe GoLive includes complete documentation in online Help, including all of the information in the *Adobe GoLive 5.0 User Guide*, a list of keyboard shortcuts, and information for advanced users on actions, AppleScript, cascading style sheets, HTML, QuickTime movies, WebDAV, and Web settings. While you work on the design of your Web site, you can open the online Help in a Web browser and read about using Adobe GoLive. To use online Help, you can select a topic from the contents, select a topic from the index, or conduct a search for a topic.

Now you'll use the online Help in three different ways to find information on using the document window. First you'll select a topic from the contents.

1 In Adobe GoLive, choose Help > GoLive Help to open the online Help in a browser. The first level of contents appears in the left pane of the online Help.

2 Click the "Looking at the Work Area" topic in the left pane to select it. A second level of contents for the selected topic appears in the right pane.

3 Click the "Using the document window" topic in the right pane to select it. If desired, read the information that appears in the right pane on using the document window.

Now you'll select a topic from the index on using the document window.

4 Click Index from the navigation bar at the top left of the online Help. The beginning of the index for the online Help appears in the left pane.

5 Click the "D" at the top right of the left pane to select it. Topics in the index beginning with the selected letter appear.

6 If necessary, scroll down the left pane until you see the "document windows" topic and the list of subtopics that appears below it.

Notice that one or more numbers appear to the right of each subtopic. When you click on a "1," you go to the first place in the online Help where the subtopic is indexed. When you click on a "2," you go to the second place in the online Help where the subtopic is indexed, and so on.

7 Click the "2" to the right of the Resizing subtopic. If desired, read the information that appears in the right pane on resizing document windows.

Now you'll search for a topic on using the document window.

8 Click Search from the navigation bar at the top left of the online Help. A text box appears in the left pane, which you can use to enter text for which you want to search.

9 Enter **document window** in the text box, and click Search. A list of topics that contain this phrase appears in the left pane.

10 If necessary, scroll down the left pane until you see the “Switching between windows” topic. Then click the “Switching between windows” topic to select it. If desired, read the information that appears in the right pane on switching between the document window and other windows.

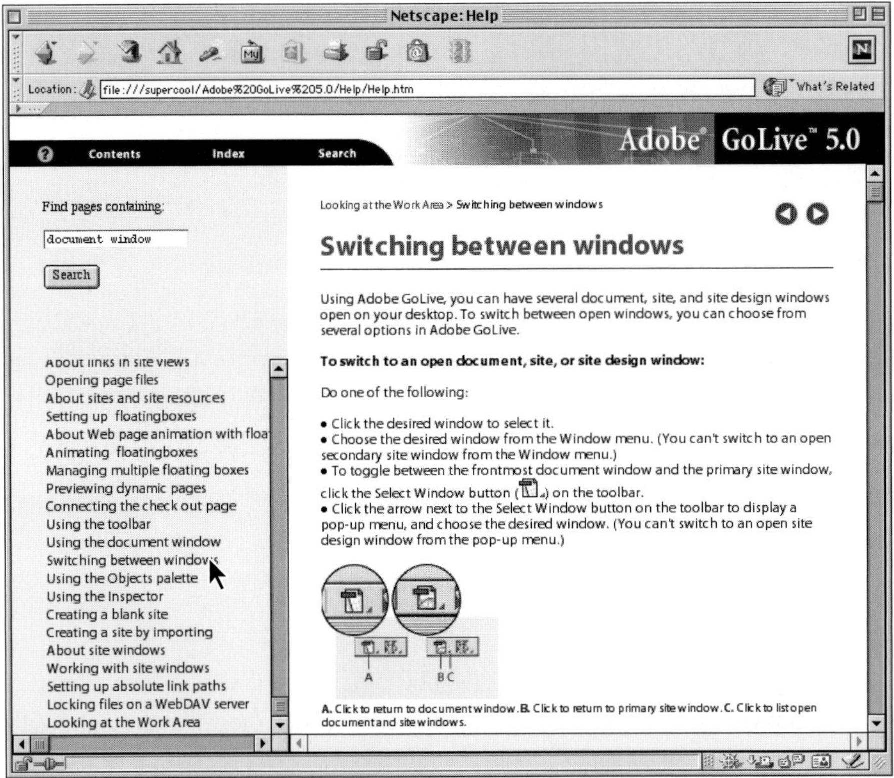

Selecting from list of topics

11 When you have finished using the online Help, close it and quit your browser.

Review questions

1 How do you open an existing Web site in Adobe GoLive?

2 What is the recommended way to set up your work area in Adobe GoLive?

3 How do you display a graphical view of a site?

4 Describe two ways in which you can use the toolbar.

5 How do you both collapse and expand a group of palettes?

6 What palette do you use to add an image placeholder to your page? What palette do you use to link an image placeholder to an image file?

7 How can you color text on your page?

8 What's the recommended way to preview a site or page that you've created in Adobe GoLive?

9 How can you open the online Help for Adobe GoLive in a Web browser?

Review answers

1 To open an existing Web site in Adobe GoLive, choose File > Open, select the file in the site folder with the .site extension, and click Open.

2 It's recommended that you set up your work area by placing the document window at the top, the site window at the bottom, and the palettes on the right side of the desktop.

3 To display a graphical view of a site, click the Navigation View button ( ) on the toolbar, or choose Design > Navigation View.

4 Among other uses, you can use the toolbar to both format text and locate a file in the Files tab of the site window.

5 To collapse a group of palettes to a tab at the right of the screen, Ctrl-click the title bar of the group window. To expand a group of palettes, click the tab at the right of the screen.

6 You use the Objects palette to add an image placeholder to your page and the Inspector to link the placeholder to an image file.

7 To color text, you can select the text in the document window, click the Text Color field on the toolbar to select it and display the Color palette, and then select a color from the Color palette.

8 In addition to previewing your page in Adobe GoLive, you should always preview it using a variety of browsers, browser versions, and platforms. You'll need to use browsers to determine potential browser differences and to preview items for which Adobe GoLive doesn't provide native support.

9 To display the online Help for Adobe GoLive in a browser, choose Help > GoLive Help.

Lesson 2

```
<TITLE>We
<STYLE TYPE=

e{color:maroon;f

</STYLE>
AD>
Y>
<!-- Begin main table -->
<TABLE BORDER="4" CELLPADDI
06">
     <TR>
          <TD><A
tp://www.adobe.com/">Adobe</A><
          <TD>GoLive</TD>
          <TD><IMG BORDER="0" HEIG
le.gif" ALT="Title"></TD>
     </TR>
     <TR>
          <TD><SPAN CLASS="head
AN></TD>
     </TR>
     <TR>
          <TD><B>DHTML an
     </TR>
</TABLE>
DY>

     P-EQUIV="content-typ
     ml;charset=iso-8859
     lcome to Adobe GoLive
     ="text/css"><!--

 main table -->
DER="4" CELLPAD

D><A
dobe.com/">Adobe</
D>GoLive</TD>
D><IMG BORDER="0" HE
="Title"></TD>

D><SPAN CLASS="hea

D><B>DHTML an
```

2 Working with Text and Tables

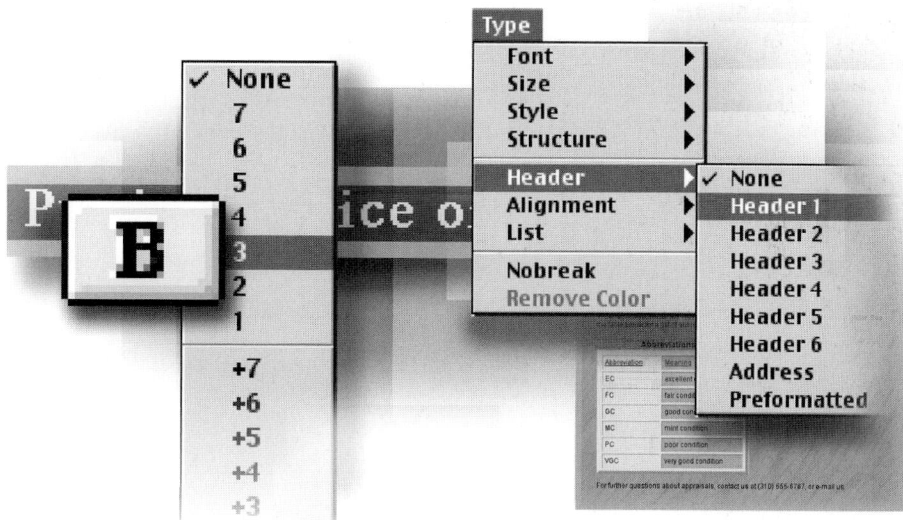

With Adobe GoLive, you can add text to a Web page using a variety of methods, including typing directly in the document window. Once the text is added, you can easily format and color it. In addition, you can use a table to control how text wraps on a page, or to present spreadsheet data or other information in rows and columns. To format a table quickly, you can apply a predefined style and sort its contents.

About this lesson

In this lesson, you'll learn how to do the following:

- Add text to a Web page by typing directly in the document window.
- Apply paragraph and physical styles to text.
- Create numbered and unnumbered lists.
- Add a line break.
- Change the color of text.
- Use tables to control how text wraps on the page and to present spreadsheet data.
- Format tables by specifying options, applying a predefined table style, and sorting the contents of a table.
- Import data into a table from another application.
- Apply a new set of fonts to the text on a page.
- Capture a table style, so that you can reuse it later.
- Preview a Web page in Adobe GoLive.

This lesson takes approximately 45 minutes to complete.

If needed, copy the Lesson02 folder onto your hard drive. As you work on this lesson, you'll overwrite the start files. If you need to restore the start files, copy them from the *Adobe GoLive 5.0 Classroom in a Book* CD.

Note: *Windows users need to unlock the lesson files before using them. For more information, see "Copying the Classroom in a Book files" on page 2.*

For information on setting up your work area, see "Setting up your work area" on page 9.

Getting started

In this lesson, you'll work on the design of a Web page for a fictional company called Gage Vintage Guitars. The page provides information about how to have your guitar appraised by the company.

First you'll view the finished page in your Web browser.

1 Start your browser.

2 Open the Appraise.html file. The path to the file is Lesson02/02End/Appraise.html.

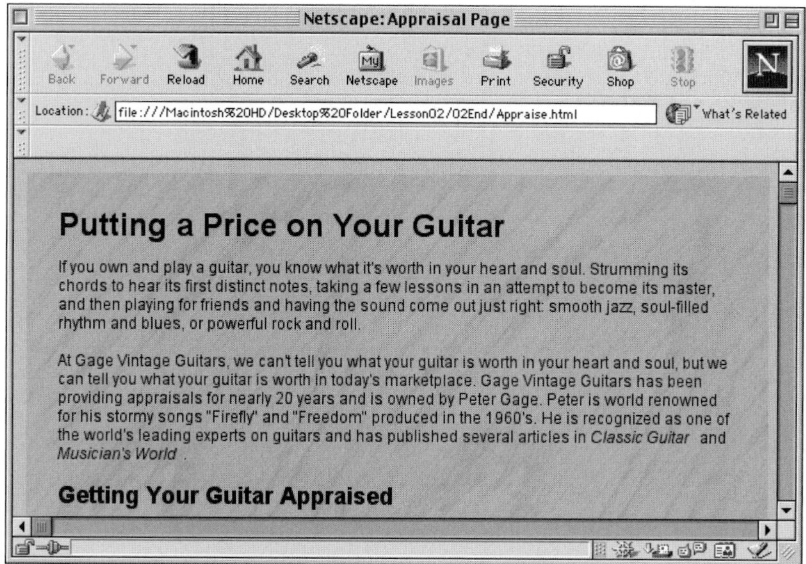

3 Scroll downward in the browser window, so that you can view all of the contents of the page.

4 When you have finished viewing the page, close it and quit your browser.

Designing a Web page

To get you started with the design of the Web page, we've created the page in Adobe GoLive and added some text. You'll open the page.

1 Start Adobe GoLive. A new document named Untitled.html opens, and several palettes are displayed in several groups by default.

Because you don't need a new document or palettes at this point in the lesson, you'll close Untitled.html and any displayed palettes.

2 Choose File > Close to close Untitled.html.

3 To hide each group of palettes, click the close box in the upper right (Windows) or upper left (Mac OS) corner of the group window.

4 Choose File > Open, select the Appraise.html file, and click Open. The path to the file is Lesson02/02Start/Appraise.html.

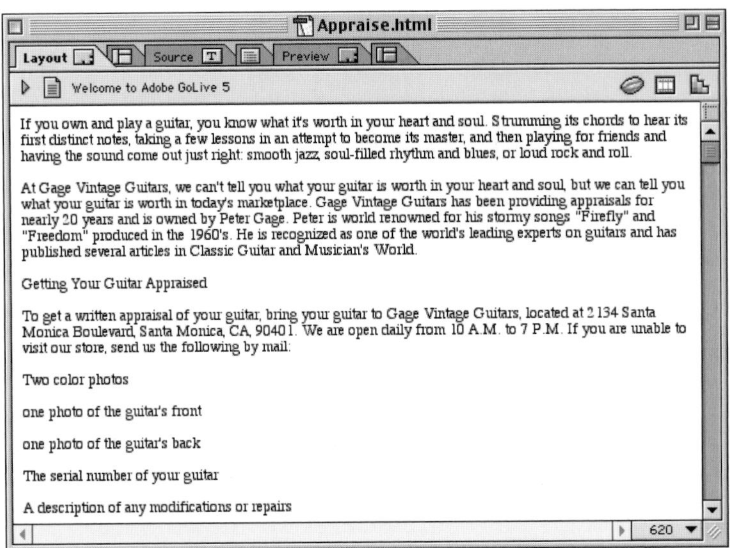

Now you're ready to begin designing the page. First you'll change the title of the page. When viewed in a Web browser, the title of the page appears in the title bar of the browser.

5 Select the page title, "Welcome to Adobe GoLive 5."

6 Type **Appraisal Page** as the new title, and press Enter or Return.

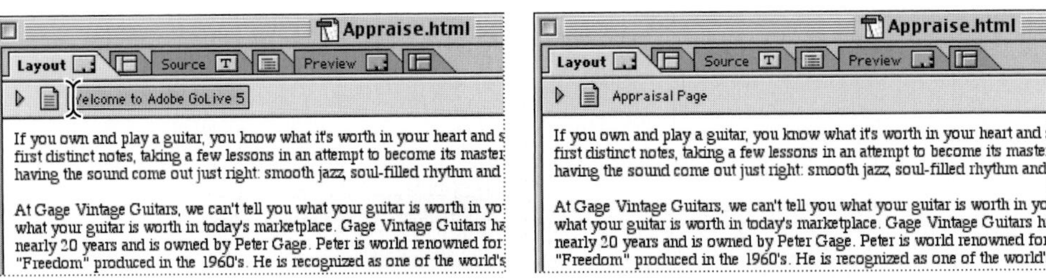

Selecting page title *New page title*

Now you'll select a window size for the page. The window size is valid only in Adobe GoLive, not browsers. However, it can help you limit the design of your page to fit within a desired window size. It's a good idea to limit the design of your page to fit within a window size of 580 pixels to accommodate viewers with 14-inch monitors.

7 Choose 580 from the Window Size menu in the lower right corner of the document window.

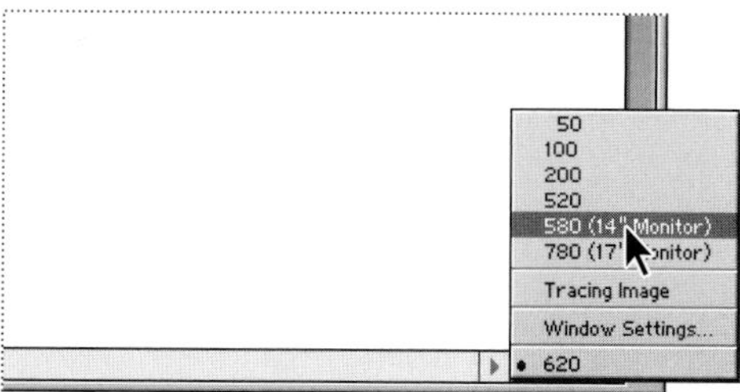

Choosing window size

Now you'll change the background color of the page from white to khaki.

8 Choose Window > Color to display the Color palette.

9 In the Color palette, click the Web Color List button (). Or, click the triangle in the upper right corner of the Color palette to display the Color palette menu, and choose Web Color List from the menu.

10 Select #CCCC99 from the list, or type **CCCC99** in the Value text box and press Enter or Return.

The selected color appears in the preview pane of the Color palette.

11 Drag the color from the preview pane of the Color palette to the Page icon () in the document window.

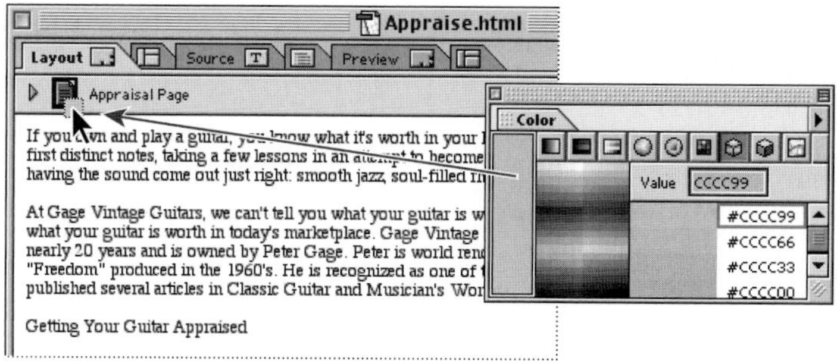

Changing page's background color

The background color of the page changes to khaki.

12 Choose File > Save.

Adding text

You can add text to an Adobe GoLive document by typing directly in the document window. Now you'll add a heading to the page.

1 Click before the first word in the document to insert a cursor.

2 Type **Putting a Price on Your Guitar**, and press Enter or Return.

Adobe GoLive provides a variety of additional methods for adding text to your documents:

• You can import text from another application into a table, which you'll do later in this lesson.

• You can add text to a page using layout text boxes and floating boxes, which you'll do in Lesson 3, "Laying Out Web Pages."

• You can copy text from a document created in another application, such as Microsoft Word, and paste the text into an Adobe GoLive document.

• You can drag text clips, created from SimpleText or Note Pad documents, from the desktop to Adobe GoLive documents.

For more information about adding text to Adobe GoLive documents, see "Creating text" in Chapter 4 of the *Adobe GoLive 5.0 User Guide*.

Formatting text

Adobe GoLive lets you format text in a variety of ways. You use paragraph styles, such as Header 1 and Header 2, to format paragraphs. You use physical styles, such as bold and italic, to emphasize text. And you use structural styles, such as Emphasis and Strong, to both emphasize and classify text.

Now you'll apply paragraph styles to format the headings in the document.

1 Click anywhere in the "Putting a Price on Your Guitar" heading on the page.

2 Choose Header 1 from the Paragraph Format menu on the toolbar.

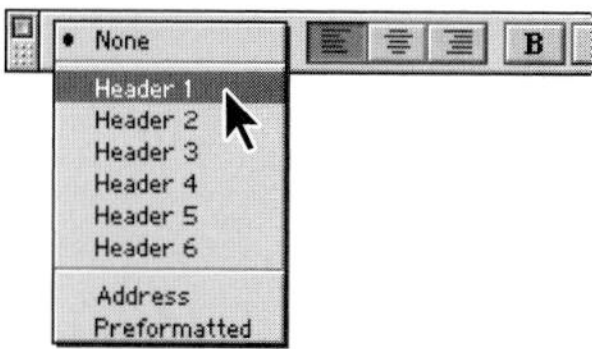

3 Click in the "Getting Your Guitar Appraised" paragraph, and choose Header 2 from the Paragraph Format menu.

Now you'll apply physical styles to some of the text in the document.

4 Select the phrase "Classic Guitar" near the end of the paragraph before the "Getting Your Guitar Appraised" heading.

5 Click the Bold button (B) on the toolbar to make the selected text bold.

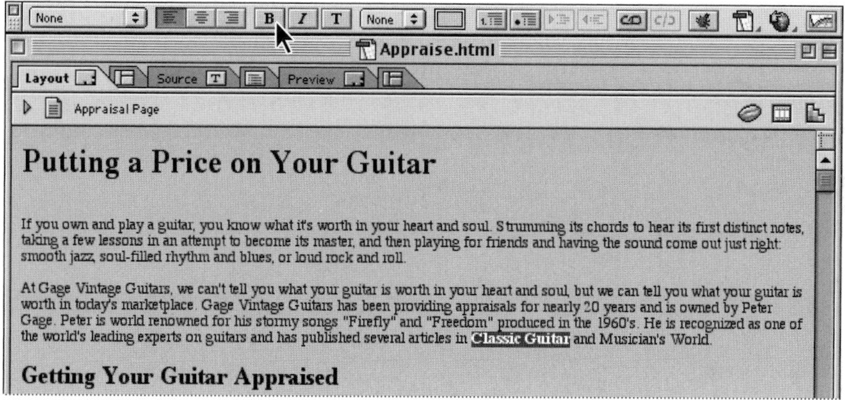

Applying physical style to text

You can easily remove a physical style and apply a new one.

6 Click the Bold button again to remove the bold style from the selected text.

7 Click the Italic button (I) on the toolbar to italicize the selected text, and click in the blank space outside the text to deselect it.

8 Apply the Italic style to the phrase "Musician's World" at the end of the same sentence.

To apply a structural style to selected text, choose an option from the Type > Structure menu. For more information about structural styles, see "Formatting text using physical and structural tags" in Chapter 4 of the *Adobe GoLive 5.0 User Guide*.

Creating lists

You can use Adobe GoLive to quickly format paragraphs as numbered or unnumbered lists. Now you'll create a numbered list from some of the text on the page.

1 Scroll downward in the document window, so that you can view the entire "Getting Your Guitar Appraised" section.

2 Select the seven paragraphs below the first paragraph in the section. (Your selection should begin with "Two color photos" and end with "$25 payable by Visa, Mastercard, or a personal check drawn from a U.S. bank.")

3 Click the Numbered List button (1.☰) on the toolbar to format the seven paragraphs as a numbered list.

By default, Adobe GoLive creates a numbered list with Arabic numerals. You can choose from several options to change the numbering style of the list.

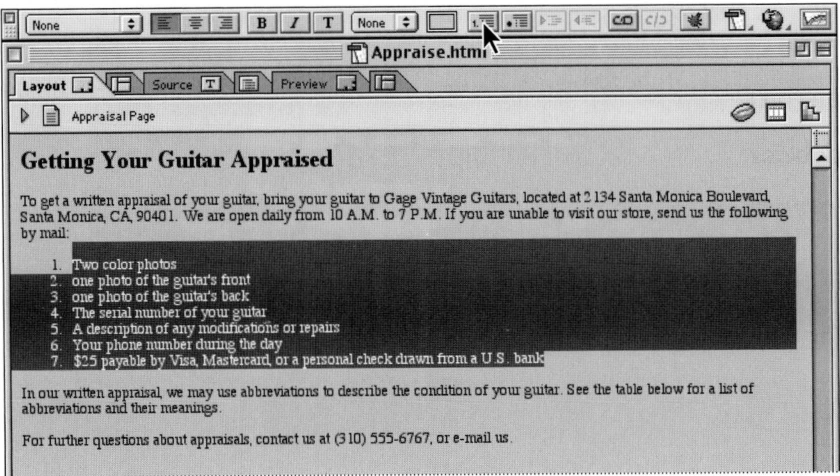

Creating a numbered list

4 Choose Type > List > Upper Roman to change the leading characters to uppercase Roman numerals.

Now you'll change the numbered list into an unnumbered list.

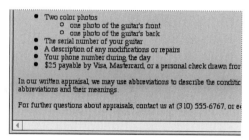

5 Click the Unnumbered List button ( ) on the toolbar to change the leading characters from numbers to bullets.

6 Click in the blank space outside the list to deselect it.

Adobe GoLive lets you easily create a hierarchical list with different numbering styles or leading characters.

7 Select the second and third items in the list.

8 Click the Increase List Level button ( ) on the toolbar to further indent the selected items and change their leading characters from bullets to circles.

Indenting list items

Adding a line break

Notice that the last item in the unnumbered list is longer than the other items. You can use a line break to make the last item flow onto two lines, rather than one.

1 Click before the word "drawn" in the last item to insert a cursor.

2 If necessary, choose Window > Objects to display the Objects palette, and make sure that the Basic tab ( ) is selected.

3 Double-click the Line Break icon in the Objects palette, or drag the Line Break icon from the Objects palette to the cursor on the page.

The line breaks, and the text beginning with "drawn" is moved to the following line.

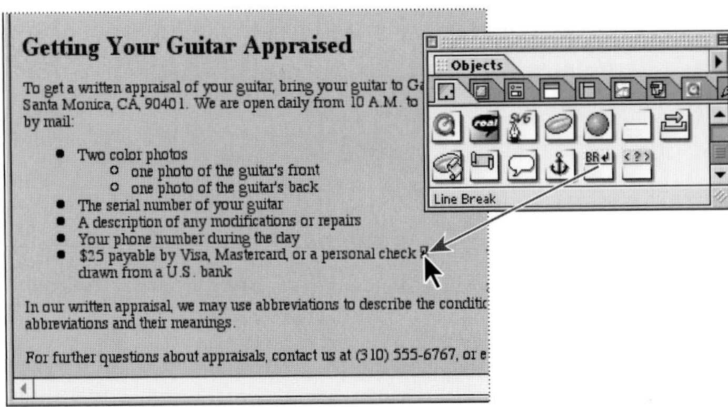

Adding line break

You can also add a line break by clicking inside a paragraph to insert a cursor and pressing Shift+Enter or Shift+Return.

Changing the color of text

Now you'll change the color of the unnumbered list to red.

1 Select the text in the unnumbered list, including the leading character of the first item in the list.

2 Click the Text Color field on the toolbar to display the Color palette.

3 In the Color palette, type **990000** in the Value text box, and press Enter or Return.

The selected color appears in the preview pane of the Color palette and the Text Color field on the toolbar. In addition, the color of the selected text changes to red.

4 Click in the blank space outside the selected text to deselect it.

5 Choose File > Save.

Adding tables

Adobe GoLive lets you quickly add tables to your documents. Tables are often used to control how text wraps on a Web page. They are also used to present information in rows and columns. In this lesson, you'll create and format tables for both purposes.

Adding a table to control how text wraps

To see how text wraps on the page without the use of a table, you'll change the window size of the document.

1 Choose 200 from the Window Size menu in the lower right corner of the document window.

Notice that the text wraps so that all of the text fits inside the smaller window. If you don't want the text to wrap to accommodate a change in window size, you can place the text inside a single-cell table. Text in a single-cell table wraps at the set width of the table, even when the window size changes.

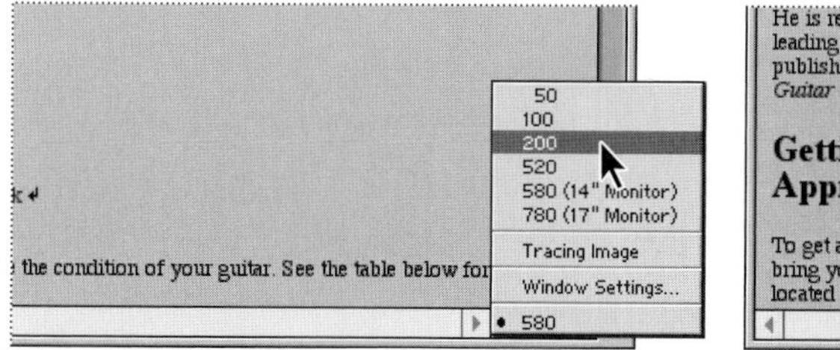

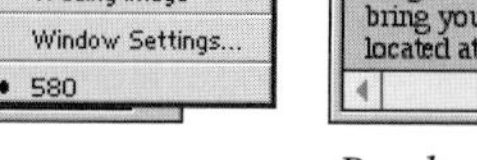

Choosing smaller window size

Result

Now you'll add a table to the page, which you'll use to control how text wraps on the page.

2 Choose 580 from the Window Size menu to return to your original window size.

3 Scroll upward in the document window, so that you can view the beginning of the document. Click before the "Putting a Price on Your Guitar" heading on the page to insert a cursor.

You'll insert a table at the cursor location.

4 Double-click the Table icon in the Objects palette, or drag the Table icon from the Objects palette to the cursor on the page.

Adding table to page

An empty table containing three rows and three columns appears at the cursor location, and the text on the page moves downward.

Using the Table Inspector, you'll remove rows and columns to create a single-cell table.

5 Choose Window > Inspector to display the Inspector.

The Inspector changes to the Table Inspector, with the Table tab selected. (As a reminder, the word "Table" appears at the bottom of the Inspector to indicate that it has changed to the Table Inspector.)

6 In the Table Inspector, enter **1** for both Rows and Columns.

Now you'll specify options for the table's appearance.

7 For Width, enter **580** to increase the width of the table.

Notice that Auto is chosen by default from the Height pop-up menu, so that the height of the table will automatically resize to accommodate the contents of the table.

8 For Border, enter **0** to remove the table's border. For Cell Pad, enter **25** to increase the horizontal and vertical spacing of the table cell.

The Cell Pad option specifies the top, left, right, and bottom margins within each table cell. When you use this option with a single-cell table that contains all of the text on the page, you're essentially specifying margins for the page.

Now you'll add a background image to the table.

9 Select BgImage, and click the Browse button (). Then select the Wood.gif file, and click Open. The path to the file is Lesson02/02Start/Wood.gif.

When you link your own Web page to an image file, we recommend that you store and manage the HTML file for the Web page and the image file in the Adobe GoLive site window. In Lesson 3, "Laying Out Web Pages," you'll create a Web site for Gage Vintage Guitars, and learn how to use the site window to store and manage your files.

Now you'll drag the text to the table cell.

10 Position the pointer before the "Putting a Price on Your Guitar" heading, and drag to select all of the text on the page.

11 Scroll upward in the document window, so that you can view the table. Position the pointer over the selected text, and drag the selected text to the table cell.

Dragging to select text on page

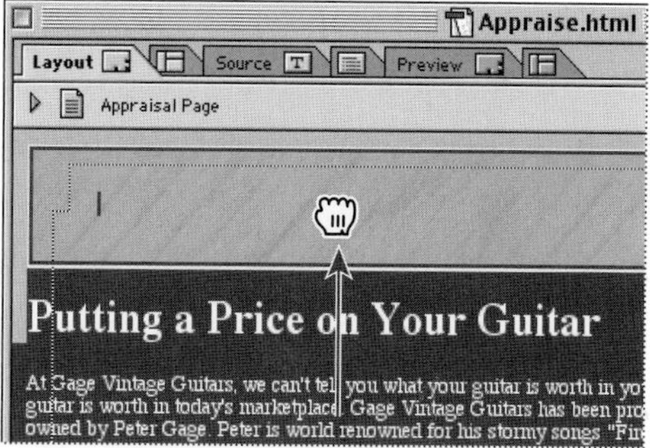

Dragging selected text to table cell

12 Scroll upward in the document window, so that you can view the beginning of the document. Click outside the selected text to deselect it.

Now you'll reduce the window size again to see how the text on the page wraps inside the table.

13 Choose 200 from the Window Size menu.

Notice that the text in the table wraps at the set width of the table, even when the window size changes.

14 Choose 580 from the Window Size menu to return to your original window size.

15 Choose File > Save.

Adding a table to present spreadsheet data

In its written appraisals, Gage Vintage Guitars uses abbreviations to describe the condition of a guitar. You'll add a second table to the page that will contain a list of abbreviations and their meanings used by the company. Then you'll import data into the table from a text-only file created in a word-processing application.

1 Scroll downward in the document window, so that you can view the end of the document. Click after the last word in the paragraph beginning with "In our written appraisal," and press Enter.

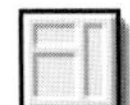

2 Drag the Table icon from the Objects palette to the cursor on the page.

An empty table appears at the cursor location, and the Inspector changes to the Table Inspector.

Notice that you placed the second table within the existing table cell on the page. Adobe GoLive lets you place a variety of objects into table cells, including text, other tables, and images.

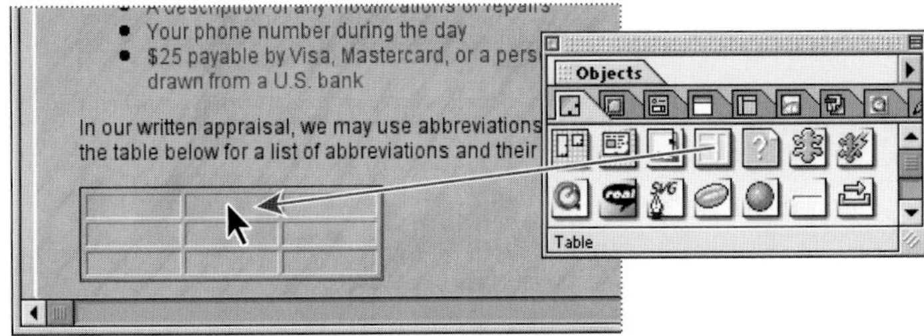

Nesting a table

Now you'll import data into the table from a text-only file. The data in the text-only file is formatted so that each line represents the contents of a row, with tabs separating the data between the columns. If you have a word-processing application installed on your system, you can open the text-only file to view its contents. If you don't have a word-processing application, skip to step 6.

3 Start your word-processing application.

4 Open the Table.txt file. The path to the file is Lesson02/02Start/Table.txt.

5 When you've finished viewing the file, close it and quit your word-processing application.

6 In the Table Inspector of Adobe GoLive, click the Browse button for the Import Tab-Text option.

7 Select the Table.txt file. The path to the file is Lesson02/02Start/Table.txt. Make sure that TAB is chosen from the Col. (Column) Separator pop-up menu, and click Open.

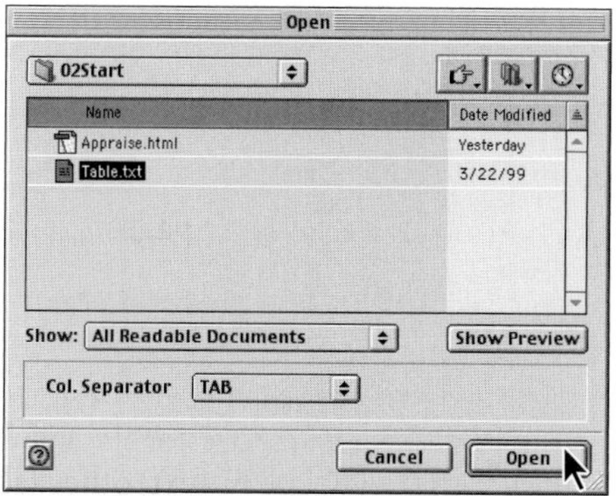

Importing file with tab as column separator

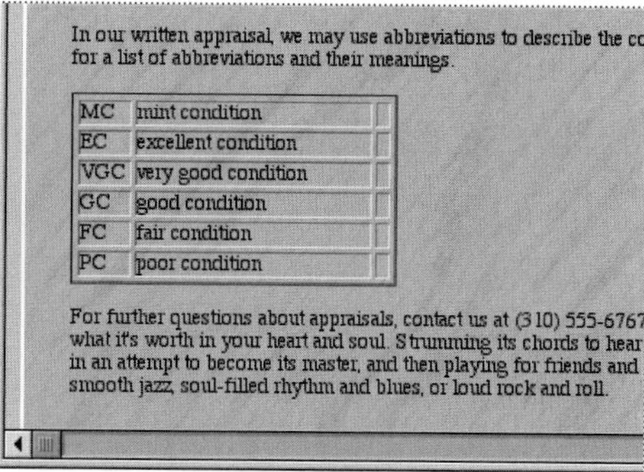

Result

Adobe GoLive adds extra columns and rows to the table as necessary to accommodate the data, and imports the data into the table.

Note: *Most spreadsheet applications can export data to a text-only file. For more information, see the documentation of your spreadsheet application.*

Formatting a table that presents spreadsheet data

You can format a table by specifying options in the Table Inspector, applying a predefined table style using the Table palette, or doing both. You need to use the Table Inspector to specify options for the table's basic appearance, such as its number of rows and columns. Predefined table styles let you quickly format specific table features, such as the color of individual table cells.

Now you'll use the Table Inspector to specify the number of rows and columns for the table. Because the third column doesn't contain data, you'll remove it from the table.

1 In the Table Inspector, for Columns, enter **2**.

Now you'll add headings to each column of the table. You'll begin by adding an empty row at the beginning of the table.

2 Click the bottom or right edge of the first cell in the left column of the table to select it. (Make sure that you select the cell, not the text.)

The Cell tab is automatically selected in the Table Inspector.

3 In the Table Inspector, click the Add Row button to add a row above the current selection.

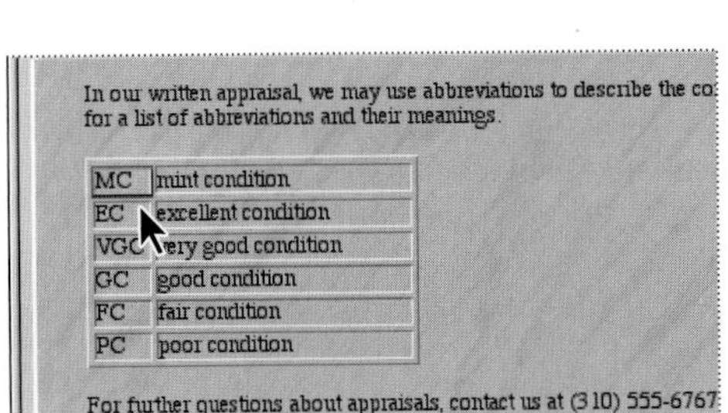

Clicking bottom edge of table cell to select it

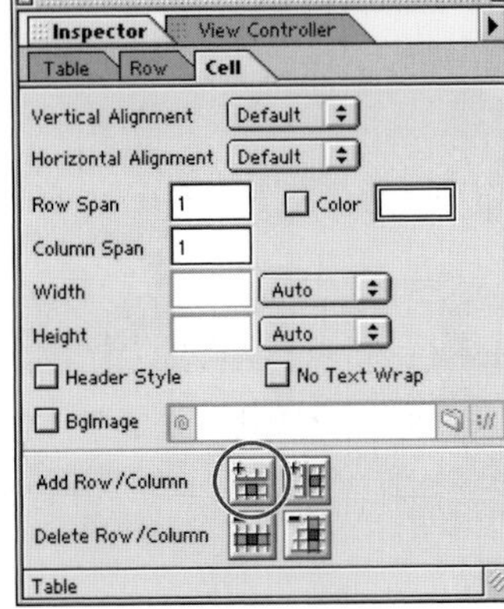

Add Row button

4 Click inside the new first cell in the left column of the table to insert a cursor.

5 Type **Abbreviation**, press Tab to move the cursor to the first cell in the right column, and type **Meaning**.

Now you'll format the table using a predefined table style included with Adobe GoLive. First, you'll preview the style in the Table palette.

6 Choose Window > Table to display the Table palette.

7 In the Table palette, click the Style tab. Then choose Green from the pop-up menu in the upper left corner of the Style tab.

8 Click Apply to apply the chosen style to the table.

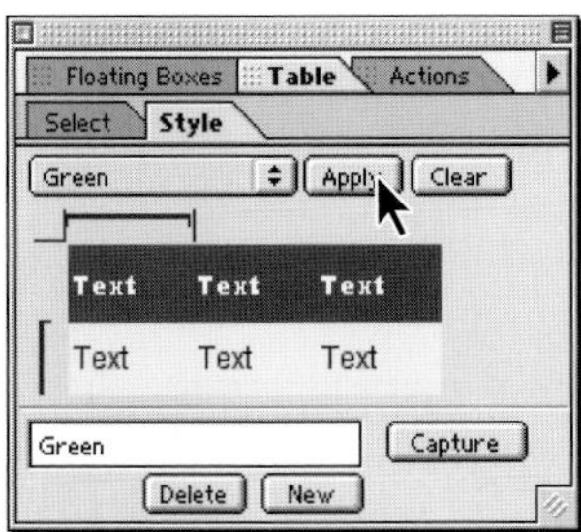

You can easily remove a predefined table style once you've applied it.

9 Click Clear to remove the chosen style from the table.

If you don't find a predefined table style that meets your needs, you can create your own style using the Table Inspector and a variety of palettes included with Adobe GoLive.

Now you'll specify options for the table's appearance using the Table Inspector.

10 In the Table Inspector, choose Auto from the Width pop-up menu.

11 For Border, enter **6** to increase the width of the table's border. For Cell Pad, enter **4** to increase the horizontal and vertical spacing of each table cell. For Cell Space, enter **4** to increase the space between table cells.

Now you'll add a caption above the table.

12 Select Caption, and make sure that Above Table is chosen from the pop-up menu.

13 Click directly above the table to insert a cursor, and type **Abbreviations**.

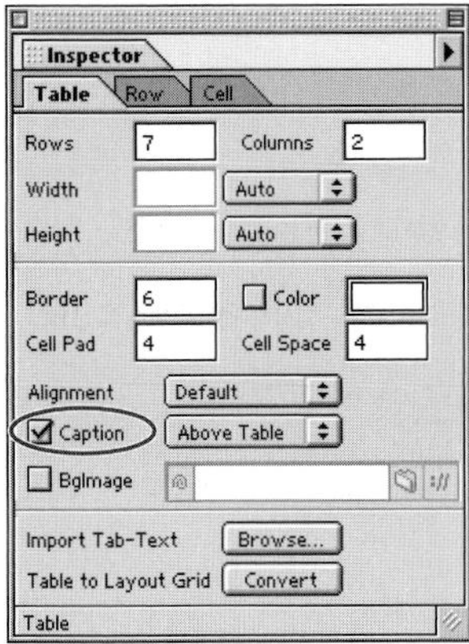

Caption and Above Table options

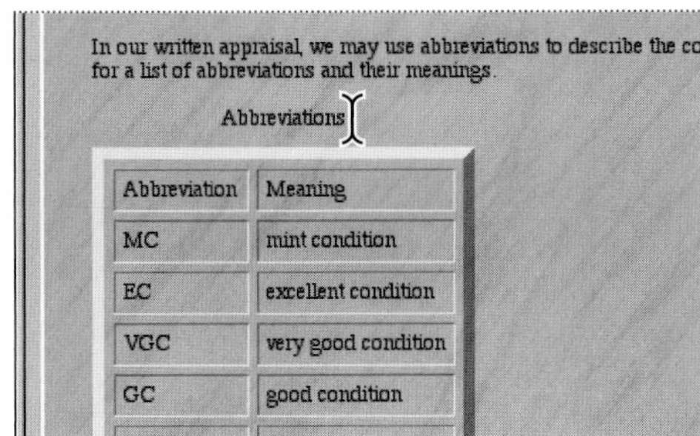

Typing caption above table

14 Click the Left Align button ( ) on the toolbar to align the caption to the left side of the table.

15 Select the "Abbreviations" text, and click the Bold button (B) on the toolbar.

Instead of selecting text by dragging, you can select a single word by double-clicking it or a line of text by triple-clicking it.

Now you'll increase the font size of the "Abbreviations" text.

You can use the Font Size menu to apply custom font sizes that override the browser's preferences. Most browsers are set to display text at 12 points. The Adobe GoLive Font Size menu includes options for setting font sizes from 1 to 7. A font size of 1 displays text at two font sizes smaller than the size set in the browser's preferences, a font size of 2 displays text at one font size smaller, a font size of 3 displays text at the same font size, a font size of 4 displays text at one font size larger, and so on.

16 Choose 4 from the Font Size menu on the toolbar, and click in the blank space outside the caption to deselect it.

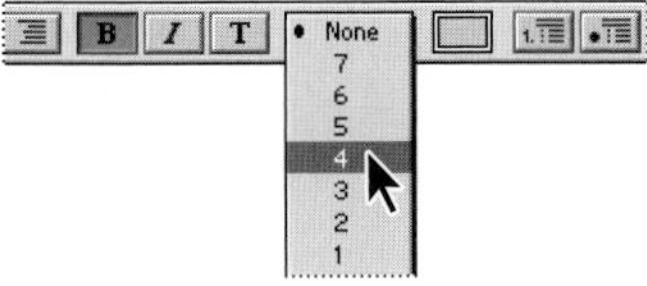

Now you'll format the column headings.

17 Select the "Abbreviation" text in the first cell of the table, and choose Type > Style > Underline to underline it. Then select the "Meaning" text, and underline it.

Now you'll adjust the width of the columns in the table.

18 Click the bottom or right edge of any cell in the left column of the table to select it.

19 In the Table Inspector, choose Pixel from the Width menu. For Width, enter **100**.

The selected cell and all other cells in its column increase in width.

20 Click the bottom or right edge of any cell in the right column of the table to select it. Choose Pixel from the Width menu. For Width, enter **140**.

You can also adjust the width of a table column by positioning the pointer on the right edge of the column so that the pointer turns into a double-headed arrow, and dragging to the left or right.

21 Choose File > Save.

Changing the color of table cells

Now you'll change the color of the cells in the table to yellow.

1 Move the pointer to the left edge of the table, and click to select the table.

The Table tab is automatically selected in the Table Inspector.

2 In the Table Inspector, click the Color field to select the field and display the Color palette. (Be sure to click the Color field, not the checkbox.)

3 In the Color palette, type **FFFFCC** in the Value text box, and press Enter or Return.

The selected color appears in the preview pane of the Color palette and the Color field in the Table Inspector. In addition, the color of the table cells changes to yellow.

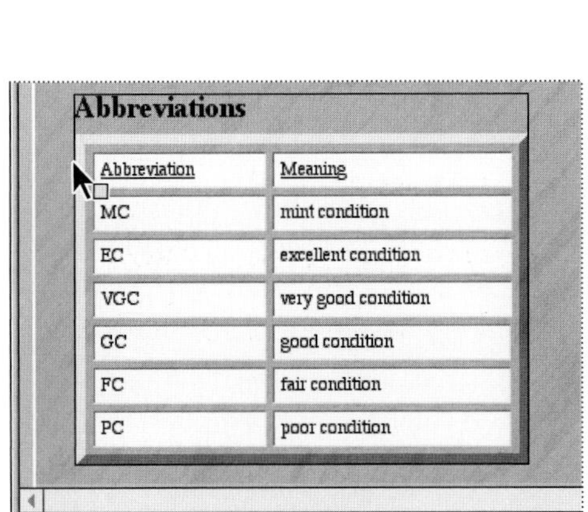

Clicking left edge of table to select it

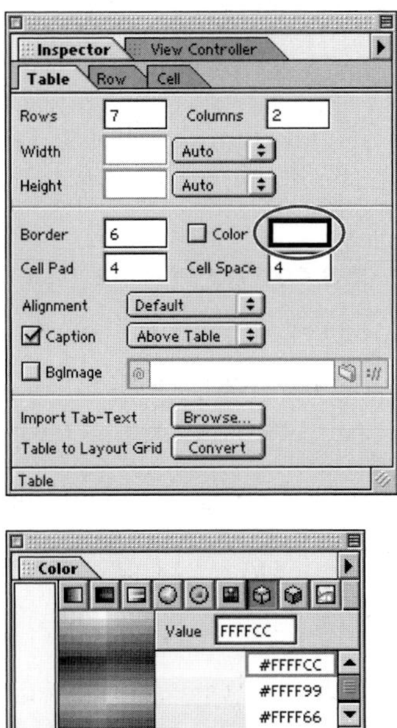

Clicking Color field in Table Inspector; choosing color in Color palette

You can also change the color of individual table cells. You'll change the color of the cells in the right column to green.

4 Shift-click the top of the right column to select all of the cells in the column.

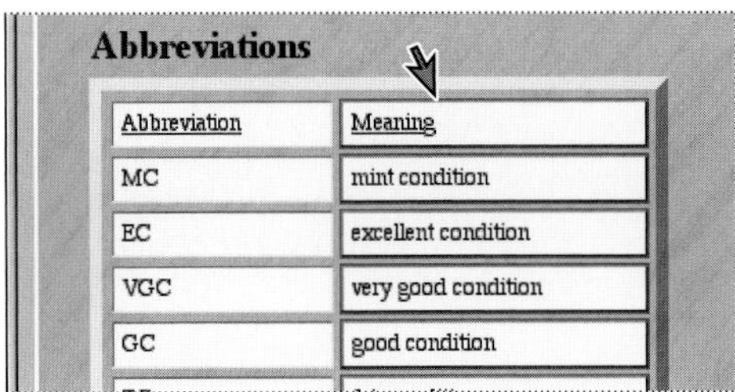

Selecting all cells in column

The Cell tab in the Table Inspector is automatically selected.

5 In the Table Inspector, click the Color field to select the field and display the Color palette.

6 In the Color palette, type **99CC99** in the Value text box, and press Enter or Return.

The selected color appears in the preview pane of the Color palette and the Color field in the Table Inspector. In addition, the color of the selected cells changes to green.

7 Click in the blank space outside the table to deselect all of its cells.

Sorting the contents of a table

Adobe GoLive makes it easy for you to sort the contents of a table, so that the contents of its rows or columns appear in alphabetical and numerical order. You can apply the sort to an entire table, specific rows, specific columns, or specific cells.

Now you'll use the Select tab of the Table palette to sort the contents of the table.

1 Move the pointer to the left edge of the table, and click to select the table.

2 In the Table palette, click the Select tab.

3 In the preview of the table that appears in the Select tab, drag to select all of the table cells except the cells in the first row.

4 Choose Rows from the Sort pop-up menu to indicate that you want to sort the order of the rows in the table. By sorting the order of the rows, you will make the contents of one or more columns appear in numerical and alphabetical order.

5 In the leftmost pop-up menu above the Sort pop-up menu, choose 1 to specify the first column as the primary column to be used when sorting the table's contents. This means that sorting the contents of the first column will be the first priority for Adobe GoLive.

You'll specify for the first column to be sorted in ascending order.

6 Make sure that the ascending order button (≜) next to the leftmost pop-up menu is displayed. If it isn't displayed, click the descending order button (⩧), so that it changes to an ascending order button.

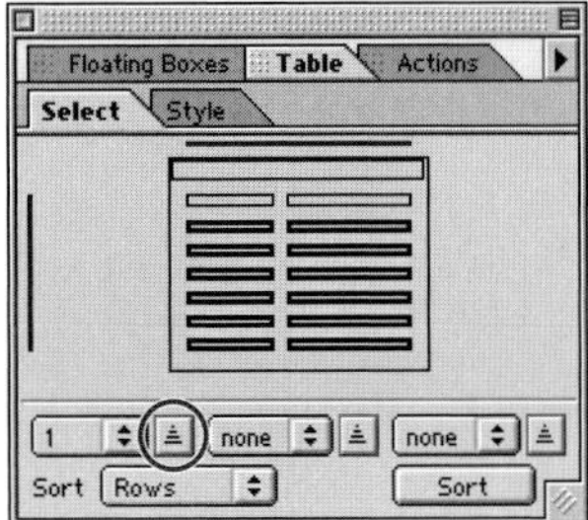

Because the table only has two columns, you don't need to specify a secondary or tertiary column to be used when sorting the table's contents. Sorting the contents of the second column will automatically be the second priority for Adobe GoLive.

7 Click Sort to sort the selected table cells using the criteria that you've specified.

Applying fonts

Adobe GoLive contains default sets of fonts that you can apply to text in your documents. One set contains the Times New Roman, Georgia, and Times fonts. If you use this set for your Web page, a visitor's browser will attempt to display text first in Times New Roman, second in Georgia, and third in Times. If none of the fonts in the set are installed on the viewer's system, the browser displays text using its default font.

Now you'll display the Font Set Editor to learn more about the sets of fonts available for your document.

1 Choose Type > Font > Edit Font Sets to display the Font Set Editor.

2 Display the default sets of fonts:

• In Windows, choose Default Font Sets from the menu in the upper left corner of the dialog box.

• In Mac OS, select Default in the left pane of the dialog box.

3 Select Arial in the Font Sets pane of the dialog box.

The Arial set of fonts appears in the Font Names pane of the dialog box.

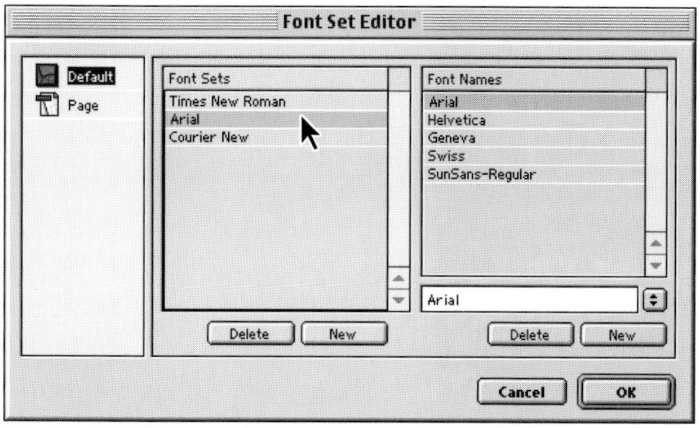

4 Click Cancel to close the dialog box.

Now you'll change the set of fonts used for the text in the document.

5 Click anywhere in the single-cell table that contains the text and nested table to insert a cursor. Then choose Edit > Select All to select all of the text in the document.

6 Choose Type > Font > Arial to choose the Arial fonts for the selected text.

7 Click inside the document to deselect the text.

Most of the text in the document changes to the Arial font. Notice that the text in the table continues to use the Times font. To change the fonts used by the text in the table, you first need to select the table caption and cells individually.

8 Select the "Abbreviations" text in the table caption, and choose Type > Font > Arial. Then click outside the selected text to deselect it.

The text in the table caption changes to the Arial font.

9 Shift-click the top of the left column to select all of the cells in the column. Shift-click the top of the right column to add its cells to the selection. Then choose Type > Font > Arial, and click outside the selected table cells to deselect them.

The text in the table cells changes to the Arial font.

You can also use Adobe GoLive to create sets of fonts that you can apply to text in your documents. For more information, see "Applying font sets" in Chapter 4 of the *Adobe GoLive 5.0 User Guide*.

Capturing a table style

Now you'll capture the table style that you've created. When you capture a table style, the style is added to the Style tab of the Table palette, so that you can reuse the style and create a consistent look for tables throughout your Web site.

1 Click the top or left edge of the table that presents spreadsheet data to select it.

2 In the Table palette, click the Style tab.

3 Click New to create a new table style.

4 In the text box above the New button, enter **Gage** as the name of the new table style.

5 Click Capture to capture the style of the selected table in the document window and save it as the new table style.

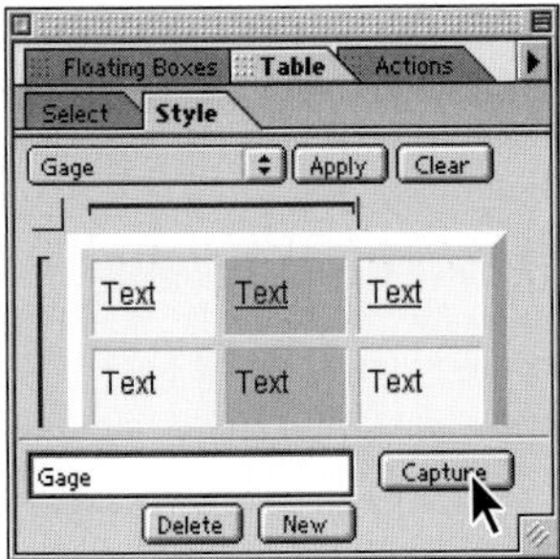

To apply the new style to another table, you can simply select the desired table in the document window, choose the new table style from the pop-up menu in the upper left corner of the Style tab, and click Apply.

Editing text

Adobe GoLive lets you edit text in your documents with the ease of using a word-processing application:

- You can delete text by selecting it and pressing Delete, choosing Edit > Cut, or pressing Ctrl+X (Windows) or Command+X (Mac OS).
- You can find and correct spelling errors by choosing Edit > Check Spelling.
- You can find and replace text by choosing Edit > Find.

Now you'll find the word "loud" and replace it with the word "powerful." You'll begin by setting preferences for finding text. You'll have Adobe GoLive keep the Find dialog box in front of the document window when a match is found.

1 Choose Edit > Preferences.

2 In the left pane of the Preferences dialog box, click the Find icon to display preferences for finding text.

3 Choose Keep Find Window In Front from the menu in the right pane, and click OK.

Now you'll search for the text to replace.

4 Scroll upward in the document window, so that you can view the beginning of the document. Then click before the main heading on the page to insert a cursor.

5 Choose Edit > Find.

6 In the Find dialog box, select the Find & Replace tab. Then type **loud** in the Find text box.

7 Click the triangle (▶) next to Replace to open the Replace text box. In the Replace text box, type **powerful**, and click Find.

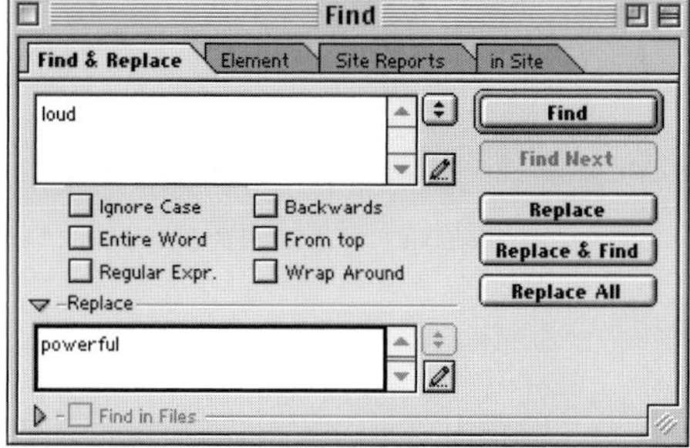

The word "loud" is highlighted in the document.

8 In the Find dialog box, click Replace. In the document, "loud" is replaced with "powerful."

9 Close the Find dialog box, and choose File > Save.

You've completed the design of the Appraisal page for this lesson. Now you're ready to preview the page in Adobe GoLive.

Previewing in Adobe GoLive

1 In the document window, click the Layout Preview tab to view the document in Preview.

If you are using Adobe GoLive for Mac OS, you can use the View Controller in conjunction with the Preview to see an approximation of what your page looks like in a variety of browsers.

2 In Mac OS, choose Window > View Controller to display the View Controller. In the View Controller, choose "Explorer 5 (Windows)" from the Root CSS menu to see how your page appears in Microsoft Internet Explorer 5 on a Windows platform. Try the different menu options and observe how your page changes in the preview. Notice that the text increases in size whenever you switch to a Windows-based browser.

3 Choose File > Close to close the Appraise.html file.

Exploring on your own

Hypertext Markup Language (HTML) is used to publish information on the World Wide Web. In this lesson, you worked in Adobe GoLive's Layout view to design a Web page. When you work in Layout view, Adobe GoLive writes HTML code for your page. Sometimes you may want to work directly with your page's HTML code. Adobe GoLive provides two different views of the HTML code, which you can use to design and edit your Web pages. Source view lets you view the HTML code directly, and Outline view lets you view the HTML code in a hierarchical, organized way.

Now that you've learned how to work in Layout view, try working in Source view and Outline view to edit the Appraisal page.

First you'll open the Appraisal page.

1 In Adobe GoLive, choose File > Open, select the Appraise.html file, and click Open. The path to the file is Lesson02/02End/Appraise.html.

2 In the Appraise.html document window, select the main heading "Putting a Price on Your Guitar."

3 Click the HTML Source Editor tab ( ) to display the document in Source view.

4 Notice that the main heading is highlighted in the HTML source code. If necessary, scroll to the right in the document window, so that you can view the highlighted text.

Now you'll use the HTML Source Editor to change the paragraph format of the main heading from Header 1 to Header 2.

5 Select the text "h1" at the beginning of the line that contains the main heading. The text that you've selected is the start tag of an h1 element, which instructs the Web browser to display the main heading using the Header 1 format.

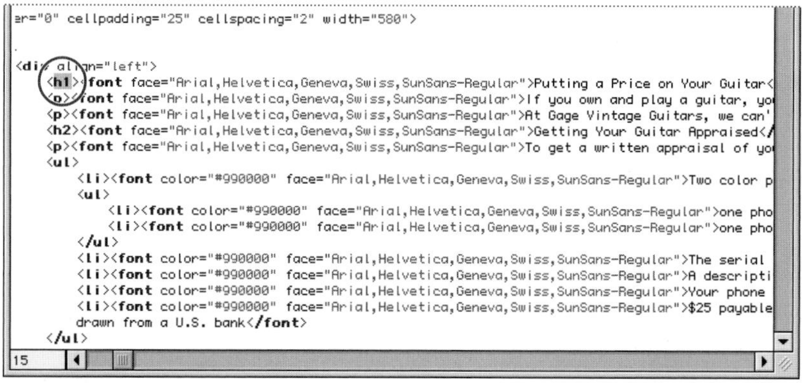

```
er="0" cellpadding="25" cellspacing="2" width="580">

<div align="left">
   <h1><font face="Arial,Helvetica,Geneva,Swiss,SunSans-Regular">Putting a Price on Your Guitar<
   <p><font face="Arial,Helvetica,Geneva,Swiss,SunSans-Regular">If you own and play a guitar, yo
   <p><font face="Arial,Helvetica,Geneva,Swiss,SunSans-Regular">At Gage Vintage Guitars, we can'
   <h2><font face="Arial,Helvetica,Geneva,Swiss,SunSans-Regular">Getting Your Guitar Appraised</
   <p><font face="Arial,Helvetica,Geneva,Swiss,SunSans-Regular">To get a written appraisal of yo
   <ul>
      <li><font color="#990000" face="Arial,Helvetica,Geneva,Swiss,SunSans-Regular">Two color p
      <ul>
         <li><font color="#990000" face="Arial,Helvetica,Geneva,Swiss,SunSans-Regular">one pho
         <li><font color="#990000" face="Arial,Helvetica,Geneva,Swiss,SunSans-Regular">one pho
      </ul>
      <li><font color="#990000" face="Arial,Helvetica,Geneva,Swiss,SunSans-Regular">The serial
      <li><font color="#990000" face="Arial,Helvetica,Geneva,Swiss,SunSans-Regular">A descripti
      <li><font color="#990000" face="Arial,Helvetica,Geneva,Swiss,SunSans-Regular">Your phone
      <li><font color="#990000" face="Arial,Helvetica,Geneva,Swiss,SunSans-Regular">$25 payable
      drawn from a U.S. bank</font>
   </ul>
15
```

Selecting "h1" text

Now you'll change the h1 element to an h2 element by modifying its start and end tags.

6 Type **h2** to replace the selected text.

7 Select the text "/h1" at the end of the line that contains the main heading. This is the end tag for the original h1 element.

8 Type **/h2** to replace the selected text.

9 Click the Layout Editor tab ( ) to return the document to Layout view. Notice that the paragraph format for the main heading now is Header 2.

Now you'll use the HTML Outline Editor to return the paragraph format of the main heading to Header 1.

10 If needed, select the main heading.

11 Click the HTML Outline Editor tab ( ) to display the document in Outline view. Notice that the main heading has a black border around it in the outline.

12 Click to select the text "h2" located two lines above the main heading.

13 Type **h1** to replace the selected text, and click in the blank space outside the selected text to deselect it.

You'll also use the HTML Outline Editor to center the main heading on the page.

14 Click the triangle to the right of the "h1" text to display a pop-up menu.

15 Choose "align" from the pop-up menu.

16 Click the triangle next to "align" to display another pop-up menu, and choose "center."

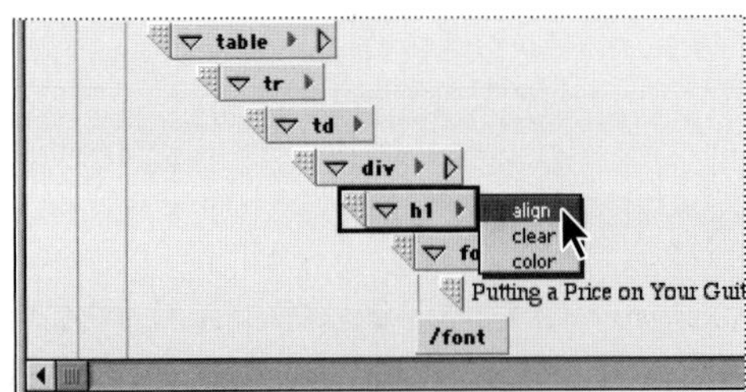

Choosing "align" from pop-up menu

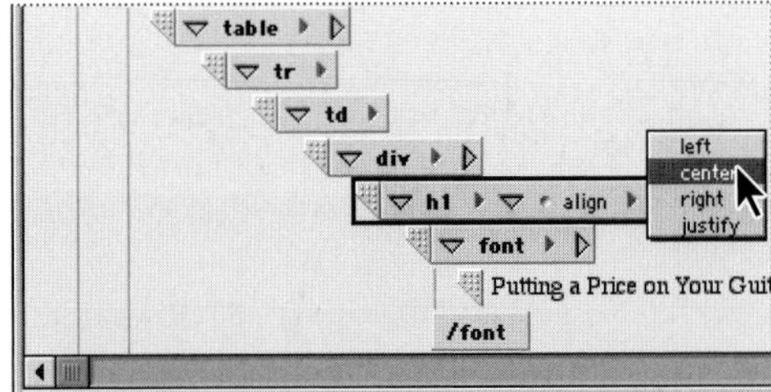

Choosing "center" from another pop-up menu

You'll also use the HTML Outline Editor to change the background color of the page to yellow.

17 Click the triangle to the right of the "body" text. The bgcolor attribute and value for the Body element appears, which determines the background color of the page.

18 In the Web Color List button of the Color palette, type **FFFFCC** in the Value text box, and press Enter or Return. The selected color appears in the preview pane.

19 Drag the color from the preview pane of the Color palette to the color field for the background color of the page. Then click outside of the color field to deselect the Body element.

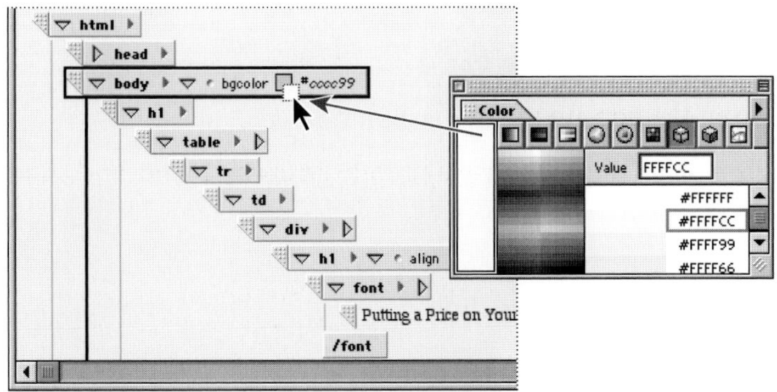

Changing page's background color

20 Click the Layout Editor tab to return the document to Layout view. Notice that the paragraph format of the main heading now is Header 1, the main heading is centered on the page, and the background color of the page is yellow.

21 Choose File > Close to close the page. You don't need to save the changes that you've made to it.

Review questions

1 Name two ways of adding text to a document.

2 How do you apply a paragraph style to text? How do you apply a physical style to text?

3 What's a common reason for putting all of the text in a document into a single-cell table?

4 Can you import data from a spreadsheet application into a table?

5 How do you apply a predefined style to a table? How do you remove a predefined style from a table?

6 How do you add a caption to a table?

7 Which palette do you use to sort the contents of a table?

8 How do you learn more about the sets of fonts available for a document?

9 How can you find and replace text in a document?

Review answers

1 You can add text to a document by typing directly in the document window; importing text from another application into a table; using layout text boxes; using floating boxes; copying text from a document created in another application and pasting it into an Adobe GoLive document; and, dragging a text clip, created from a SimpleText or Note Pad document, from the desktop to an Adobe GoLive document.

2 To apply a paragraph style, click anywhere in a paragraph, and choose a paragraph style from the Paragraph Format menu on the toolbar or the Type > Header submenu. To apply a physical style, select the text, and click the Bold, Italic, or Teletype button on the toolbar or choose a physical style from the Type > Style submenu.

3 A common reason for putting all of the text in a document into a single-cell table is to control how text wraps on the page. Text in a single-cell table wraps at the set width of the table, even when the window size changes.

4 Yes, you can import data from most spreadsheet applications into a table. First, you need to export data from the spreadsheet application to a text-only file. The data in the text-only file needs to be formatted so that each line represents the contents of a row with column separators (tabs, commas, spaces, or semicolons). For more information, see the documentation for your spreadsheet application.

5 To apply a predefined style to a table, choose a style from the pop-up menu in the upper left corner of the Style tab of the Table palette, and click Apply. To remove a predefined style from a table, make sure that the table is selected, and click Clear in the Style tab of the Table palette.

6 To add a caption to a table, select Caption in the Table Inspector, and choose Above Table or Below Table from the pop-up menu in the Table Inspector. Then click above or below the table to insert a cursor and type the text for the caption.

7 To sort the contents of a table, you use the Select tab of the Table palette.

8 To learn more about the sets of fonts available for a document, choose Type > Font > Edit Font Sets to display the Font Set Editor. In the Font Set Editor, select a set of fonts to display its contents.

9 You can choose Edit > Find to find and replace text in a document.

Lesson 3

```
<TITLE>We
<STYLE TYPE=
e{color:maroon;
</STYLE>
AD>
Y>
<!-- Begin main table -->
<TABLE BORDER="4" CELLPADD
06">
    <TR>
        <TD><A
tp://www.adobe.com/">Adobe</A
        <TD>GoLive</TD>
        <TD><IMG BORDER="0" HEIGH
le.gif" ALT="Title"></TD>
    </TR>
    <TR>
        <TD><SPAN CLASS="hea
AN></TD>
    </TR>
    <TR>
        <TD><B>DHTML ani
    </TR>
</TABLE>
DY>

EQUIV="content-typ
charset=iso-885
come to Adobe GoL
text/css"><

main table -
ER="4" CELLPADD

D><A
dobe.com/">Adobe</
D>GoLive</TD>
D><IMG BORDER="0" HEI
="Title"></TD>

D><SPAN CLASS="head

D><B>DHTML
```

3 Laying Out Web Pages

Adobe GoLive provides multiple ways for you to lay out your Web pages, so that you can precisely place text, images, and other objects on each page. It also provides several ways for you to save time when laying out your pages, so that you can quickly add objects and apply colors that are frequently used in your Web site. In this lesson, you'll explore the various tools for page layout as you work on the design of three pages.

About this lesson

In this lesson, you'll learn how to do the following:

- Create a new Web site, and add files to the site.
- Create a dynamic component that stores frequently used page content, and add the component to a page.
- Create a new page.
- Use a layout grid to place objects precisely on a page.
- Add images to a page using a variety of methods.
- Move, align, and distribute objects on a layout grid.
- Add a background image to a page.
- Add text to a page using layout text boxes.
- Create a custom color palette that stores frequently used colors, and add the colors to a page.
- Extract color from a region below the pointer.
- Use floating boxes to place overlapping objects on a page.

This lesson takes approximately 1 hour to complete.

If needed, copy the Lesson03 folder onto your hard drive. As you work on this lesson, you'll overwrite the start files. If you need to restore the start files, copy them from the *Adobe GoLive 5.0 Classroom in a Book* CD.

***Note:** Windows users need to unlock the lesson files before using them. For more information, see "Copying the Classroom in a Book files" on page 2.*

For information on setting up your work area, see "Setting up your work area" on page 9.

Getting started

In Lesson 2, "Working with Text and Tables," you designed a Web page for Gage Vintage Guitars. In this lesson, you'll create a Web site for the company and work on the design of three pages for the site.

First you'll view the finished Web pages in your browser.

1 Start your Web browser.

2 Open the Index.html file. The path to the file is Lesson03/03End/Gage Folder/Gage/Index.html.

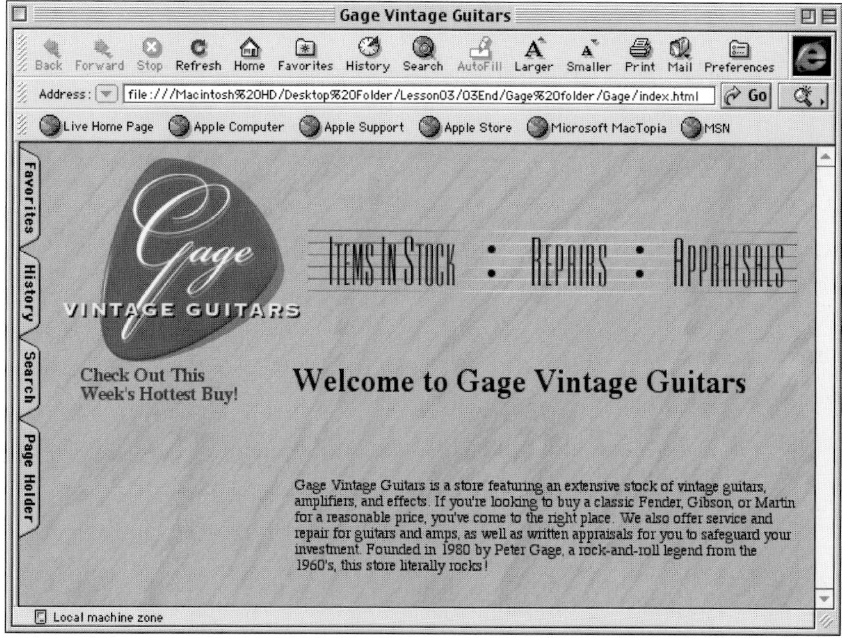

3 Open the Appraise.html file. The path to the file is Lesson03/03End/Gage Folder/Gage/Pages/Appraise.html.

4 Open the Hottest.html file. The path to the file is Lesson03/03End/Gage Folder/Gage/Pages/Hottest.html.

5 When you have finished viewing the pages, close them and quit your browser.

Creating a new Web site

You'll begin this lesson by creating a new Web site using Adobe GoLive.

1 Start Adobe GoLive. A new document named Untitled.html opens. You don't need a new document for this part of the lesson.

2 Choose File > Close to close Untitled.html.

Now you're ready to create a new Web site.

3 Choose File > New Site > Blank.

4 Type **Gage** as the name of the new site.

5 Do one of the following:

- In Windows, click Browse and use the pop-up dialog box to select the Lesson03 folder.
- In Mac OS 8, select the Lesson03 folder, and don't open it.
- In Mac OS 9, select and open the Lesson03 folder.

6 Make sure that Create Folder is selected so that Adobe GoLive creates a folder for you.

7 In Windows, click OK. In Mac OS 8, click Choose. In Mac OS 9, click Save.

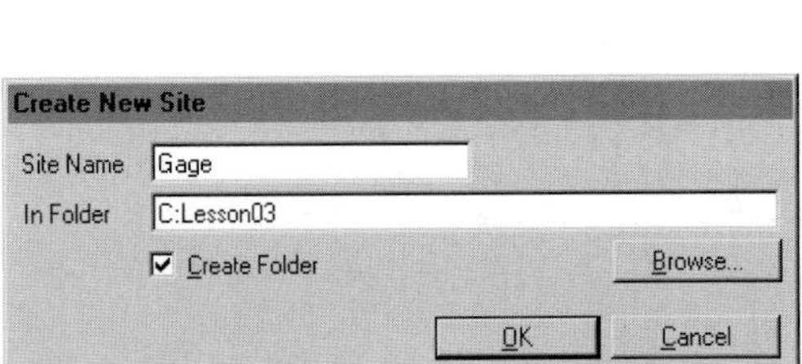

Creating new site (Windows)

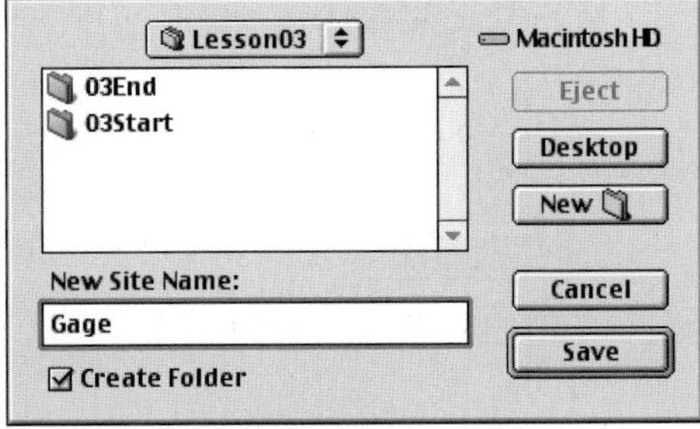

Creating new site (Mac OS)

A folder named Gage Folder is created within the Lesson03 folder. The site window appears with the Files tab selected displaying the contents of the Gage site.

8 Use Explorer (Windows) or the Finder (Mac OS) to open the Gage Folder, and examine its contents.

The Gage Folder contains the following:

- A folder called Gage, which stores the pages and media for your site. When you create a new site, this folder already contains a blank home page named Index.html.
- The Gage.data folder, which stores auxiliary material needed to build and maintain the site.
- The Gage.site file, which stores information about the structure of your site. When you open this file, the site window displays in Adobe GoLive.

Adding files to the Web site

Now you're ready to add files to the Web site. First you'll add a folder of image files. Later in this lesson, you'll use the image files when adding images to the pages for the site.

1 Using Explorer (Windows) or the Finder (Mac OS), select the Images folder, located inside the Lesson03/03Start folder. Drag the Images folder to the Files tab of the site window.

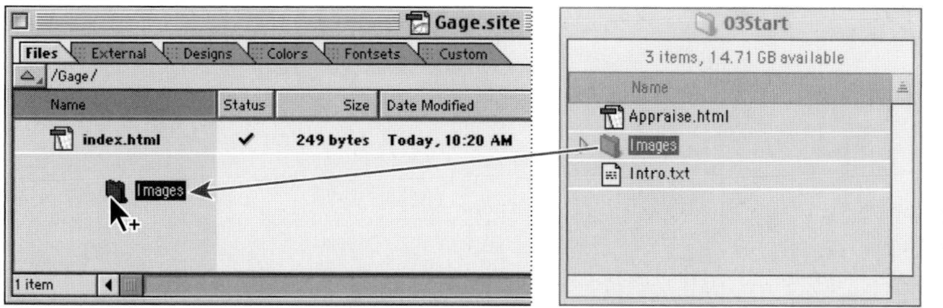

Dragging folder to Files tab of site window

2 Click the symbol next to the Images folder icon in the site window to display the contents of the Images folder. Click in a blank area of the site window to deselect the Images folder.

Now you'll add a new folder to the site. This folder will store the pages for the site.

3 Choose Site > New > Folder. A new untitled folder appears in the site window.

4 Type **Pages** to rename the folder, and click in the blank space outside the folder to deselect it.

Now you'll add the finished Web page from Lesson 2, "Working with Text and Tables," to the Pages folder. Later in this lesson, you'll update the design of the page.

5 Using Explorer (Windows) or the Finder (Mac OS), select the Appraise.html file, located inside the Lesson03/03Start folder. Drag the Appraise.html file from the desktop to the Pages folder in the site window.

Note: *If you pause too long over the Pages folder, it opens and the Files tab displays only its contents. To return to the root level of the Gage site, click the ( ) icon at the top left of the site window to go up one level in the site hierarchy.*

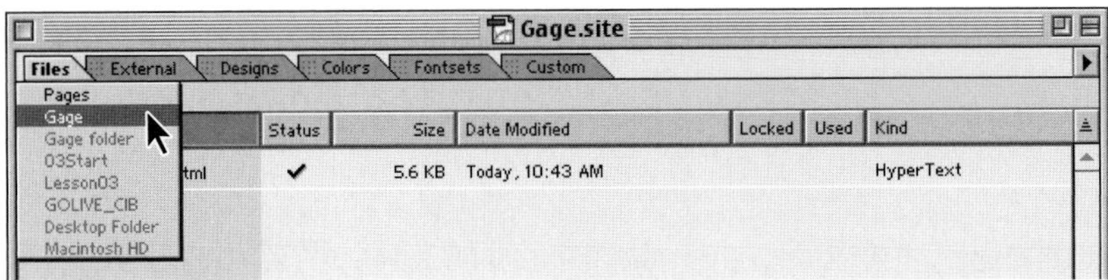

Returning to Gage folder

6 When the Copy Files dialog box appears, click OK.

7 Click the symbol next to the Pages folder icon in the site window to display the folder's contents.

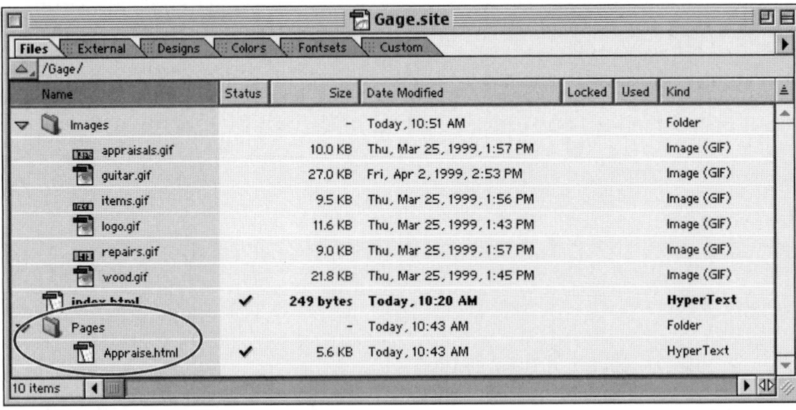

Displaying folder's contents

For detailed information on managing Web sites with Adobe GoLive, see "Managing Web Sites" on page 367.

Creating a component

Now you're ready to begin designing the pages for the Web site. At the top of each page, you'll place the Gage Vintage Guitars logo and a navigation bar for the site. Instead of creating this page content multiple times, you'll create it once and save it as a *component* that you can quickly add to your pages.

Using components

Components let you create elements in one source file that you can use on multiple pages. This feature is useful for buttons, logos, headers, and other items that you want to use throughout your site.

About components

You can use Adobe GoLive components to reference other HTML pages and embed them in your page, complete with text, images, and other visual content. When you embed an element as a component instead of writing the HTML code in your pages, you can change the object simply by double-clicking it to open the source file (an HTML page containing only the element) and then editing the object. When you save the source page, Adobe GoLive automatically updates all pages that contain the element.

Adobe GoLive encloses the embedded HTML page in a custom element that the browser ignores at run time (although its content is understood and interpreted correctly), and marks it as dynamic page content that needs to be updated each time the source file changes.

***Note:** Components are updated only while you work on your local hard disk. Pages on the Web server are not updated by just uploading the source file. You need to upload all pages that reference a component to update your site after changing the source file.*

Now you'll create a new page that you'll save as a component.

1 Place the site window at the bottom of your desktop, so that the window is visible when you create a new page. To move a window, drag its title bar.

2 Choose File > New to create a new page.

If needed, you can resize the document window and the site window, so that they take up less space on the desktop. To resize a window, drag its lower right corner.

3 Select the page title, "Welcome to Adobe GoLive 5."

4 Type **Navigation Bar** as the new title, and press Enter or Return.

5 If necessary, choose Window > Inspector to display the Inspector.

6 Click the Page icon (▤) in the upper left corner of the document window. The Inspector changes to the Page Inspector.

7 In the Page Inspector, click the HTML tab. Then click Component to set up the current page for use as a dynamic component.

8 Choose File > Save, rename the page **Navbar.html**, and save it in the Components folder. The path to the folder is Lesson03/Gage Folder/Gage.data/Components.

The Components folder stores dynamic components for the site. You can view the contents of this folder in the site window.

9 Click the double-arrow icon in the bottom right corner of the site window to expand the site window. The expanded pane of the site window is displayed, with the Extras tab selected and the Gage.data folder open.

10 Click the symbol next to the Components folder in the Extras tab of the expanded site window to see the folder's contents.

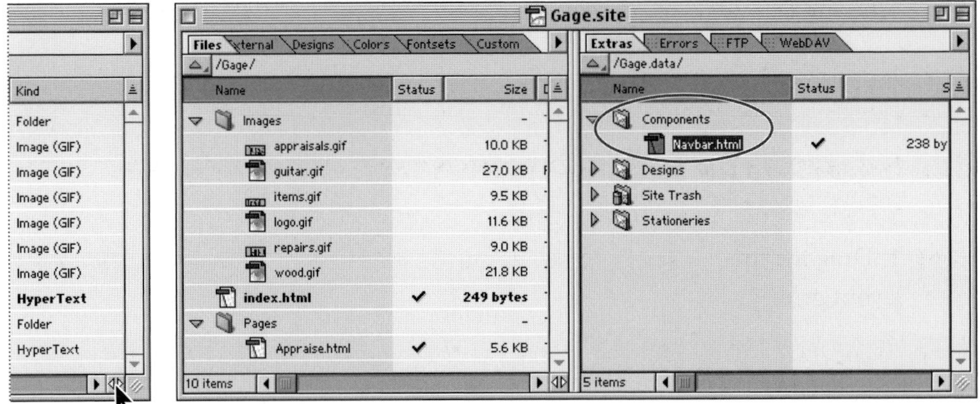

Components folder in expanded pane of site window

Adding a layout grid

You can use a layout grid to place text, tables, images, and other objects precisely on a page. When you add a layout grid to a page, Adobe GoLive actually generates tables in the HTML source code for the page. It uses these tables to place the objects on the page with 1-pixel accuracy.

Now you'll add a layout grid to the page.

1 Click the Navbar.html window to make it active.

2 If necessary, choose Window > Objects to display the Objects palette, and make sure that the Basic tab ( ) is selected.

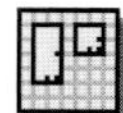

3 Drag the Layout Grid icon from the Objects palette to the page.

A layout grid is added to the page, and the Inspector changes to the Layout Grid Inspector.

Now you'll specify a width for the layout grid.

4 In the Layout Grid Inspector, enter **600** for Width.

You can also resize a layout grid by selecting it and dragging one of its handles.

Adding an image using the Point and Shoot button

Now you'll add four images to the page using a variety of methods. Adobe GoLive supports the standard image formats for the Web: Graphical Interchange Format (GIF), Joint Photographic Experts Group (JPEG), or Portable Network Graphics (PNG). Typically, GIF images are used for line art and JPEG images are used for photographs and other images with more than 256 colors. In this lesson, you'll use GIF images.

For information on using non-Web format images, such as native Photoshop, Illustrator, or LiveMotion images, see "Using Smart Objects" on page 109.

First you'll add the company logo to the page using the Point and Shoot button in the Image Inspector.

1 Drag the Image placeholder from the Objects palette to the upper left corner of the layout grid.

An image placeholder appears on the layout grid, and the Inspector changes to the Image Inspector.

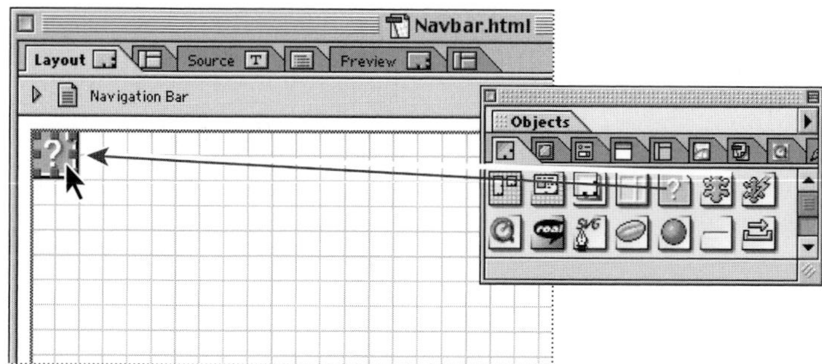

Adding image placeholder to page

2 In the Image Inspector, make sure that the Basic tab is selected.

Notice that the Source text box in the Image Inspector shows "Empty Reference!" This indicates that the image placeholder does not refer to an image yet. You'll use the Point and Shoot button to connect a specific image file in the site window with the image placeholder on the page.

3 Drag from the Point and Shoot button ( ) in the Image Inspector to Logo.gif in the Images folder within the site window. Release the mouse button when Logo.gif is highlighted.

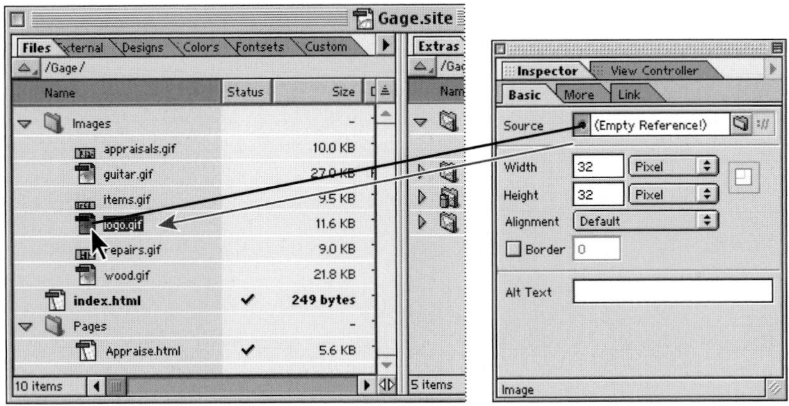

Using Point and Shoot button to specify image

The company logo is added to the page, and the Source text box in the Image Inspector shows the path to Logo.gif. If needed, you can easily adjust the position of the image by dragging it to the desired location.

Adobe GoLive supports the use of low-resolution images, which are displayed in the viewer's browser while high-resolution images are loading. You can get low-resolution images from another source, or generate them quickly using Adobe GoLive, as you'll do now.

4 Click the More tab in the Image Inspector, and then click Generate.

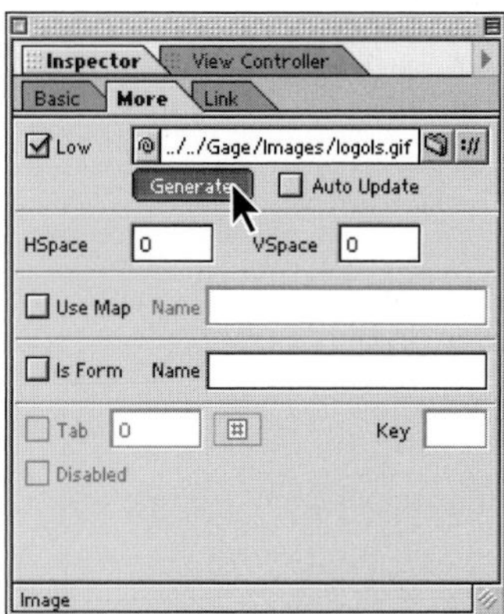

A low-resolution image named Logols.gif appears in the Images folder in the site window, and the Low option in the Image Inspector is automatically selected.

Now you'll add an alternative text message for the image. In browsers that don't support images or have image loading turned off, the text message is displayed instead of the image.

5 Click the Basic tab in the Image Inspector. Enter **Gage Vintage Guitars Logo** in the Alt Text box.

6 Choose File > Save to save the page.

Adding an image using a keyboard shortcut

Now you'll add a second image to the page using a keyboard shortcut. This image is part of the navigation bar for the site.

1 Drag the Image icon from the Objects palette to the right of the company logo on the page.

2 Hold down Alt (Windows) or Command (Mac OS), and drag from the image placeholder on the page to Items.gif in the Images folder in the site window.

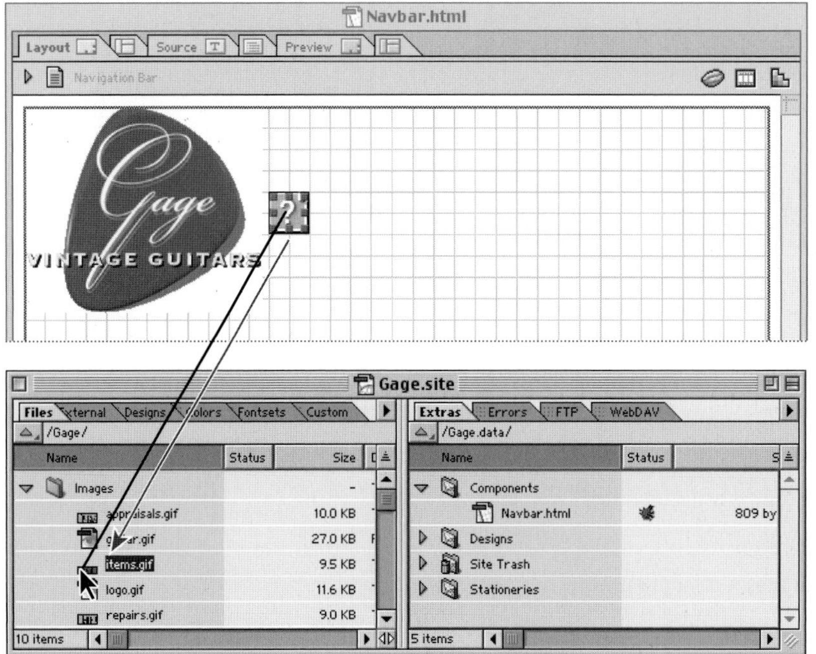

Using keyboard shortcut to specify image

3 In the Basic tab of the Image Inspector, type **Items In Stock** in the Alt text box, and press Enter or Return to add an alternative text label for Items.gif.

Because Items.gif is small in file size (1K), you don't need to create a low-source image for it.

Adding images by dragging

You'll add the third and fourth images to the page by dragging. These images also are part of the navigation bar for the site.

Now you'll add the third image to the page.

1 Drag the Image icon from the Objects palette to the right of the Items In Stock image on the page.

2 Drag Repairs.gif from the Images folder in the site window to the image placeholder on the page.

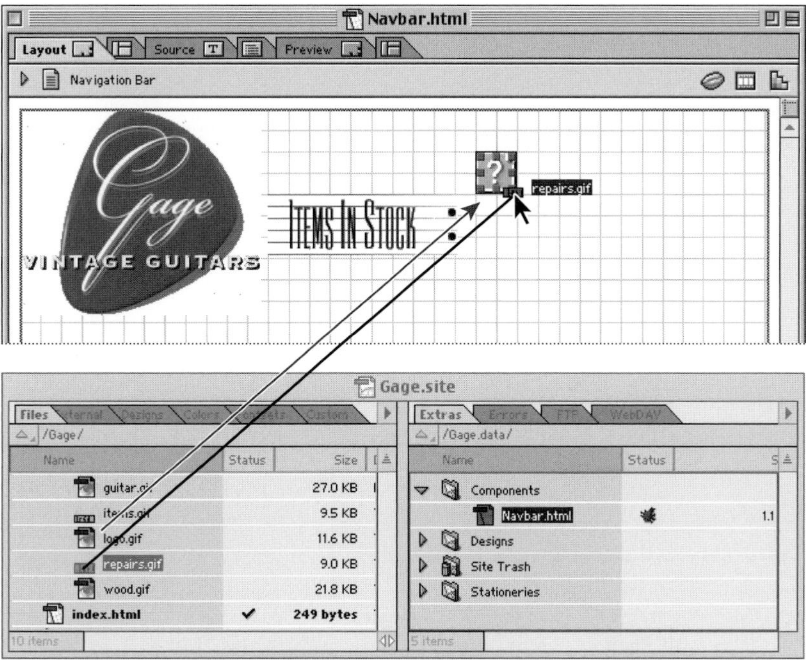

Dragging image file from site window to image placeholder

3 In the Image Inspector, type **Repairs** in the Alt text box, and press Enter or Return.

Now you'll add the fourth image to the page.

4 Drag the Image icon from the Objects palette to the right of the Repairs image on the page.

5 Drag Appraisals.gif from the Images folder in the site window to the image placeholder on the page.

6 In the Image Inspector, type **Appraisals** in the Alt text box, and press Enter or Return.

7 Choose File > Save to save the page.

To add an image, you can also drag the image file from the site window to the page, without using an image placeholder. Using an image placeholder gives you more control over the initial placement of the image.

Aligning and distributing multiple objects

Now that you've added all of the images, you're ready to align and distribute them on the page, using the Align palette. While the toolbar lets you align objects relative to the layout grid, the Align palette lets you both align and distribute objects relative to each other or their parents.

Now you'll align the tops of the three images that make up the navigation bar.

1 Choose Window > Align to display the Align palette.

2 Click the Items In Stock image to select it. Then Shift-click the Repairs image and the Appraisals image to add them to the selection.

3 In the Align palette, click the Vertical Align Top button ( ) in the Align Objects area to align the tops of the selected objects. (The button is dimmed if the tops of the selected objects are already aligned.)

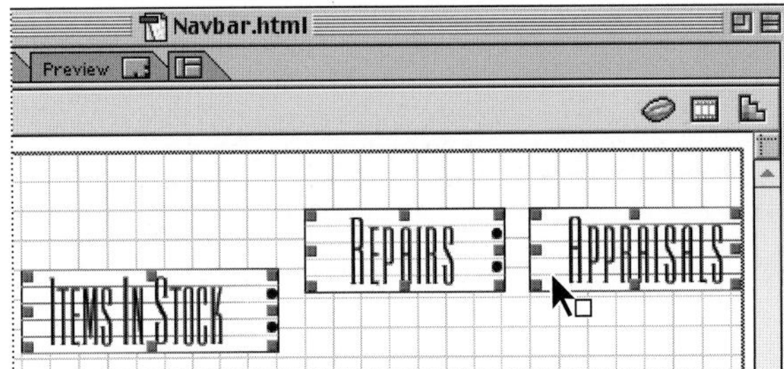

Shift-clicking to select multiple objects

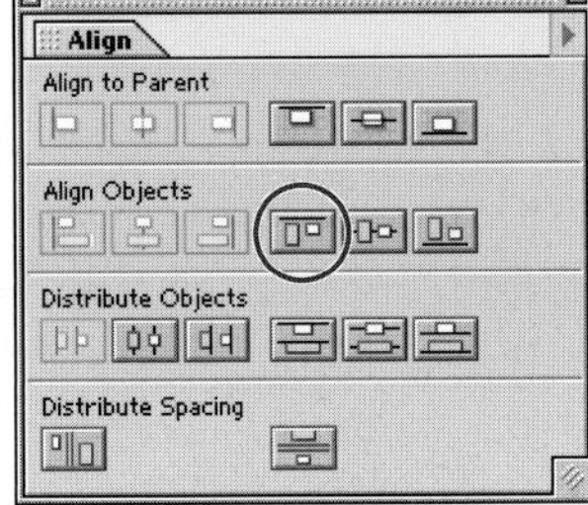

Align Top button

4 With the three images still selected, click the Vertical Align Top button in the Align to Parent area of the Align palette. This aligns the three images with the top of the layout grid.

Now you'll use a keyboard shortcut to move the three images together.

5 Select just the Repairs image on the page, and press Option+left arrow (Mac OS) or Ctrl+Alt+left arrow (Windows) repeatedly until the image moves no further.

6 Select the Appraisals image, and press Option+left arrow (Mac OS) or Ctrl+Alt+left arrow (Windows) repeatedly until the image moves no further.

The selected objects are moved horizontally on the page so that their edges touch each other.

Note: *You can move a selected object on a layout grid using the arrow keys. By default, pressing an arrow key moves the object 16 pixels, the spacing between the horizontal and vertical lines of the grid. If a layout grid has options selected to snap objects to the grid, you can easily move a selected object on the grid by 1 pixel. Hold down Ctrl+Alt (Windows) or Option (Mac OS), and press an arrow key.*

7 Click the blank space beneath the selected images to deselect them.

You might have noticed that the layout grid may have increased in size as necessary to accommodate the images that you added to it. When you've finished placing objects on a layout grid, it's a good idea to optimize the grid. Optimizing a grid reduces its size, so that it takes up less space on the page.

8 If necessary, click the layout grid to select it. Then click Optimize in the Layout Grid Inspector.

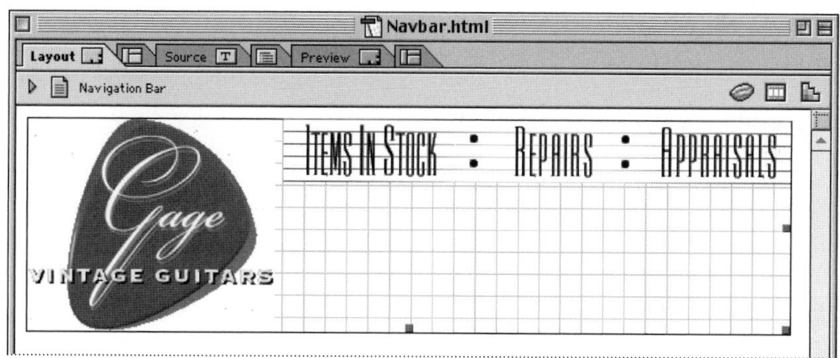

Optimized layout grid

9 Choose File > Save to save the page. Then choose File > Close to close it.

Designing the home page

Now you're ready to design the home page for the Web site.

1 In the site window, double-click Index.html to open it.

2 Change the title of the page to **Gage Vintage Guitars**.

Adding a background image

Now you'll add a background image to the home page. When choosing a background image, you can choose an image that's smaller in size than your page. Adobe GoLive, as well as Web browsers, treats the background image as a tile that it repeats to cover the page.

First you'll preview the image. You can use the File Inspector to obtain detailed information about a file, including a preview of its contents.

1 In the site window, click the icon for Wood.gif in the Images folder. (Be sure to click the icon, not the filename.) The Inspector changes to the File Inspector.

2 Click the Content tab of the File Inspector. A preview of Wood.gif appears in the File Inspector.

Now you'll add a background image to the page using Wood.gif.

3 Click the Page icon ( ) in the upper left corner of the document window. The Inspector changes to the Page Inspector.

4 In the Page Inspector, click the Page tab, if necessary. Click the check box next to Image to select the Image option.

5 Drag from the Point and Shoot button (▣) in the Page Inspector to Wood.gif in the Images folder within the site window.

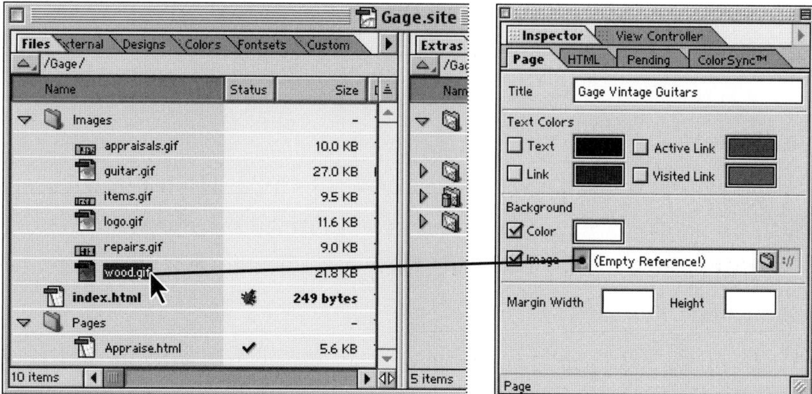

Specifying image to tile for page's background

The image of the wood is tiled to cover the page.

Adding a component

Now you'll add the navigation bar to the home page using the component that you created earlier in this lesson.

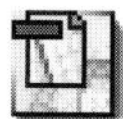

1 Click the Smart tab (▣) in the Objects palette. Then drag the Component icon to the upper left corner of the page.

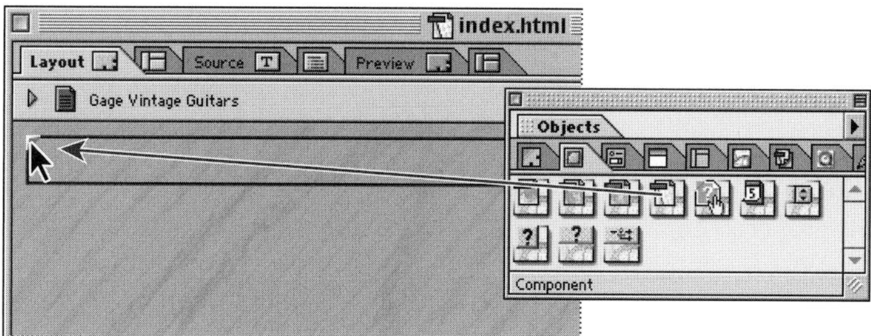

Adding component placeholder to page

2 Click the Component placeholder.

The Inspector changes to the Component Inspector.

3 Drag from the Point and Shoot button (◎) in the Component Inspector to Navbar.html in the Components folder in the site window. (Remember that the Components folder is displayed in the expanded pane of the site window.)

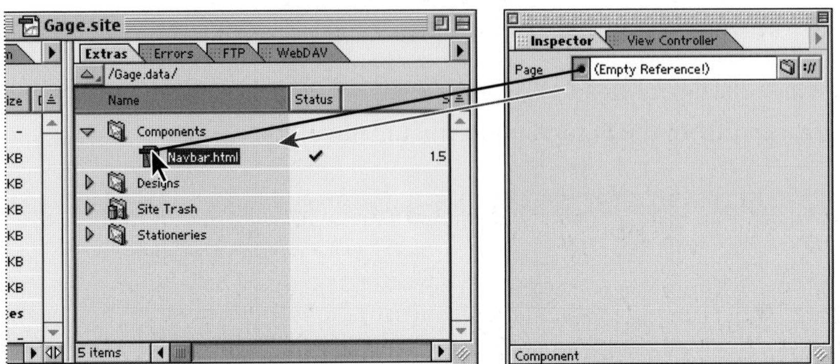

Using Point and Shoot button to specify component

The navigation bar is added to the top of the home page. Adobe GoLive also automatically generates a GeneratedItems folder in the site window. Inside this folder is a file called CSScriptLib.js where Adobe GoLive stores common code related to your pages. Don't delete this folder or its contents.

4 Choose File > Save to save the page.

Adding text using layout text boxes

Now you'll add text to the page using layout text boxes. Before you can add layout text boxes to the page, you must add a layout grid to the page. You place the layout text boxes on the grid and then type text in the boxes. With layout text boxes, you can easily rearrange the location of text on your page by moving or aligning the boxes.

First you'll add a layout grid to the home page.

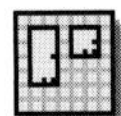

1 Click the Basic tab (▣) in the Objects palette. Then drag the Layout Grid icon from the palette to below the component on the page.

2 Type **580** for Width in the Layout Grid Inspector, and press Enter or Return.

3 Type **300** for Height in the Layout Grid Inspector, and press Enter or Return.

Now you're ready to add the first layout text box to the page. You'll use this box to add a main heading to the page.

4 Drag the Layout Text Box icon from the Palette to the upper center of the new layout grid.

A layout text box is added to the page. If needed, you can easily adjust the position of the box. Move the pointer to an edge of the box, so that the pointer turns into a little box with an arrow. Then drag the box to the desired location.

5 Click inside the layout text box, and type **Welcome to Gage Vintage Guitars**. Then choose Header 1 from the Paragraph Format menu on the toolbar.

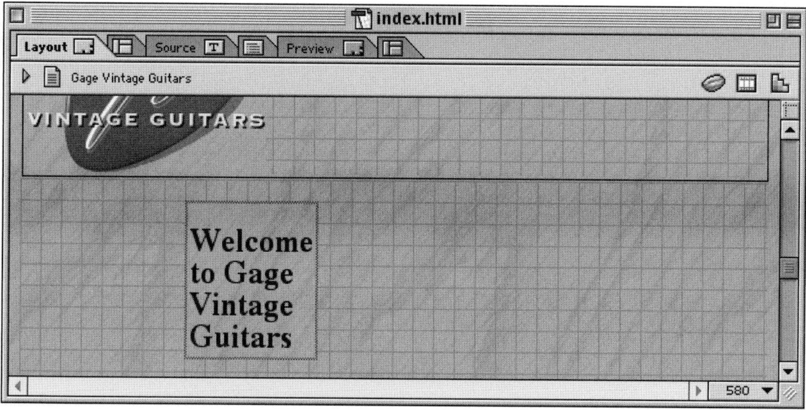

Text in layout text box, reformatted as Header 1

You can use the toolbar to position a selected object precisely on a layout grid.

6 Click an edge of the layout text box to select it.

7 On the toolbar, type **179** in the Horizontal Position text box, and press Tab to position the box 179 pixels from the left edge of the grid, and jump to the next entry box. Type **0** in the Vertical Position text box, and press Tab to position the box 0 pixels from the top of the grid, and jump to the next entry box.

You can also use the toolbar to resize a selected object.

8 On the toolbar, type **400** in the Width text box, and press Tab to make the box 400 pixels in width, and to jump to the next entry box. Type **80** in the Height text box, and press Enter or Return to make the box 80 pixels in height.

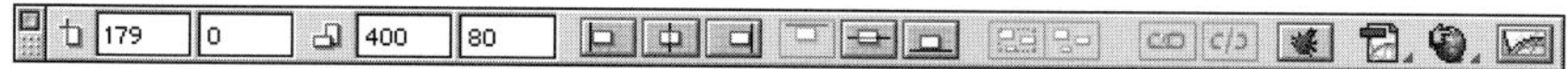

Now you'll add a second layout text box to the page. You'll use this box to add a subheading to the page.

9 Drag the Layout Text Box icon from the Objects palette to the upper left of the layout grid.

10 Click inside the layout text box, and type **Check Out This Week's Hottest Buy!** Then select the text you've just typed, click the Bold button (B) on the toolbar, and choose 4 from the Font Size menu on the toolbar.

If needed, you can resize the layout text box using its handles. Click an edge of the box to select it, and drag one of its handles.

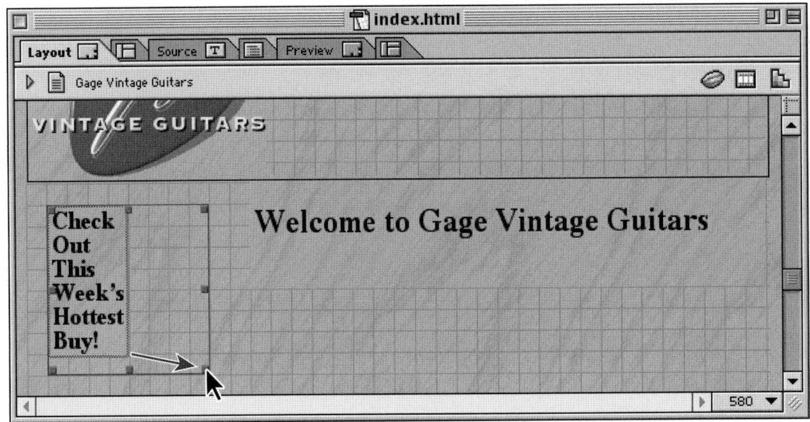

Resizing layout text box

11 Click in the blank space outside the layout text box to deselect it.

Adding text using a table

Now you'll add text to the page that introduces Gage Vintage Guitars. You'll begin by creating a single-cell table. Then you'll import text into the table from a text-only file created in a word-processing application.

For more information about working with tables, see "Adding tables" on page 43.

1 Drag the Table icon from the Objects palette to below the main heading on the layout grid.

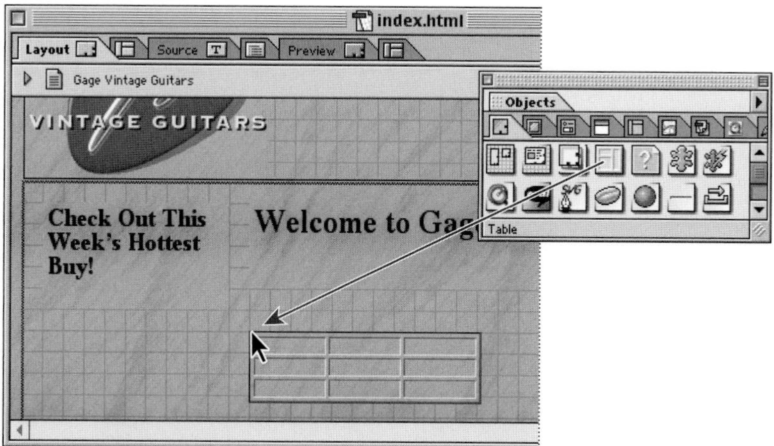

Adding table to page

The Inspector changes to the Table Inspector, with the Table tab selected.

2 In the Table Inspector, type **1** for Rows, and press Tab. Type **1** for Columns, and press Tab.

3 Choose Pixel from the menu to the right of the Width text box, if necessary. For Width, type **400**, and press Enter or Return.

4 Type **0** for Border, and press Enter or Return to remove the table's border.

5 Click the Browse button for the Import Tab-Text option.

6 Select the Intro.txt file, located inside the Lesson03/03Start folder, and click Open.

7 On the toolbar, type **179** in the Horizontal Position text box, and press Tab. Type **80** in the Vertical Position text box, and press Enter or Return.

8 Click the layout grid to select it. Then click Optimize in the Layout Grid Inspector.

9 Choose File > Save to save the page.

Creating a custom color palette and adding color to text

Now you'll add color to some of the text on the page. You'll begin by adding a color to the Colors tab in the site window. You can use the Colors tab as a custom color palette to store colors that you frequently use in your site.

1 Click the Colors tab in the site window.

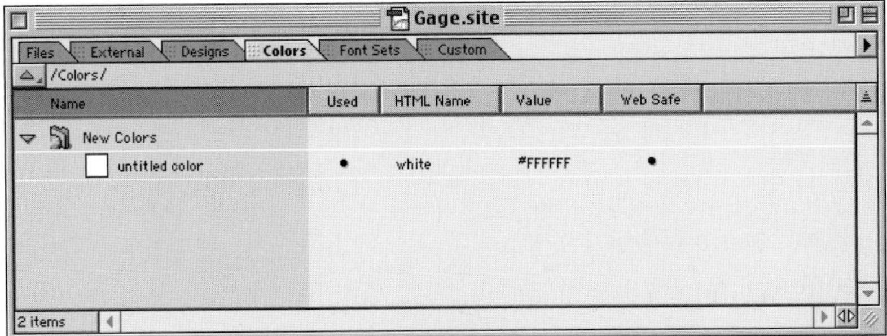

Colors tab in site window

Notice that the Colors tab contains a New Colors folder and an untitled color within it. When you create a new site, Adobe GoLive automatically adds these contents to the Colors tab. The untitled color represents the default white background color used on the home page, Index.html.

First you'll name the untitled color.

2 Click the name of the untitled color to select it. (Be sure to click the name, not the icon.) Rename the color **White**, and click in the blank space beneath the name to deselect it, or press Enter or Return. The easiest way in Windows to rename a color is to select the untitled color and then press F2. This selects just the color label.

Now you'll add a custom color to the Colors tab.

3 If necessary, choose Window > Color to display the Color palette.

4 In the Color palette, make sure that the Web Color List button (icon) is selected. In the Value text box, enter **990000**, and press Enter or Return. The selected color appears in the preview pane.

5 Drag the color from the preview pane to the New Colors folder in the Colors tab of the site window.

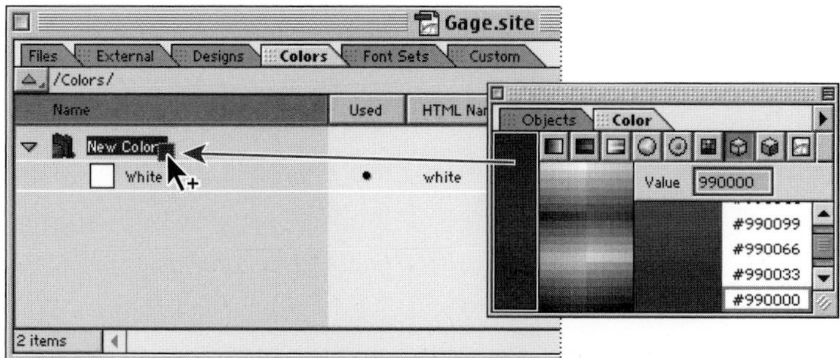

Dragging color from preview pane to Colors tab in site window

6 Rename the color **Red**, and then press Enter or Return. The easiest way in Windows to rename a color is to select the untitled color and then press F2.

Now you'll color some of the text on the page using the Red color.

7 Select the text "Check Out This Week's Hottest Buy!" (Make sure that you select the text, not the text box.)

8 Drag the Red color from the Colors tab of the site window to the selected text on the page.

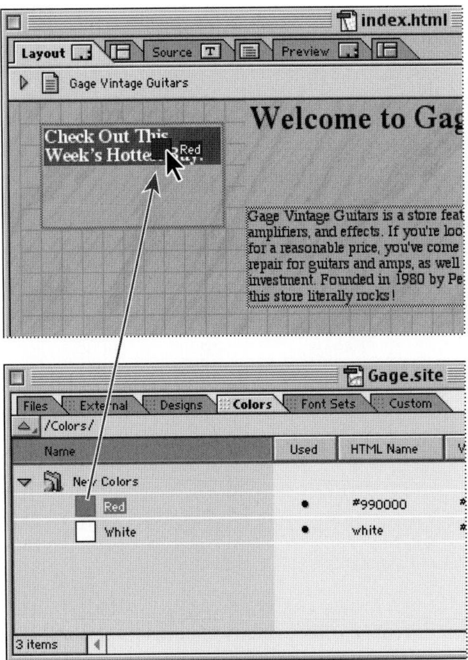

Dragging color from site window to selected text

9 Click in the blank space outside the selected text to deselect it.

You can also extract color from a region below the pointer and add the color to your custom color palette. This feature is useful when you want to match the colors of two objects.

10 Move the pointer over the checkerboard colors field in the Color palette, so that it turns into an eyedropper.

11 Drag from the checkerboard colors field to the shadow of the guitar pick on the page, and release the mouse button. The color of the shadow appears in the preview pane of the Color palette.

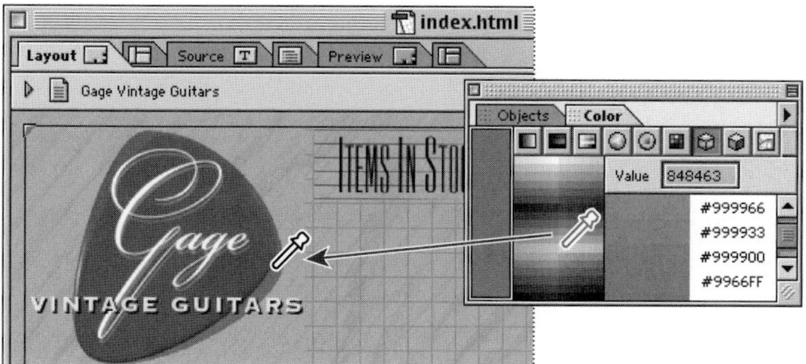

Extracting color from image on page

12 Drag the new color from the preview pane to the New Colors folder in the Colors tab of the site window.

13 Type **Olive** as the name of the color, and then click in the blank space beneath the name to deselect it.

If desired, you can now match objects on the page with the color of the shadow. The site window provides information about whether or not a color is Web safe. In the Web Safe column of the site window, the Olive color does not have a bullet, indicating that the color will dither on a system set to 256 display colors (standard PCs).

14 Choose File > Save to save the home page. Then choose File > Close to close it.

Now you're ready to design two other pages for the Gage Vintage Guitars Web site.

Updating the design of the Appraisal page

First you'll update the design of the finished Web page from Lesson 2, "Working with Text."

Adding a component

Currently, the page does not contain the navigation bar for the site. You'll add the navigation bar quickly using the component you created earlier in this lesson. You've learned how to add a component by first adding a Component placeholder to the page. Now you'll learn how to add a component without using a placeholder.

1 Click the Files tab in the site window.

2 In the site window, double-click Appraise.html in the Pages folder to open it.

3 Click the Site Extras tab (▣) in the Objects palette.

4 Choose Components from the menu in the lower right corner of the Objects palette. An icon of the component, Navbar.html, appears in the Objects palette.

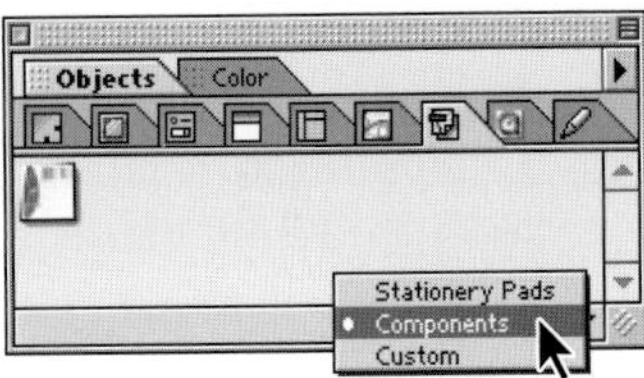

5 Drag the icon of Navbar.html in the Objects palette to the upper left corner of the page.

Using icon in Objects palette to add component

6 If necessary, scroll up to bring the beginning of the document into view.

The navigation bar is added to the top of the Appraisal page. Notice that the Page text box in the Component Inspector shows the path to Navbar.html. Adobe GoLive also automatically creates a GeneratedItems folder in the site window. Inside this folder is a file called CSScriptLib.js where Adobe GoLive stores common code related to your pages. Don't delete this folder or its contents.

Updating a custom color palette

Now you'll update your custom color palette with any colors from the Appraisal page that aren't already in the palette.

1 Click the Colors tab in the site window, and then click the Update button (✓) in the toolbar.

The new background colors from the page and the table cells are added to the New Colors folder in the colors tab of the site window. You'll name each of the colors.

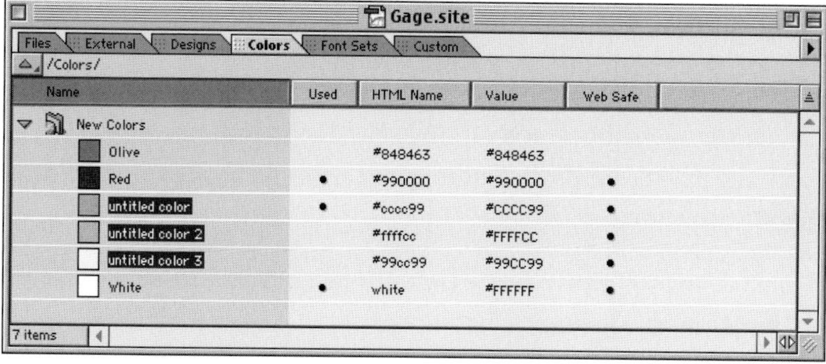

Updated custom color palette

2 Click in the blank space outside the selected colors to deselect them.

3 Click the name of the first untitled color to select it. Type **Green**, and then click in the blank space beneath the name to deselect it.

4 Change the name of the second untitled color to **Khaki**, and change the name of the third untitled color to **Yellow**.

Now you'll change the name of the New Colors folder.

5 Click the name of the New Colors folder to select it. Type **Gage Colors**, and then click in the blank space beneath the name to deselect it.

6 Click the title bar of the Appraisal page to activate it. Choose File > Save to save the page. Then choose File > Close to close it.

Designing the Hottest Buy page

Now you'll design a new page using floating boxes. Floating boxes let you place objects on the page intuitively, without using a table or layout grid. They also let you overlap objects on a page in layers. You can add text, tables, images, and other objects to floating boxes.

First you'll create a new page.

1 Choose File > New.

2 Change the title of the page to **Hottest Buy**.

3 Choose File > Save, rename the page **Hottest.html**, and save it in the Pages folder. The path to the folder is Lesson03/Gage Folder/Gage/Pages.

Now you'll change the background color of the page. Using your custom color palette, you can easily match the background color of the page with the background color of the Appraisal page.

4 Drag the Khaki color from the Colors tab in the site window to the Page icon ( ) in the upper left corner of the document window.

The background color of the page changes to khaki.

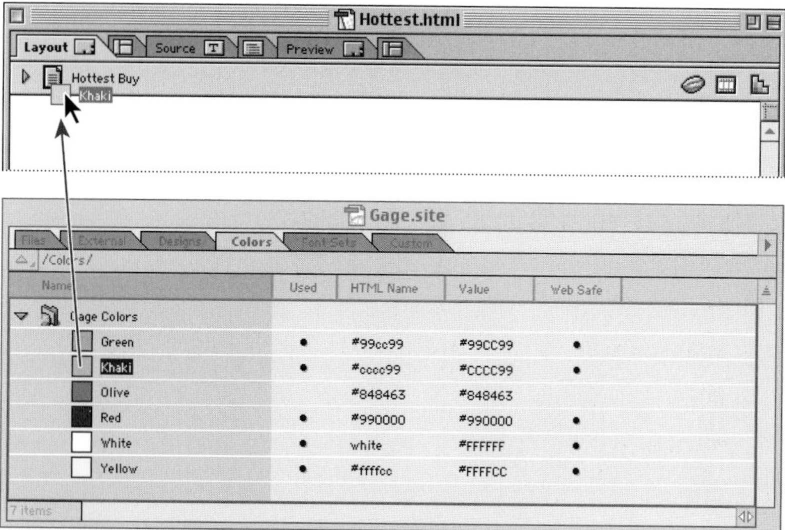

Using Colors tab in site window to change page's background color

Now you'll add the navigation bar to the page, as you did with the other pages for the site.

5 Drag the icon of Navbar.html in the Site Extras tab of the Objects palette to the upper left corner of the page.

6 Choose File > Save to save the page.

Adding the first floating box

Now you'll add a floating box to the page. You'll use this floating box to add an image of a guitar to the page.

1 Click the Basic tab in the Objects palette. Then drag the Floating Box icon from the Objects palette to the page. You can also just double-click the Floating Box icon in the Objects palette to insert it, if you have an insertion point already on the page.

A floating box appears on the page in the upper left corner below the component, and the Inspector changes to the Floating Box Inspector.

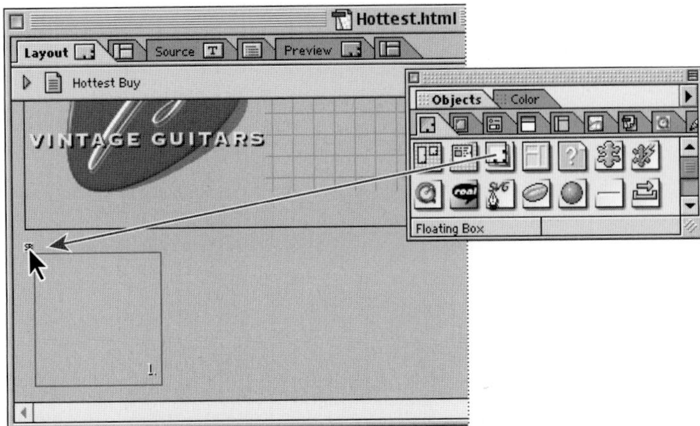

Adding floating box to page

Now you'll name the floating box, so that you can differentiate it from other floating boxes that you'll add to the page.

2 In the Floating Box Inspector, type **Image** in the Name text box, and press Enter or Return.

Now you'll add the guitar image to the floating box.

3 Click the Files tab in the site window. Then drag Guitar.gif from the Images folder in the site window to the floating box on the page.

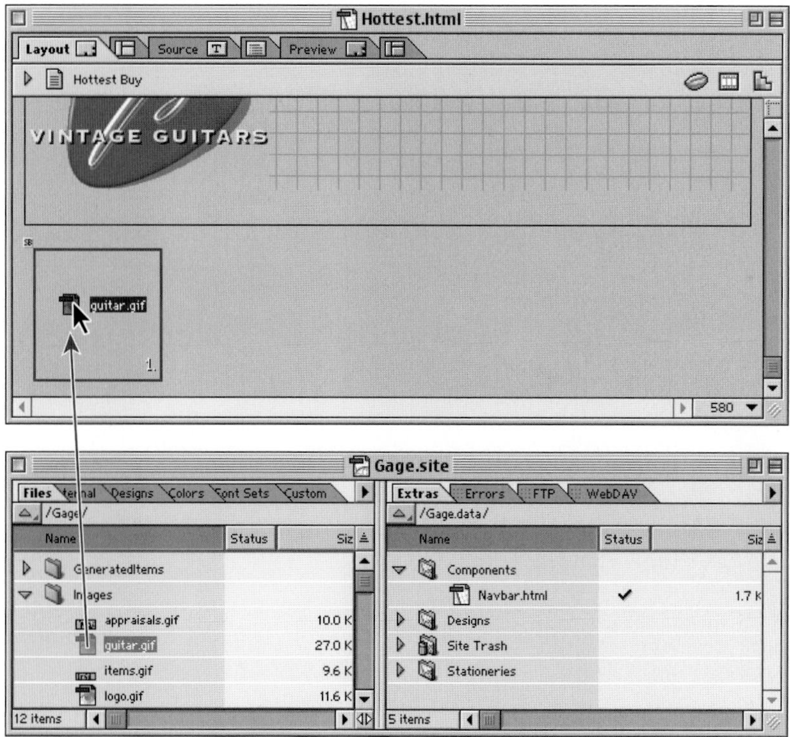

Dragging image file from site window to floating box

The guitar image appears in the floating box.

4 Click in the blank space outside the image to deselect it.

Adding the second floating box

You'll add a second floating box to the page that will contain a description of the guitar you've just added to the page.

1 Double-click the Floating Box icon in the Objects palette. The second floating box appears on top of the first one.

2 In the Floating Box Inspector, type **Description** in the Name text box, and press Enter or Return.

For now, you'll move the Description floating box to an empty area of the page.

3 Move the pointer over an edge of the Description floating box, so that the pointer turns into a hand pointing left.

4 Drag the Description floating box to the right of the Image floating box.

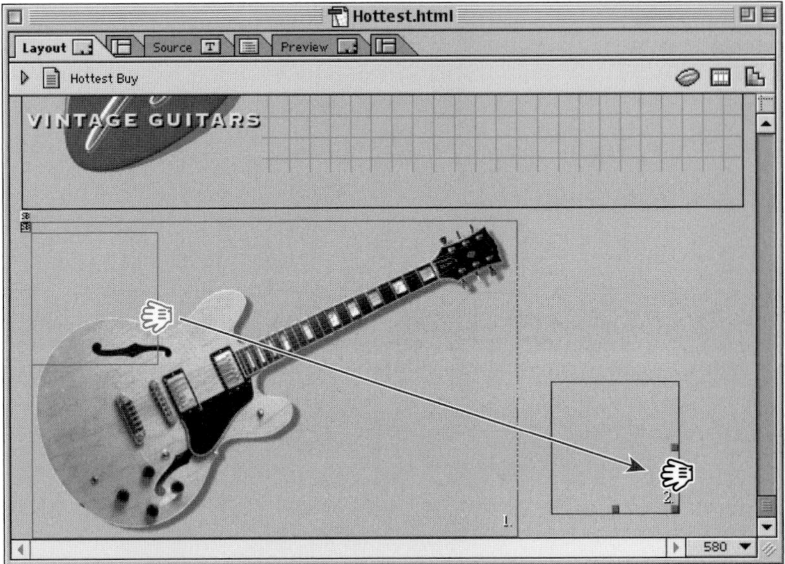

Dragging second floating box to right of first one

Now you'll add text to the Description floating box. You'll enter a description of the guitar shown on the page.

5 Click inside the Description floating box, and type **1981 Gibson ES-347**. Then select the text you've just typed, click the Bold button (B) on the toolbar, and choose 6 from the Font Size menu on the toolbar.

6 Click the Colors tab in the site window. Then drag the Red color from the site window to the selected text on the page.

7 Click in the blank space outside the selected text to deselect it.

You can also display custom colors for your site in the Site Colors tab of the Color palette. Then you can use the Color palette instead of the site window to apply colors to the page.

Now you'll move the Description floating box using the Floating Box Inspector.

8 Move the pointer over an edge of the Description floating box, so that the pointer turns into a hand pointed to the left. Then click an edge of the floating box to select it.

9 In the Floating Box Inspector, type **250** for Left, and press Enter or Return to position the floating box 250 pixels from the left edge of the page. Type **300** for Top, and press Enter or Return to position the floating box 300 pixels from the top of the page.

Now you'll resize the floating box using the Floating Box Inspector.

10 Type **200** for Width, and press Enter or Return to make the floating box 200 pixels in width. Type **100** for Height, and press Enter or Return to make the floating box 100 pixels in height.

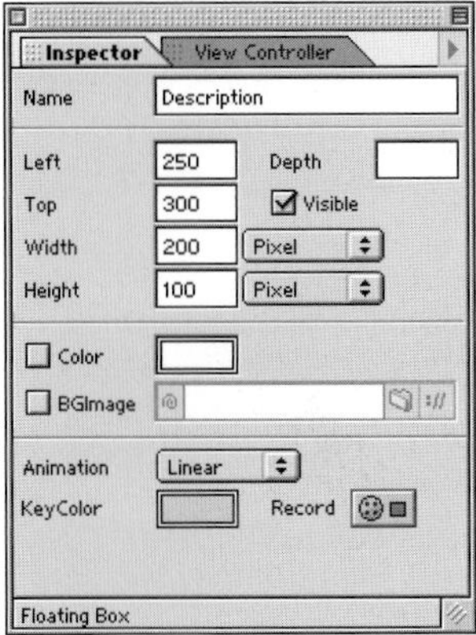

You can also resize a floating box by selecting it and dragging one of its handles.

11 Choose File > Save to save the page.

Notice that the Items In Stock, Repairs, and Appraisals images on the Hottest Buy page are aligned to the top of the grid. You'll move these images down so that they're vertically centered on the grid.

12 Try to click the Items In Stock image to select it for editing. Notice that you selected the entire component instead.

You can't edit the objects in the component from this page. Instead, you must open the file in which you created them.

13 Choose File > Close to close the page.

Using floating boxes

Floating boxes let you manipulate page content to create dynamic effects and multilayered displays. Floating boxes let you divide your page into rectangles that you can format individually, fill with HTML content, and stack. The boxes can be opaque or transparent to reveal objects in the background.

Note: *To display properly, floating boxes require Web browsers version 4.0 or later. Although floating boxes may soon be used as commonly as HTML tables, viewers with older browsers may have trouble viewing pages that contain floating boxes.*

About floating boxes

Floating boxes are based on the DIV element, which has been available since HTML 3.2 but not commonly used. HTML 4.0 substantially enhances the DIV element's functionality, allowing it to be absolutely positioned, and stacked to accept a background image or background color. The DIV element is also a core element of Dynamic HTML, and a major building block for absolute positioning with cascading style sheets.

Two concepts are key to understanding floating boxes:

- *Layering is a key feature of floating boxes. Floating boxes can overlap or even be placed on top of each other. The stacking order is controlled by an attribute called the z-index (z is from the z-axis in a three-dimensional coordinate system). Elements with a higher z-index display on top of elements with a lower z-index. For example, an element with a z-index of 2 appears to float above an element with a z-index of 1. By default, floating boxes are superimposed on the normal flow of HTML and the Adobe GoLive layout grid.*
- *As an independent division within the page, a floating box accepts any other HTML element—such as an image or simple HTML text with formatting. It also has the same background image and color properties as an HTML page.*

Editing a component

An additional benefit of using a component to place frequently used page content throughout your site is that you only need to edit a single file to make changes to the component. When you save your changes to the component, Adobe GoLive automatically updates all files that use it.

Now you'll open Navbar.html to edit it.

1 Click the Extras tab in the expanded site window.

2 In the Components folder in the site window, double-click Navbar.html to open it.

3 Click the Items In Stock image to select it. Then Shift-click the Repairs image and the Appraisals image to add them to the selection.

4 Click the Vertical Align Center button ( ) on the toolbar to center the images vertically on the grid.

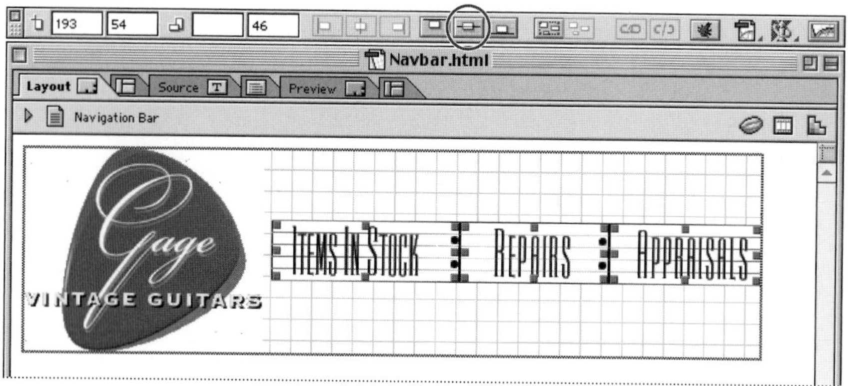

Images centered vertically on grid

5 Click in the blank space outside the selected images to deselect them.

6 Choose File > Save to save the page. Click OK for Adobe GoLive to automatically update the files that use Navbar.html as a dynamic component.

7 Choose File > Close to close the page.

You've completed the design of the Web site for this lesson. Now you're ready to preview the pages in Adobe GoLive.

Previewing in Adobe GoLive

To preview each Web page, do the following:

1 In the site window, double-click Index.html, Appraise.html, or Hottest.html to open it. (The Appraise.html and Hottest.html files are located inside the Pages folder.)

2 In the document window, click the Preview tab.

Adobe GoLive displays a preview of the page. Notice that the location of the navigation bar has moved down on the page to reflect the change you made to the component.

3 When you have finished viewing the page, choose File > Close to close it.

4 When you have finished viewing all of the pages, choose File > Close to close the site window.

For additional information on previewing pages, see "Previewing in Adobe GoLive" on page 24 and "Previewing in a Web browser" on page 25.

Exploring on your own

Sometimes you may want several pages in your Web site to be similar in page layout and design. Instead of creating each page from scratch, you can create the page once and save it as stationery. In Adobe GoLive, stationery is equivalent to page templates available in most word-processing applications. You save a page as stationery and use the stationery to create new pages that are fully editable.

Try creating stationery from the home page for the Gage Vintage Guitars site. Then use the stationery to create a new page.

1 Choose File > Open, and open the Gage.site file. The path to the file is Lesson03/03End/Gage Folder/Gage.site.

2 In the site window, double-click Index.html to open it.

3 Choose File > Save As, and then choose Stationeries from the pop-up button menu in the Save As dialog box.

4 Rename the page **Master.html**, and then click Save. The new stationery is saved to the Stationeries folder of the site.

5 Choose File > Close to close the page.

6 Click the Site Extras tab ( ) in the Objects palette.

7 Choose Stationery Pads from the menu in the lower right corner of the Objects palette, if necessary. An icon of the stationery, Master.html, appears in the Objects palette.

8 Drag the icon of Master.html in the Objects palette to the Pages folder in the site window. A new page from the Master.html stationery appears in the site window.

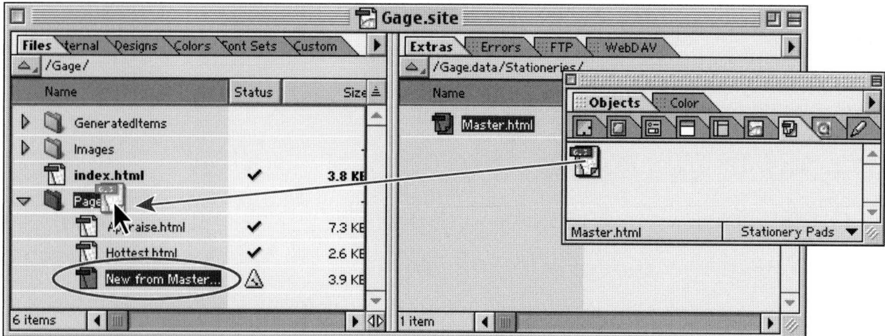

Creating new page from stationery

9 Type **New.html** to rename the page, and press Enter or Return. Then click in the blank space outside the filename to deselect it.

10 In the site window, double-click New.html in the Pages folder to open it.

11 Click the navigation bar at the top of the page. Notice that you selected the entire component. As with other pages that use the component, you can't edit the objects in the component from this page. Instead, you edit the objects in the component from the file in which you created them.

12 Select the text "Check Out This Week's Hottest Buy!"

13 Type new text as desired to replace the selected text. (We used "Click Here for a Free Appraisal!") Notice that you can edit the text in the layout text boxes on the page.

You can also remove objects from the page.

14 Click the left edge of the single-cell table to select it. (The table contains the text that introduces Gage Vintage Guitars.) Press Delete to remove the table.

You can also add objects to the page.

15 Click the Basic tab (▣) in the Objects palette, and drag the Layout Text Box icon from the Objects palette to the lower layout grid on the page. A layout text box is added to the page.

16 If desired, continue to make changes to the page. When you have finished, choose File > Close to close the page. You don't need to save your changes. Then choose File > Close to close the site window.

Review questions

1 Which file displays in the site window?

2 Name two benefits of using a component.

3 How can you add a component to a page?

4 What are the three standard image formats for the Web?

5 Name two ways that you can specify an image for an image placeholder on a page.

6 What object needs to be present before adding a layout text box to a page?

7 How do you create a custom color palette?

8 Can you extract color from an image that you've added to a page? If so, how?

9 Why do you name floating boxes?

10 How do you move a floating box?

Review answers

1 The file with the .site extension displays in the site window.

2 Using a component, you can create repetitive page content once and then quickly add it to the pages for your site. You can also make edits to repetitive page content in a single file and then have Adobe GoLive automatically update pages in your site that use the component.

3 You can add a component to a page by doing one of the following:

• Drag the Component icon from the Smart tab in the Objects palette to the page. Then drag from the Point and Shoot button in the Component Inspector to an HTML file in the Components folder in the site window.

• Choose Components from the menu in the lower right corner of the Site Extras tab in the Objects palette. Then drag the icon of the HTML file from the Objects palette to the page.

4 The three standard image formats for the Web are Graphical Interchange Format (GIF), Joint Photographic Experts Group (JPEG), and Portable Network Graphics (PNG).

5 You can specify an image for an image placeholder by doing one of the following: drag from the Point and Shoot button in the Image Inspector to an image file in the site window; hold down Alt (Windows) or Command (Mac OS), and drag from the image placeholder to an image file in the site window; or drag an image file from the site window to the image placeholder.

6 A layout grid needs to be present before adding a layout text box to a page.

7 Using the Color palette, choose a color that you want in your custom color palette. Then drag the color from the preview pane of the Color palette to the Colors tab in the site window. When the Colors tab in the site window is selected, you can also quickly create a custom color palette by opening a new page that has color applied and clicking the Update button on the toolbar.

8 Yes, you can extract color from an image that you've added to a page. Drag from the checkerboard colors field of the Color palette to a specific area of the image on the page, and release the mouse button. The color of the area of the image appears in the preview pane of the Color palette. You can then drag from the preview pane to the Colors tab of the site window.

9 You name floating boxes so that you can differentiate them from one another.

10 Move the pointer over an edge of the floating box, so that the pointer turns into a hand pointed to the left. Drag the floating box to move it. You can also enter specific values in the Floating Box Inspector to position a selected floating box precisely.

Lesson 4

```
TITLE>We
STYLE TYPE=

{color:maroon;

/STYLE>
D>
>
!-- Begin main table -->
TABLE BORDER="4" CELLPADD
6">
    <TR>
        <TD><A
p://www.adobe.com/">Adobe</A>
        <TD>GoLive</TD>
        <TD><IMG BORDER="0" HE
e.gif" ALT="Title"></TD>
    </TR>
    <TR>
        <TD><SPAN CLASS="head
N></TD>
    </TR>
    <TR>
        <TD><B>DHTML an
    </TR>
/TABLE>
DY>

    P-EQUIV="content-typ
    charset=iso-8859-
    come to Adobe GoLi
    text/css"><

main table -->
ER="4" CELLPADD

D><A
dobe.com/">Adobe</A
D>GoLive</TD>
D><IMG BORDER="0" HE
="Title"></TD>

D><SPAN CLASS="head

D><B>DHTML an
```

4 Using Smart Objects

Adobe GoLive lets you insert Smart Objects on your Web pages that maintain links to images in their original formats, including Photoshop, Illustrator, and LiveMotion files. You can edit the images in their own applications, and the links ensure that Web pages containing the images are updated. Smart Object technology revolutionizes the traditional workflow for creating Web graphics, making it more efficient and flexible.

About this lesson

In this lesson, you'll learn how to do the following:

- Learn about Smart Object technology and see it in action.
- Learn how to place, resize, and edit a Smart Photoshop Object.
- Learn how to place and edit Illustrator files.
- Learn how to place and edit LiveMotion files.

Note: *To complete this lesson fully, you'll need Adobe Photoshop 5.5, Adobe Illustrator 9.0, and Adobe LiveMotion 1.0 installed on your hard disk.*

This lesson takes approximately 1 hour to complete.

If needed, copy the Lesson04 folder onto your hard drive. As you work on this lesson, you'll overwrite the start files. If you need to restore the start files, copy them from the *Adobe GoLive 5.0 Classroom in a Book* CD. Also, be sure to install the special fonts, as instructed in "Installing the Classroom in a Book fonts" on page 2, because these fonts are used in some of the graphics that you'll work with in this lesson.

Note: *Windows users need to unlock the lesson files before using them. For more information, see "Copying the Classroom in a Book files" on page 2.*

For information on setting up your work area, see "Setting up your work area" on page 9.

Getting started

You'll begin this lesson by using your Web browser to view a copy of the finished Web page.

1 Start your browser.

2 Choose File > Open, and open the End.html file. The path to the file is Lesson04/04End/Farm Folder/Farm/End.html.

3 Scroll through the page, examining the placement of the images, especially the three in the top of the table. Those are the ones that you'll be placing. Be sure to wait for the animation.

4 If you want, print the finished page to use as a reference as you go through the lesson.

5 When you have finished viewing the page, close your browser.

About Smart Objects

Smart Objects provide an easy way to incorporate native Adobe Photoshop, Illustrator, and LiveMotion images on your Web pages. The general procedure for any kind of Smart Object is similar: drag a Smart Object icon from the Smart tab of the Objects palette to your Web page, and set the Smart Object's source file. Once placed, you can open any Smart Object in its creating application by double-clicking the Smart Object on the page.

Adobe GoLive can automatically convert a source file from any of these programs to one of the formats supported by current Web browsers, optimize the image, and maintain smart links between the Web-safe copy and the source file for easy editing and automatic updating. Smart Objects provide an easier, better way to enliven your Web pages with graphics.

In this lesson, you'll be creating a highly graphical home page for a bed and breakfast inn in the countryside. The starting page is partially done for you, but you'll add several graphics, and work on them using Smart Objects technology and Adobe GoLive.

For information on placing images that are already in a Web-safe format, see "Adding an image using the Point and Shoot button" on page 75.

Using Smart Photoshop Objects

In this first section of the lesson, you'll place two Smart Photoshop objects, resize one of them, and edit the color table in the other to achieve a special effect—all without leaving Adobe GoLive. Adobe Photoshop files can be in any of several supported formats: RGB 8-bit PSD, BMP, PICT (Mac OS only), PCX, Pixar, Amiga IFF, TIFF, and TARGA.

Placing a Smart Photoshop Object

The first step involves placing a Smart Photoshop Object on the page. The graphic is a Photoshop file that has been sliced in Adobe ImageReady.

1 Open the Farm site. The path to the file is Lesson04/04Start/Farm Folder/Farm.site.

2 Right-click (Windows) or Control-click (Mac OS) in the site window, and choose New Folder from the context menu. Name the folder Images. You'll be placing all your images here to keep the site window better organized.

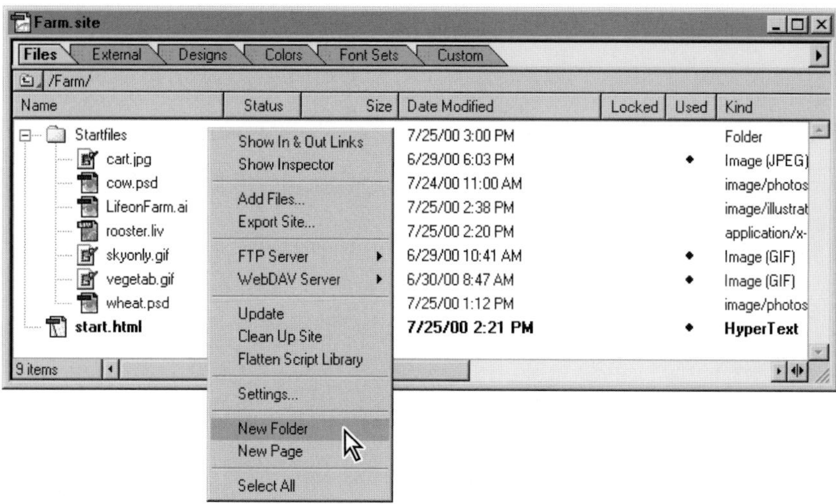

Choosing New Folder from context menu

3 Double-click Start.html in the site window to open the page. Notice that the page consists of a seven-cell table with three images already in the bottom three cells.

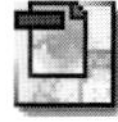

4 From the Smart tab (▣) of the Objects palette, drag a Smart Photoshop Object to the top left cell of the table.

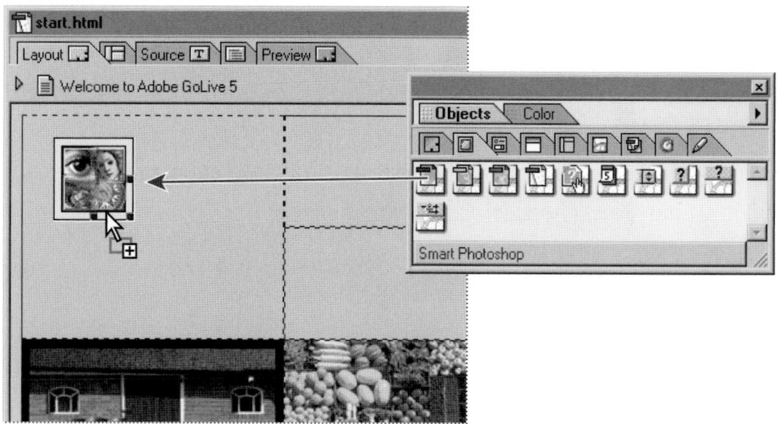

Dragging Smart Photoshop object icon to table cell

5 In the Live Image Inspector, click the Browse button ( ) for Source, and locate Cow.psd in the Startfiles folder. The path to the file is Lesson04/04Start/Farm Folder/Farm/Startfiles/Cow.psd. Click Open.

6 Select the Images folder you created when prompted. Since this image has been sliced in ImageReady (there are four slices: the cow itself, and three sky slices to the left, right, and below the cow), you are prompted to select a location for the Cow.data folder that will be created automatically to store all the slices in a Web-safe format.

The Save for Web dialog box appears.

7 Click the Optimized tab, and select the Slice Select tool ( ).

8 With the Slice Select tool, click on the cow slice in the optimized image.

9 Select JPEG High from the Settings pop-up menu.

10 Shift-click the three slices containing the sky. They are located on the left, the right, and just below the cow slice.

11 Select GIF 32 No Dither from the Settings pop-up menu.

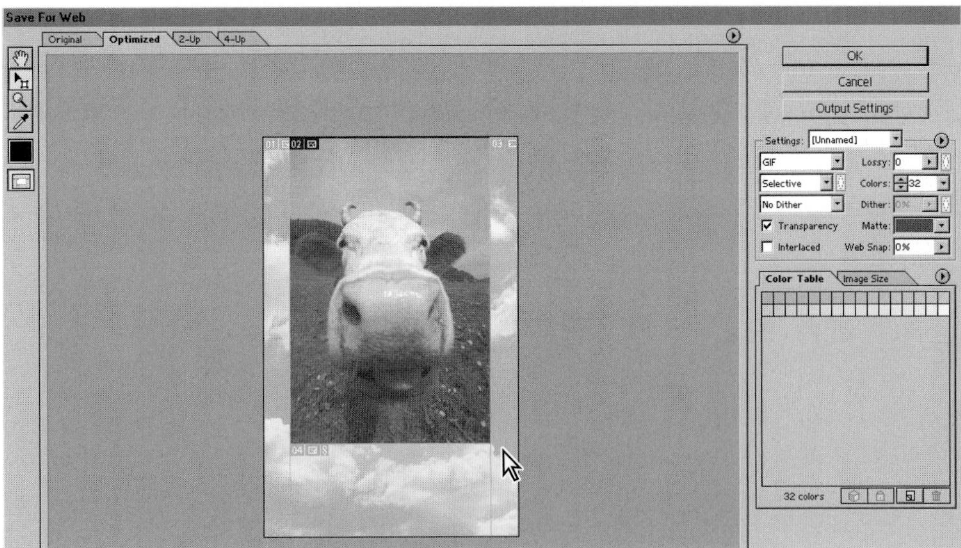

12 Click OK in the Save for Web dialog box.

Adobe GoLive converts the sliced Photoshop image into several Web-safe images, adding the appropriate extension to each image. In this example, there will be three GIF images and one JPEG image. All remain linked to the original Photoshop file. Note that when you import sliced images, as you did here, you can set different conversion settings for each slice.

Resizing a Smart Photoshop Object

Now you'll need to resize the image that you just placed. Resizing GIF or JPEG images themselves often provides less than satisfactory results. Smart Objects technology lets you return to the source image (in this case, a sliced Photoshop file), and create new, resized Web-safe images from the original file. The new file uses the settings that you already applied in the Save for Web dialog box when you first placed the Smart Photoshop Object. The original Photoshop file remains unchanged.

1 With the image still selected, Shift-drag the bottom right handle until the cow image is approximately the same width as the milk wagon image in the cell below. The Updating from Source File progress bar tells you that Adobe GoLive is creating the resized Web-safe version using the original Photoshop source file.

Note: *To select the entire sliced image and not just a slice, move the pointer over the top right corner. When the cursor changes to this ( ), click to select the entire sliced image. If you click when the cursor looks like this ( ), you will select a slice rather than an entire image, and the Settings button will be disabled.*

2 Save the document as Working.html in the Lesson04/04Start/Farm Folder/Farm.

You can also resize an image by going back to the Save for Web dialog box. We want the cow image to have exactly the same width as the wagon image in the cell below it.

3 Select the wagon image and note its width in the Image Inspector. (The width was 204 in our document.)

4 Select the entire cow image (not just a slice), and click Settings in the Live Grid Inspector. You'll be prompted again for a location to save the Cow.data folder and images. Make sure you're saving to the Images folder, and click Save.

Selecting cow image

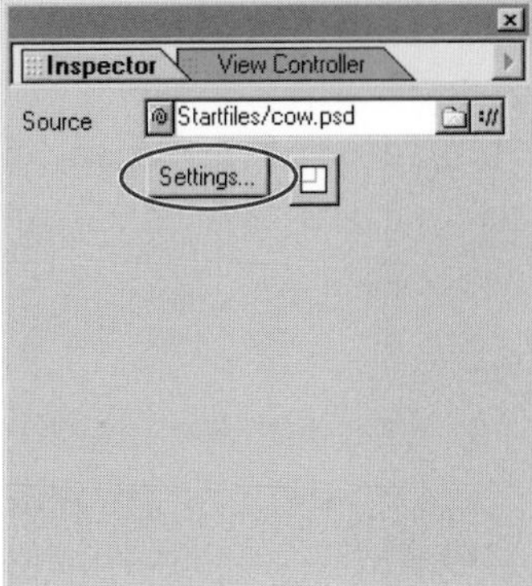

Clicking Settings

5 In the Save for Web dialog box, click the Image Size tab. Make sure the Constrain Proportions option is checked, and enter **204** as the width and press Enter or Return. Note the image size (our image was 204 by 309). You'll need these dimensions later when you resize the image that you'll place in the top right cell.

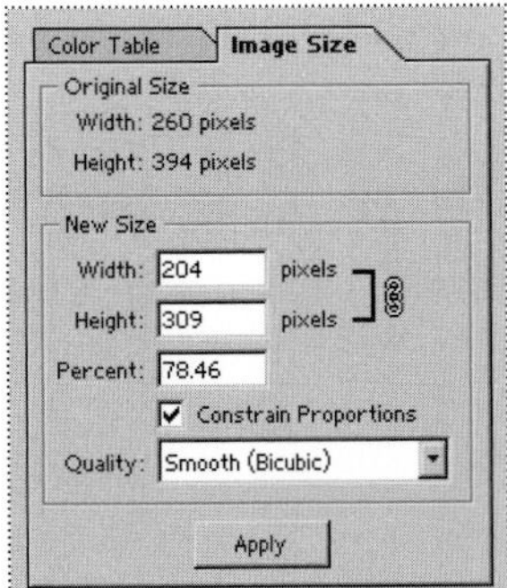

6 Click Apply, and then click OK.

Note: *You can return to the Save for Web dialog at any time and experiment with different settings.*

Editing a Smart Photoshop Object

Next you'll add another Smart Photoshop Object to the page, and edit the image's color table to achieve a special effect—again, without ever leaving Adobe GoLive.

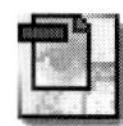

1 From the Smart tab of the Objects palette, drag a Smart Photoshop Object icon to the top right cell of the table.

2 In the Live Image Inspector, click the Browse button, and locate Wheat.psd in the Start-files folder. The path to the file is Lesson04/04Start/Farm Folder/Farm/Start-files/Wheat.psd. Click Open.

3 In the Settings panel of the Save for Web dialog box, select GIF 32 No Dither from the Settings pop-up menu, and view Optimized.

4 Reduce Colors to 20.

5 In the Color Table tab, double-click the darkest brown color.

Double-clicking color

6 In the Color (Windows) or Color Picker (Mac OS) dialog box, choose a color, and click OK. (We used red.) All of the areas of the image with the dark brown color are now changed to the new color. Replacing colors using this technique is an easy way to achieve some eye-catching special effects.

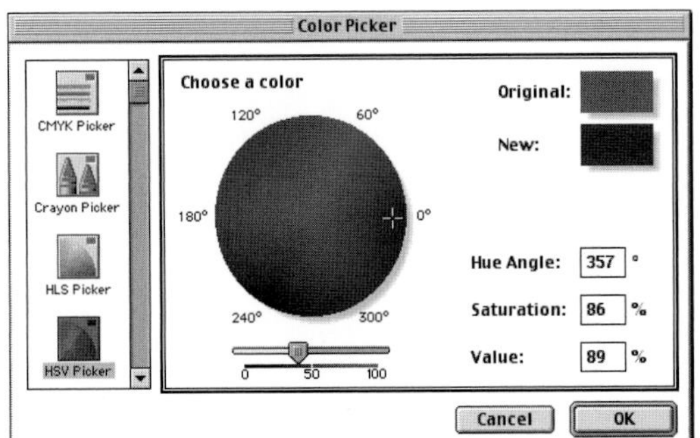

Color Picker dialog box (Mac OS)

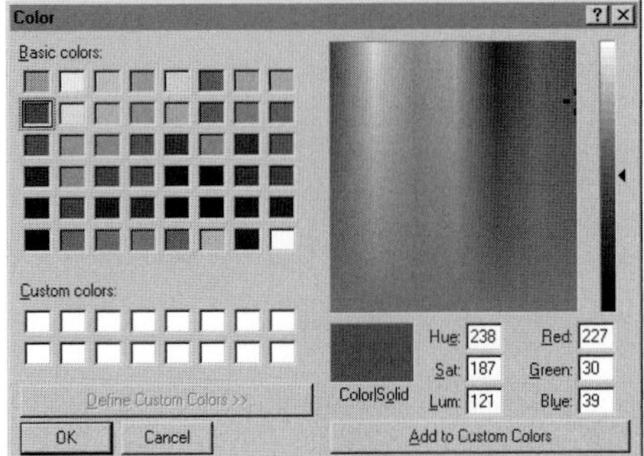

Color dialog box (Windows)

7 Click OK in the Save for Web dialog box, and click Save to save the converted image (Wheat.gif) to your Images folder.

8 The wheat image should be about the same size as the cow image (ours was 204 by 309), so select the Wheat.gif Smart Photoshop Object in the top right cell.

9 In the Basic tab of the Live Image Inspector, enter the dimensions that you noted for the cow image earlier. Press Enter or Return after you type each dimension, and notice that the Updating from Source File progress bar tells you that Adobe GoLive is updating the Web-safe image from its linked source file. The cow and wheat images should be the same size now.

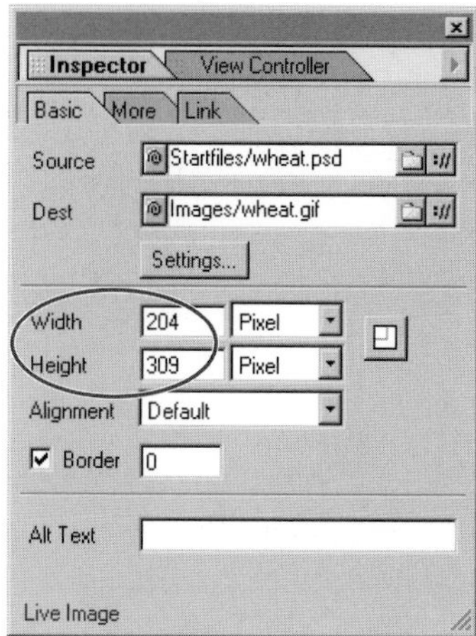

Using Smart Adobe Illustrator Objects

You can also place Smart Illustrator Objects on a Web page just as easily as Photoshop images.

Note: *You must have Adobe Illustrator 9.0 or later installed on your hard disk to complete this section of the lesson.*

Placing a Smart Illustrator Object

You'll now add a Smart Illustrator Object to the page and resize it.

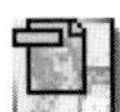

1 From the Smart tab of the Objects palette, drag a Smart Illustrator Object icon to the top middle cell of the table.

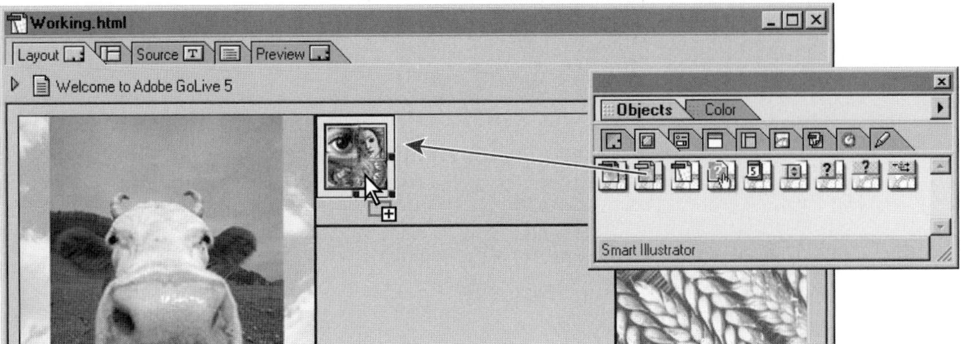

Dragging Smart Illustrator Object icon to table cell

2 In the Live Image Inspector, click the Browse button ( ), and locate Lifeonfarm.ai in the Startfiles folder. The path to the file is Lesson04/04Start/Farm Folder/Farm/Startfiles/Lifeonfarm.ai. Click Open.

3 The Conversion Settings dialog appears. Choose GIF, and click OK. Adobe Illustrator opens in the background, if it is not already open, and the Updating from Source File progress bar tells you that the file is being converted.

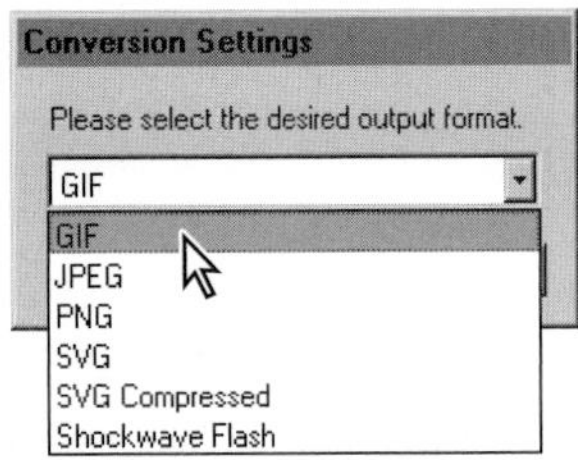

Choosing GIF

4 In the Settings panel of the Save for Web dialog box, select GIF 32 Dither, and reduce the Colors to 20.

5 Click OK, and save the file to your Images folder.

6 Resize the placed Illustrator file to the same size (232 by 174) as the Vegetables image in the cell just below it either by Shift-dragging, or using the Image Inspector.

Note: *Automatic updating does not occur if the resized Web graphic is in the SWF or SVG format, since those formats are vector-based and scale well. Accordingly, Illustrator does not have to open in the background.*

7 Double-click the Smart Illustrator Object on your page. Illustrator starts, if it's not open, and the original Lifeonfarm.ai source file appears. Make some changes to the file (for example, change the color of the white rectangle to yellow as we did), and save the file.

Note: *If the Smart Object's application does not open, choose Edit > Preferences, expand General preferences icon in the left pane, select User Interface, and make sure that the Launch Other Applications To Edit Media Files option displayed in the right pane is enabled.*

8 Go back to Adobe GoLive. When you do, Adobe GoLive automatically updates the Smart Illustrator Object on your page to reflect the changes you just made to the source file in Illustrator.

Using Smart Adobe LiveMotion Objects

You can add LiveMotion files to your Web pages in the SWF format. This lets you add lively animated images to your site that remain linked to LiveMotion native source files. Any changes you make in Adobe GoLive or in LiveMotion are updated for you.

Note: *You must have LiveMotion installed on your hard disk to complete this section of the lesson.*

Prior to using Smart LiveMotion objects in Adobe GoLive, you must make the following export settings in LiveMotion itself.

1 Start LiveMotion, if it is not already running.

2 Choose Window > Export.

3 Select SWF in the top pop-up menu of the Export palette.

4 Close LiveMotion.

Placing a Smart LiveMotion Object

1 From the Smart tab of the Objects palette, drag a Smart LiveMotion Object icon to the top middle cell of the table just below the Smart Illustrator Object.

Dragging Smart Live Motion Object icon to table cell

2 In the Live Image Inspector, click the Browse button (), and locate Rooster.liv in the Startfiles folder. The path to the file is Lesson04/04Start/Farm Folder/Farm/Startfiles/Rooster.liv. Click Open.

3 The Conversion Settings dialog appears. Choose Shockwave Flash, and click OK. Adobe LiveMotion opens in the background, if it is not already open, and the Updating from Source File progress bar tells you that the file is being converted. You'll also see Generating a SWF File and Generating a Report progress bars. A save dialog box appears.

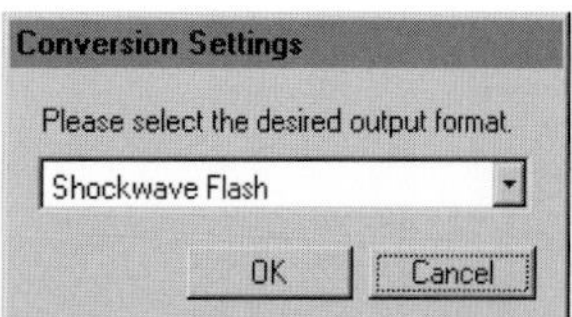

4 Save the image to your Images folder. Note the .swf extension. This tells you the file is in the SWF format.

5 Preview the Farm working.html page in your browser to see the animation by choosing Special > Show in Default Browser. When you're done, close your browser and return to Adobe GoLive.

6 Double-click the Smart LiveMotion Object on your page. LiveMotion starts, if it's not open, and the original Rooster.liv source file appears. Make some changes to the file (for example, change the color of the black rectangle), and save the file.

Note: *If the Smart Object's application does not open, choose Edit > Preferences, expand General preferences icon in the left pane, select User Interface, and make sure the Launch Other Applications To Edit Media Files option displayed in the right pane is enabled.*

7 Go back to Adobe GoLive. When you do, Adobe GoLive automatically updates the Smart LiveMotion Object on your page to reflect the changes that you just made to the source file in LiveMotion.

Note: *Since Smart LiveMotion Objects are always placed as SWF, a vector-based format that scales well, LiveMotion does not have to be open in the background when you resize a Smart LiveMotion Object on your Web page.*

8 Save your document, and preview it again in your browser.

Review questions

1 How does an image placed with the Image icon differ from one placed as a Smart Object?

2 How do you place a Smart Object?

3 What happens to the source file when you resize a Smart Object on your page?

4 Which dialog box contains all the settings you can use when you place a Smart Photoshop Object?

5 How do you open the source file for a Smart Object within Adobe GoLive?

Review answers

1 An image placed on a Web page with the Image icon has to be in a Web-safe format such as GIF, JPEG, or PNG. An image placed as a Smart Object can be in a variety of non-Web-safe bitmapped and vector-based formats created by Adobe Photoshop, Illustrator, and LiveMotion. Adobe GoLive converts the image to a Web-safe format and retains a live link to the underlying source file. If you change the source file in its native application, your Web page will be updated automatically the next time you open the page in Adobe GoLive. If you resize the image on the Web page, Adobe GoLive goes back to the source file and creates new Web-safe images for optimal appearance of the resized files without changing the source image.

2 To place a Smart Object of any kind (Photoshop, Illustrator, or LiveMotion), simply drag the corresponding Smart Object icon from the Smart tab of the Objects palette to your Web page. Then you set the source file for the Smart Object in the Live Image Inspector. A series of prompts leads you the rest of the way.

3 Nothing! The great thing about Smart Objects is that your source files remain unchanged. Adobe GoLive recreates only the Web-safe versions that appear on your Web page, leaving the source files untouched.

4 The Adobe GoLive Save for Web dialog box appears whenever you place a Smart Photoshop Object. It appears for Smart Illustrator Objects, if you choose a bitmapped format such as GIF, JPEG, or PNG in the initial Conversion Settings dialog box. It never appears for Smart LiveMotion Objects since they are always in the vector-based SWF format.

5 You can open the source file in its native application of any Smart Object by double-clicking the Smart Object on your Web page. If this doesn't work, Choose Edit > Preferences, expand General preferences icon in the left pane, and choose User Interface. Select the Launch Other Applications To Edit Media Files option displayed in the right pane.

Lesson 5

```
<TITLE>Wel
<STYLE TYPE="te

e{color:maroon;fon

</STYLE>
AD>
Y>
<!-- Begin main table -->
<TABLE BORDER="4" CELLPADDI
06">
    <TR>
        <TD><A
tp://www.adobe.com/">Adobe</A
        <TD>GoLive</TD>
        <TD><IMG BORDER="0" HEIG
le.gif" ALT="Title"></TD>
    </TR>
    <TR>
        <TD><SPAN CLASS="headl
AN></TD>
    </TR>
    <TR>
        <TD><B>DHTML an
    </TR>
</TABLE>
DY>

P-EQUIV="content-typ
ml;charset=iso-8859-
come to Adobe GoLi
="text/css"><!

main table -->
ER="4" CELLPAD

D><A
dobe.com/">Adobe</A
D>GoLive</TD>
D><IMG BORDER="0" HEI
="Title"></TD>

D><SPAN CLASS="head

D><B>DHTML an
```

5 Creating Links

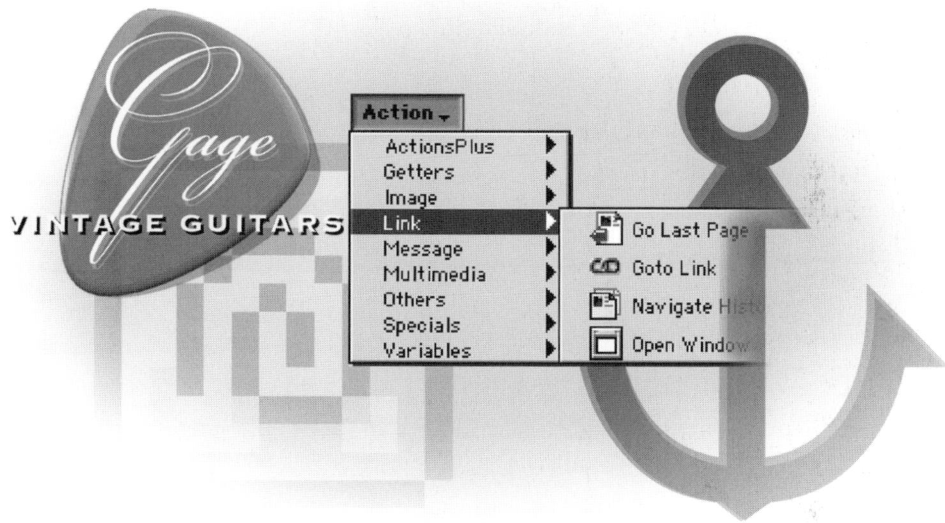

Once you've created content for your Web pages, you need to provide visitors with a way to get from one page to another. Links let visitors jump from text or graphics on one page, to other pages in the site or other sites.

About this lesson

In this lesson, you'll learn how to do the following:

- Add links to graphics on a Web page.
- Add hypertext links to a page.
- Add anchors that act as targets for links within a page.
- Add an action to a link.
- Change a link's color and highlight.
- Verify links.
- Create image maps and link them to a page.
- Add hotspots to an image map and change their shape.
- Edit links and anchors.
- Fix broken links and change link preferences.

This lesson takes approximately 45 minutes to complete.

If needed, copy the Lesson05 folder onto your hard drive. As you work on this lesson, you'll overwrite the start files. If you need to restore the start files, copy them from the *Adobe GoLive 5.0 Classroom in a Book* CD.

Note: *Windows users need to unlock the lesson files before using them. For more information, see "Copying the Classroom in a Book files" on page 2.*

For information on setting up your work area, see "Setting up your work area" on page 9.

About links

Links allow users to jump:

- Locally within a site.
- To locations on the same page as the link (called anchors).
- Across the Web.
- To non-Web resources such as FTP servers, newsgroups, and e-mail addresses.

Getting started

In this lesson, you'll explore linking from graphics and text, creating image maps, and adding an action to a link. You'll start the lesson by viewing the final lesson file in your browser, to see what you'll accomplish.

1 Start your browser.

2 Choose File > Open, and open the Index.html file. The path to the file is Lesson05/05End/Gage Folder/Gage/Index.html.

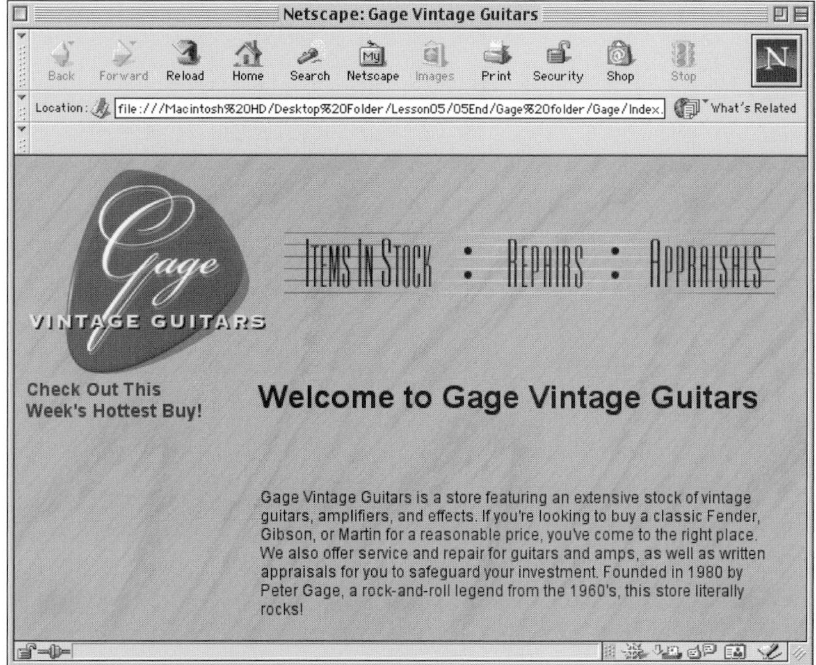

Final Index.html file, previewed in Netscape browser

3 Click the links in the Index.html file, and explore the site.

4 When you've finished viewing the file, close your browser.

Opening a site

Follow these steps to open the site and begin this lesson.

1 Start Adobe GoLive.

2 Close the Untitled.html document.

3 Choose File > Open, and open the Gage.site file. The path to the file is Lesson05/05Start/Gage Folder/Gage.site.

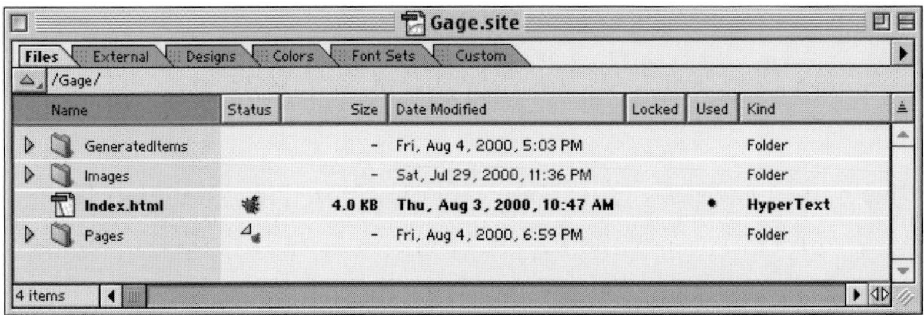

Gage site window

This site consists of the Index.html file; the Images folder, which contains images for the site; and, the Pages folder which contains separate HTML pages that you'll link.

4 In the site window, double-click the Index.html file to open it. This is the home page for the Gage Vintage Guitars Web site.

Creating a link from a graphic

Adding links to a page lets viewers jump to other pages in the site. Now you'll create a link from the Index.html file to the Stock page, so that viewers can jump from the home page to a list of items in stock for the company.

You'll start by seeing whether the Index.html file contains any links, and determining where and how to add a link to the file.

1 Click the Layout Preview tab (▣) at the top of the Index.html file document window, so that you can work for a moment in Preview.

2 Using the pointer, click various places in the document window. Notice that the file has no links.

3 Click the Layout Editor tab (▣) of the Index.html file to return to Layout view.

4 In the document window of the Index.html file, click the Items In Stock image to try to select it. You won't be able to select the image because it's actually part of a component—an element that is updated automatically across a site when you change the source file.

Selecting unlinked graphic within component

To create the link, you must open the component and add the link to that file. You'll do that in the next steps.

Components let you easily manage repetitive content, such as headers, footers, and other recurring design elements, by storing them in a single file instead of inserting them physically wherever they occur. (For instructions on creating a component, see "Creating a component" on page 73.)

You'll add the link to the component so that any changes you make later to the link will be applied automatically across the site.

5 Open the Navbar.html file using any of these techniques:

• Double-click the component in the document window.

• Choose File > Open, and open the file. The path to the file is Lesson05/05Start/Gage Folder/Gage.data/Components/Navbar.html.

• Click the icon at the bottom right of the site window to display all of the site's contents. In the right pane of the site window, the Extras tab displays the site's Gage.data folder and its contents. The Navbar.html file is located inside the Components folder.

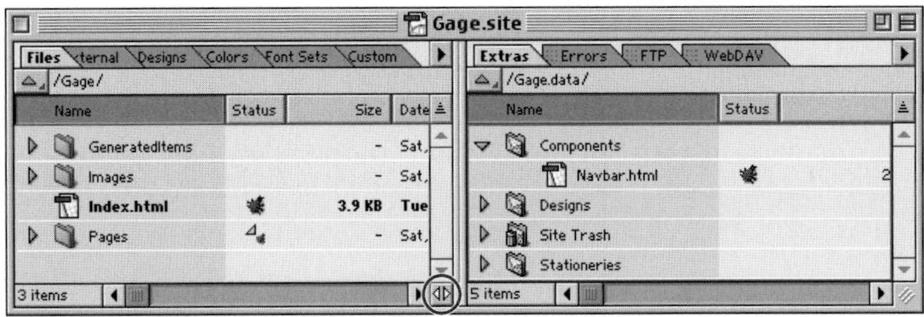

Expanded site window

When a component is embedded in your pages, you can easily edit the component by editing the source file (in this case, the HTML page containing only the header) and then letting Adobe GoLive automatically update all pages.

6 If it isn't open, choose Window > Inspector to display the Inspector.

7 In the document window, click the Items In Stock graphic to select it. The Image Inspector becomes active.

8 Click the Link tab of the Image Inspector. You use this tab to specify links.

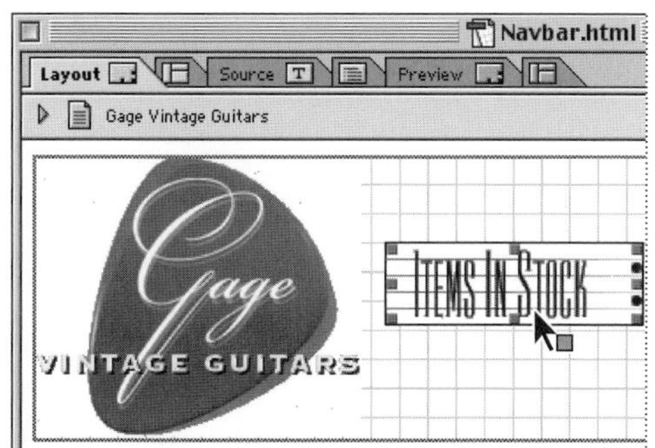

Selecting graphic within component

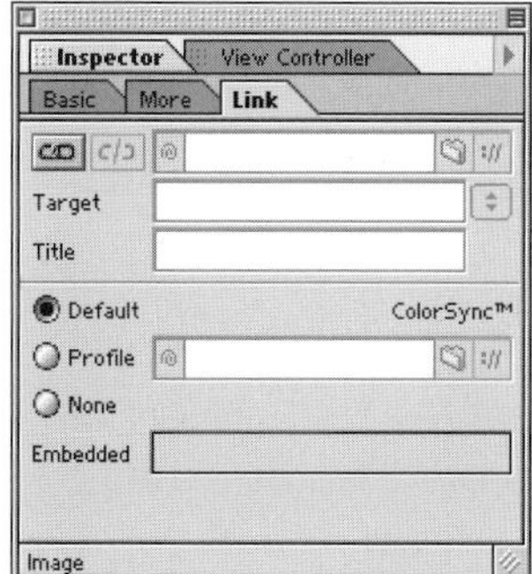

Link tab of Image Inspector

You can also create a new link by clicking the New Link button on the toolbar, as you'll do later in this lesson.

You'll create your first link by using the Point and Shoot button in the Image Inspector to link to a file in the site window.

9 If necessary, arrange the document window, site window, and Image Inspector so that all three are visible on your desktop.

10 In the Link tab in the Image Inspector, click the New Link button ( ), or press Ctrl+L (Windows) or Command+L (Mac OS). Then drag from the Point and Shoot button ( ) to the Stock.html file inside the Pages folder in the site window. If the Stock.html file isn't visible, position the pointer over the icon to the left of the Pages folder until the folder opens, and then drag to select the file.

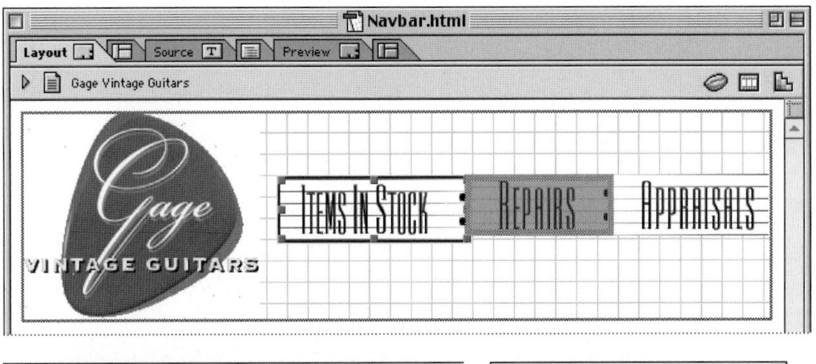

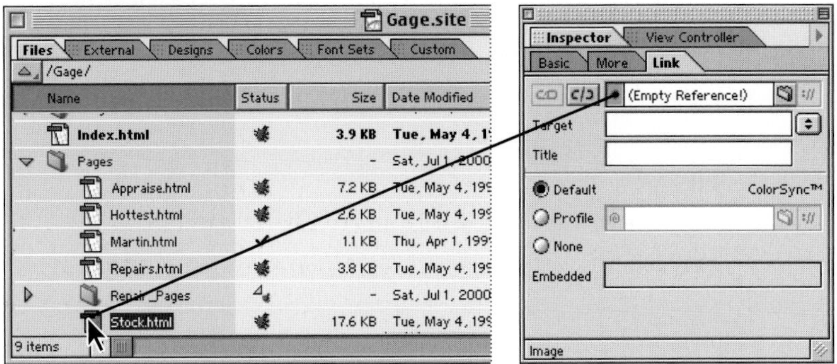

Using Point and Shoot button to link from Items In Stock image to Stock.html file

The filename and directory path appear in the URL text box in the Image Inspector. You've created your first link. (If the link can't be made, the line snaps back to the Point and Shoot button.)

11 Click the Basic tab of the Image Inspector. In the Alt Text box, enter **Items In Stock** and press Enter or Return. The alternative text appears if a browser can't display the image.

12 Choose File > Save to save the Navbar.html file. When prompted to update the files that use the component, click OK. Close the Navbar.html file.

Now you'll test the link to make sure that it works as you expect.

Testing a link

You can test your links using the Layout Preview tab in the document window.

1 Return to the home page by clicking the Index.html page to make it active.

2 Click the Layout Preview tab (), and then click the Items In Stock graphic. The Stock.html file opens in its own document window.

Clicking linked graphic

Result

Creating anchors

In this section, you'll create a link from a bulleted item to its corresponding topic later in the page. Anchors act as targets for links within the same page. Using an anchor lets viewers jump to the information without having to scroll. You can create a single link that connects to a single anchor. Or, you can create several links that point to a single anchor point.

Now you'll work with the Stock page and add links to it. You'll start by creating a link from a bulleted list item to an anchor in a topic further down the page. You'll use the Point and Shoot feature, which will simultaneously create the anchor and the link to the anchor.

1 If necessary, click the Stock.html document window to make it active. You opened the file when you tested the link that you just created.

This file describes the Gage Vintage Guitars product line of acoustic and electric guitars, amps, pedals, and other equipment.

2 Using the text cursor, triple-click the second item in the bulleted list, "Electric Guitars," to select the line. You'll create a link from this item to an anchor that you'll place in the corresponding topic (the "Electric Guitars" section) further down the page.

It's best to place anchors in the flow of HTML text, inside a layout text box, or inside a table. (You can add a small layout text box to the layout grid to hold the anchor.) You'll get more consistent results if you put the anchor near the left margin of the page. You cannot anchor directly to a graphic because HTML does not yet support this feature; instead, place the anchor near the top left of the graphic.

3 Hold down Alt (Windows) or Command (Mac OS), and drag from the selected text to a point directly to the left of the Electric Guitars heading. An elastic line extends from your start point and a cursor (short vertical line) follows the mouse pointer. To scroll through the document, hold down the mouse button with the pointer on the bottom border of the window.

After you release the mouse button, the document window springs back to the link point (the Electric Guitars item in the bulleted list). The URL field in the Link tab of the Text Inspector displays the unique name of the new anchor. Scroll back down to the Electric Guitars heading to see the anchor icon that was inserted next to it.

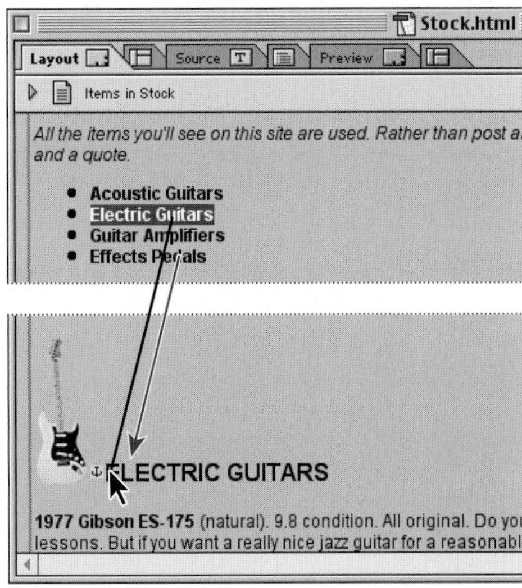

Alt/Command-dragging from bullet; anchor set in Electric Guitars heading

The point and shoot method is the easiest way to create an anchor. You can also use the Objects palette, which you'll do now.

4 Click the Basic tab ( ) of the Objects palette. Then drag the Anchor icon from the palette to the "Guitar Amplifiers" section of the Stock.html page. Place the anchor to the left of the heading.

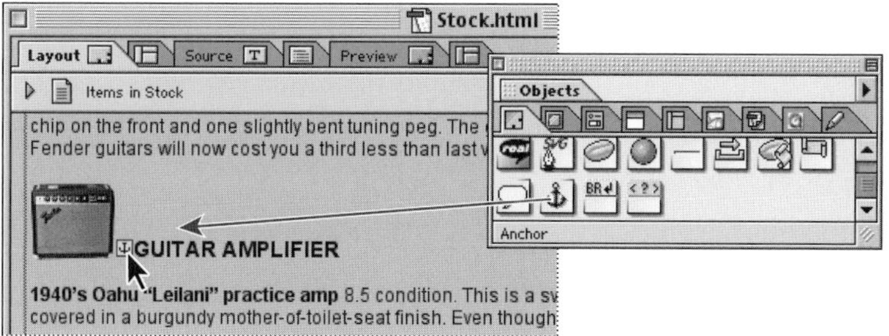

Dragging Anchor icon from Objects palette to text in document window

5 In the Anchor Inspector, enter a descriptive name for the anchor (we used "Amps"). Naming anchors lets you update them more easily, and helps you find and correct broken links when you're managing your site.

6 In the document window, scroll up to the bulleted list and triple-click to select "Guitar Amplifiers."

7 In the Text Inspector, click the New Link button. Drag from the Point and Shoot button to the Amps anchor that you just inserted.

You've created a link between the list item and the topic later in the page. The anchor name (Amps) appears in the URL field of the Text Inspector (anchor names are always preceded by a "#" symbol).

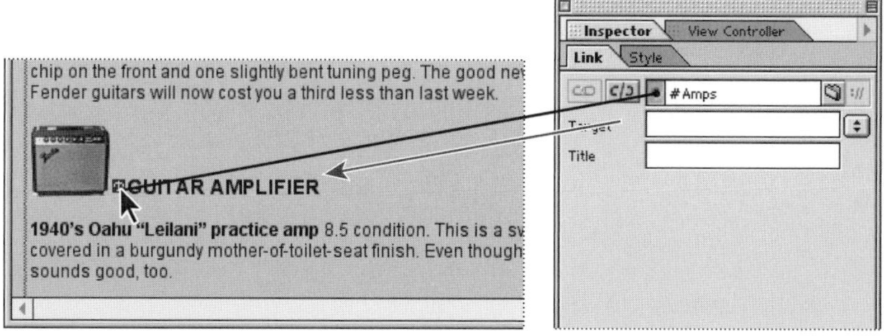

8 Choose File > Save to save your file.

Verifying anchors

You've tried out previewing links using Adobe GoLive's Preview mode. You can also see how links and anchors work in a Web browser, by opening the file in a browser and testing the links. Now you'll preview the anchors that you just created.

1 Click the Show in Browser button in the upper right corner of the toolbar. The document appears in the Web browser that you specified in the Preferences dialog box.

Show in Browser button

2 Click the bulleted text to see how the links jump to the corresponding heads in the document.

3 When you have finished previewing, close or quit your browser. Then click the document window to return to the Stock.html file.

4 Close all open files except Stock.html and Gage.site.

Creating hypertext links

Now you'll create some hypertext links. You'll select some text in the Stock page and link the text to another page. The technique is similar to creating a graphic link or a link to an anchor.

1 In the Stock.html document window, scroll to the bottom of the page. You'll create hypertext links from the last line in the document: "Home | Stock | Appraisals | Repairs."

2 Double-click the word "Home" to select it. The Inspector changes to the Text Inspector.

3 Click the New Link button ( ) in the Text Inspector, or press Ctrl+L (Windows) or Command+L (Mac OS).

You'll create your first hypertext link using the Point and Shoot button in the Text Inspector to link to a file in the site window.

4 Drag from the Point and Shoot button ( ) in the Text Inspector to Index.html in the site window.

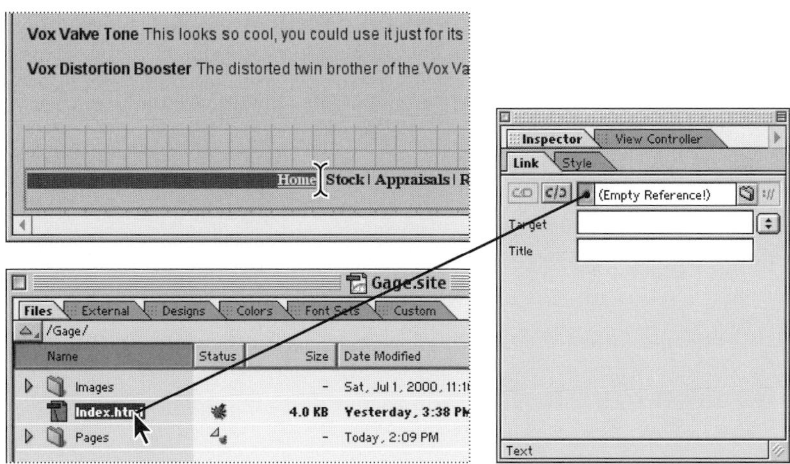

Creating link from Home text to Index.html file using point and shoot method

If Index.html file isn't visible, position the pointer over the Gage folder icon in the site window until the folder opens, then drag to the file.

5 If you make a mistake, select the Home text in the document window, and click the Remove Link button ( ) on the toolbar. Then repeat steps 3 and 4 to create the link.

You can also use the Remove Link button to unlink graphics.

Now you'll create a hypertext link to another file within the site by using the Inspector's Browse button to locate a file.

6 Select the text "Appraisals." Then click the New Link button ( ) on the toolbar.

7 In the Text Inspector, click the Browse button ( ), select Appraise.html, and click Open. The path to the file is Lesson05/05Start/Gage folder/Gage/Pages/Appraise.html.

Another way to specify a link in the Inspector is to enter the file's pathname in the URL text box. Now you'll create the final hypertext link.

8 Select the "Repairs" text in the document window. Click the New Link button ( ) on the toolbar. In the Link tab of the Text Inspector, enter the file's relative pathname in the URL text box: **Repairs.html.** (In this case no path is necessary, as Repairs.html is in the same directory as Stock.html.)

When you browse for the link destination or enter the URL, you can enter just the relative path (with the site folder name implied). Absolute URLs include the complete pathname of a file, including the site folder name. Relative URLs don't include the full pathname, and can refer to a file in a subdirectory from which the file is linked. By default, Adobe GoLive is aware of the site folder, so that you don't need to enter it in the URL text box.

9 Choose File > Save to save the Stock.html file.

10 To preview the links that you just created, click the Layout Preview tab. In Preview, click the Home, Appraisals, and Repairs links to test them. Each file opens in its own window.

You can also test these links in your browser by clicking the Show in Browser button on the toolbar, and then clicking a link to test it. (If you've connected each link correctly, the information it's linked to appears in the document window. If not, the browser will display an error message.)

11 Close all open files except Stock.html and Gage.site. Then click the Layout Editor tab ( ) in the Stock.html document window to return to Layout view.

About absolute link paths

Site pages contain paths to a variety of linked files: other pages in the site (<HREF>), images displayed on the page (<IMG>), media items embedded in the page (<EMBED>), and so on. When you make such a path absolute, *the entire path from the root folder to the linked file is provided. Otherwise only a relative path is provided.*

Example *A page* /root/pages/info/page.html *(where root is the name of the root folder) contains the image* /root/images/image.gif. *The absolute path to the image file is* /images/image.gif. *The relative path is* ../../images/image.gif.

Absolute paths are useful in the following cases:

- *If a form references a CGI script at the root level of the site directory (or any other subdirectory), any references to that file are usually written as absolute.*

- *If a common navigation bar is used on many pages that reside in folders at various hierarchical levels, you can use an absolute path specification throughout to reference its image files, allowing you to copy and paste the same HTML snippet onto all the pages.*

However, absolute paths work only at sites where there is a Web server providing information about the location of the site's root folder. For the same reason, using absolute paths prevents you from previewing pages in a Web browser; that is, a previewing browser has no way of locating this root folder.
Note: *An absolute path in Adobe GoLive is not a full path from the file system root or a fully qualified URL.*

Setting up absolute link paths

You can specify absolute paths for all new links or for specific links.

To make all new link paths absolute:

1. *Choose Edit > Preferences, expand General, and click URL Handling in the left panel.*

2. *Select Make New Links Absolute.*

3. *Click OK.*

To make a specific link path absolute:

1. *Open the page containing the link or reference in a document window.*

2. *Display the Inspector.*

3. *Select the link.*

4. *Click the Absolute Link button (://) to the right of the Source or URL text box in the appropriate Inspector or dialog box—for example, in the Basic tab of the Image inspector or the Link tab of the Text Inspector.*

–From the Adobe GoLive 5.0 User Guide, Chapter 17

Creating external links

Until now, the links that you've created have been within pages (using anchors), and between pages in your site. You can also create links from your site to other sites on the Web. To do this, you'll create a link to an external URL.

First, you need to store the URL that you want to use in the External tab of the site window. The External tab is useful for storing information that you may want to use in more than one place on your site. If you later need to update an item in the External tab, it is automatically updated wherever it appears in the site.

1 Click the External tab in the site window.

2 Click the Site tab in the Objects palette. This tab contains elements for sites, such as pages, URLs, and e-mail addresses. Drag the URL icon from the palette to the site window.

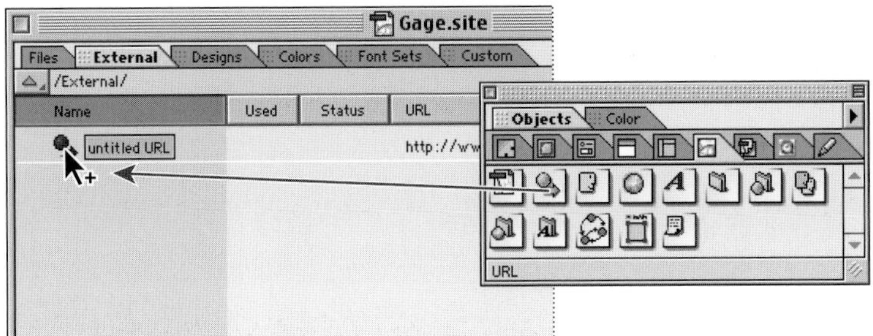

A new, untitled URL entry is added to the External tab, and the Inspector changes to the Reference Inspector (in Mac OS, click on the Inspector to change it). For this exercise, you'll create an external link to the Adobe home page.

3 Rename the URL, using either the Name field in the External tab or the Name field in the Reference Inspector. (This name is for reference only, to help you keep track of stored URLs.)

4 In the URL field of the Reference Inspector, change the URL text to the correct text for the URL to which you want to link. For the Adobe home page, change "http://www.untitled.1/" to "http://www.adobe.com". Make sure that you leave "http://" at the beginning of the URL.

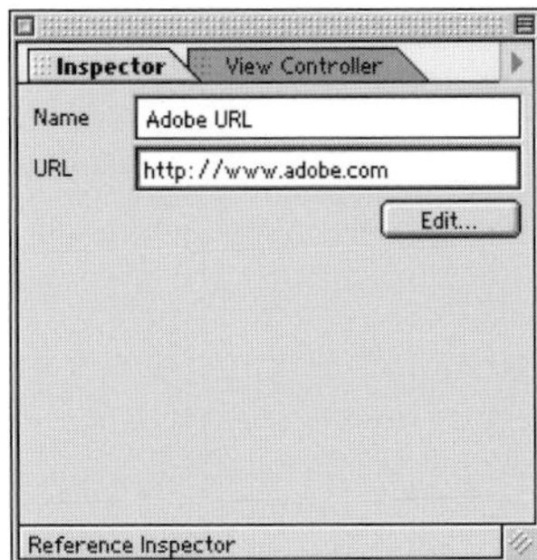

5 Click Enter or Return. The URL is updated in the External tab.

Note: *You can also add URLs to the External tab by dragging them from an open Web browser. For more information, see "Using site URLs and e-mail addresses" on page 397 of the* Adobe GoLive 5.0 User Guide.

Now that the URL is added to the External tab, you'll create a link to it from text in the Appraise.html page.

6 Click on the Files tab in the site window. Then double-click the Appraise.html page in the site window to open the page.

7 Locate the text "Classic Guitar" at the end of the second paragraph of text, and drag to select it.

8 Click the New Link button ( ) in the Link tab of the Text Inspector.

9 Drag from the Point and Shoot button to the Adobe URL in the External tab of the site window.

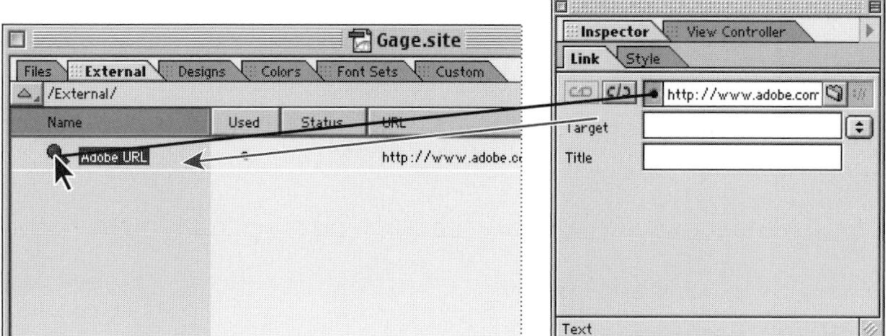

10 Choose File > Save to save the Appraise.html file.

11 To preview the link that you just created, click the Show in Browser button. Click the Classic Guitar link. The external Web site (www.adobe.com, in our example) replaces the Appraise.html page in the browser window.

Creating e-mail links

Now you'll add a link to the Appraise.html page that brings up an e-mail window with an e-mail address in it. Like URLs, e-mail addresses can be stored in the External tab.

1 Click the External tab in the site window.

2 Click the Site tab ( ) in the Objects palette.

3 Drag the Address icon from the palette to the site window.

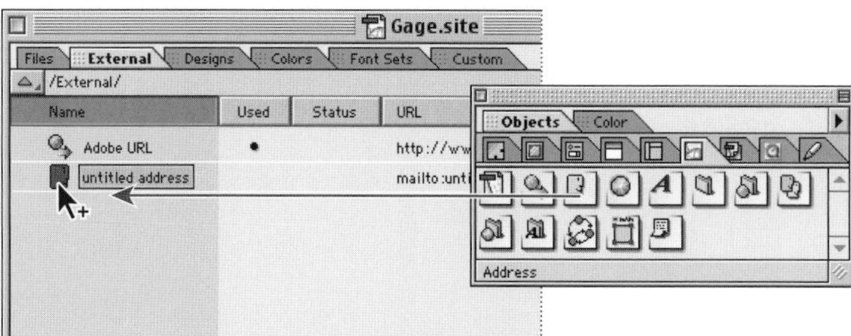

4 Double-click the Address icon in the site window to change the Inspector to the Reference Inspector. (In Windows, the Inspector changes automatically after you dragged the address.)

5 In the Name field of the Reference Inspector, enter a name for the address. For example, change "untitled address" to "Anne's Address." Although it's not required, entering names helps you manage addresses in a site.

6 In the URL text box, change the text after "mailto:" to a real e-mail address. For example, change "mailto:untitled@1/" to "mailto:AnneSmith@mycompany.com". Make sure that you leave "mailto:" in the text box and that there are no spaces between it and the e-mail address.

7 Select the text "e-mail us" at the bottom of the list of abbreviations in the Appraise.html page.

8 Click the New Link button ( ) in the Text Inspector.

The link is highlighted and underlined. Now you can attach the text as a link to the e-mail address you just created.

9 Drag from the Point and Shoot button ( ) in the Text Inspector to the Address icon in the site window.

10 Choose File > Save.

11 Choose a Web browser from the Show in Browser menu ( ) on the toolbar. Then use the Appraise.html page displayed in the browser to click the e-mail link and display an e-mail editor.

12 Close your browser and the Appraise.html page in Adobe GoLive.

Changing a link's color and highlight

Now that you've created some links, you'll see how easy it is to change their color. You'll use the Page Inspector to change a link's color and highlight.

1 Click the Page icon (📄) in the upper left corner of the Stock.html document window. The Inspector changes to the Page Inspector.

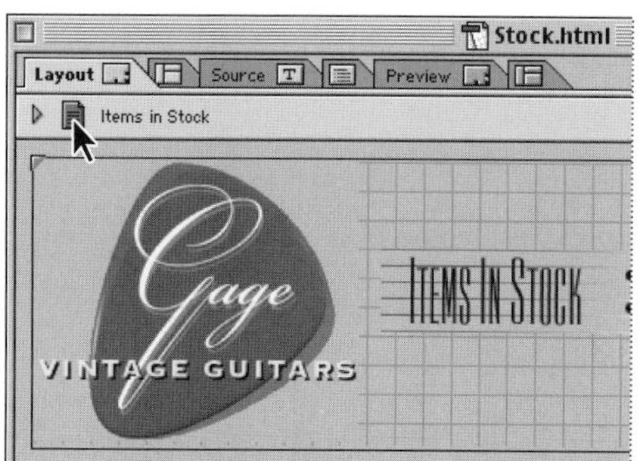

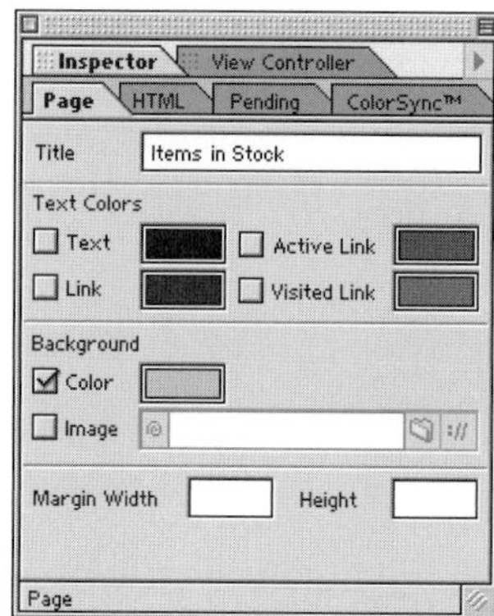

Clicking Page icon to display Page Inspector

2 Click the Link color field to display the Color palette, if it's not already displayed. In the Color palette, click the Web Color List button (🎲). This button lets you select Web-safe colors for consistent color across platforms and browsers.

3 In the Color palette, select another color either by clicking a color swatch or by entering a value. The color that you choose should provide enough contrast between the page's background and text color so that it stands out, but not so much that it's distracting to the viewer (we used 006600). As you try different colors, you can view the effect on the links at the bottom of the Stock.html page.

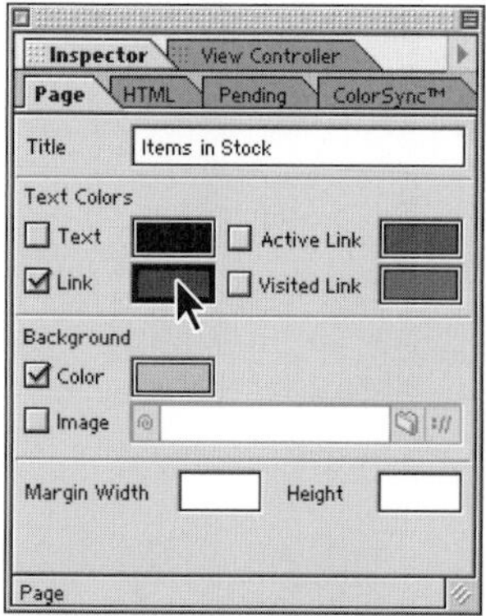

Clicking Link color field

Selecting color from Color palette

4 Repeat steps 2 and 3 for the Active Link and Visited Link color fields, selecting each field in turn. (We used 6600FF for Active Link and FF3300 for Visited Link.)

When selecting a color for visited links, it's helpful to viewers to pick a color that's opposite the link color on the color wheel. So, for example, if the link color is red, you could use green for the visited link color.

5 Choose File > Save to save your work.

6 To preview the link color and how it changes when the link is clicked, click the Show in Browser button in the upper right corner of the toolbar. The document appears in your Web browser.

7 In the browser, scroll to the end of the document, and click the Appraisals link to test it. Notice how the color changes when you click the link (the active link color) and after you've clicked it (the visited link color).

Note: *Depending on how they've set browser preferences, some visitors won't be able to see the link colors that you've set.*

8 When you've finished testing the links, close or quit your browser.

9 Click the Stock.html document window to return to Adobe GoLive.

Creating an action

You can add actions to links that increase their interactivity. For example, you can use actions that open a second window when a link is clicked. Or you can add an action that displays or hides information when the mouse pointer is over a link. You can also add an e-mail action to a link that lets viewers send comments to an address you set up. For more information on actions, see Lesson 9, "Using Actions and JavaScript."

Now you'll link the Custom Acoustic Guitar text on the Stock page to a page that contains a guitar image. Then you'll add an action to the link that opens the page in a separate window at a preset size.

1 In the Stock.html page, select the text "1927 Martin 0-28K" in the first paragraph of the Acoustic Guitar section

Keep in mind that text used as a link should be short and descriptive. Try to keep the text to no more than five words, so that it captures attention without requiring too much effort. If you inadvertently select too much text for a link, you can unlink the extraneous text using the Remove Link button.

2 Click the New Link button ( ) in the Link tab of the Text Inspector.

3 Choose Window > Actions to open the Actions palette.

4 In the Events pane, select Mouse Click. Then click the New Action button ( ) above the Actions pane to activate the Action pop-up menu.

5 From the Action pop-up menu, choose Link > Open Window.

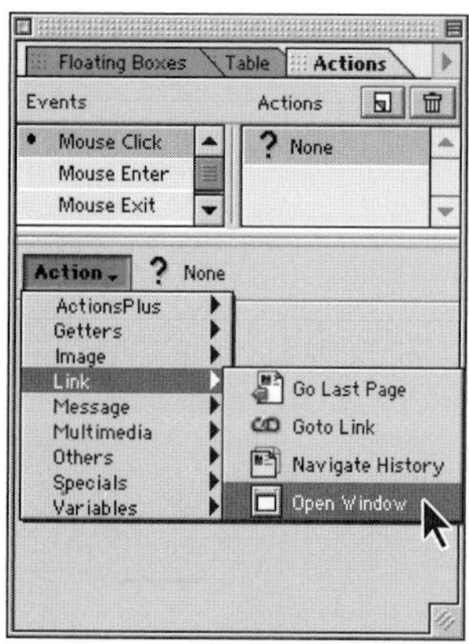

6 Click the Browse button (next to the Link text box) and locate the Martin.html file in the Gage/Pages folder. Click Open.

7 For size, enter **170** in the first text box and **325** in the second text box. Deselect Resize, Scroll, Menu, and Dir. You don't want the second window to resize, be scrollable, have a menu, or show a directory toolbar in some browsers.

8 Choose File > Save to save the file.

9 Click the Show in Browser button to view the Stock.html file, then click the "1927 Martin 0-28K" text to test the action. Close your browser.

Previewing Open Window action

10 Close the Martin.html and Stock.html files.

Using image maps

Image maps are images with hotspots. You can link image maps to other resources, and connect the hotspots in the map to other scripted actions such as forms or mailing addresses.

Now you're ready to work on the final page of your site. You'll add an image map to an image of a guitar, and link the hotspots in the map to other pages. You'll start by opening the page in which you'll create the image map.

1 In the site window, double-click Repairs.html, inside the Gage/Pages folder, to open the file.

2 Drag the Image icon from the Basic tab (▣) of the Objects palette to the document window, so that the placeholder is centered beneath the Navbar component. It's unnecessary to resize the placeholder, because it will resize automatically when you insert the image.

3 If necessary, click the Basic tab of the Image Inspector.

4 Insert the Map.gif image, located in the Gage/Images folder within the Gage folder, using any of these techniques:

• Drag from the Point and Shoot button (◎) to Map.gif located in the Gage/Images folder in the site window.

• Click Browse, navigate to the Map.gif file inside the Gage/Images folder, and click Open.

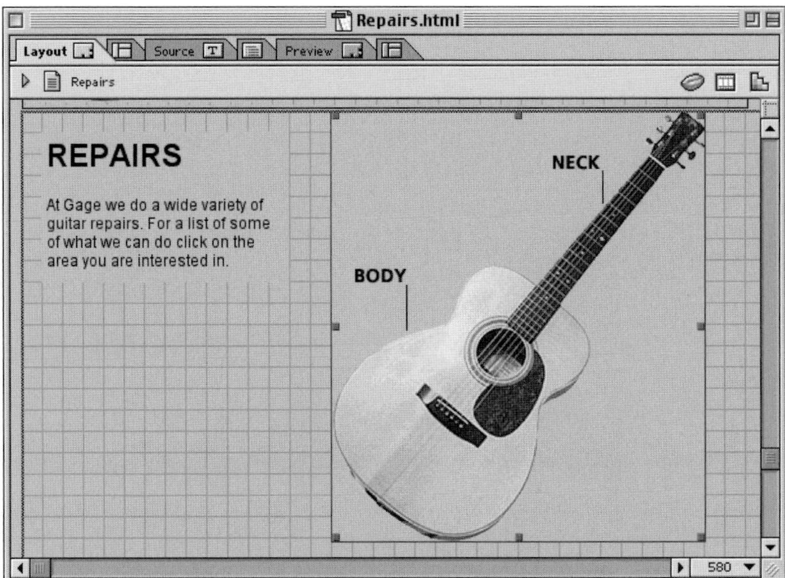

5 If necessary, drag the image to reposition it under the component.

Creating hotspots on an image map

You'll use the Guitar image to show specific repairs that guitars might need. First you'll create hotspots for the types of repairs on the guitar. Then you'll create links from the hotspots to information on repair stores.

1 In the Basic tab of the Image Inspector, type **Repair map** in the Alt Text box. This is the alternative text that appears if a browser can't display the image.

2 Click the More tab of the Image Inspector. Then select the Use Map option. This option lets you add an image map to an image, and activates the map tools on the toolbar.

You use the map tools to create an image map. The map tools include drawing tools for creating the hotspots of an image map.

3 In the Map Name text box, enter a name for the map, with the suffix **.map**. (We named the map Guitar.map.)

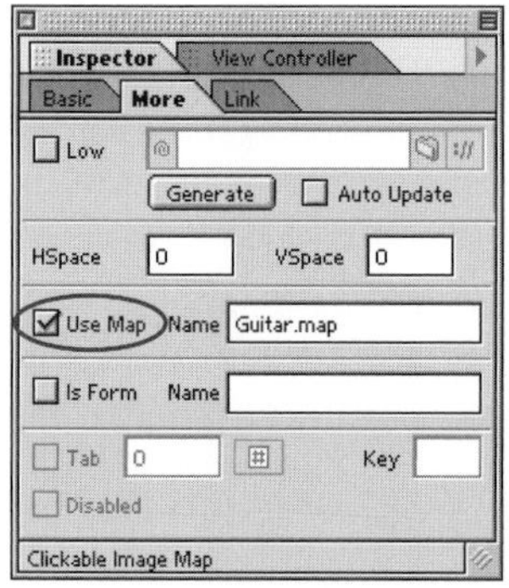

Selecting Use Map option

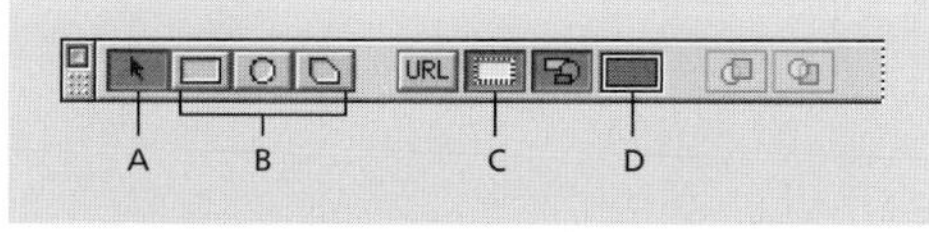

***A.** Select Region button **B.** Region creation tools*
***C.** Frame Regions button **D.** Select Color button*

4 Click the rectangle region tool (▭) on the toolbar.

5 In the document window, drag a rectangular area that includes all of the guitar neck. Handles appear at the sides and corners of the hotspot. You can use these handles to adjust the hotspot or simply drag the hotspot to reposition it.

6 Click the circle tool ( ) on the toolbar. In the document window, drag a circular hot spot over the guitar body that overlaps the rectangular hotspot.

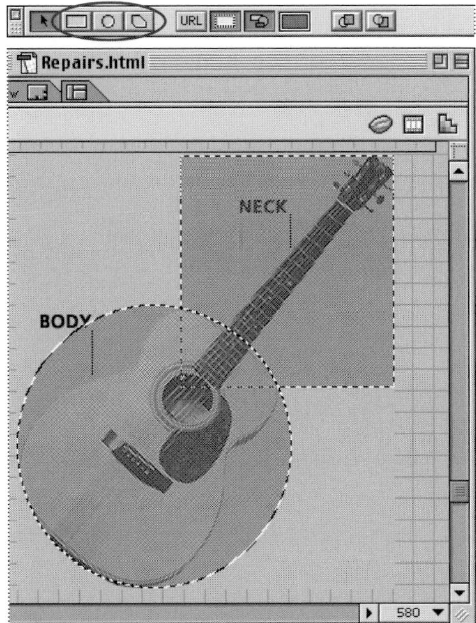

Hotspot drawing tools in Map tab; overlapping rectangular and circular hotspots

Editing hotspots

You can edit an image map's hotspots to change their shape, color, or border, as well as reposition hot spots and change how they overlap. Now you'll change the color and positioning.

1 Click the Select Color button (the eighth button from the left) on the toolbar to open the Color palette. Click a color or enter a number to change the fill color for the hotspot. (Blue is the default.)

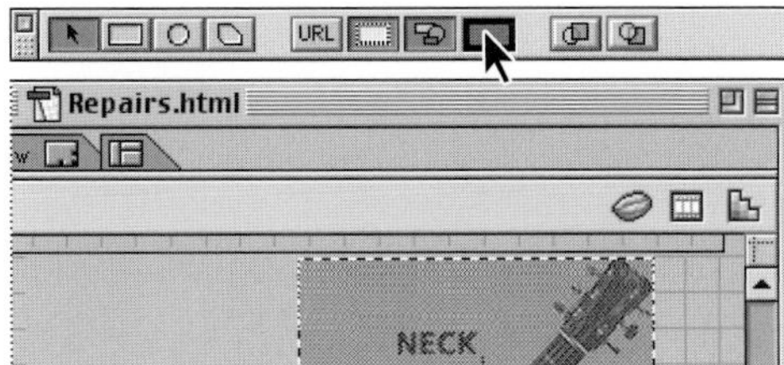

Clicking Select Color button

Selecting color in Color palette

2 If desired, click the Frame Regions button (the sixth button from the left) on the toolbar to activate the border around the hotspot.

When two hotspots overlap, you can change which is on top by selecting one of the hotspots and clicking either the Bring Region to Front or Send Region to Back button.

Instead, you'll reposition the hotspots so that they don't overlap.

3 Click the Select Region button (the leftmost button on the toolbar). In the document window, click the rectangular hotspot to select it. Handles appear around it.

4 Drag the handles of the rectangular hotspot to adjust it so that it no longer overlaps the circular one.

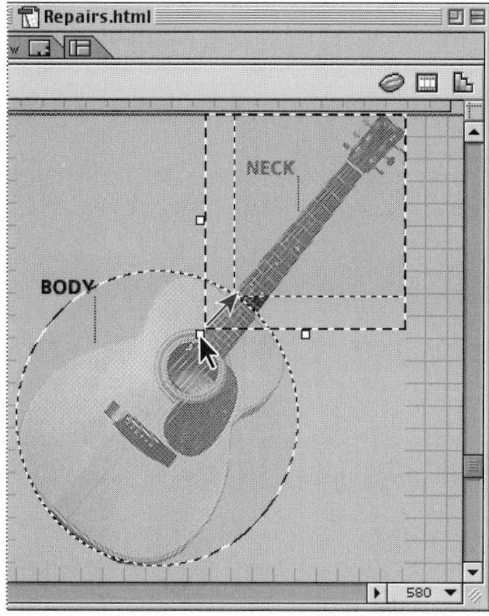

Dragging handles to adjust hotspot

Linking an image map with a Web page

To link an image map with a Web page, you use a technique similar to creating a hypertext link.

1 Select the rectangular hotspot.

2 In the Map Area Inspector, link the rectangular hotspot to the Neck.html file using any of these techniques:

• Drag from the Point and Shoot button (◎) to the Neck.html file, located in the Gage/Pages/Repair_Pages folder, in the site window.

• Click Browse, navigate to the Neck.html file, in the Gage/Pages/Repair_Pages folder, and click Open.

• In the URL text box, type the URL **Repair_Pages/Neck.html**, and press Enter or Return. (It's OK to use a relative pathname.)

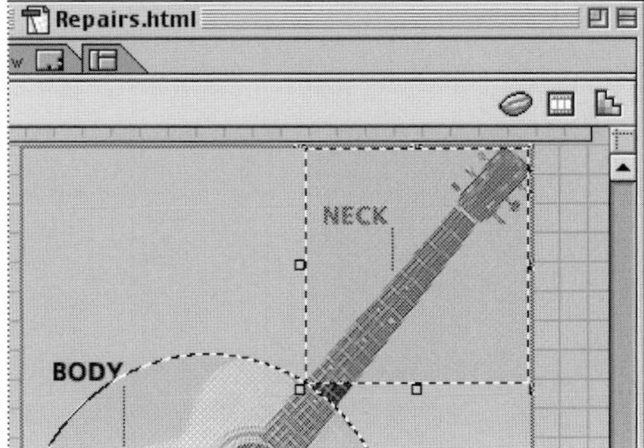

Rectangular hotspot in Repair.html

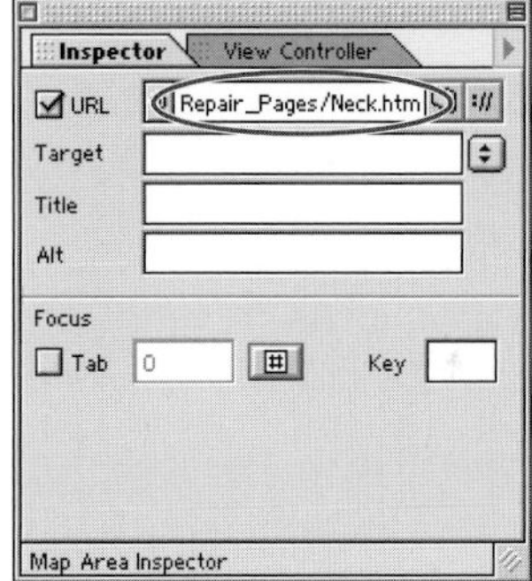

Link to Neck.html in Map Area Inspector

3 Repeat steps 1 and 2 to link the circular hotspot to the Body.html file in the Gage/Repair_Pages folder.

4 Choose File > Save to save the Repair.html file.

5 To test the hotspots, click the Layout Preview tab in the document window, and click the hotspot. When you have finished previewing them, close the Neck.html and Body.html files.

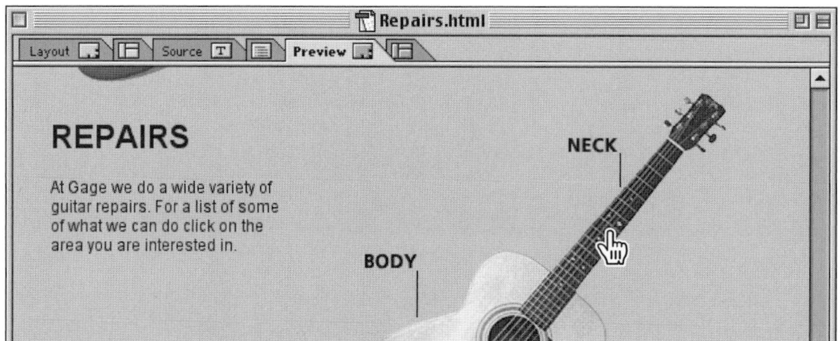

Clicking hotspot

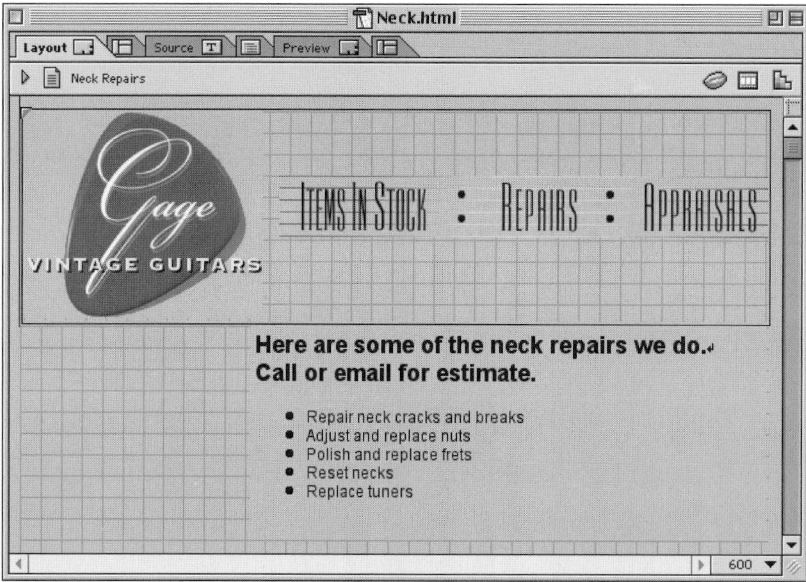

Result

6 Click the Layout Editor tab in the Repairs.html document window to return to Layout view.

Setting preferences for link warnings

Adobe GoLive signals broken links on pages within your site with link warnings. You can control the appearance of link warnings, including their text and background color and box size. The default color for broken links is red.

1 Choose Edit > Preferences.

2 On the left side of the Preferences dialog box, click the symbol next to the General option to display more options. Click the User Interface option.

3 To select a different color for link warnings, click the Link Warning color field. The system color picker appears.

4 Select a color, and then click OK.

5 To set the size of the color box that marks link warnings in the text or around images, choose an option from the Frame Border pop-up menu. Click OK.

6 Choose File > Save to save the file, and close the Repairs.html file.

Finding and fixing broken links

In this final exercise, you'll fix some broken links in Navbar.html, the component that is used in the Index.html page. By default, broken links appear outlined in red in the document window and the Inspector URL text box.

1 Double-click the Navbar.html file in the Extras tab of the site window. This file contains several broken links. (You can also locate the file in the Gage/Gage.data/Components folder, and open it from the desktop.)

2 Click the Layout Editor tab ( ) of the Navbar.html file to display it in Layout view.

3 To activate the display of link warnings, click the Link Warnings button ( ) on the toolbar, or choose Edit > Show Link Warnings.

Images with broken links appear with a border in the size and color that you set in the previous section for the link warnings.

4 Select the Repairs image in the document window.

5 Click the Link tab of the Image Inspector. Notice that the link appears broken, as indicated by the highlight color in the URL text box.

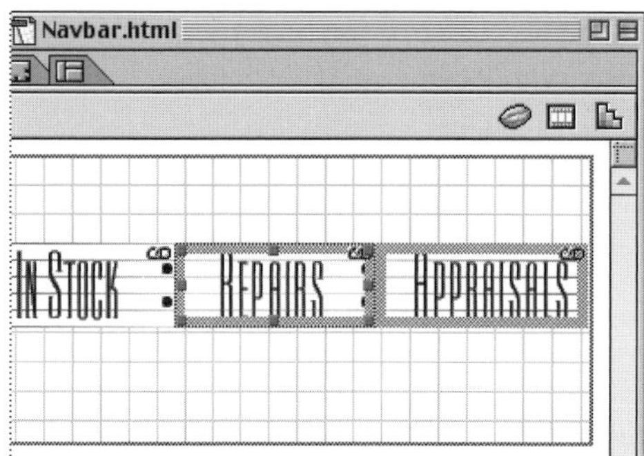

Broken link

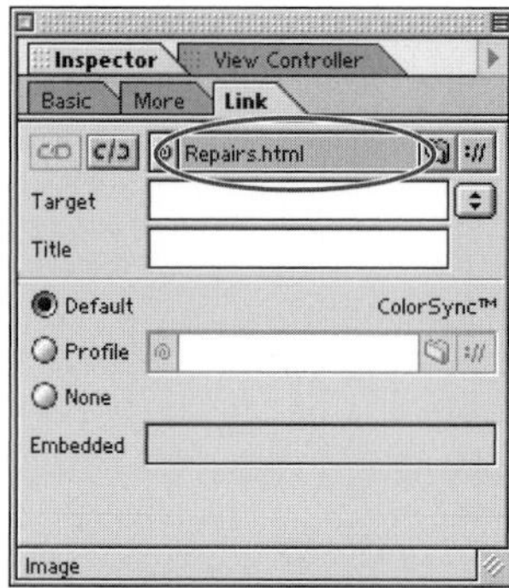

Link tab of Image Inspector

6 In the Link tab, fix the link by dragging from the Point and Shoot button to the correct file, Repairs.html, inside the Pages folder in the site window.

You'll repeat steps 4 through 6 to relink the Appraisals image to the corresponding file.

7 Select the Appraisals image in the document window. This link also appears as broken in the Link tab in the Image Inspector.

8 Now relink this image to the Appraise.html file by dragging from the Point and Shoot button in the Link tab to the Appraise.html file, inside the Pages folder in the site window. The Link Warning border will disappear after you deselect the Appraisals image.

9 Choose File > Save to save the file. When prompted to update the file, click OK.

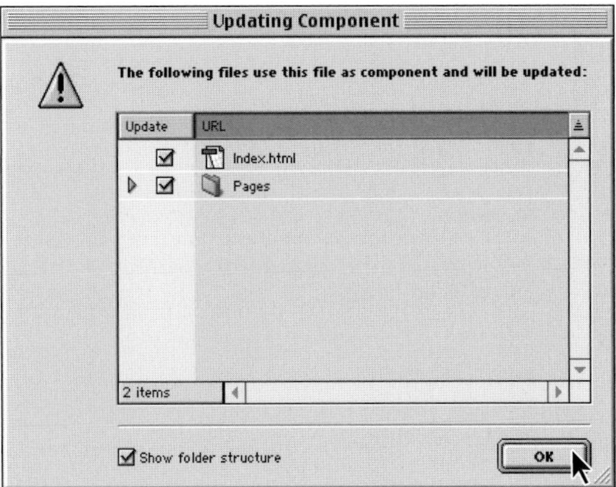

Updating component

10 Close the Navbar.html file.

Previewing links

As a final step, you should make sure all your links work as expected by previewing them in your Web browser.

1 Start your browser.

2 Locate and open your completed Index.html file. Choose File > Open. Select the Index.html file, located in the Lesson05/05Start/Gage Folder/Gage folder, and click Open.

3 Click the links in the Index.html file, and explore the site.

4 When you have finished viewing the file, close it.

5 Close and quit your browser.

For additional practice in fixing broken links, see Lesson 13, "Managing Web Sites."

Review questions

1 What is a link? How do you create one?

2 What is an anchor? How do you create one?

3 What is the best location for an anchor?

4 How do you add an action to a link?

5 How do you create a link in a component?

6 What is the difference between relative and absolute pathnames? Why is this difference significant for links?

7 What is an image map? How do you create one?

8 What is the purpose of a link warning?

Review answers

1 A link is a jump from one location in a Web page to another location—on the same page (to an anchor), locally within a site, across the Web, or to non-Web resources such as FTP servers, newsgroups, and e-mail addresses.

You create a link from text or an image by selecting it in the document window, and then clicking the Link button in the Text Inspector or the New Link button on the toolbar. You then use the Point and Shoot button or Browse button to link to another file in the site, or enter the file pathname in the URL text box. You can also link to external URLs stored in the External tab of the site window.

2 Anchors act as targets for links within the same page. You can create a single link that connects to a single anchor. Or you can create several links that point to a single anchor.

To create a link from one location on the page to another, you can select the link text, and Alt-drag (Windows) or Command-drag (Mac OS) to the link destination on the page, creating a link and anchor in one step. Or you can drag an Anchor icon from the Objects palette to the target text in the document window. Then click the New Link button in the Text Inspector and use the Point and Shoot feature to select the anchor. Adobe GoLive automatically generates a name for a new anchor, which you can change using the Anchor Inspector.

3 It's best to place anchors in the flow of HTML text, inside a layout text box, or inside a table. (You can add a small layout text box to the layout grid to hold the anchor.) You'll get more consistent results if you put the anchor near the left margin of the page. You cannot anchor directly to a graphic because HTML does not yet support this feature; instead, place the anchor near the top left of the graphic.

4 To add an action to a link, you first make a selection and create a link using the New Link button on the toolbar, or in the Link tab of the Text Inspector. Then you use the Actions palette to add an action to the link.

5 When a component is updated, all the files that refer to it are also updated to pick up the change. To add a link to a component, you use the same technique as when adding other links, but you must first open the component file.

6 Absolute URLs include the complete pathname of a file, including the site folder name. Relative URLs don't include the full pathname, and can refer to a file in a subdirectory from which the file is linked. When you browse for the link destination or enter the URL, you can enter just the relative path (with the site folder name implied). By default, Adobe GoLive is aware of the site folder, so you don't need to enter it in the URL.

7 Image maps are images with hotspots. You can link image maps to other resources and connect the hotspots in the map to other scripted actions such as forms or mailing addresses. To create an image map, you insert an image in your document, specify the image as an image map using the More tab in the Image Inspector, and add hotspots using the map tools on the toolbar. You then add links to the hotspots as you would any other links.

8 Link warnings appear as a highlighted URL text box in the Link tab of the Inspector (or as bug icons in the site window). Link warnings alert you to files with broken links that require fixing before uploading the files to a Web server (and frustrating viewers who can't find the linked information).

Lesson 6

```
<TITLE>Wel
<STYLE TYPE=

e{color:maroon;fon

</STYLE>
AD>
Y>
<!-- Begin main table -->
<TABLE BORDER="4" CELLPADDI
06">
     <TR>
          <TD><A
tp://www.adobe.com/">Adobe</A
          <TD>GoLive</TD>
          <TD><IMG BORDER="0" HEIGH
le.gif" ALT="Title"></TD>
     </TR>
     <TR>
          <TD><SPAN CLASS="head
AN></TD>
     </TR>
     <TR>
          <TD><B>DHTML ani
     </TR>
</TABLE>
DY>

     EQUIV="content-ty
     charset=iso-8859-
     ome to Adobe GoL

main table -->
ER="4" CELLPADD

D><A
dobe.com/">Adobe</A
D>GoLive</TD>
D><IMG BORDER="0" HEIGH
="Title"></TD>

D><SPAN CLASS="head

D><B>DHTML ani
```

6 Working with Frames

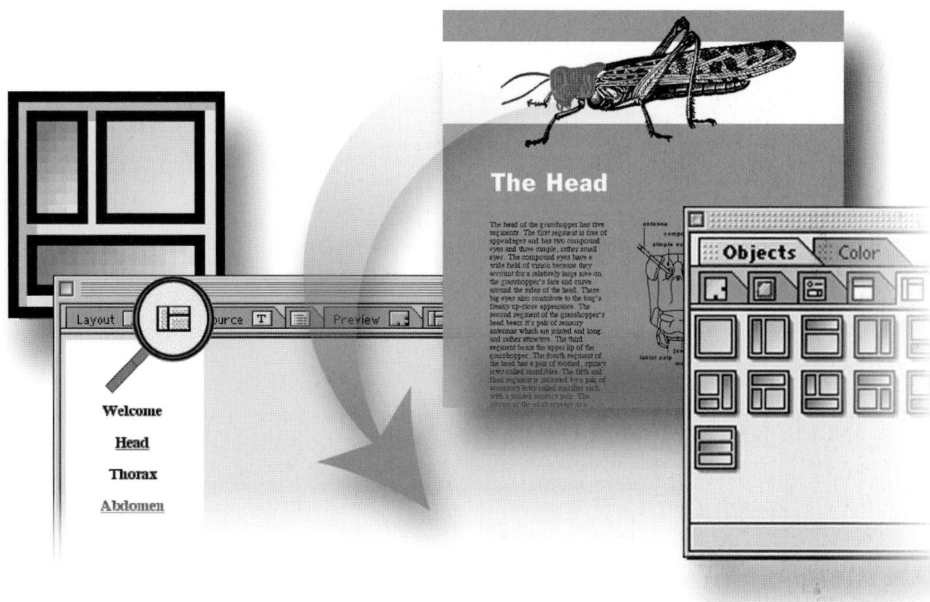

Frames are very useful for controlling the layout and structure of your Web site. They can be used both as a navigation tool and to show more than one type of information at the same time. In this lesson, you'll create a frame set with three frames and add their content.

About this lesson

In this lesson you'll learn how to do the following:

- Create a frame set.
- Change frame set options using the Frame Set Inspector.
- Configure individual frames using the Frame Inspector.
- Add, move, and delete a frame.
- Add content to frames.
- Create targeted links within the frame set.
- Link the frame set to your home page.

This lesson takes approximately 1 hour to complete.

If needed, copy the Lesson06 folder onto your hard drive. As you work on this lesson, you'll overwrite the start files. If you need to restore the start files, copy them from the *Adobe GoLive 5.0 Classroom in a Book* CD.

Note: *Windows users need to unlock the lesson files before using them. For more information, see "Copying the Classroom in a Book files" on page 2.*

For information on setting up your work area, see "Setting up your work area" on page 9.

About frame sets

A frame set is an HTML page that holds several frames and that allows you to show a different document in each frame. Using a frame structure, you can display several HTML documents at once, each in its own pane within the Web browser window. Each pane works independently and can be scrollable or static, depending on its purpose.

A frame set doesn't contain the individual HTML pages that are displayed. It simply provides them with a structure. If you look at the source code for a page containing a frame set, it just has basic HTML meta-information and a few lines of code defining the frame set—nothing else.

The simplest frame set contains two frames, one for navigation purposes and one to display content. The one you will create in this lesson will have three: a navigation frame, a main page frame, and a banner image frame.

Note: *You will not be nesting frame sets in this lesson. While this is allowed in HTML, it can cause serious navigational problems.*

Structure of a frame set

In this lesson, you'll create a frame set titled Frameset.html and then import various content pages into it, as shown in the following illustration.

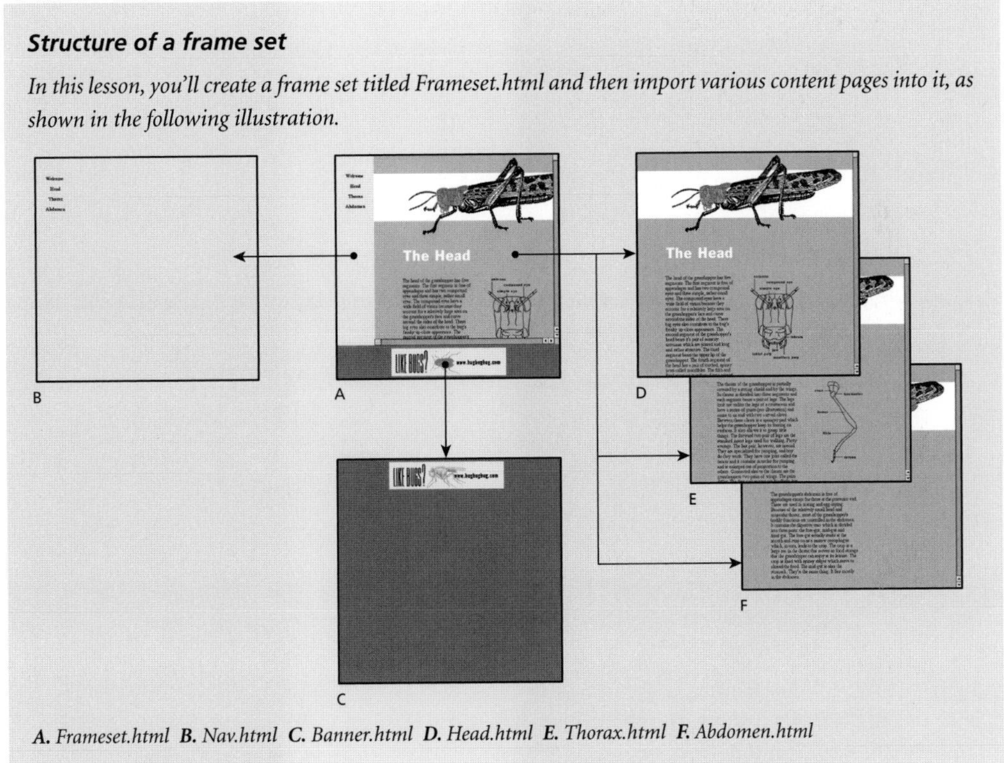

A. *Frameset.html* ***B.*** *Nav.html* ***C.*** *Banner.html* ***D.*** *Head.html* ***E.*** *Thorax.html* ***F.*** *Abdomen.html*

Getting started

In this lesson, you'll create a frame set for a Web site called BugBody and then add the content to the frames. First, you'll view the finished site in your Web browser.

1 Use your browser to open the Web page Index.html. The path to the file is Lesson06/06End/BugBody Folder/BugBody/Index.html.

This is the BugBody site's home page. As it is not part of the frame set, it appears as one page across the whole browser.

2 Click Enter. This link is to an HTML page called Frameset.html.

Although you can see content in this page, Frameset.html only contains code for the site's frame set. The content pages open up inside the frame set.

Notice that the page has three frames: the information about the grasshopper's head is the main frame, the list of contents is another frame, and the animated image at the bottom of the page is another.

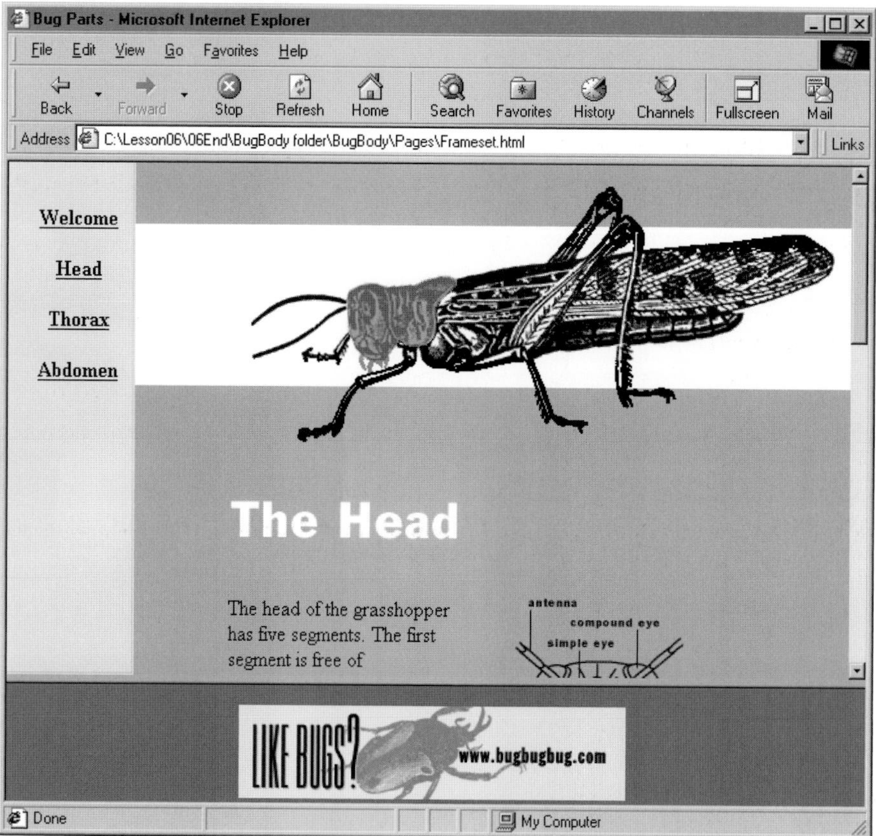

3 Click the links in the list of contents and explore the site.

4 When you have finished viewing the site, quit your browser.

Creating a frame set

When you create a new Web site using frames, you need to set up the page containing your frame set first, and then carefully consider how you want the frames to look. Only then should you start adding and formatting your content pages.

You'll begin this lesson by opening the BugBody Web site and creating a new HTML page containing a frame set.

1 Start Adobe GoLive.

2 Choose File > Open, and open the BugBody.site file. The path to the file is 06Lesson/06Start/BugBody Folder/BugBody.site.

This site contains a home page (Index.html) and several content pages. These pages are not currently set out in frames. You'll create a frame set for the site's content pages.

3 Choose File > New to create a new page.

4 Select the page title, "Welcome to Adobe GoLive 5."

5 Type **Bug Parts** as the new title, and press Enter or Return.

Now that you've created a new page, you can add a frame set to it. When you work with frames, you start by selecting a frame set from the Objects palette, and then configuring it in the Frame Editor of the document window.

6 Click the Frame Editor tab (▤) of the document window to display the Frame Editor. It currently says No Frames.

7 Click the Frames tab (▤) of the Objects palette.

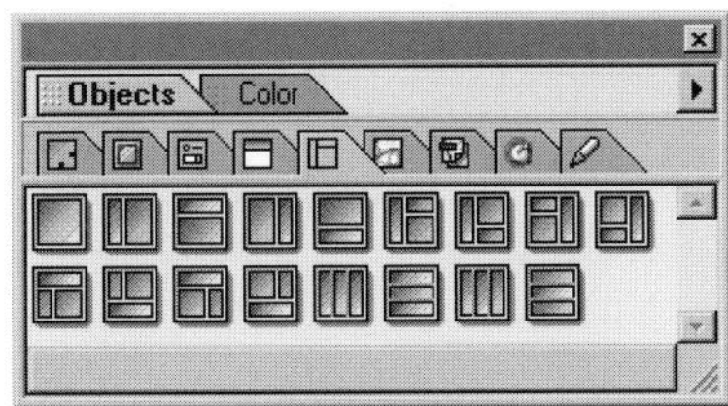

Frames tab of Objects palette

The Frames tab contains a variety of frame set templates, with up to three frames in them. Each template shows you how the frames will appear on the page.

***Note:** The first icon on the top row shows just one frame. You can use this to add an additional frame to a frame set.*

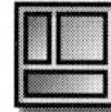

8 In the Frames tab of the Objects palette, select the icon shown at left and drag it from the Frames tab to the Frame Editor. A frame set appears in the document window.

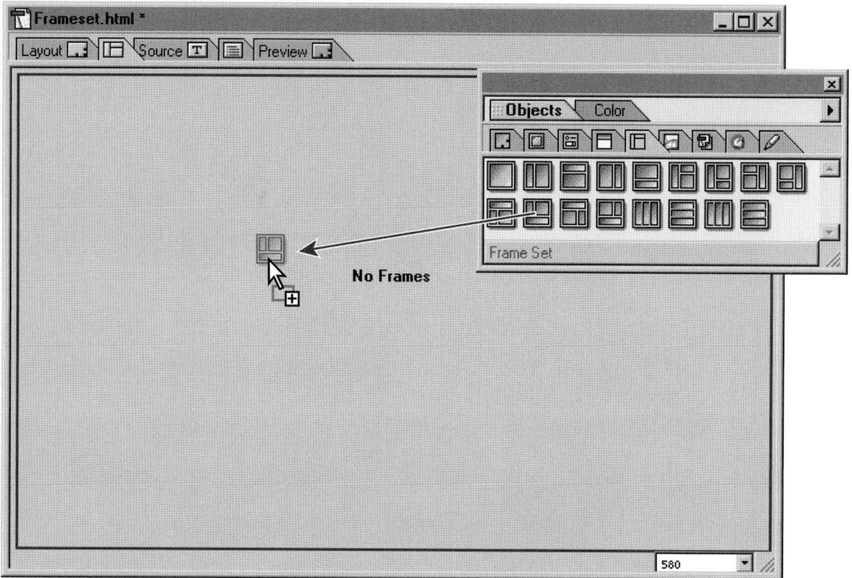

Dragging frame set to Frame Editor

Notice that each frame contains the words "No Name" and has a question mark icon in it and the words "Empty Reference!". You'll name each frame and fill it with content later in this lesson. But now is a good time to take a look at the source code for the new frame set.

9 Click the HTML Source Editor tab (T) of the document window to display the Source view. The source code for this page consists of the frame tags and some meta-information.

10 Return to the Frame Editor.

11 Choose File > Save, and save the page as **Frameset.html** in the Lesson06/06Start/ BugBody Folder/BugBody/Pages folder.)

Note: *To delete a frame set, click on a frame border and press Delete.*

Making changes to the frame set

You can make several changes to a frame set, such as changing its orientation or borders, by using the Frame Set Inspector.

1 If the Inspector is not already open, choose Window > Inspector to open it.

2 Click the internal border above the bottom frame to change the Inspector to the Frame Set Inspector.

You can select any internal border of the frame set to change the Inspector to the Frame Set Inspector.

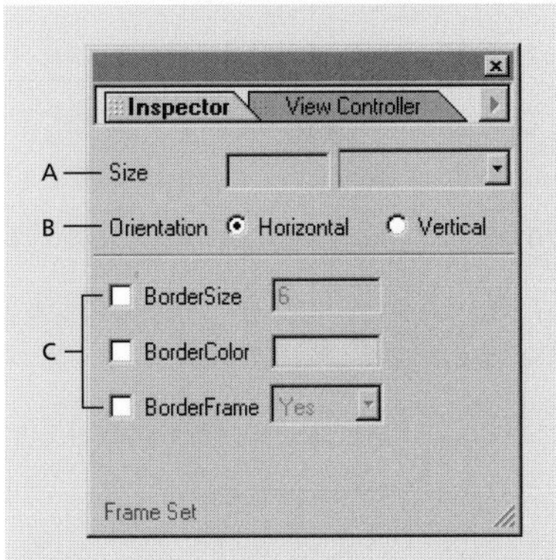

A. Size ***B.*** *Orientation* ***C.*** *Border properties*

3 Select the Horizontal Orientation option and notice how this changes the appearance of the frames on both sides of the selected border. Then reselect the Vertical Orientation option.

Note: *These options do not change the orientation of the entire frame set, but only of the frames adjacent to the selected border.*

4 Select the BorderSize option, enter **5** in the text box, and press Enter or Return. Notice how the change applies only to the border that you selected in the Frame Set Inspector.

5 Select the BorderColor option, and click the gray color field to open the Color palette.

6 Click the Web Color List button (icon) of the Color palette, and then select a color by either clicking in the color grid, or typing a value and pressing Enter or Return. (We entered 99CC99 in the Value field.) Notice how this changes the color of *all* the internal borders.

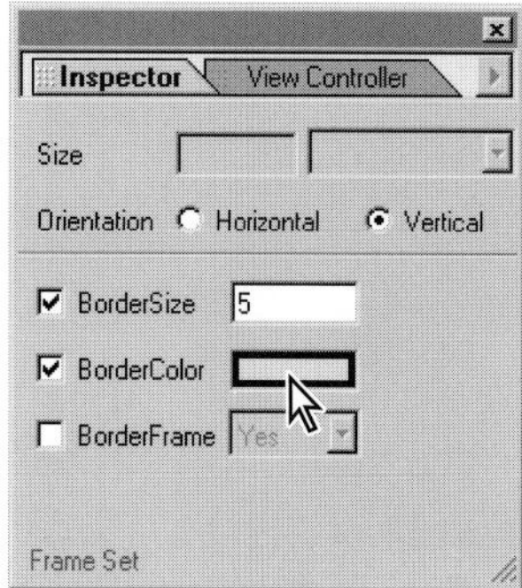

Selecting BorderColor field in Frame Set Inspector

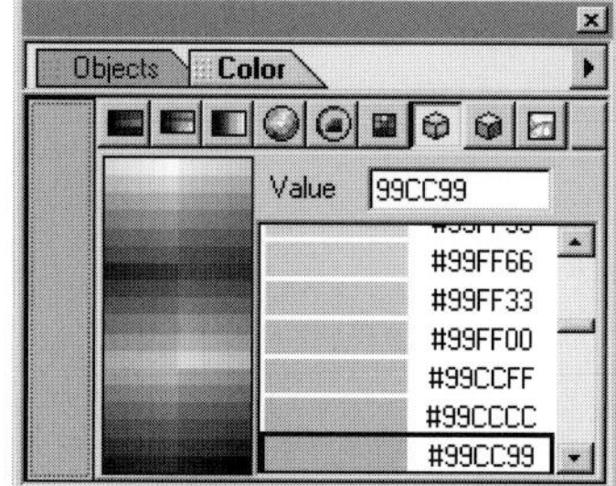

Choosing color in Color palette

7 Select the internal border between the top two frames.

Notice that this frame is set to a horizontal orientation. Select the Vertical Orientation option to see how this affects the orientation of the frames and then reselect the Horizontal Orientation option.

8 Select the BorderSize option and enter **0** in the text box. Then select the BorderFrame option and choose No from the pop-up menu. The border will not appear in a browser, although you can still see a black line in the Frame Editor.

Note: *Many Web designers use borderless frames with the same background color to give the impression of a frameless Web site.*

9 Choose File > Save to save your work.

Setting up the content frames

Now you'll use the Frame Inspector to name the content frames in your frame set, resize them, and specify their scrolling behavior.

1 Select the top left frame. This opens the Frame Inspector.

The Frame Inspector lets you specify options for a selected frame. You can resize and name a frame, link it to a content page, and set its scrolling and resizing properties. You can also turn content viewing on or off.

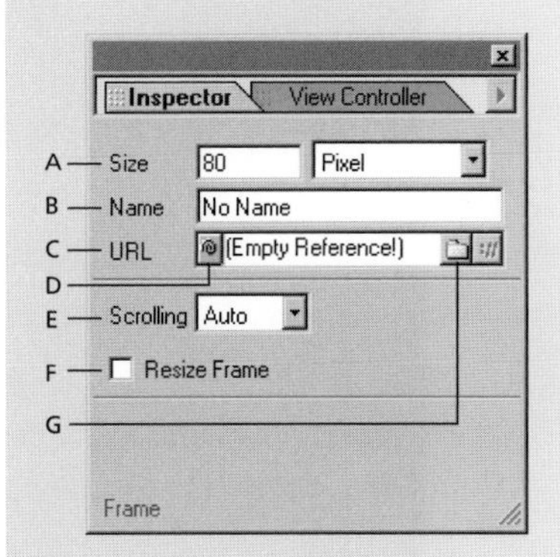

A. *Size* ***B.*** *Name* ***C.*** *URL typed entry*
D. *Point and Shoot button to URL link*
E. *Scrolling* ***F.*** *Resize Frame* ***G.*** *Browse to URL link*

2 In the Name text box of the Frame Inspector, enter **Navigation** as the name of the frame.

Now, you'll set the size of the frame. You can do this in several ways:

- Enter a precise pixel size for each pane.
- Enter a percentage of the browser window for each pane.
- Scale a frame to fit the browser window.

You'll set the size of the Navigation frame to a precise pixel size. Because this frame will contain a navigation bar, it should be the same width in all browsers and at all screen resolutions, to ensure that the wording for the links can be seen at all times.

3 Choose Pixel in the Size pop-up menu, enter **110** in the Size text box, and press Enter or Return to resize the frame. Notice that the left-hand frame is now slightly larger than it was.

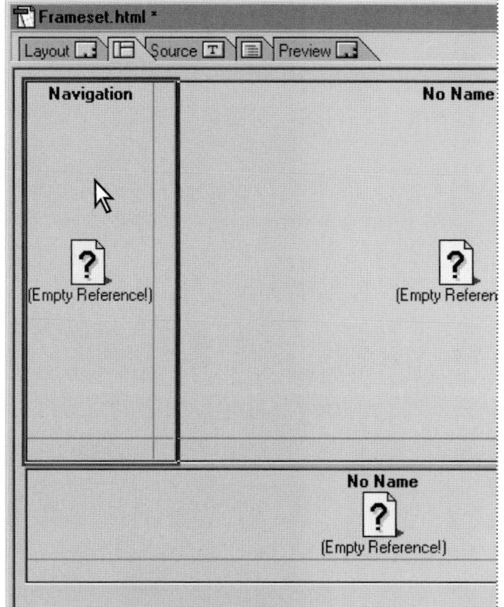

Selecting Navigation frame

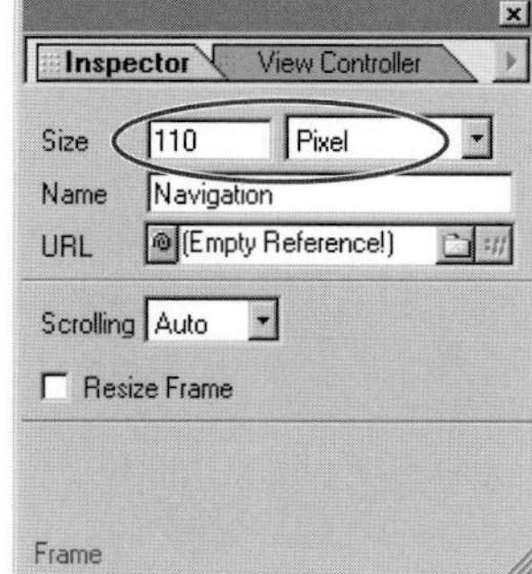

Specifying pixel size

4 Leave Resize Frame deselected. This prevents viewers from changing the layout of your frames.

5 Choose No from the Scrolling pop-up menu to make the pane nonscrolling.

A navigation pane is more useful if it's nonscrolling. Rather than force site viewers to scroll through links, you should cut the pane's content. If your site has too many pages to show on the navigation pane, consider reorganizing the site into areas and using the navigation pane to take a viewer to those areas, rather than straight to individual pages. Each area can have its own contents list, showing its pages.

Now, you'll format the main content frame.

6 Select the top right frame. In the Frame Inspector, choose Scale from the Size pop-up menu.

If a viewer resizes the browser window, the Scale option allows this frame to expand or contract to fill all of the browser window to the right of the Navigation frame.

7 In the Name text box, enter **Main.**

8 Choose Yes from the Scrolling pop-up menu. This will add vertical and horizontal scrollbars to the frame.

Now, you'll format the bottom frame.

9 Select the bottom frame, and name it **Banner**.

10 Set its size to 90 pixels. This is slightly larger than the image that will fill this frame, to allow for shifting in different browsers.

11 Choose the No Scrolling option.

12 Choose File > Save to save your work.

Adding, moving, and deleting frames

You can add frames to the frame set, move them around, and delete them. First, you'll add a fourth frame to your set.

1 In the Frames tab of the Objects palette, drag a new frame (the first icon on the top row) to the bottom frame of your frame set. It appears to the right of the existing frame.

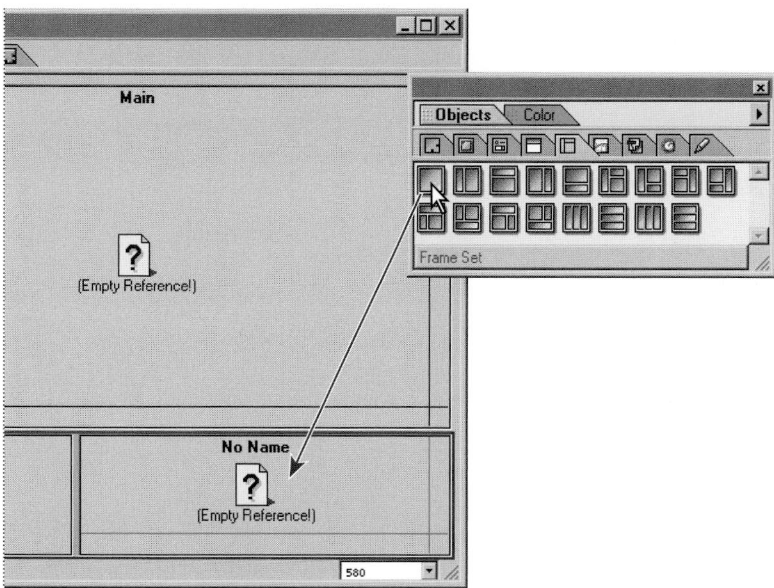

Dragging new frame from Objects palette to frame set

2 In the Frame Inspector, choose Percent from the Size pop-up menu, enter **20** in the Size text field, and press Enter or Return to resize the frame.

You'll now move the new frame to the left of the original frame.

3 Drag the new frame over the original bottom frame until it turns black (Windows) or gray (Mac OS), and then drop it onto the frame. The new frame appears to the left of the original one.

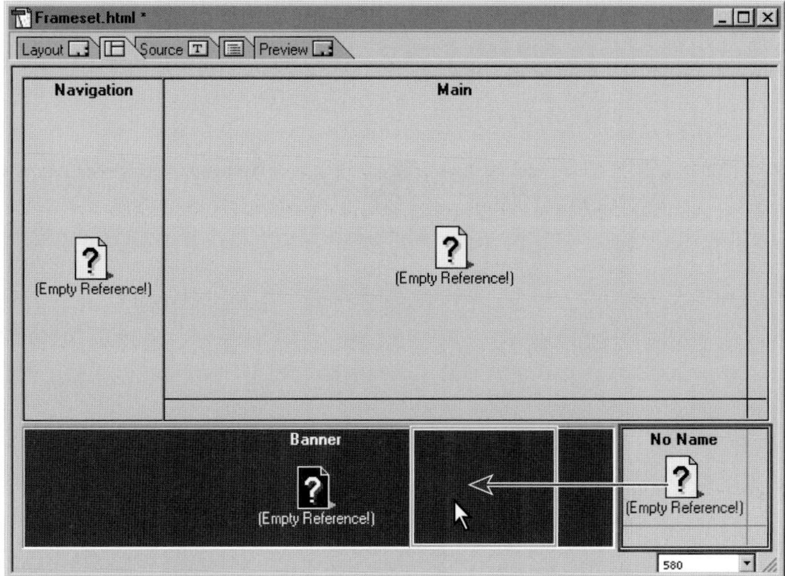

Dragging new frame to left of original one

4 Select the new frame, and press Delete. This removes the new frame and restores the Banner frame to its original size of 90 pixels.

Adding content to frames

It's time to add content to each of your three frames by linking them to content pages. You'll do this in several ways:

- By using the Browse button in the Frame Inspector.
- By using the Point and Shoot button (@) in the Frame Inspector.
- By dragging a content file directly to a frame.

You're going to use each method as you add content to the three frames.

First, you'll browse for a file. This technique is particularly useful if the content file does not reside in the same folder as the rest of your Web site.

1 Select the Navigation frame on the left of the page. In the Frame Inspector, click the Browse button, navigate to Nav.html in the BugBody/Pages folder, and click Open. An icon representing the file appears in the frame.

In Mac OS, click the Preview Frame button (▶) in the Frame Inspector. The contents list in Nav.html appears in the frame. (You can click the button again to turn off the display, but leave it on for now.)

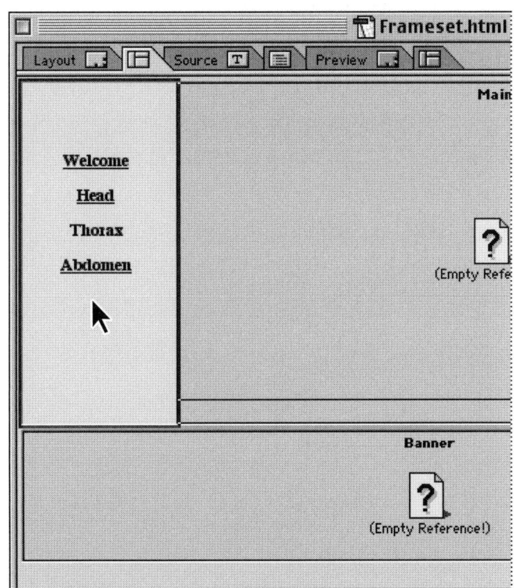

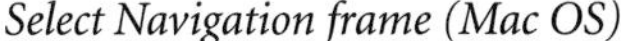

Select Navigation frame (Mac OS)

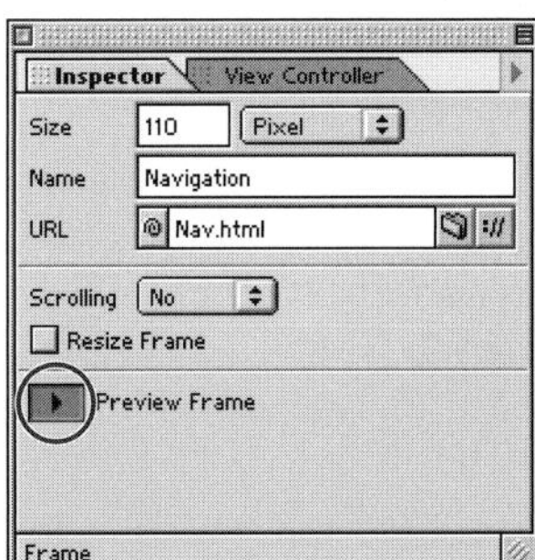

Click Preview Frame button in Frame Inspector (Mac OS)

Now, you'll try another technique for adding a content file. If the file resides in your Web site, you can use the Point and Shoot button in the Frame Inspector to add content to a frame.

2 If necessary, drag the document window to a place on your screen where you can see both the Main frame of your frame set and the files in your site window.

3 In the site window, open the Pages folder.

4 In the document window, select the Main frame.

5 In the Frame Inspector, drag from the Point and Shoot button ( ) to the Head.html file in the site window to create a link.

The final method for adding content to a frame is perhaps the easiest. This is by dragging.

6 If necessary, drag the document window to a place on your screen where you can see both the bottom frame of your frame set and the files in your site window. (You may need to resize Frameset.html to do this.)

7 Drag Banner.html from your site window to the bottom frame. The Banner.html file is now linked to the frame.

8 Click the Layout Preview tab (Windows) or the Frame Preview tab (Mac OS) in the document window to display the contents of all three frames.

Note: *When you want to add an image as the content of a frame, you must first put the image into an HTML page. A frame will not show a plain image file.*

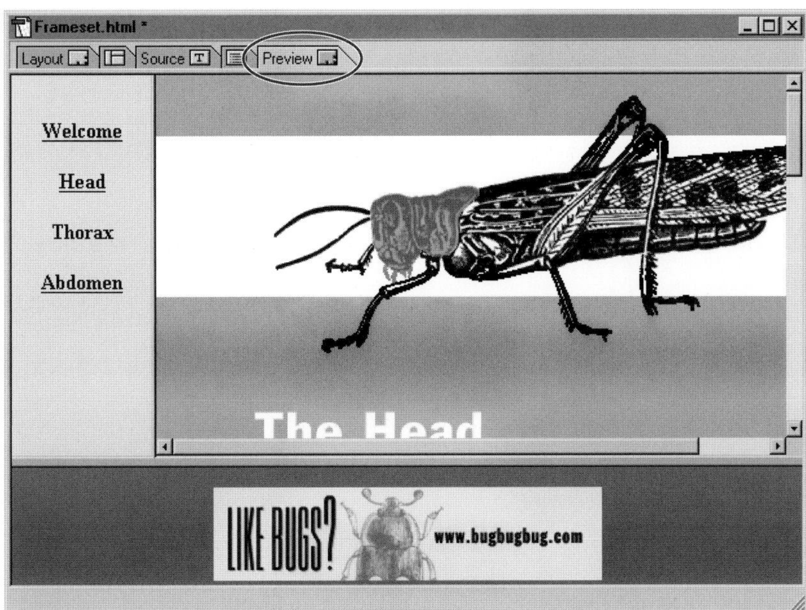

Layout Preview tab (Windows)

Frame Preview tab (Mac OS)

9 Choose File > Save to save your frame set.

Creating targeted links

Although your frames can be used simply to display these three Web pages, they are much more powerful when used to navigate and view your entire site. You'll enable a viewer to change the content of the Main frame by using targeted links from the Navigation (contents) pane to other pages.

1 In the site window, open Nav.html.

2 Select the word "Thorax" in the Nav.html file.

3 In the Text Inspector, click the New Link button ( ), and then use the Point and Shoot button to create a link to Thorax.html.

This creates a link between the two pages. But which frame will it appear in? You want it to appear in the Main frame, so you must select that frame as the target.

4 In the Text Inspector, choose Main from the Target pop-up menu.

Selecting Main frame as target

Now, when a visitor clicks on this link in the Contents, Thorax.html will replace Head.html in the Main frame.

Creating a return link to the home page

You are going to target the Welcome link on this page to the home page. This will allow viewers to return to the home page at any time, and from anywhere in your site.

1 Select the Welcome link.

2 In the site window, make sure that Index.html is visible.

3 In the Text Inspector, click the New Link button, and then use the Point and Shoot button to create a link to Index.html.

4 This time, in the Text Inspector, choose _parent from the Target pop-up menu.

The _parent option specifies the browser window as the target and causes the browser to change the content of the entire window. The browser will replace the frame set with one pane that shows the home page; it will no longer display the navigation bar or banner.

The other two links have already been done for you.

5 Save and close the Nav.html file.

6 Choose File > Save to save Frameset.html.

7 Be sure that Frameset.html is selected and not one of the frames inside of it. Then choose Special > Show in Browser > [your favorite browser] to open Frameset.html in your browser.

8 Click each of the links in the Contents pane (select the Welcome link last). The linked pages appear in the Main pane.

Notice that when you click the Welcome link, the site's home page fills the entire browser window. This shows the effect of setting the link's target to _parent. However, you will also notice that nothing happens when you click Enter.

Linking the frame set to your home page

Now you need to create a link from your home page to the new frame set. This link usually says something like Enter. When a viewer clicks it, the frame set opens, displaying your site's opening content pages.

Note that you don't create a link to a content page. Instead you create a link to Frameset.html, which will open showing the three content pages in its frames.

1 Close your browser.

2 In the site window, open Index.html. Make sure that the site window is visible, and that the Pages folder is open.

3 In Index.html, select the text Enter.

4 In the Text Inspector, click the New Link button ( ), and then use the Point and Shoot button to create a link to Frameset.html.

5 Choose File > Save to save both Index.html and Frameset.html.

Adding an action to always load the frame set

As the BugBody site is set up now, it's still possible to browse an individual page (such as Abdomen.html) without the frame set, so that it fills the entire browser window. This could produce unwanted consequences if the site were actually on the Web. For example, a search engine might locate content in the Abdomen.html page, and return the URL for that page to a viewer. Clicking on that URL would open Abdomen.html in the entire browser window, with no access to the navigation bar or any other page in the site.

To prevent this from happening, you can add a ForceFrame head action to the individual content pages in your site. The Force Frame action identifies the frame set associated with the page and instructs the browser to load the page in the frame set, thus preserving the site structure.

1 In the site window, double-click the Abdomen.html file in the Pages folder to open it.

2 Click the triangle at the top left of the page to open the head section pane of the document window.

3 In the Objects palette, click the Smart tab (▣).

4 Drag the Head Action icon from the Objects palette to the head section pane.

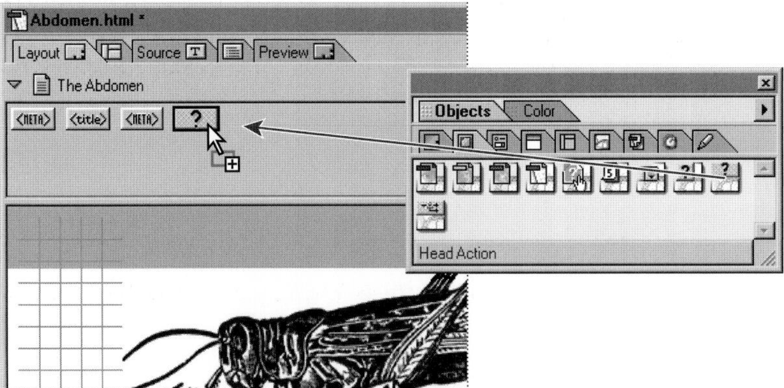

5 In the Action Inspector, choose OnLoad from the Exec. pop-up menu. From the Action pop-up menu, choose ActionsPlus > ForceFrame.

6 Now you need to select the frame set. Either use the Point and Shoot button and create a link to Frameset.html in the site window, or use the Browse button to select Frameset.html.

7 Choose File > Save to save both Abdomen.html and Frameset.html.

Now you're ready to test the ForceFrame action. Open a browser, and then open the Abdomen.html page. The page displays in the frame set, along with the navigation bar and banner frames.

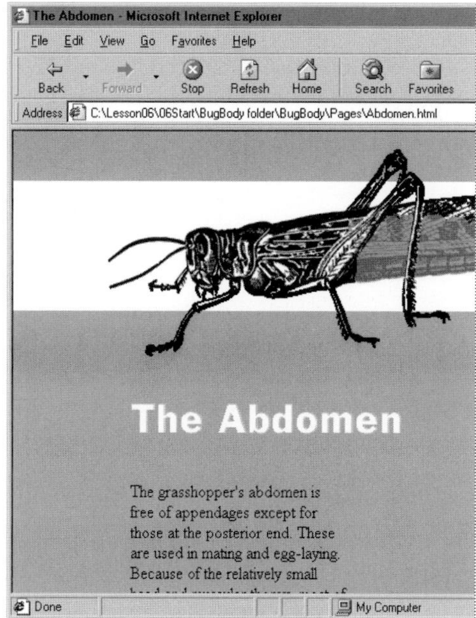

Page viewed without ForceFrame action

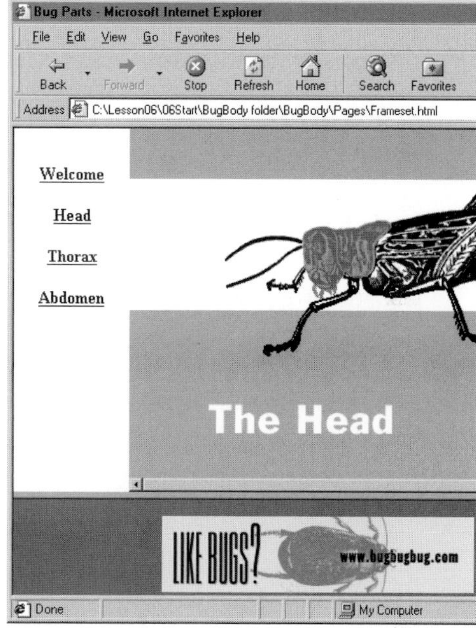

Page viewed with ForceFrame action

8 Close Abdomen.html and Frameset.html.

Previewing in a Web browser

Now that you've created a frame set and content frames for your Web site, you can preview the finished site in a browser.

1 Start your browser.

2 Locate and open the completed Index.html file. Choose File > Open. Select the Index.html file, located in the Lesson06/06Start/BugBody Folder/BugBody folder.

3 Click the Enter link in the Index.html file, and explore the site.

4 When you've finished viewing the pages in the site, close your browser.

Review questions

1 Where will you find a set of ready-made frame layouts?

2 How do you set a frame size to a specific number of pixels?

3 How do you add color to a frame border?

4 How do you add a scrollbar to a frame?

5 How do you add a new frame to your frame set?

6 What are the three ways to fill a frame with content?

7 How can you preview the content in your frame set without launching a browser?

8 Why would you add a ForceFrame head action to a Web page?

Review answers

1 You will find a set of ready-made frame layouts in the Frames tab of the Objects palette.

2 Select the frame. In the Frame Inspector, choose Pixel from the Size pop-up menu and enter the number of pixels in the Size text box.

3 Select the frame border. In the Frame Set Inspector, select the BorderColor option, and then click on the color field to open the Color palette. Click the Web Color List button in the Color palette and select the color that you want.

4 Select a frame. In the Frame Inspector, choose Yes from the Scrolling pop-up menu.

5 Drag a Frame icon from the Frames tab of the Objects palette to your frame set. Drop it into the frame that you want.

6 Select a frame. You can fill it with content:

- By browsing for a file in the Frame Inspector.
- By using the Point and Shoot button on the Frame Inspector to link to a file.
- By dragging a file from the site window to the frame.

7 Click the Layout Preview tab (Windows) or Frame Preview tab (Mac OS) of the document window, or double-click on the page icon in a frame to open its content file in another window.

8 You add a ForceFrame head action to make sure that the page is always viewed as part of a frame set, rather than as an individual page filling the browser window.

Lesson 7

```
<TITLE>Wel
<STYLE TYPE=

e{color:maroon;

</STYLE>
AD>
Y>
<!-- Begin main table -->
<TABLE BORDER="4" CELLPADDIN
06">
    <TR>
        <TD><A
tp://www.adobe.com/">Adobe</A>
        <TD>GoLive</TD>
        <TD><IMG BORDER="0" HEIG
le.gif" ALT="Title"></TD>
    </TR>
    <TR>
        <TD><SPAN CLASS="head
AN></TD>
    </TR>
    <TR>
        <TD><B>DHTML
    </TR>
</TABLE>
DY>

 main table -->
DER="4" CELLPAD

D><A
dobe.com/">Adobe</A
D>GoLive</TD>
D><IMG BORDER="0" HE
T="Title"></TD>

D><SPAN CLASS="head

D><B>DHTML
```

7 Creating Rollovers

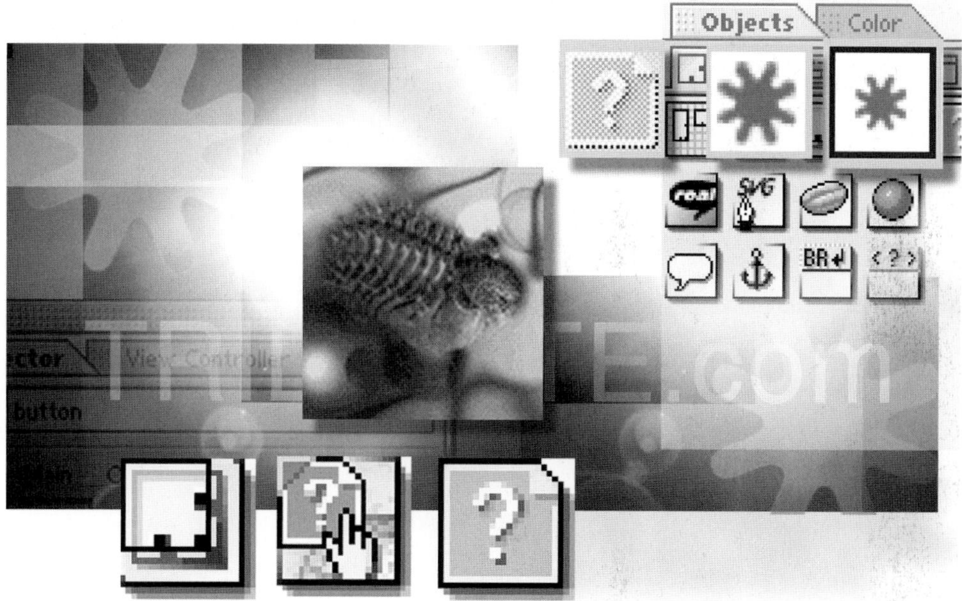

In this lesson, you'll design a navigation bar for the home page of a Web site. First, you'll create rollover buttons that change in appearance when your mouse moves over them. Next you'll assign actions to the rollover buttons so that floating boxes appear when your mouse moves over them. Lastly, you'll assign an action to a rollover button to create a drop-down menu effect.

About this lesson

In this lesson, you'll learn how to do the following:

- Add floating boxes to a page, so that you can overlap objects.
- Create rollover buttons inside floating boxes on a page.
- Add images inside floating boxes on a page.
- Add actions to rollover buttons for showing and hiding floating boxes.
- Add actions to a rollover button to create a drop-down menu effect.
- Link a rollover button to a page on the Web.
- Preview a page in a Web browser.

This lesson takes approximately 45 minutes to complete.

If needed, copy the Lesson07 folder onto your hard drive. As you work on this lesson, you'll overwrite the start files. If you need to restore the start files, copy them from the *Adobe GoLive 5.0 Classroom in a Book* CD.

***Note:** Windows users need to unlock the lesson files before using them. For more information, see "Copying the Classroom in a Book files" on page 2.*

For information on setting up your work area, see "Setting up your work area" on page 9.

Getting started

In this lesson, you'll work on the design of the home page of a Web site for a fictional company called Trilobite.com, which specializes in selling trilobites, collectible fossils of one of the first arthropods. You'll work on the design of a navigation bar for the page by adding rollover buttons to the page and then assigning actions to these buttons.

Rollover buttons are buttons that change in appearance when your mouse moves over them or clicks them. You can assign actions to rollover buttons that are triggered by the same mouse events. Examples of actions that you can assign to a rollover button are showing and hiding a floating box. For more complete information on using actions, see Lesson 9, "Using Actions and JavaScript."

First you'll view the finished home page in your Web browser.

1 Start your browser.

2 Open the Index.html file, the home page for the site. The path to the file is Lesson07/07End/Trilobite folder/Trilobite/Index.html.

The home page welcomes viewers to Trilobite.com. It contains a green button in the upper left area of the page.

3 Move your mouse over the green button. Notice how the button changes in appearance and text associated with the button appears below it.

4 Click the green button. Notice how two other buttons appear to the right of it.

***Note:** If the button doesn't work as expected when you click it, you may be experiencing problems with your browser. If you are using Microsoft Internet Explorer, you may need to click the button twice to display the other buttons.*

5 Move your mouse over the new buttons on the page. Notice how each button changes in appearance and text associated with each button appears below it.

The buttons are designed to function as a navigation bar that viewers can use to explore the site. Currently, the buttons aren't linked to other pages in the site, because the site contains only the home page. For the sake of this lesson, we linked the blue button to the Adobe Web site, so that you can see how a button can be linked to another page on the Web.

6 Click the blue button to go to the Adobe Web site.

7 Click the Back button in your browser to return to the home page for the Trilobite.com Web site.

8 Click the green button again. Notice how the other buttons disappear.

9 When you have finished viewing the home page, close it and quit your browser.

Opening the home page

You'll begin this lesson by opening the home page for the Trilobite.com Web site in Adobe GoLive.

1 Start Adobe GoLive.

2 Choose File > Open, select the Trilobite.site file, and click Open. The path to the file is Lesson07/07Start/Trilobite Folder/Trilobite.site.

The primary site window for the Trilobite Web site appears with the Files tab selected.

Now you'll open the home page for the Trilobite Web site.

3 Double-click the Index.html file in the Files tab of the site window.

The home page appears with the Layout tab selected. The page contains a single, large image and a floating box that contains an animated GIF image.

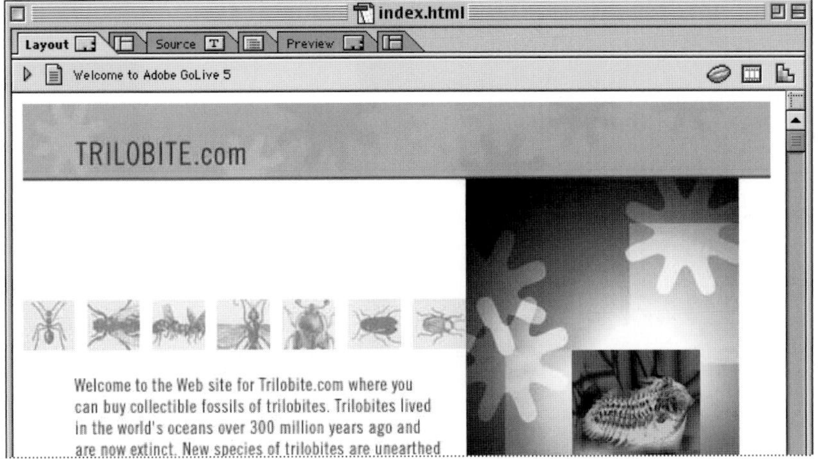

4 Choose Window > Inspector to display the Inspector.

5 Click anywhere on the home page except on the floating box that contains the animated GIF image. Notice how most of the content of the page is selected. In addition, the Inspector changes to the Image Inspector, indicating that you have selected an image. (As a reminder, the word "Image" appears at the bottom of the Inspector to indicate that it has changed to the Image Inspector.)

Creating a rollover button

Now that you've opened the home page, you're ready to begin creating the navigation bar for the page. The navigation bar will contain three rollover buttons. You'll place each rollover button inside a floating box on the page. Floating boxes are useful because they allow you to overlap objects on a page. Using floating boxes, you can position the rollover buttons on top of the single, large image on the page. As an alternative to using floating boxes, you can also place rollover buttons directly on a page, on a layout grid, or inside a table cell.

Now you'll add your first rollover button to the home page. First you'll add a floating box to the page. Then you'll place the rollover button inside the floating box.

1 Scroll downward in the document window until you reach its end. Notice that a small icon appears in the lower left corner of the home page. This is a marker for the floating box that contains the animated GIF image. When you change the position of a floating box, its icon remains at the original point of insertion. You can click this icon to select the floating box.

2 Click in the blank space to the right of the small icon, so that a cursor appears.

3 Choose Window > Objects to display the Objects palette.

4 In the Objects palette, make sure that the Basic tab (▣) is selected. Drag a Floating Box icon from the Objects palette to the cursor in the document window.

An empty floating box is added to the document window, and the Inspector changes to the Floating Box Inspector.

5 Scroll downward in the document window, so that you can view the floating box that you've added to the page.

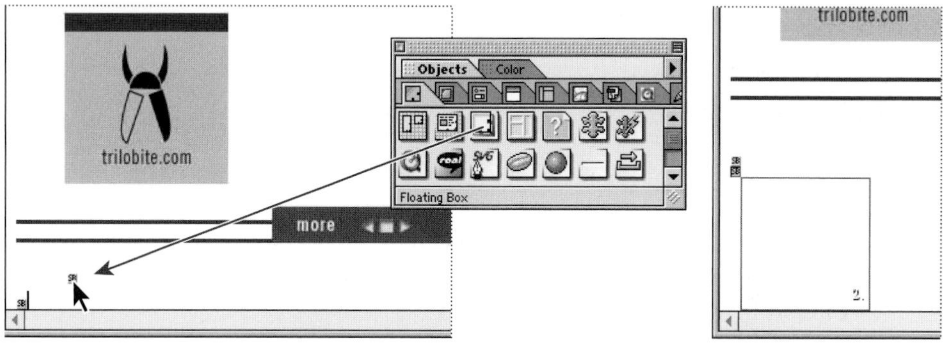

Dragging Floating Box icon to cursor *Result*

Now you'll use the Floating Box Inspector to set attributes for the floating box. First you'll name the floating box, so that you can differentiate it from other floating boxes that you'll add to the page. Then you'll specify its position on the page and its size.

6 Make sure that the floating box is selected. To select a floating box, move the pointer over an edge of the floating box, so that the pointer turns into a hand pointing left. Then click an edge of the floating box to select it.

7 In the Floating Box Inspector, enter **Button01** for Name, enter **50** for Left, enter **76** for Top, and enter **40** for both Width and Height.

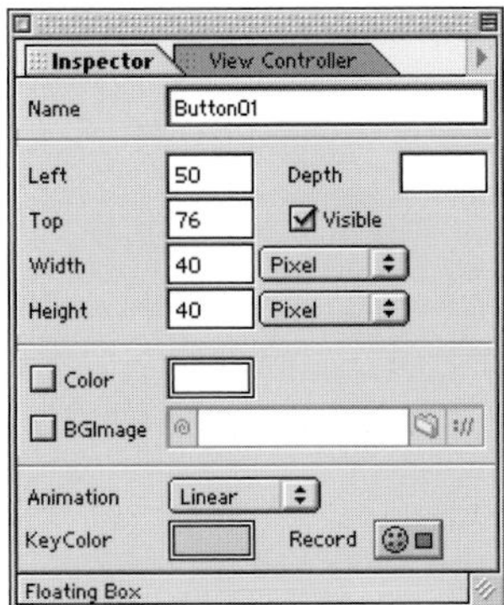

8 If needed, scroll upward in the document window, so that you can see the new position and size of the floating box.

Now you'll add a placeholder for a rollover button to the floating box.

9 In the Objects palette, click the Smart tab (▣). Drag the Rollover icon from the Objects palette to the floating box in the document window.

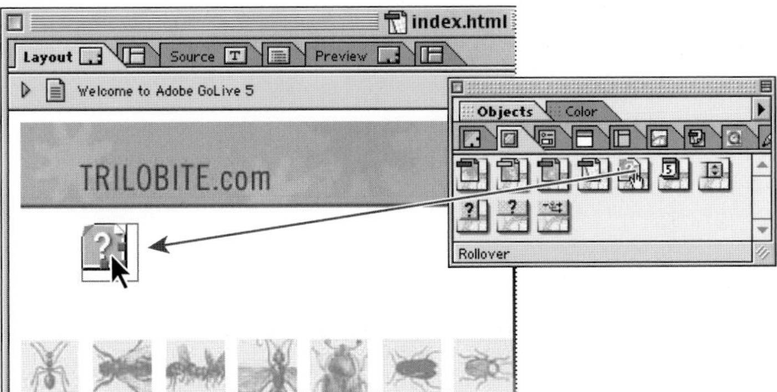

Dragging Rollover icon to floating box

The Inspector changes to the Rollover Inspector. The Rollover Inspector lets you specify three different images for three different states of a rollover button: how the button appears by default, how the button appears when your mouse moves over it, and how the button appears when clicked.

First you'll specify an image for how the button appears by default.

10 In the Files tab of the site window, locate the 01_main.gif file inside the Images folder.

11 In the Rollover Inspector, make sure that the Main icon is selected. Then drag from the top Point and Shoot button (@) to the 01_main.gif file in the Files tab of the site window.

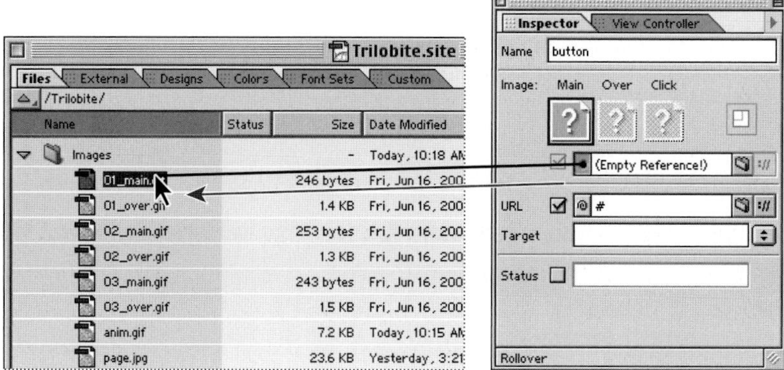

Dragging from Point and Shoot button to image file in site window

The path to the file appears in the Source text box of the Rollover Inspector, and the main button image appears in the document window.

Now you'll specify an image for how the button appears when your mouse moves over it.

12 In the Rollover Inspector, click the Over icon to select it. Then click the check box below the icons representing the different button states, so that the top Point and Shoot button reappears.

13 Drag from the top Point and Shoot button (◎) in the Rollover Inspector to the 01_over.gif file inside the Images folder in the Files tab of the site window.

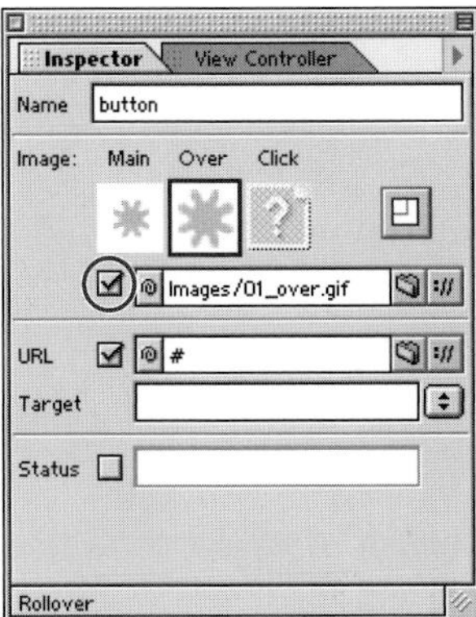

14 Choose File > Save to save the Index.html file.

Creating additional rollover buttons for a navigation bar

Now you'll add two more rollover buttons to the home page, using the same method that you used to add the first rollover button. To test your knowledge, the instructions for adding these rollover buttons is less detailed. If needed, see "Creating a rollover button" on page 193 for more detailed information.

First you'll add the second rollover button to the home page.

1 Scroll downward in the document window until you reach its end. Notice that two small icons now appear in the lower left corner of the home page.

2 Click in the blank space to the right of the second small icon, so that a cursor appears.

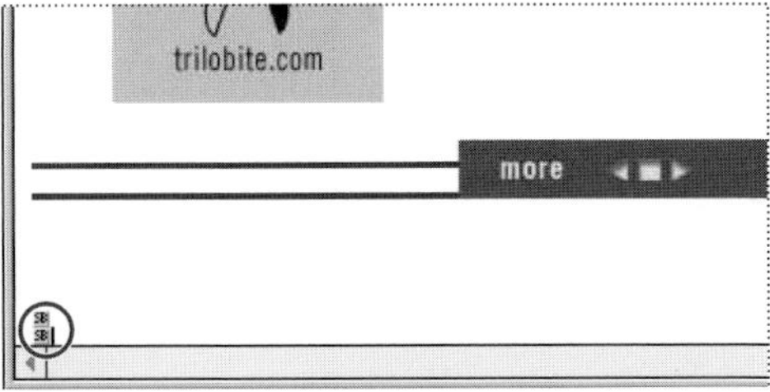

3 Using the Basic tab of the Objects palette, add a third floating box to the document window at the location of the cursor.

4 Using the Floating Box Inspector, name the third floating box **Button02**, position it 90 pixels from the left of the document window and 76 pixels from the top, and specify its width and height to be 40 pixels. (Remember that you need to select the floating box before you can specify its properties in the Floating Box Inspector.)

5 Using the Smart tab of the Objects palette, add a rollover placeholder to the Button02 floating box on the page.

6 Using the Rollover Inspector, specify the Main image for the button to be the 02_main.gif file inside the Images folder in the Files tab of the site window.

7 Using the Rollover Inspector, specify the Over image for the button to be the 02_over.gif file inside the Images folder in the Files tab of the site window. (Remember that you need to first click the necessary check box in the Rollover Inspector, before you can use the top Point and Shoot button.)

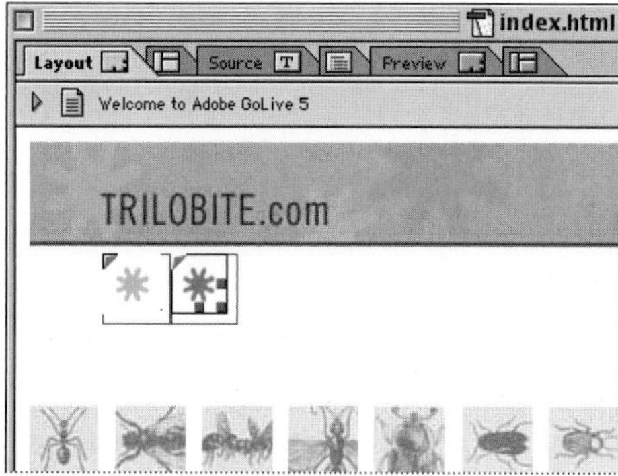

Now you'll add the third rollover button to the home page.

8 Scroll downward in the document window until you reach its end.

9 Click in the blank space to the right of the third small icon, so that a cursor appears.

10 Using the Basic tab of the Objects palette, add a fourth floating box to the document window at the location of the cursor.

11 Using the Floating Box Inspector, name the fourth floating box **Button03**, position it 130 pixels from the left of the document window and 76 pixels from the top, and specify its width and height to be 40 pixels.

12 Using the Smart tab of the Objects palette, add a rollover placeholder to the Button03 floating box on the page.

13 Using the Rollover Inspector, specify the Main image for the button to be the 03_main.gif file inside the Images folder in the Files tab of the site window.

14 Using the Rollover Inspector, specify the Over image for the button to be the 03_over.gif file inside the Images folder in the Files tab of the site window.

15 Choose File > Save.

Adding images inside floating boxes

Now you'll add three images to the page. Each image contains text that is associated with each rollover button on the page. Like the rollover buttons, you'll place each image inside a floating box, so that you can position the image on top of the single, large image on the page. Later in this lesson, you'll assign an action to each rollover button to display its associated image when you move your mouse over the button.

Now you'll add the first image inside a floating box to the page.

1 Scroll downward in the document window until you reach its end.

2 Click in the blank space to the right of the fourth small icon, so that a cursor appears.

3 In the Objects palette, click the Basic tab (). Then drag a Floating Box icon from the Objects palette to the cursor in the document window.

A fifth floating box is added to the document window, and the Inspector changes to the Floating Box Inspector. Now you'll use the Floating Box Inspector to name the floating box, specify its position, and specify its size.

4 In the Floating Box Inspector, enter **Text01** for Name, enter **45** for Left, enter **116** for Top, enter **300** for Width, and enter **30** for Height.

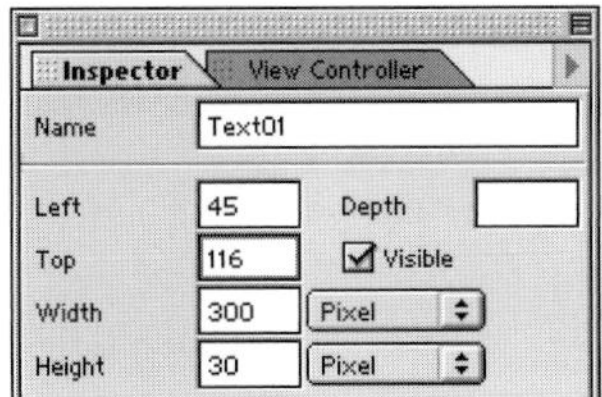

5 If needed, scroll upward in the document window, so that you can see the new position and size of the Text01 floating box.

Now you'll add a placeholder for an image to the Text01 floating box.

6 Drag the Image icon from the Objects palette to the floating box in the document window.

The Inspector changes to the Image Inspector. Now you'll link the image placeholder to an image file.

7 Drag from the Point and Shoot button (◉) in the Image Inspector to the text01.gif file inside the Images folder in the Files tab of the site window.

The path to the file appears in the Source text box in the Image Inspector and the image appears in the document window.

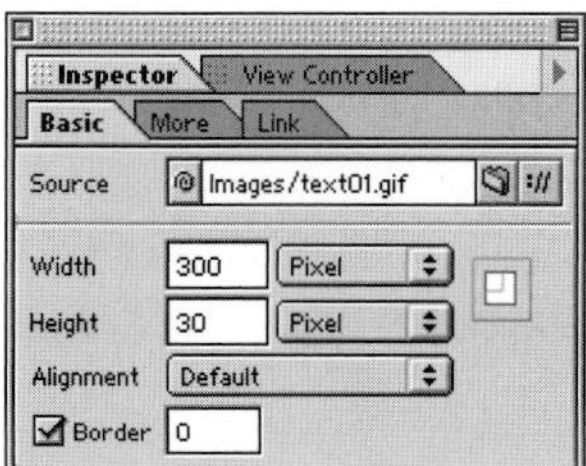

Now you'll add the second and third images to the home page, using the same method that you used to add the first image. To test your knowledge, the instructions for the rest of this section are less detailed. If needed, see the steps at the beginning of this section for more detailed information.

First you'll add the second image to the home page.

8 Scroll downward in the document window until you reach its end.

9 Click in the blank space to the right of the fifth small icon, so that a cursor appears.

10 Using the Basic tab of the Objects palette, add a sixth floating box to the document window at the location of the cursor.

11 Using the Floating Box Inspector, name the sixth floating box **Text02** and specify its width to be 300 pixels and its height to be 30 pixels.

You'll first add an image to the Text02 floating box before repositioning it on the page. When you move the Text02 floating box to the same position as the Text01 floating box, the Text02 floating box will appear on top.

12 Using the Basic tab of the Objects palette, add an image placeholder to the Text02 floating box on the page.

13 Using the Image Inspector, link the image placeholder to the text02.gif file inside the Images folder in the Files tab of the site window.

Now you can reposition the Text02 floating box.

14 Move the pointer over an edge of the floating box, so that the pointer turns into a hand pointing left. Then click an edge of the floating box to select it.

15 Using the Floating Box Inspector, position the floating box 45 pixels from the left of the document window and 116 pixels from the top.

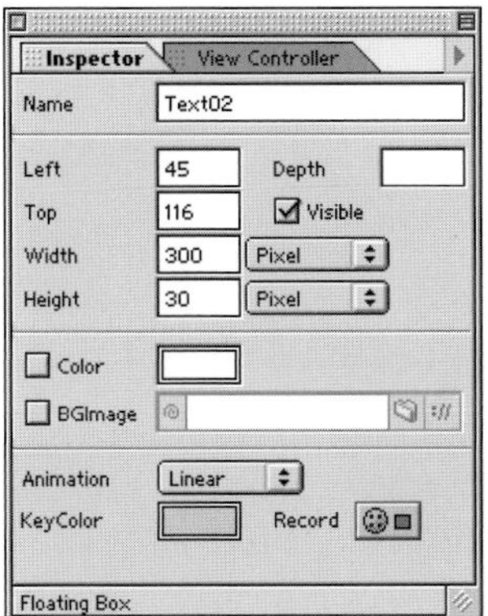

Specifying position in Floating Box Inspector

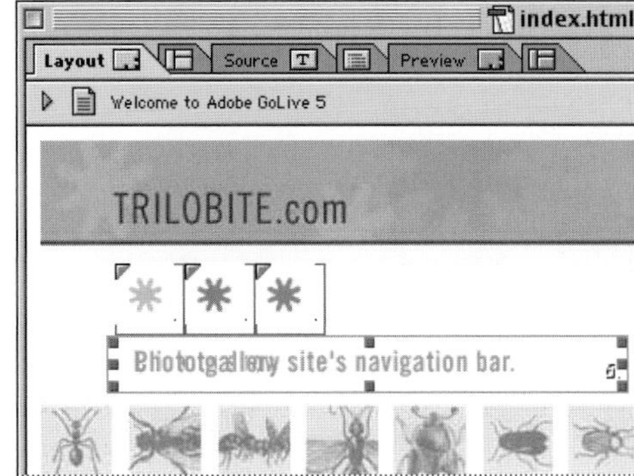

Result

Now you'll add the third image to the home page.

16 Scroll downward in the document window until you reach its end.

17 Click in the blank space to the right of the sixth small icon, so that a cursor appears.

18 Using the Basic tab of the Objects palette, add a seventh floating box to the document window at the location of the cursor.

19 Using the Floating Box Inspector, name the seventh floating box **Text03** and specify its width to be 300 pixels and its height to be 30 pixels.

20 Using the Basic tab of the Objects palette, add an image placeholder to the Text03 floating box on the page.

21 Using the Image Inspector, link the image placeholder to the text03.gif file inside the Images folder in the Files tab of the site window.

Now you can reposition the Text03 floating box.

22 Select the floating box. Using the Floating Box Inspector, position the floating box 45 pixels from the left of the document window and 116 pixels from the top.

23 Choose File > Save.

Adding actions for showing and hiding floating boxes

Now you'll add actions to each rollover button, so that its associated image appears when you move your mouse on top of the button and disappears when you move your mouse off of the button.

First you'll add actions to the first rollover button on the home page.

1 Click the first rollover button (the left button) to select it.

2 Choose Window > Actions to display the Actions palette.

3 In the Actions palette, under Events, select Mouse Enter to specify an action to occur when the mouse moves on top of the button. Then click the New Action button ( ) to add an action to the Actions list box.

4 From the Action pop-up menu, choose Multimedia > ShowHide. From the Floating Box pop-up menu, choose Text01. From the Mode pop-up menu, choose Show.

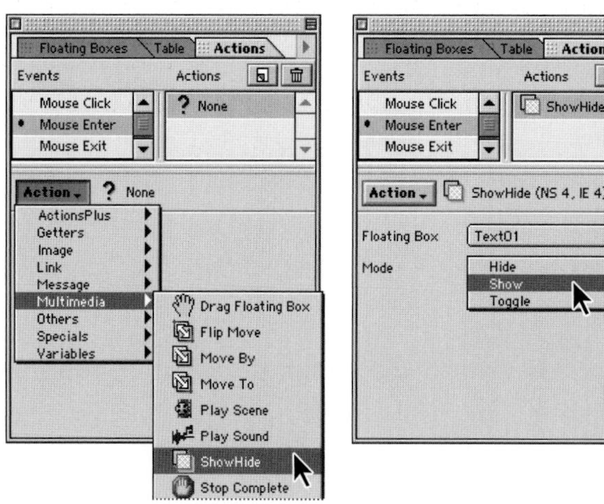

Choosing ShowHide action *Choosing Show mode*

5 In the Actions palette, under Events, select Mouse Exit to specify an action to occur when the mouse moves off of the button. Then click the New Action button ( ) to add an action to the Actions list box.

6 From the Action pop-up menu, choose Multimedia > ShowHide. From the Floating Box pop-up menu, choose Text01. From the Mode pop-up menu, choose Hide.

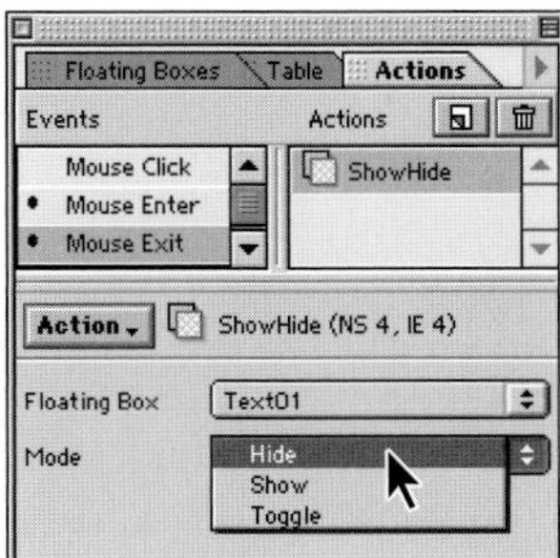

Choosing Hide mode

Now you'll add actions to the second and third rollover buttons on the home page, using the same method that you used to add actions to the first rollover button. To test your knowledge, the instructions for the rest of this section are less detailed. If needed, see the steps at the beginning of this section for more detailed information.

7 Select the second rollover button (the middle button). Using the Actions palette, specify for the Text02 floating box to show when the mouse moves on top of the button. Then specify for the Text02 floating box to hide when the mouse moves off of the button.

8 Select the third rollover button (the right button). Using the Actions palette, specify for the Text03 floating box to show when the mouse moves on top of the button. Then specify for the Text03 floating box to hide when the mouse moves off of the button.

9 Choose File > Save.

Linking rollover buttons to pages

Currently, the buttons aren't linked to other pages in the site, because the site contains only the home page. For the sake of this lesson, you'll link the blue button to the Adobe Web site, so that you can learn how to link a button to a page on the Web. For more information on adding links to pages, see Lesson 5, "Creating Links."

1 Click the blue button on the home page to select it.

The Inspector changes to the Rollover Inspector.

2 In the Rollover Inspector, enter **http://www.adobe.com** in the URL text box.

3 Choose File > Save.

Adding actions to create a drop-down menu effect

Now you'll create a drop-down menu effect. You'll specify for the first rollover button in the navigation bar to be the only button that is visible when the home page is loaded. You'll also add actions to the first button so that the other buttons toggle between showing and hiding when it's clicked.

Now you'll add actions to the first rollover button.

1 Select the first rollover button (the left button) on the home page.

2 In the Actions palette, under Events, select Mouse Click to specify an action to occur when the mouse clicks the button. Then click the New Action button ( ) to add an action to the Actions list box.

3 From the Action pop-up menu, choose Multimedia > ShowHide. From the Floating Box pop-up menu, choose Button02. From the Mode pop-up menu, choose Toggle.

4 Using the Actions palette, add another action to the first rollover button that specifies for the Button03 floating box to toggle between showing and hiding when the button is clicked.

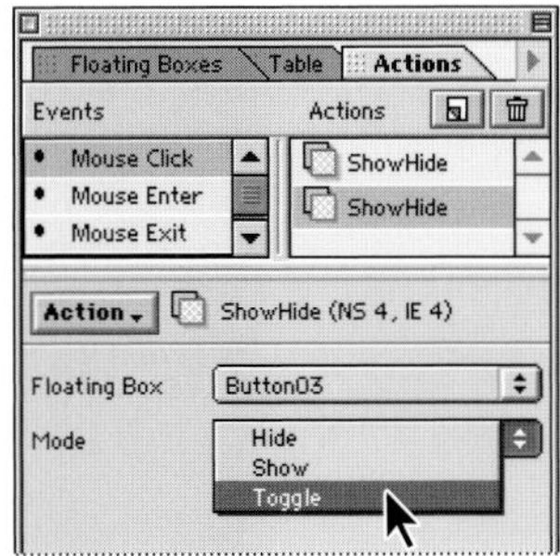

Choosing Toggle mode

Now you'll complete the drop-down menu effect by specifying for the floating box that contains the first rollover button and the floating box that contains the animated GIF image to be the only floating boxes visible when the home page is loaded.

5 Choose Window > Floating Boxes to display the Floating Boxes palette.

6 In the Floating Boxes palette, select Button01 to select the Button01 floating box in the document window.

7 In the Floating Box Inspector, make sure that Visible is selected, indicating that the Button01 floating box will be visible when the page is loaded.

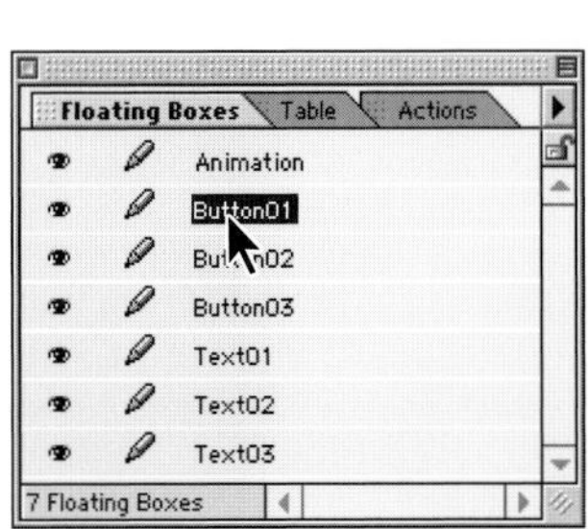

Selecting floating box in Floating Boxes palette

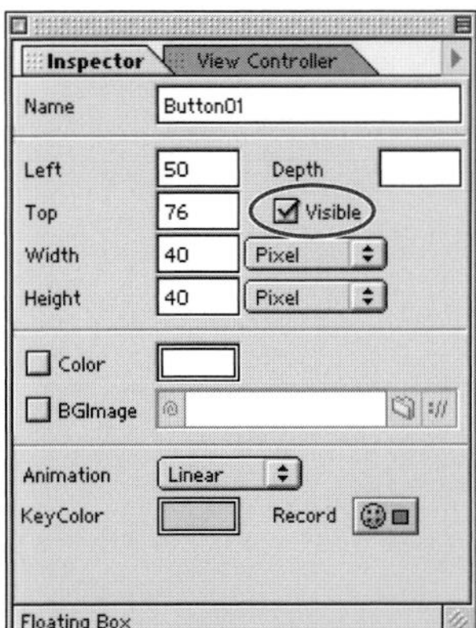

Selecting Visible option in Floating Box Inspector

8 In the Floating Boxes palette, select Button02 to select the Button02 floating box in the document window.

9 In the Floating Box Inspector, deselect Visible so that the Button02 floating box will not be visible when the page is loaded.

10 Using the Floating Boxes palette and Floating Box Inspector, set options so that all other floating boxes (with the exception of Button01 and Animation) will not be visible when the page is loaded.

11 Choose File > Save.

Previewing in a Web browser

Now that you've finished modifying the home page of the Trilobite.com Web site, you'll preview the page in a browser.

1 Click the triangle in the lower right corner of the Show in Browser button ( ) on the toolbar, and then choose the desired browser from the pop-up menu.

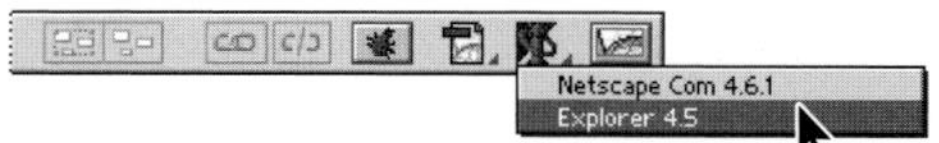

Choosing browser from Show in Browser pop-up menu

2 When you have finished viewing the home page, close it and quit your browser.

Review questions

1 Can you add a rollover button directly on a page?

2 Name two reasons why you would add a rollover button inside a floating box.

3 What is the purpose of the small icon that appears when you add a floating box to a page?

4 What is the purpose of the Rollover Inspector?

5 Which palette do you use to add an action to a rollover button?

6 Which objects on a page can you show or hide using the ShowHide action?

Review answers

1 Yes, you can add a rollover button directly on a page, on a layout grid, inside a table cell, or inside a floating box.

2 You would add a rollover button inside a floating box if you want the rollover button to overlap another object on the page, such as a large image. You would also add a rollover button inside a floating box if you want to show or hide the button using actions assigned to other buttons on the page.

3 The small icon marks the original position of the floating box on the page. You can select this icon to select its floating box.

4 You can use the Rollover Inspector to specify three different images for three different states of a rollover button: how the button appears by default, how the button appears when your mouse moves over it, and how the button appears when clicked. You can also use the Rollover Inspector to link the a rollover button to a Web page.

5 You use the Actions palette to add an action to a rollover button.

6 You can show or hide floating boxes using the ShowHide action.

Lesson 8

```
<TITLE>We
<STYLE TYPE=
{color:maroon;
</STYLE>
D>
>
<!-- Begin main table -->
<TABLE BORDER="4" CELLPADD
06">
    <TR>
        <TD><A
p://www.adobe.com/">Adobe</A>
        <TD>GoLive</TD>
        <TD><IMG BORDER="0" HE
e.gif" ALT="Title"></TD>
    </TR>
    <TR>
        <TD><SPAN CLASS="head
N></TD>
    </TR>
    <TR>
        <TD><B>DHTML
    </TR>
</TABLE>
Y>
EQUIV="content-typ
charset=iso-8859-
come to Adobe GoLi
main table -->
ER="4" CELLPAD
)><A
lobe.com/">Adobe</A>
)>GoLive</TD>
)><IMG BORDER="0" HE
="Title"></TD>
)><SPAN CLASS="hea
)><B>DHTML
```

8 Creating Animations

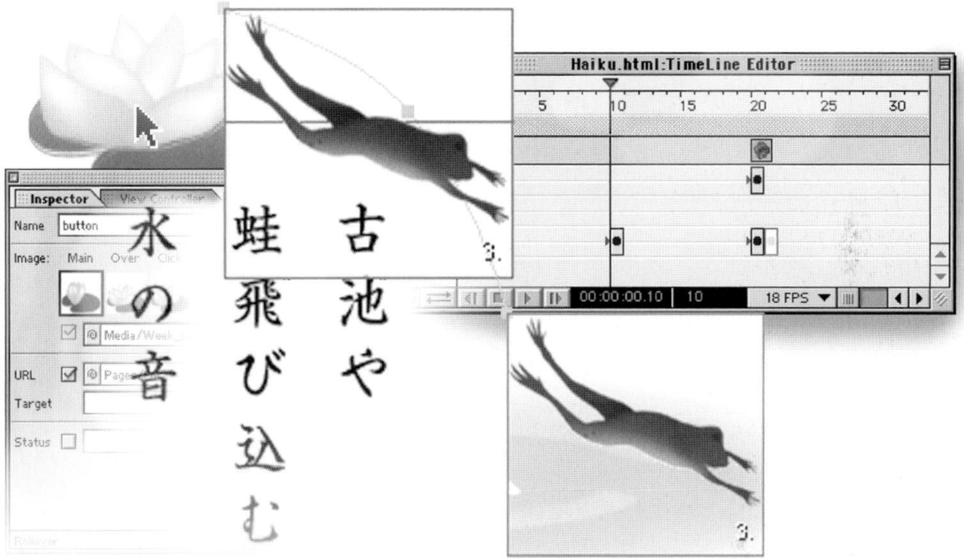

Adobe GoLive supports Dynamic HTML, which lets you add floating boxes and animations to your Web pages. You can animate floating boxes to move their contents around the page. You can even make floating boxes that pass in front of and then behind each other as they move.

About this lesson

In this lesson, you'll learn how to do the following:

- Change the layering of floating boxes.
- Create animations with a single floating box and multiple floating boxes.
- Use actions to add transition effects to animations.
- Create multiple animation scenes.
- Use actions to control multiple scenes on a Web page.

This lesson takes approximately 1 hour to complete.

If needed, copy the Lesson08 folder onto your hard drive. As you work on this lesson, you'll overwrite the start files. If you need to restore the start files, copy them from the *Adobe GoLive 5.0 Classroom in a Book* CD.

Note: *Windows users need to unlock the lesson files before using them. For more information, see "Copying the Classroom in a Book files" on page 2.*

For information on setting up your work area, see "Setting up your work area" on page 9.

Getting started

You'll begin this lesson by using your Web browser to view the finished Web pages in the poetrypond.com site, a fictitious Web site about an international poetry organization.

1 Start a DHTML-compliant Web browser, such as Netscape Communicator 4 or Microsoft Internet Explorer 4. (If the browser is not compliant, features such as animation or actions will not be visible.)

2 Use the browser to open the Web page Index.html. The path to the file is Lesson08/08End/Poetry Folder/Poetry/Index.html.

3 Click the Poetry Sampler link at the top of the Web page Index.html to go to the Poetry Sampler page.

There are four pages linked to the Poetry Sampler page, each using a variety of floating boxes and animation effects. Click on the links to explore the pages. You'll work on each page in order during this lesson, modifying some of the existing animations and creating new ones.

4 When you have finished viewing the Web site, quit your browser.

Working with floating boxes

In Lesson 3, "Laying Out Web Pages," you learned how to add floating boxes to a page. Now, you'll learn how to overlap two floating boxes, and how to control their stacking order. In this part of the lesson, you'll create two floating boxes and add them to the Forever page (the first link on the Poetry Sampler page). You'll fill one floating box with text and the other with an image.

1 Start Adobe GoLive.

2 Choose File > Open, and open the poetrypond.com Web site. The path to the file is Lesson08/08Start/Poetry Folder/Poetry.site.

3 Double-click the file Forever.html in the Pages folder in the site window to open the Web page.

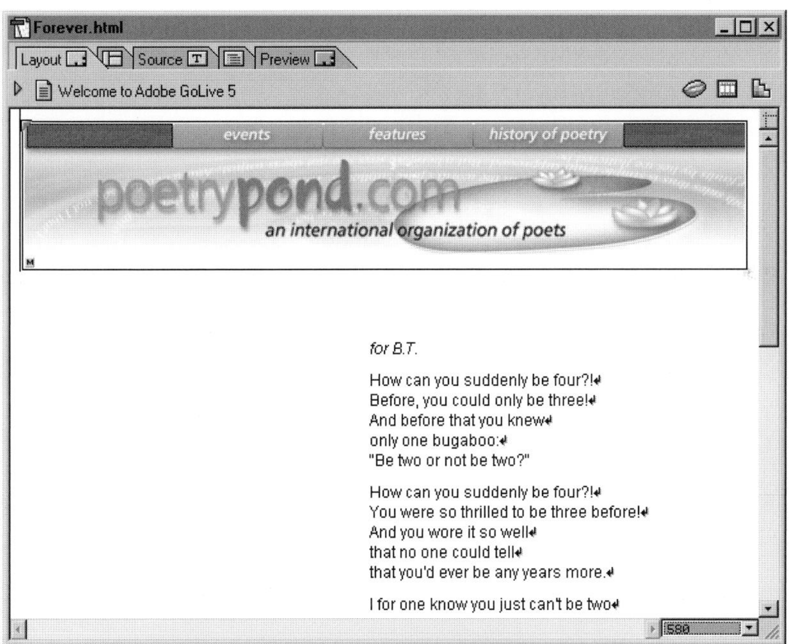

4 Click the Basic tab ( ) of the Objects palette.

You'll place the anchor for the floating box between the banner graphic at the top of the page and the poem. To do so, you'll need to set the insertion point just past the banner graphic. The easiest way to do this is to move the pointer onto the right side of the banner graphic. Because Adobe GoLive can't place the anchor directly onto the banner graphic, the anchor will go to the next available place after the graphic.

5 Drag the Floating Box icon from the Objects palette to the right side of the banner graphic on the Web page.

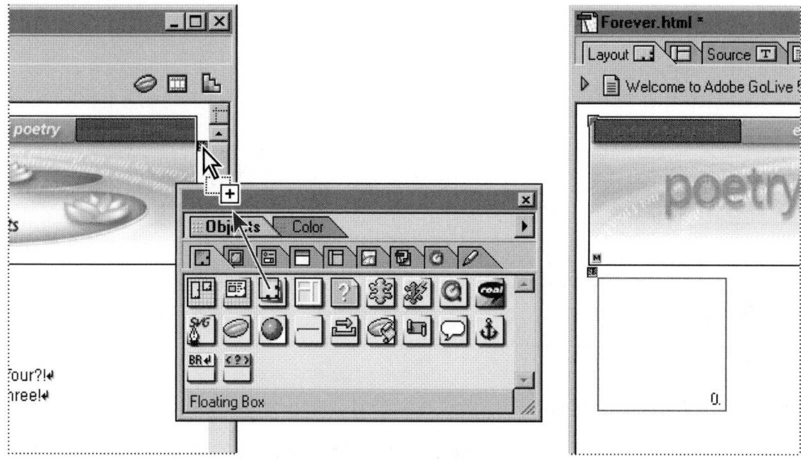

Dragging Floating Box icon *Result*

The Inspector changes to the Floating Box Inspector.

You can place text, images, JavaScript applets, and QuickTime movies inside a floating box. Here, you'll place text inside the floating box.

6 Click inside the floating box and type **Forever Four**, the title of the poem.

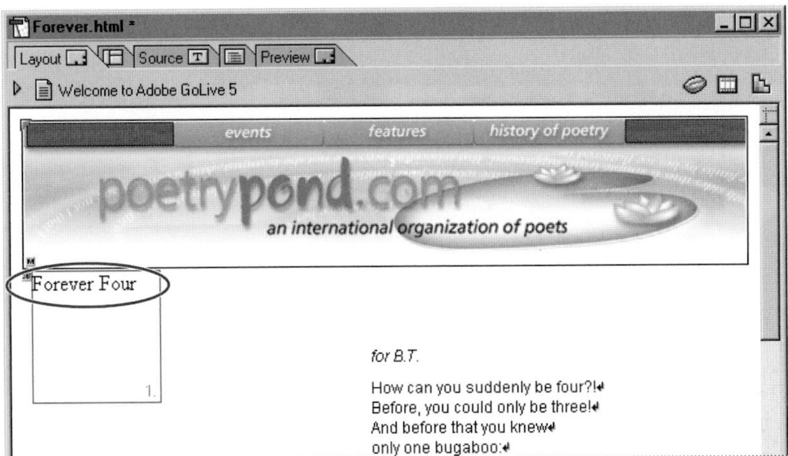

7 Drag to select the type.

8 In the toolbar, click the Bold button (B) and choose 6 from the Font Size menu (None).

9 Choose Type > Font > Arial for the typeface.

10 Move the pointer over the floating box until the pointer changes to a hand pointing left. Then click to select the floating box.

In the Floating Box Inspector, enter **Title** for Name. This names the floating box so it's easier to work with when you have multiple boxes.

You can resize the floating box so that the title fits on one line.

11 Move the mouse pointer to the bottom right corner of the floating box.

12 When the pointer changes to an arrow, drag the corner of the floating box so that both words in the title fit on the same line. Drag again to fit the floating box closely around the title.

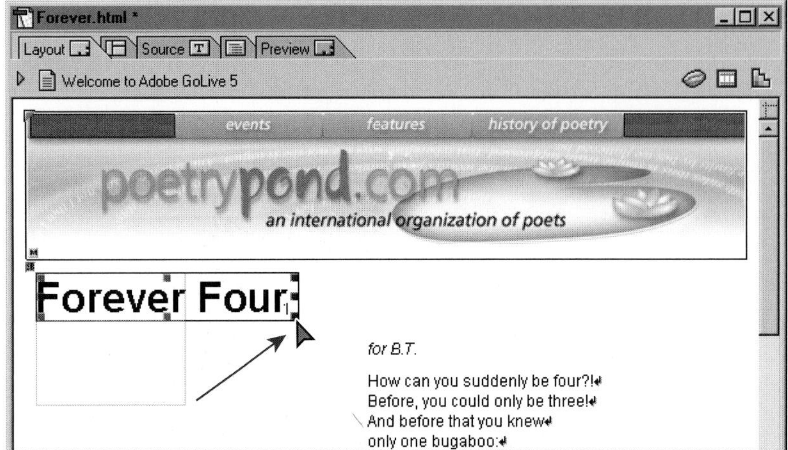

13 In the Floating Box Inspector, enter **185** for Left, and press Enter or Return. Then enter **125** for Top, and press Enter or Return to specify an exact location for the floating box.

You've finished making your first floating box.

14 Choose File > Save.

Stacking floating boxes

Now you'll add a second floating box. This one will contain an image.

1 Drag the Floating Box icon from the Objects palette just to the right of the small yellow anchor of the first floating box. (You can tell you are dragging to the correct location when a blinking vertical cursor appears to the right of the first floating box's anchor. The resulting floating box should appear as shown in the illustration.)

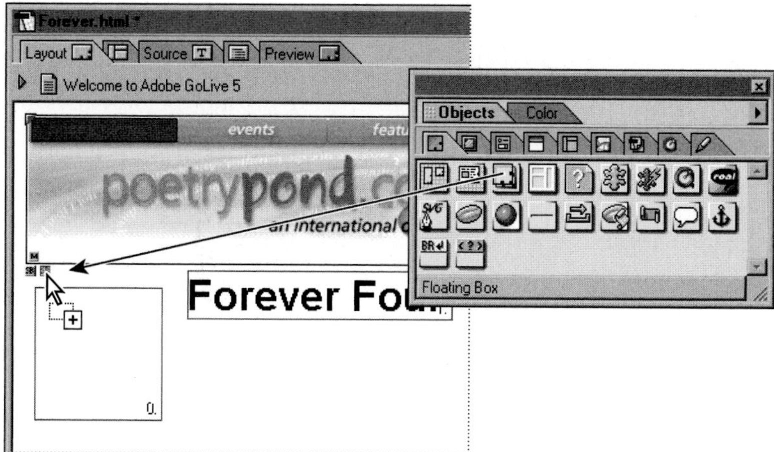

2 In the Floating Box Inspector, enter **Duck** in the Name text box. This lets you differentiate it from the Title floating box that you added earlier.

3 Drag the Image icon from the Objects palette into the floating box that you just made.

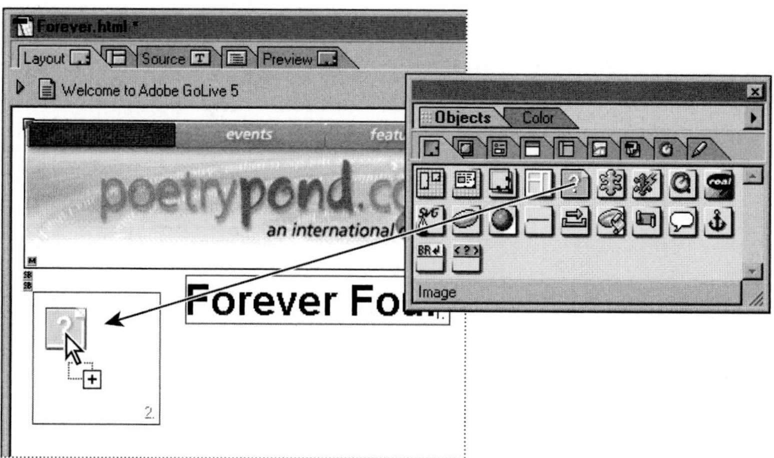

The image placeholder is now inside the floating box and the Inspector changes to the Image Inspector.

Now you'll connect the image placeholder to an image file.

4 Hold down Alt (Windows) or Command (Mac OS) and drag from the image placeholder on the Web page to the file Duck.gif in the Media folder in the site window. (This method has the same effect as dragging from the Point and Shoot button in the Image Inspector to a file in the site window.)

The image of a duck appears in the floating box.

This time, rather than specifying values in the Floating Box Inspector, you'll drag the floating box to place it.

5 Click the side of the new floating box to select it. Make sure the floating box is selected, and not just the image within it. You can tell the floating box is selected when the pointer changes to a hand pointed to the left.

6 Drag the new floating box so that its right side is against the left edge of the poem, and its top is lined up with the title "Forever Four." The duck is now blocking part of the title.

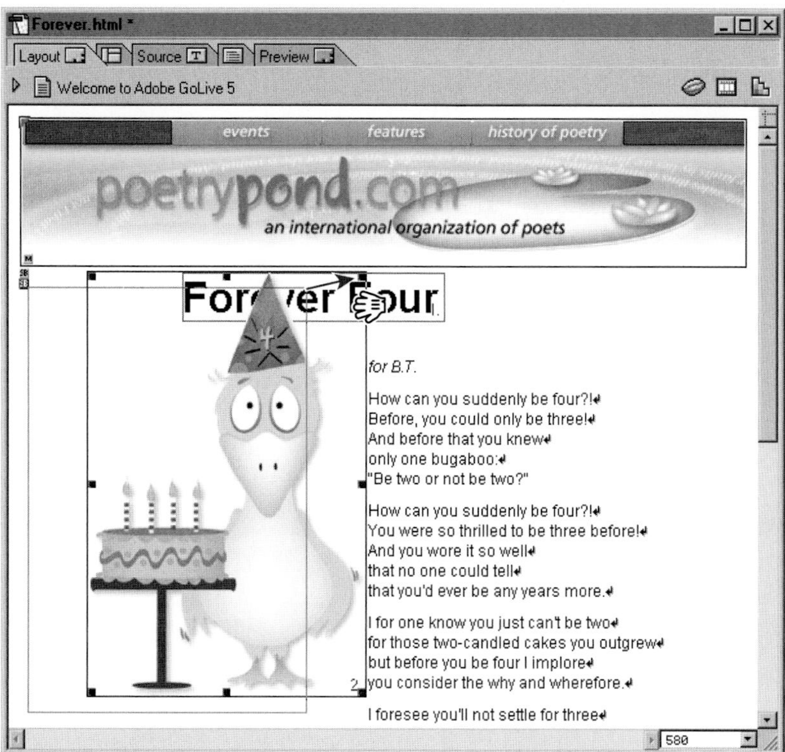

7 Choose File > Save.

Notice that you didn't use a layout grid on this page to locate objects precisely. That's because floating boxes enable you to move objects around without the need for tables or layout grids. In fact, as more people design and view pages using HTML 4.0-compliant applications, the need to use tables to position items may disappear.

Changing the stacking order

You can change the order in which floating boxes are stacked on top of each other. Here, you'll change the stacking order so that the floating box containing the title is on top of the floating box with the duck image.

The stacking order is initially determined by the location of the anchor on the page. That is, the further down and to the right a floating box's anchor is compared to others on the page, the higher in the stack it is. However, specifying a depth in the Floating Box Inspector overrides the default stacking order. The number that appears in the bottom right corner of the floating box indicates the order in which that floating box was added to the page.

1 Select the floating box containing the duck. (Remember, the floating box is selected when the hand points to the left.)

2 In the Floating Box Inspector, enter **1** for Depth, and press Enter or Return.

3 Select the right side of the floating box containing the title "Forever Four" (where it isn't under the other floating box).

4 In the Floating Box Inspector, enter **2** for Depth, and press Enter or Return.

Because the floating box with the title has a higher number, it moves on top.

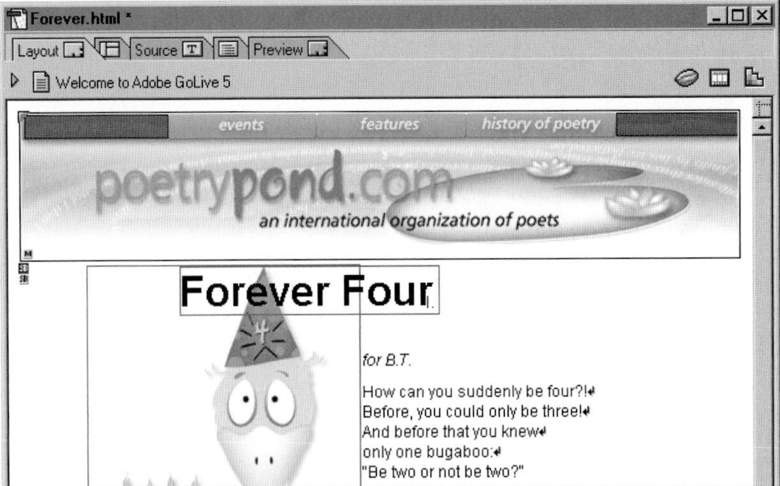

5 Choose File > Save.

6 Close the page Forever.html.

Animating a floating box

In this part of the lesson, you'll learn how to animate a floating box so that it moves across the page. You'll work with the Night.html page, the second link from the Poetry Sampler page.

The page contains an image of a singing bird, some text, and a floating box containing an image of musical notes. You'll create an animation that moves the musical notes across the page. First, though, you need to add a special action to your page to ensure the animation will display correctly in all browsers.

Adding a head action to display animations correctly

Netscape Navigator contains a program error that causes Web pages to have trouble displaying animations when visitors resize the page. You can add a head action to the page that prevents this problem. It's a good idea to add this action to any page containing animated floating boxes. (We've already added this action to the other pages that you'll use in this lesson.)

1 Double-click the file Night.html in the Pages folder in the site window to open the Web page.

2 Click the triangle next to the Page icon (▤) in the document window to display the head section pane.

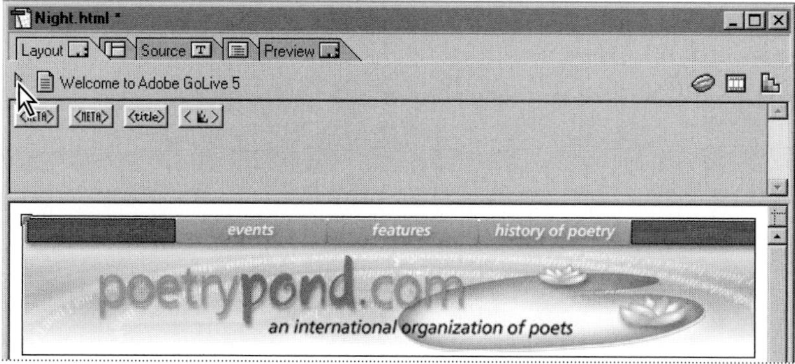

Result of clicking triangle

3 Click the Smart tab (▣) in the Objects palette.

4 Drag the Head Action icon from the palette to the head section pane of the document window.

The Inspector changes to the Action Inspector.

5 In the Action Inspector, choose OnLoad from the Exec. (Execute) menu (this is the default). Then choose Others > Netscape CSS Fix from the Action menu.

6 Click the triangle next to the Page icon in the document window to close the head section pane.

7 Choose File > Save.

Using keyframes

Keyframes indicate particular points (called "frames") along the timeline of the animation. You add keyframes to the Timeline Editor. Then you select a keyframe and move the floating box to a location on the Web page. As the animation runs and the time indicator reaches that keyframe, the floating box moves to the location on the Web page.

1 Click the Timeline Editor button (▦) at the top right of the document window.

The Timeline Editor appears. The Timeline Editor gives you precise control over each frame of an animation while you're building and testing it. The Timeline Editor contains an animation track, or *Time Track*, for each floating box on the web page. This animation has one Time Track, for the floating box containing the musical notes.

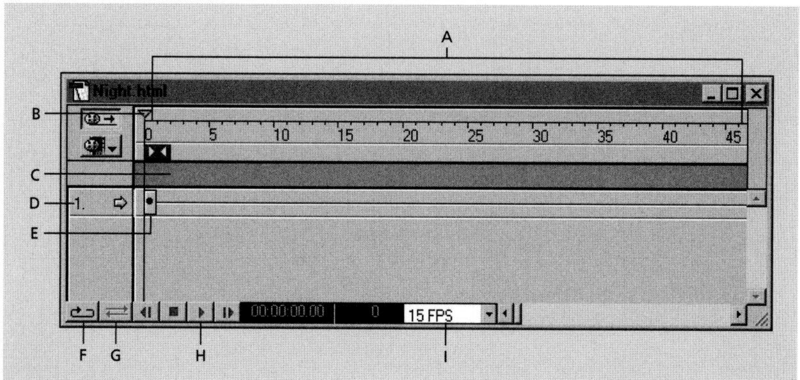

A. Frame markers ***B.*** *Time Indicator* ***C.*** *Action Track* ***D.*** *Time Track for floating box* ***E.*** *First keyframe* ***F.*** *Loop button* ***G.*** *Palindrome ("back and forth") button* ***H.*** *Play button* ***I.*** *Frames per second menu*

2 Click the initial keyframe in the Time Track to select it.

3 Select the floating box containing the musical notes. (Remember, the hand points to the left when the floating box is selected.)

Note: *Throughout this lesson, in Windows, click once in the document window to select the window before dragging the floating box. Then click back on the Timeline Editor to make it active before moving or adding frames.*

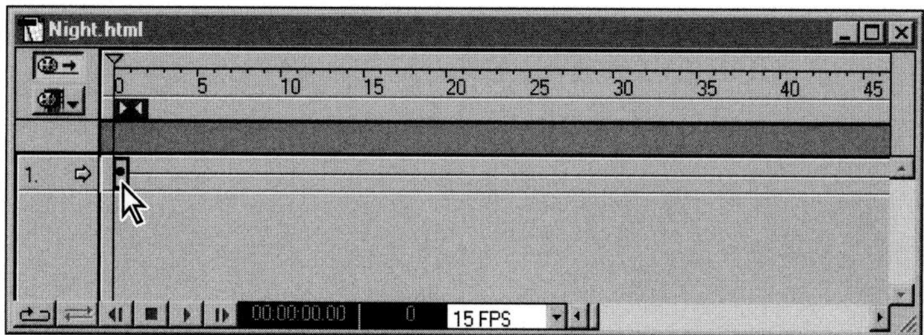

4 With the keyframe selected, drag the floating box just to the right of the nightingale's beak. This specifies where the floating box should be when the animation starts.

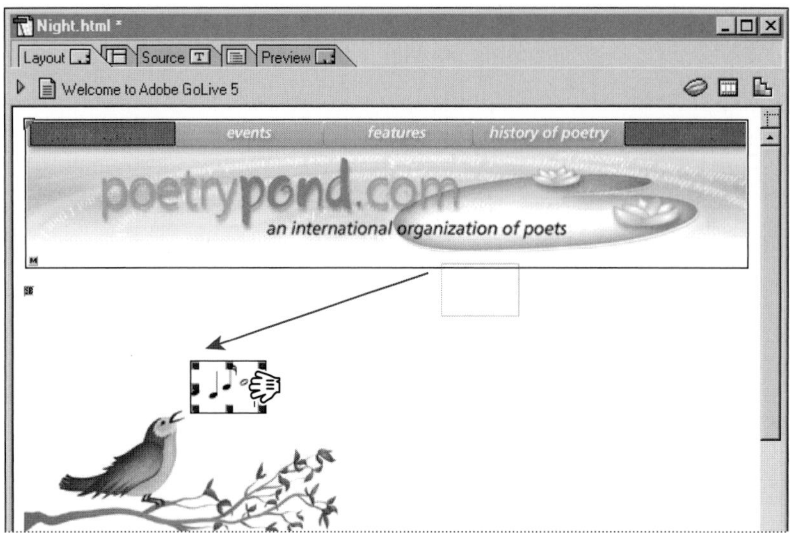

Now you'll add another keyframe and move the floating box to its next position in the animation.

5 Ctrl-click (Windows) or Command-click (Mac OS) in the time track to add another keyframe at the 30 frame mark. (If you don't create the keyframe at the correct frame mark, you can drag it into position.)

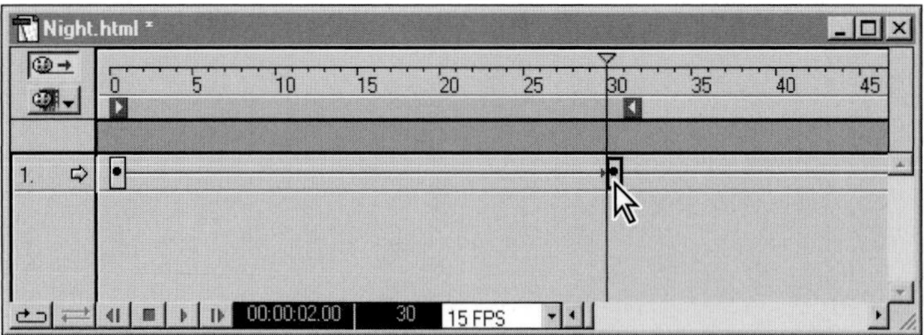

6 Drag the floating box to just below the bottom right corner of the banner.

Now you can play the animation.

7 Click the Play button ( ) near the bottom left of the Timeline Editor. If you are at the end of an animation, you'll need to click the Play button a second time to restart the animation from the beginning.

The animation plays once and stops. Now you'll make it loop back and forth, and change its speed.

8 Click the Loop button ( ), then the Play button on the Timeline Editor to see the animation repeat continually. Then click the Palindrome button ( ) on the Timeline Editor to see the animation loop forward and backward.

9 Choose different speeds from the FPS (Frames Per Second) pop-up menu at the bottom of the timeline to see the animation move faster or slower.

10 When you're through experimenting, choose 20 FPS from the Frames Per Second pop-up menu.

11 Click the Stop button ( ) to stop the animation.

12 Choose File > Save.

Editing keyframes

1 Ctrl-click (Windows) or Command-click (Mac OS) to add another two keyframes between the two existing ones, one at the 10 frame mark and the other at the 20 frame mark.

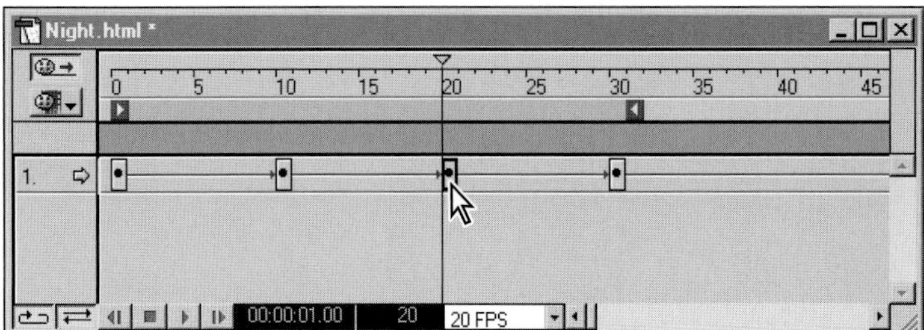

2 Select the keyframe at the 10 frame mark, and drag the floating box to a spot just below the middle of the banner.

3 Select the keyframe at the 20 frame mark, and drag the floating box to a location above the title.

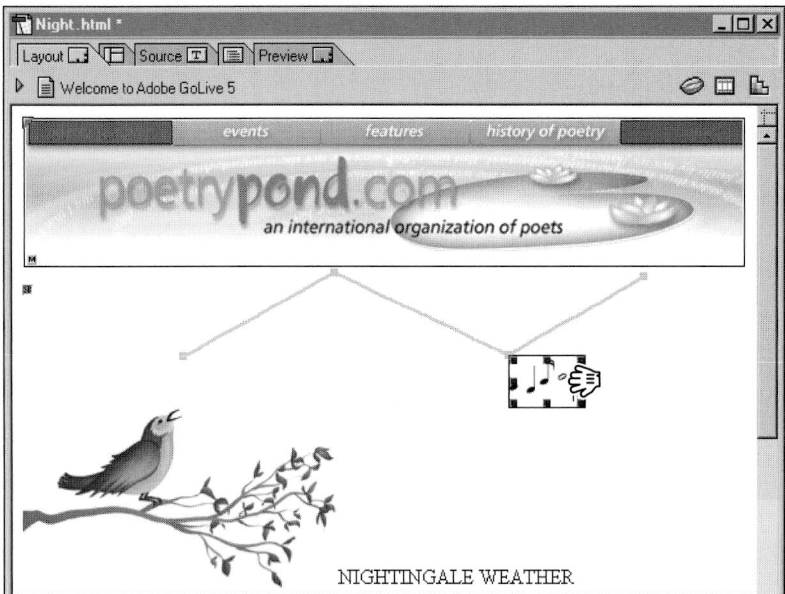

4 Click the Play button ( ) to play the animation again.

5 Click the Stop button ( ) to stop the animation.

Rather than have the floating box move in sharp angles from keyframe to keyframe, you'll smooth out the animation path.

6 Shift-click each keyframe, or drag from the side or below to select all four keyframes.

Note: *If you use the drag method, you must first move the time indicator until it is aligned with one of the keyframes in the animation. Click a keyframe to move the time indicator directly to that keyframe.*

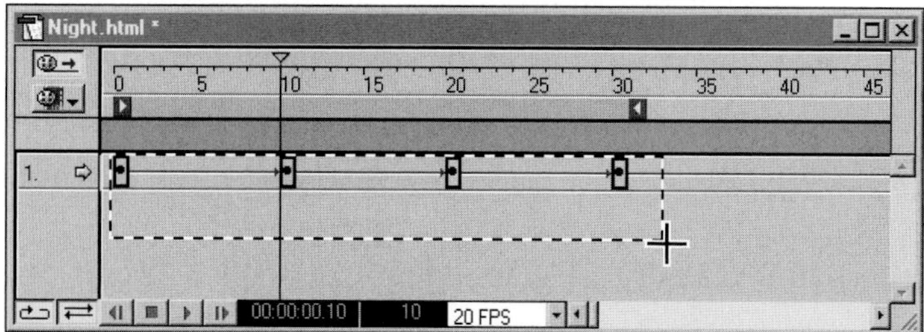

7 In the Floating Box Inspector, choose Curve from the Animation pop-up menu.

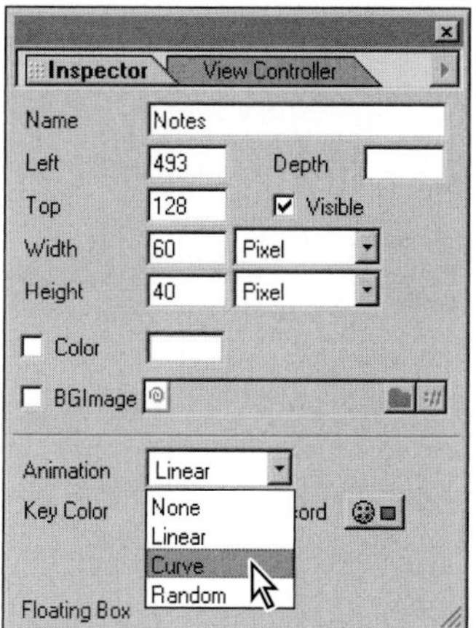

8 Play the animation. Notice how much smoother the motion is now.

9 Stop the animation.

10 Choose File > Save.

11 Close the Timeline Editor and the Night.html Web page.

Animating multiple floating boxes

Now that you've animated a single floating box, you're ready to work with an animation that uses multiple floating boxes. In this part of the lesson, you'll modify an animation on the Haiku.html page, the third link from the Poetry Sampler page.

1 Double-click the file Haiku.html in the Pages folder in the site window to open the Web page.

This page already contains the following objects:

- A large floating box named Poem, with an image of a poem, pond, and reeds in it.
- An animated floating box named Jumper with an image of a jumping frog in it. This animated floating box becomes invisible at the end (before it loops) and contains a transition effect called a Wipe. You'll learn how to create these effects later in the lesson.
- A floating box named Dragonfly with an image of a dragonfly in it.

For this exercise you'll animate the Dragonfly floating box so that it passes in front of, and then behind the reeds.

2 Click the Timeline Editor button (▦) at the top right of the document window to display the Timeline Editor.

Notice that the Timeline Editor displays a separate track for each floating box on the page. This enables you to animate each floating box separately. The number in the bottom right corner of each floating box corresponds to the track numbers in the Timeline Editor.

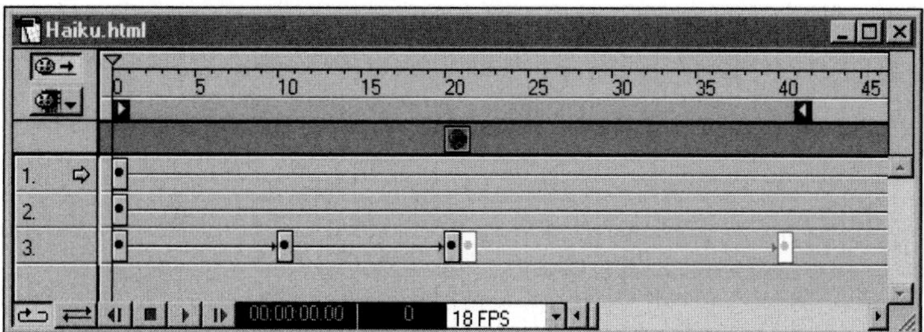

3 Click on the first keyframe in track 1 to select it. The Dragonfly floating box is also selected on the Web page.

Since you need to work only with the Dragonfly floating box, you can use the Floating Boxes palette to temporarily lock the other two floating boxes in place so you don't accidentally select or move them.

4 If necessary, choose Window > Floating Boxes to display the palette.

5 In the Floating Boxes palette, click the Pencil icons next to Poem and Jumper so that they are dimmed. The Poem and Jumper floating boxes are now locked in place for the current keyframe.

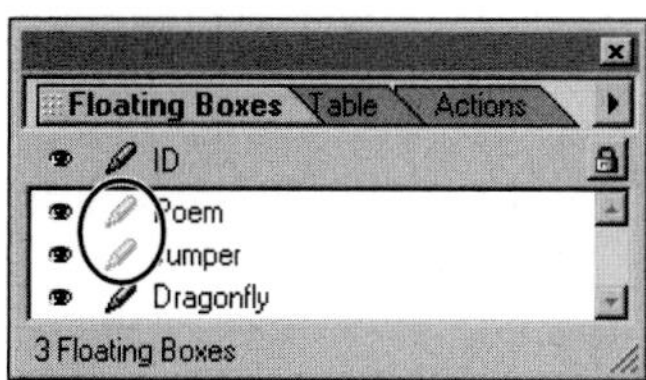

6 Click on the document window to make it active, and then drag the Dragonfly floating box to a position near the top center of the Poem floating box.

7 Ctrl-click (Windows) or Command-click (Mac OS) to create a second keyframe for the floating box at frame 20 in the Timeline Editor.

8 In the document window, drag the Dragonfly floating box down and to the right of the reeds.

Notice that when you select the keyframe at frame 20, the other floating boxes are shown in their positions at frame 20 as well.

9 Ctrl-click/Command-click to create a third keyframe for the floating box at frame 40.

10 Select the keyframe, and drag the floating box back to its starting position at the middle of the page.

To get the floating box to the same starting position, you can select the first keyframe (at frame 0) and note the left and top coordinates in the Floating Box Inspector. Then select the keyframe at frame 40 and enter the coordinates from the keyframe at frame 0. Or, you can Alt-click (Windows) or Option-click (Mac OS) the first keyframe, and then drag to frame 40 to create a new keyframe with the same coordinates.

11 Play the animation.

The dragonfly goes back and forth in front of the reeds and the frog jumps into the pond. Now you'll make the dragonfly go behind the reeds as it passes them from right to left.

12 Stop the animation.

13 Click to select the first keyframe for track 2, which is the track of the floating box containing the reeds.

14 In the Floating Box Inspector, enter **2** for Depth, and press Enter or Return. This sets the depth of the Poem floating box (which contains the reeds) in the stacking order of floating boxes on the page. By giving it a depth of 2, you have room to give the Dragonfly floating box a higher and lower depth.

15 Click to select the first keyframe in the track of the Dragonfly floating box (it's in track 1). Then enter **3** for Depth in the Floating Box Inspector, and press Enter or Return.

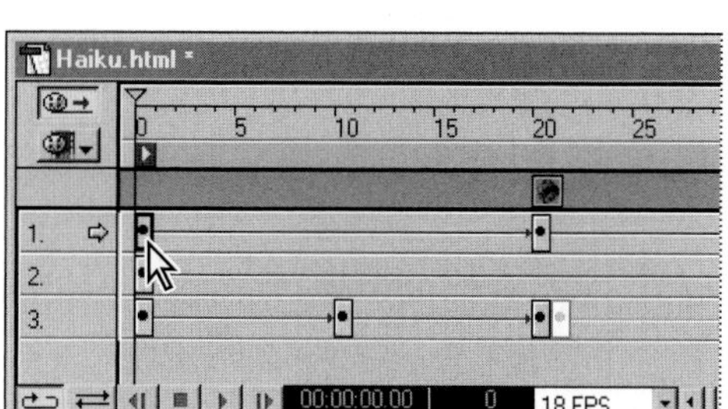

16 Select the second keyframe in that track, enter **1** for Depth, and press Enter or Return. The lower depth will put the Dragonfly floating box behind the reeds beginning at this keyframe.

17 Select the last keyframe for the track of the Dragonfly floating box, enter **3** for Depth, and press Enter or Return. This places the Dragonfly floating box in front of the reeds in the stacking order.

18 Play the animation.

Notice that the dragonfly now seems to circle the reeds, first passing in front of and then passing behind them.

19 Stop the animation, and choose File > Save.

20 Close the Timeline Editor and close the Haiku.html file.

Adding actions to animations

Actions are premade scripts that let you trigger events and control different processes on the page. Actions can be attached to text, images, and floating boxes. You can use actions to control transition effects for animated floating boxes, and to control which animations play on a page. (For more information on actions, see Lesson 9, "Using Actions and JavaScript.")

In this part of the exercise you'll add actions to two animated floating boxes on the Prince.html page (the last link off the Poetry Sampler page). The floating boxes contain a poem and a poem title. When the page loads, the boxes are invisible. As the animation runs, the title box appears and moves to the right, and then the poem appears. The actions you add will make both boxes appear more gradually on the page.

1 Double-click the Prince.html file in the Pages folder in the site window to open the Web page.

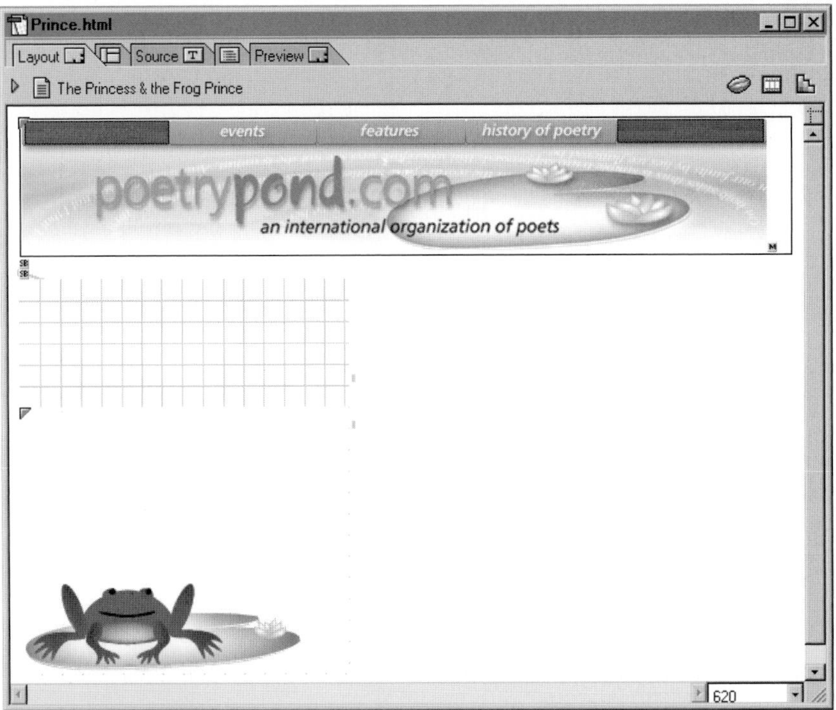

2 Click the Timeline Editor button (▦) at the top right of the document window to display the Timeline Editor.

This animation contains two Time Tracks. Track 1 controls the floating box that contains the poem's title and track 2 controls the floating box that contains the poem. Note that in the first frame of the animation, both keyframes are dimmed. This means the floating boxes are invisible in that frame. You can control the visibility of a floating box using the Visible option in the Floating Box Inspector.

3 Select the first keyframe in track 1. In the Floating Box Inspector, select the Visible option. Note how the keyframe becomes fully visible, and the Title box becomes visible in the document window. Now deselect the Visible option to make the floating box disappear.

4 Click the Play button ( ) in the Timeline Editor. Notice that at frame 10 of the animation the title suddenly appears and begins moving across the page. Then at frame 50, the text of the poem appears.

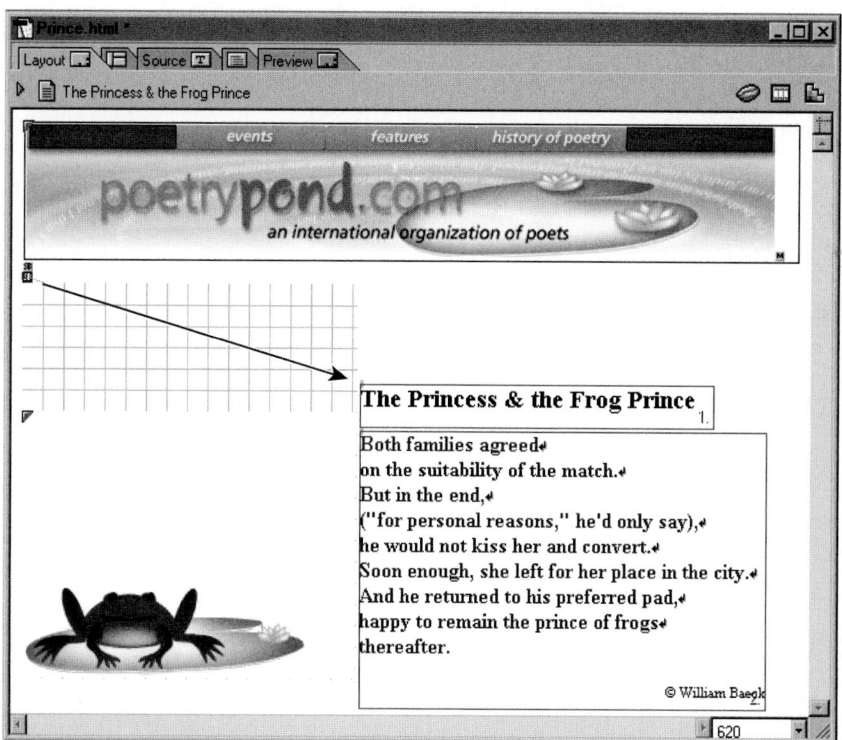

5 Use the scroll buttons at the bottom of the Timeline Editor to scroll back to the first frames of the animation track.

6 In track 1 of the Timeline Editor, click to select the keyframe at frame 10. Notice that the floating box now displays the title. You'll add an action so that instead of the title becoming visible suddenly, it will gradually appear from left to right as it floats across the page.

7 Ctrl-click (Windows) or Command-click (Mac OS) in the Action track (the gray track) in the Timeline Editor, directly over the keyframe at frame 10.

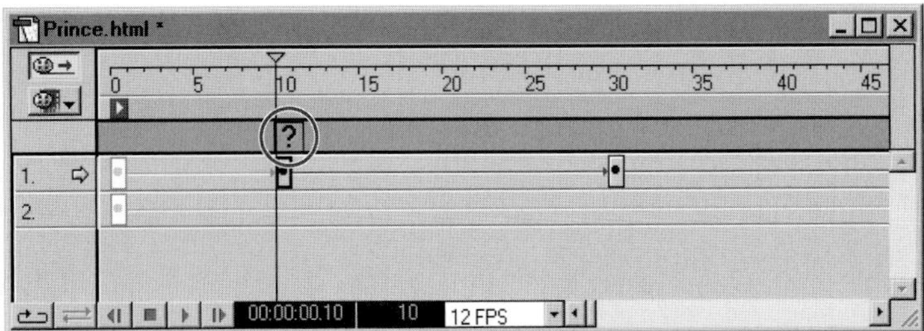

The Inspector changes to the Action Inspector.

8 Choose Multimedia > Wipe Transition from the Action menu in the Action Inspector.

9 Choose Title from the Floating Box menu to select that floating box.

10 Choose Wipe In From Left To Right from the Transition menu to specify the kind of transition that you want. Then enter **30** in the Steps text box to make the transition occur in 30 steps. (More steps make the transition longer and smoother.)

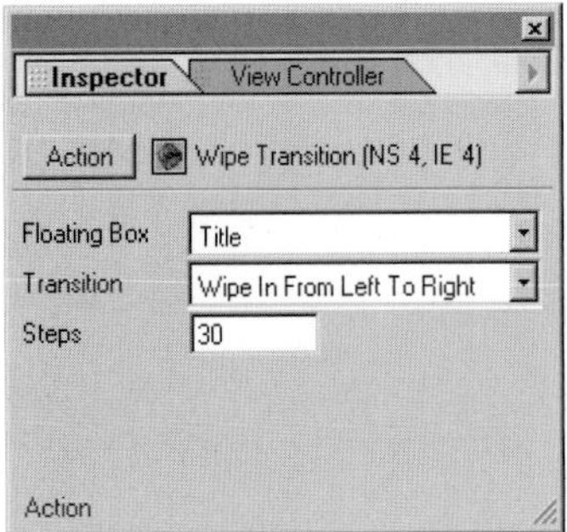

11 Choose File > Save to save the page.

Now, you'll add an action to the Time Track for the floating box with the poem in it.

12 Use the scroll buttons at the bottom of the Timeline Editor to scroll to frame 50 of the animation track.

13 In track 2 of the Timeline Editor, select the keyframe at frame 50.

The floating box now displays the poem as well as the title over it. You'll add an action so that instead of becoming visible suddenly, the poem will gradually appear line by line from top to bottom.

14 Ctrl-click (Windows) or Command-click (Mac OS) in the Actions track in the Timeline Editor, above the keyframe at frame 50.

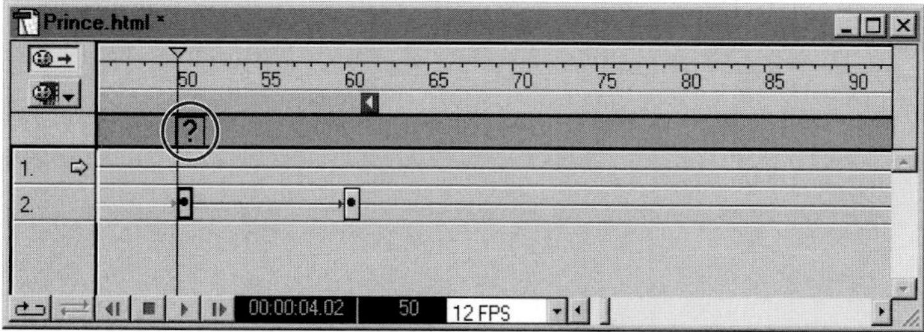

15 From the Action menu in the Action Inspector, choose Multimedia > Wipe Transition.

16 Choose Poem from the Floating Box menu to select that floating box.

17 Choose Wipe In From Top To Bottom from the Transition menu to specify the kind of transition you want. Then enter **15** in the Steps text box to make the transition occur slowly.

18 Choose File > Save to save the page.

19 Click on the Show in Web Browser button. Start a Web browser that supports DHTML, such as Netscape Communicator 4.0 or Microsoft Internet Explorer 4.0.

View the actions that you've added to the animated floating boxes. Note how the title now appears more gradually, wiping in from left to right. The poem now wipes in gradually from top to bottom.

Creating a new scene

The animation that you've been working with is called a scene. In Adobe GoLive, one Web page can contain multiple scenes. All scenes share the same document window and the same floating boxes. However you can position the floating boxes differently in each scene, and give them different behaviors. You can also use actions to start and stop scenes, or to play different scenes in sequence.

For the last part of the lesson, you'll add a second animation scene to the Prince.html page. This will be a short animation that makes the Title floating box disappear. Then you'll create an action that plays the scene. You'll set the action to be triggered by the Frog rollover image.

1 Click the Timeline Editor for the Prince.html page to make it active.

2 In the Timeline Editor, click the Options ( ) pop-up menu. At the bottom of the menu, the name of the current scene appears: Scene 1. Choose New Scene from the menu.

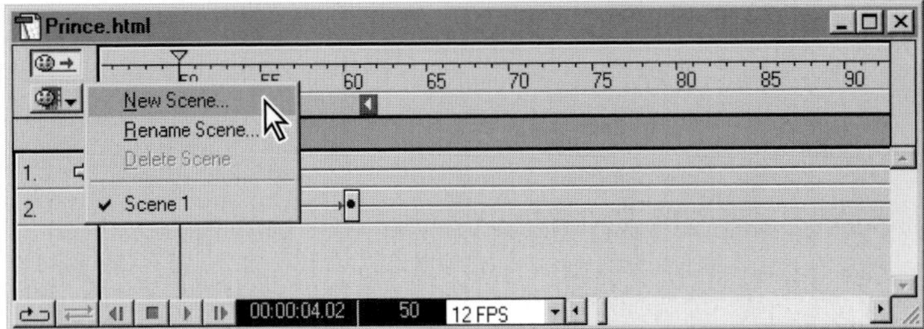

3 Enter a name for the new scene, and click OK. (We used Scene 2.)

The Timeline Editor displays a new timeline for Scene 2. Note that the timeline contains initial keyframes for the two floating boxes that appear in Scene 1.

In the first frame of Scene 2, the Title floating box should be positioned above the Poem floating box, where it was in the last frame of Scene 1. You'll take the coordinates from the Scene 1 frame and copy them to the first frame in Scene 2.

4 Choose Scene 1 from the Options pop-up menu.

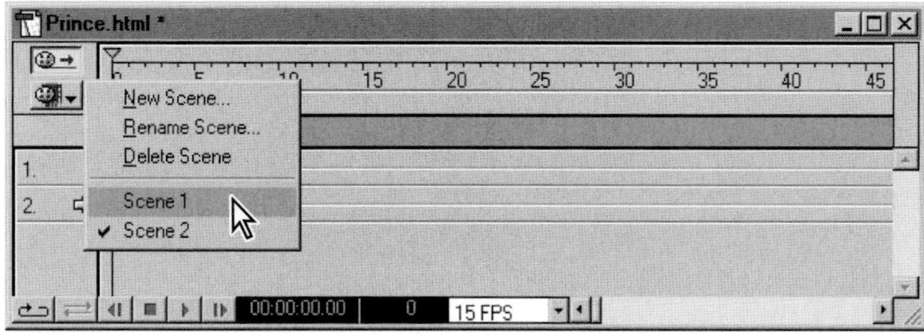

5 In the time track for the Title box, click on the third keyframe. From the Floating Box Inspector, copy the Left and Top position settings.

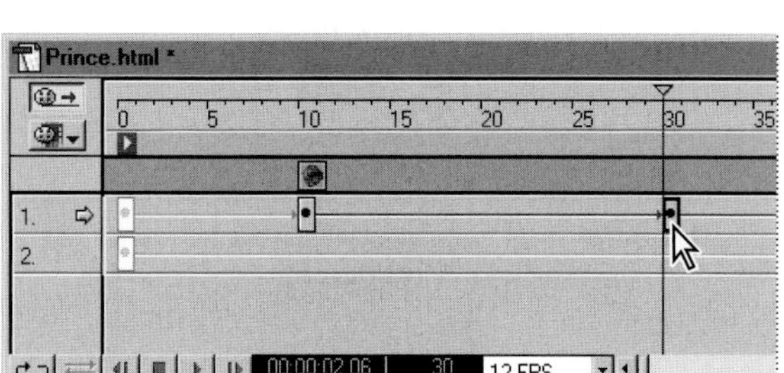

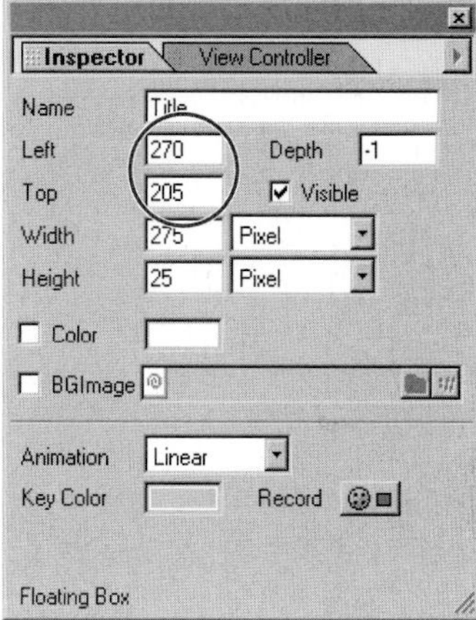

6 Use the Options menu to switch back to Scene 2.

7 Select the keyframe for the Title box in the first time track. In the Floating Box Inspector, select the Visible option. Then enter the Left and Top settings that you copied from the other keyframe.

Now the Title box is in the correct position and visible in the first frame. You need to add another frame to make it invisible, and then add a Wipe Transition.

8 Ctrl-click (Windows) or Command-click (Mac OS) in the time track to add another keyframe at the 5 frame mark.

9 Select the keyframe. In the Floating Box Inspector, deselect the Visible option.

The second keyframe is dimmed, and the floating box disappears from the document window.

10 In the Timeline Editor, Ctrl-click (Windows) or Command-click (Mac OS) in the Action track directly over frame 5.

11 Choose Multimedia > Wipe Transition from the Action menu in the Action Inspector.

12 Choose Title from the Floating Box menu to select the floating box.

13 Choose Wipe Out From Left To Right from the Transition menu. Then enter **10** in the Steps text box to make the transition occur in 10 steps.

14 Click the Autoplay button ( ) to turn Autoplay off.

For a new scene, Autoplay on is the default setting. Autoplay means the scene will play automatically when the page loads in the browser.

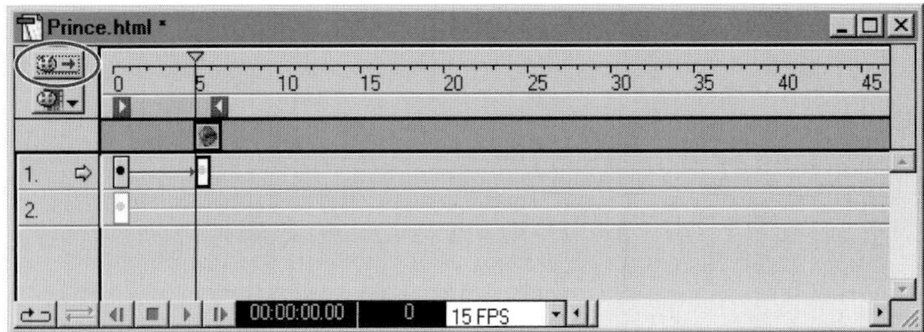

15 Choose File > Save to save the page.

Now that you've added another scene to your page, you have two animations available for use with this page. The first animation, Scene 1, will play automatically when the page loads. The second animation, Scene 2, won't play at all unless you set up an action to trigger it. You'll do that next.

Adding an action to play the scene

Now you'll add an action to the Frog rollover button to play Scene 2.

1 Make the Prince.html document window active. Make sure that the Actions palette is visible as well.

2 Select the image of the frog on the page. The Inspector changes to the Rollover Inspector.

3 Select Mouse Click listed under Events in the Actions palette. This specifies an action to be triggered when a visitor to the Web page clicks the rollover.

4 Click the New Action button ( ) in the Actions palette. This activates the Action pop-up menu.

Now you'll choose the action that you want to occur. In this case, you'll link it to the new animation scene that you just created.

5 From the Action menu, choose Multimedia > Play Scene.

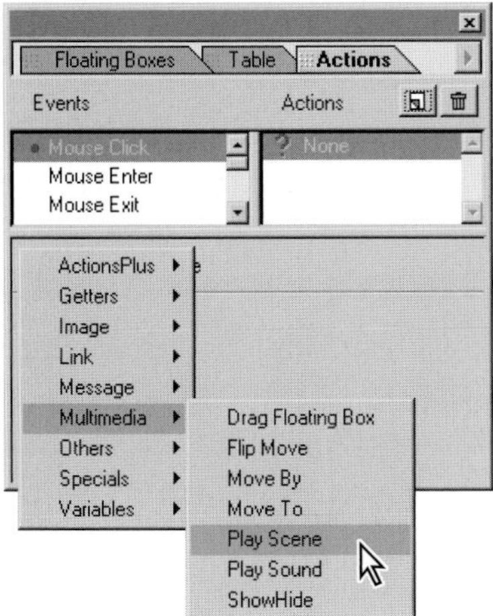

6 Choose Scene 2 from the scene pop-up menu.

7 Choose File > Save to save the page.

You can also start and stop scenes using actions inside a scene. To use one scene to start another, add a Play Scene action to the Actions Track of the first scene. (If the first scene is a looped animation or palindrome, you may need to insert a Play Scene action followed by a Stop Scene action.) For more details, see "Controlling the playback of scenes" on page 228 of the Adobe Golive 5.0 User Guide.

Previewing in a Web browser

Now that you've finished creating and modifying all the animations in the poetrypond.com site, you can preview the finished site in a browser.

1 Start your browser.

2 Locate and open the poetrypond.com home page. Choose File > Open. Select the Index.html file, located in the Lesson08/08Start/Poetry folder, inside the Lessons folder.

3 Click the Poetry Sampler link at the top of the Index.html page to go to the Poetry Sampler page, then explore the links on that page.

4 When you've finished viewing the pages in the site, close your browser.

Review questions

1 What are two ways of creating animations?

2 What determines the stacking order of floating boxes?

3 What does the Floating Box Controller do?

4 How do you smooth out an animation path?

5 How do you create a Wipe Transition for an animated floating box?

6 What are scenes?

7 How do you control when a scene will play?

Review answers

1 You can create animations quickly by using the Record button in the Floating Box Inspector and dragging a floating box to record the motions. For more control, you can use the Timeline Editor.

2 Initially, a floating box's stacking order is determined by its anchor's location on the page, with the top leftmost anchor indicating a floating box lowest in the stacking order, and so on down and across the page. You can control the stacking order by changing the Depth value in the Floating Box Inspector.

3 The Floating Box Controller lets you lock floating boxes in place. In animations, the floating boxes are locked only for the selected key frame.

4 To smooth out an animation path, first select all the keyframes that make up the animation: Shift-click each keyframe, or drag from the side or bottom to select all the keyframes (make sure the time indicator is aligned with a keyframe). Then choose Curve from the Animation pop-up menu in the Floating Box Inspector.

5 To create a Wipe Transition, Ctrl-click (Windows) or Command-click (Mac OS) in the Action track in the Timeline editor directly over a keyframe. Then choose Multimedia > Wipe Transition from the Action menu in the Action Inspector. Choose the floating box to which you want to apply the transition and the number of steps (more steps for a faster transition, fewer steps for a slower one).

6 Scenes are used to store multiple animations for the same Web page. All scenes share the same floating boxes, but you can create different behaviors for the boxes in different scenes. Each Web page contains one scene by default. To create a new scene, choose New Scene from the Options pop-up menu in the Timeline Editor.

7 Turn Autoplay On to play a scene automatically when the Web page loads. You can also start a scene with user input, such as clicking on a rollover button. Select the rollover button, and then click the New Action button in the Actions palette. From the Action pop-up menu, select Multimedia > Play Scene, and then choose the scene from the Scene pop-up menu.

Lesson 9

```
<TITLE>We
<STYLE TYPE=

e{color:maroon;fon

</STYLE>
AD>
Y>
<!-- Begin main table -->
<TABLE BORDER="4" CELLPADDI
06">
    <TR>
        <TD><A
tp://www.adobe.com/">Adobe</A
        <TD>GoLive</TD>
        <TD><IMG BORDER="0" HEIGH
le.gif" ALT="Title"></TD>
    </TR>
    <TR>
        <TD><SPAN CLASS="headl
AN></TD>
    </TR>
    <TR>
        <TD><B>DHTML an
    </TR>
</TABLE>
DY>

    EQUIV="content-ty
    charset=iso-885
    lcome to Adobe GoL

main table -->
ER="4" CELLPADD

D><A
dobe.com/">Adobe</
D>GoLive</TD>
D><IMG BORDER="0" HE
="Title"></TD>

D><SPAN CLASS="head

D><B>DHTML
```

9 Using Actions and JavaScript

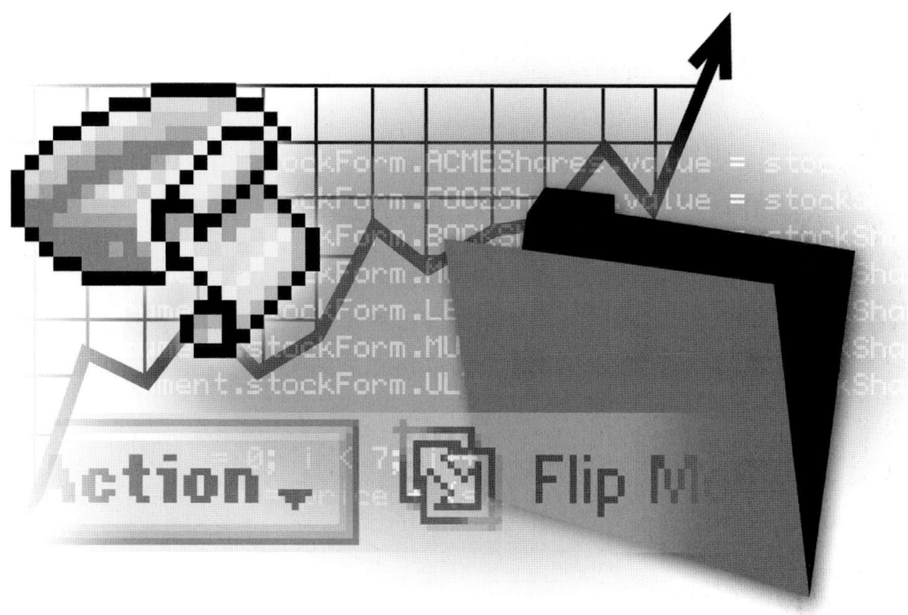

Adobe GoLive lets you attach premade scripts called actions to links, images, and floating boxes. Actions can trigger events such as playing animations, switching a viewer with an older Web browser to a special version of your Web site, and changing the contents of images. You can add your own JavaScript scripts to Adobe GoLive's repertoire for even greater flexibility.

About this lesson

In this lesson, you'll learn how to do the following:

- Create head actions that run automatically when a page is loaded in a Web browser.
- Create a browser switch action.
- Create an action that automatically resizes the browser window.
- Apply actions to floating boxes, images, and links.
- Add JavaScript scripts to page elements.

If needed, copy the Lesson09 folder onto your hard drive. As you work on this lesson, you'll overwrite the start files. If you need to restore the start files, copy them from the *Adobe GoLive 5.0 Classroom in a Book* CD.

Note: *Windows users need to unlock the lesson files before using them. For more information, see "Copying the Classroom in a Book files" on page 2.*

For information on setting up your work area, see "Setting up your work area" on page 9.

Getting started

You'll begin this lesson by using your Web browser to view a copy of the finished Web page.

1 Start your browser.

2 Choose File > Open and open the Index.html file. The path to the file is Lesson09/09End/Stockblock Folder/Stockblock/Index.html.

3 Scroll through the page, and experiment with its buttons and interface. Notice the automatic resizing of the window when the page opens, the pop-up ticker box, the appearance of info boxes, live update of stock transactions, and the dynamic browser status bar that notifies you when you buy, sell, or dump stocks.

4 When you have finished viewing the page, close your browser.

Creating head actions

Head actions are special premade scripts inserted into the header of a Web page. Some automatically run just before or after the viewer opens the page in a Web browser. Others are "on call" and only run in response to something the viewer has done; for example, clicking a link or image. You'll insert several head actions into the page for this lesson. The first three actions are among the most common Web designers find necessary to implement in a site.

Creating a browser switch action

Visitors using older Web browsers may not see a Web page correctly if it contains features and technology such as JavaScript, frames, floating boxes, or tables. It's important to provide a way for those viewers to see an alternative page when they view your Web site. A browser switch action automatically takes viewers with older browsers to any page you designate, even if it's only a page saying that your site doesn't support their browser.

The page you're building in this lesson uses functions specific to version 4.0 browsers, so adding a browser switch action to the page is necessary.

1 Start Adobe GoLive.

2 Choose File > Open, and open the Index.html file. The path to the file is Lesson09/09Start/Stockblock Folder/Stockblock/Index.html.

3 Click the triangle next to the page title at the top of the document window to open the head section of the page. Notice that there are five JavaScript objects already in the header. You'll use them later in this lesson to calculate stock transaction information.

Clicking triangle to open head section

4 From the Smart tab of the Objects palette, drag the Browser Switch icon to the head section of the document window.

Dragging Browser Switch icon to head section

5 If the Inspector is not open, double-click the icon that you just placed in the head section of the page to bring up its attributes in the Inspector.

The default attributes are correct and don't need to be changed. If you already had an alternate page designed, you could enter the page's name in the alternate link box. This is the page that viewers with older browsers would see instead of the current page.

6 Drag the Browser Switch icon so that it is as far to the left as possible. You want this action to run before any others, so that visitors with older browsers will be switched to the alternate page right away before the rest of the page loads.

Dragging Browser Switch icon to left

7 Choose File > Save.

Adding a Netscape CSS fix action

Netscape Navigator contains a program error that causes Web pages with animations in floating boxes to have trouble displaying properly when viewers resize the page. Now you'll add a head action that prevents this problem. It's a good idea to add this action to any page containing animated floating boxes.

1 From the Smart tab of the Objects palette, drag the Head Action icon to the head section of the document window.

Dragging Head Action icon to head section

2 If the Inspector is not open, double-click the icon that you just placed in the head section of the page to bring up its attributes in the Inspector.

You want this action to run when the page is loading, so you'll leave the Exec. pop-up box set to OnLoad in the Inspector.

3 Choose Others > Netscape CSS Fix from the Action pop-up menu.

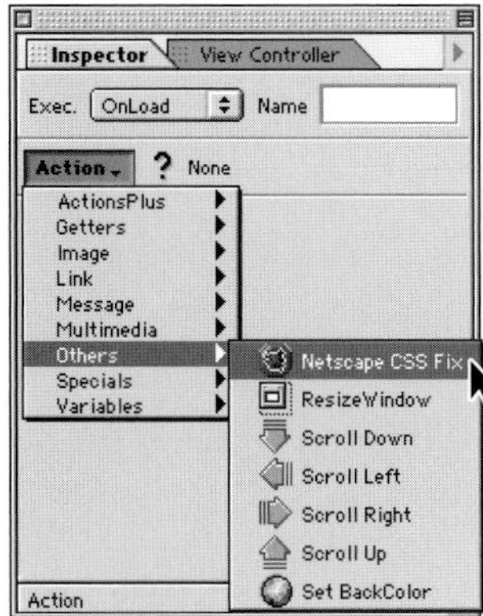

Choosing Others > Netscape CSS Fix from Action pop-up menu

4 Choose File > Save.

Resizing a browser window automatically

Now you'll insert a head action that automatically resizes the browser window to fit the design of your Web page, so that viewers see the page exactly as you intended.

1 From the Smart tab of the Objects palette, drag the Head Action icon to the head section of the document window.

2 If the Inspector is not open, double-click the icon that you just placed in the head section of the page to bring up its attributes in the Inspector.

You want this action to run when the page is loading, so you'll leave the Exec. pop-up box set to OnLoad in the Inspector.

3 Choose Others > Resize Window from the Action pop-up menu.

4 Set both the Width and Height resize value to 550. This ensures that the browser window will be 550 pixels tall and wide—just big enough to display the More Info copy.

5 Choose File > Save.

6 Choose Special > Show in Default Browser to preview the page, and see how the resize window head action that you just created works.

Applying actions to page elements

In this part of the lesson, you'll start applying actions to elements on the page. You can apply actions to various elements, including floating boxes, images, and links.

Using actions to manipulate floating boxes

You'll be using actions in this section to make the stock ticker already at the top of the page (a floating box called Quotes) retractable, so that it won't take up space when it's not needed. You'll do this by creating another floating box containing an image that will extend or collapse the ticker when clicked. For additional information on floating boxes, see "Working with floating boxes" on page 213.

1 Scroll to the bottom of the page. From the Basic tab of the Objects palette, drag the Floating Box icon to the bottom of the page away from any other object. You'll set the exact position of the new floating box using the Floating Box Inspector. Make sure that the box is still selected. You may have to scroll down to see it.

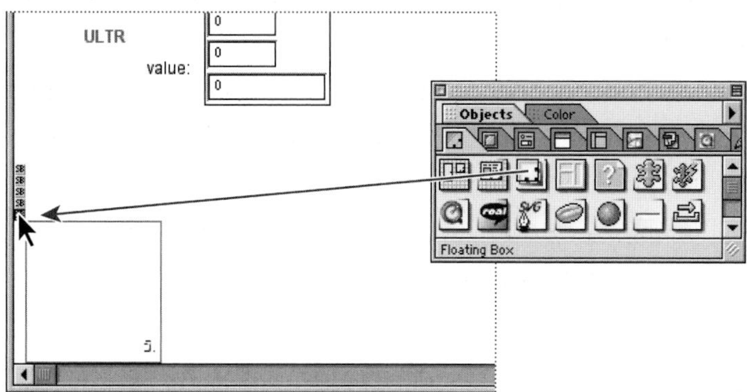

Dragging Floating Box icon to bottom of page

2 In the Floating Box Inspector, rename the box **QuoteTrigger**, and set the Left value to **451** and the Top value to **94**. The stock jumps to the right of the stock ticker at the top of the page. You may have to scroll up to see it.

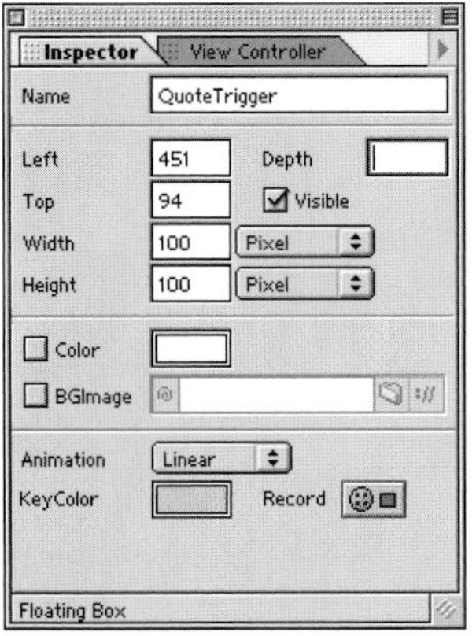

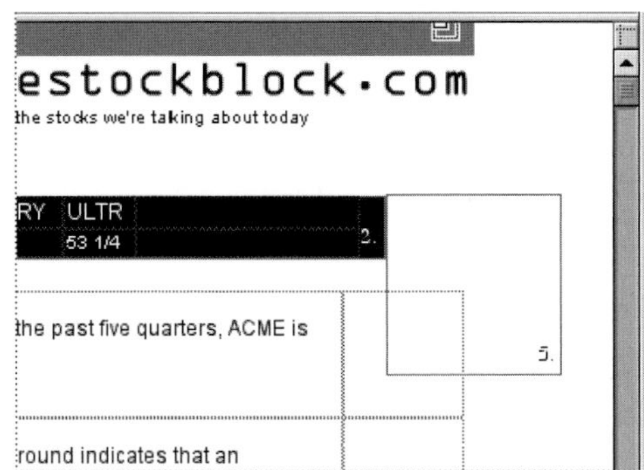

3 From the Basic tab of the Objects palette, drag the Image icon to the floating box that you just created and renamed.

4 With the Image icon still selected in the floating box, set its Source, using the Browse button in the Image Inspector, to the image Tab.gif located in the Lesson09/09Start/ Stockblock Folder/Stockblock/Images folder.

5 Select the QuoteTrigger floating box. Resize it using the Floating Box Inspector to set its dimensions to 26 by 40 (the same size as the Tab.gif image). This image will be the trigger for the stock ticker's motion.

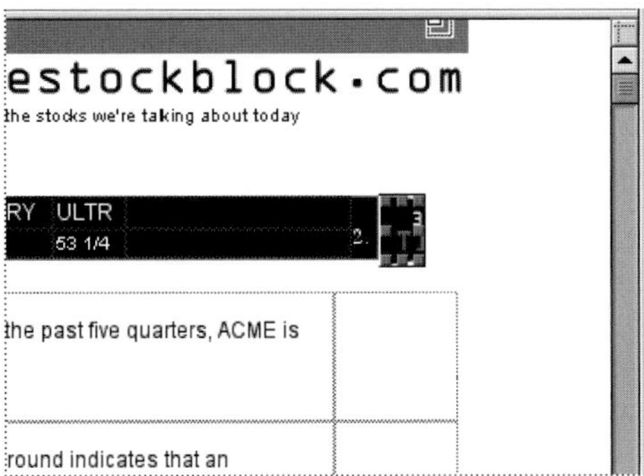

6 Select the Tab.gif image. In the Image Inspector, select the Border option and set it to 0 so that the image does not have a border.

7 Click the Link tab in the Image Inspector, and click the Link button.

8 Change (Empty Reference!) to #. Linking an object to # simply links the object to an empty anchor on the current page—in others words, to nowhere. You can only apply actions to an image that is assigned a link. This technique lets you apply an action to an image and remain on the current page. For additional information on creating links, see Lesson 5, "Creating Links."

Now that you have the floating box created and positioned, and the image set up to serve as a trigger, you can begin applying actions.

9 Choose Window > Actions to open the Actions palette. Listed on the left are several events. You want the ticker to be displayed when a viewer clicks the image, so select the Mouse Click event and click the New Action button ( ) at the top of the Actions palette.

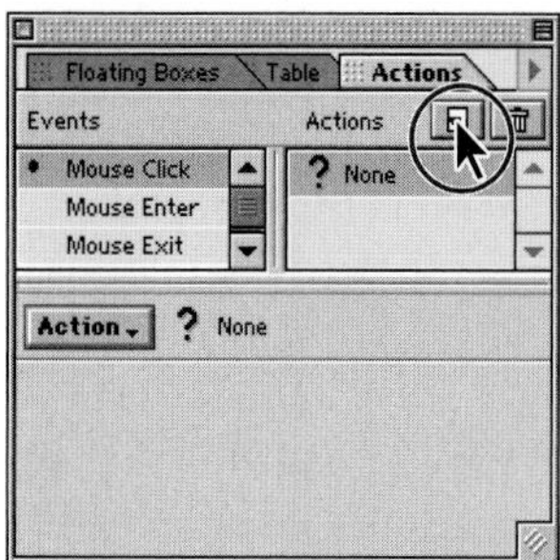

Clicking New Action button

10 Make sure that the None action is selected. The Action pop-up menu for None is now enabled. Choose Multimedia > Flip Move from the Action pop-up menu. The Flip Move action toggles a floating box between two positions each time the action is triggered.

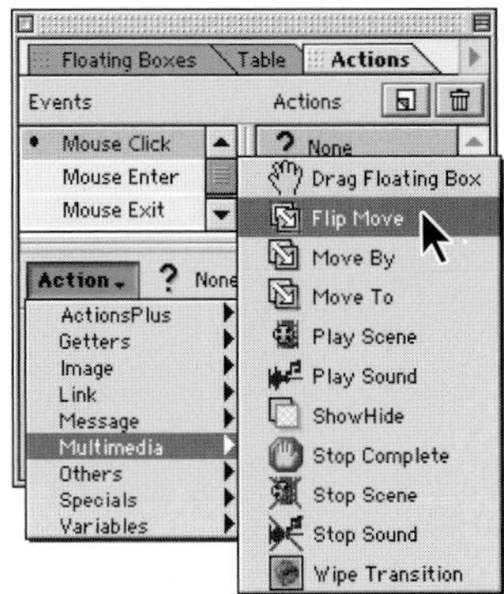

Choosing Multimedia > Flip Move from Action pop-up menu

11 Choose QuoteTrigger from the Floating Box pop-up menu. Position1 refers to the first position to which you want the floating box to jump. In this case, that's the current position of the box, so click the Get button. The values for the current position of the QuoteTrigger box are added.

12 Set the Position2 values to 1 and 94—almost flush left with the left side of the window. This will place the floating box all the way to the edge.

13 Make sure the Animation (Anim) option is selected, and enter **3** in the Ticks box. This will animate the movement so that the box moves out and in, in a series of three steps and doesn't simply pop into place.

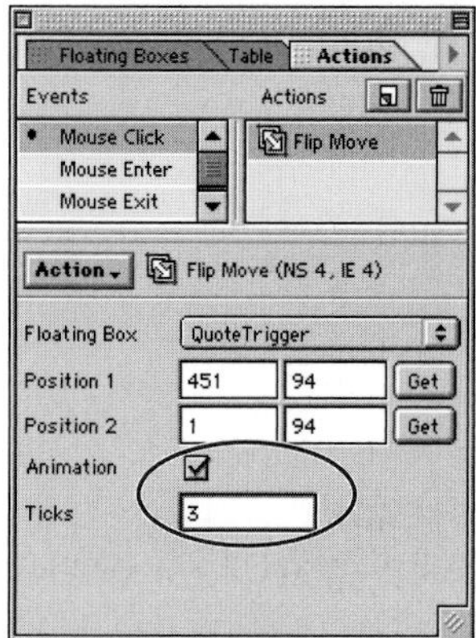

14 Click the New Action button ( ) again to add another action to the Mouse Click event, and again choose Multimedia > Flip Move from the Action pop-up menu.

15 Choose Quotes from the Floating Box pop-up menu, and again click the Get button next to Position1.

16 Set the Position2 values to -450 and 95. This positions the Quote floating box outside the browser window until it moves in when triggered.

17 Make sure that the Animation option is selected, and set the Ticks value to 3.

18 You'll now want to move the Quotes and QuoteTrigger floating boxes to their starting positions. Choose Window > Floating Boxes to open the Floating Boxes palette. Select the Quotes floating box in the Floating Boxes palette. In the Floating Box Inspector, set its Left value to **-450** and the Top value to **95**.

19 Select QuoteTrigger in the Floating Boxes palette. In the Inspector, set its Left value to **1** and the Top value to **94**.

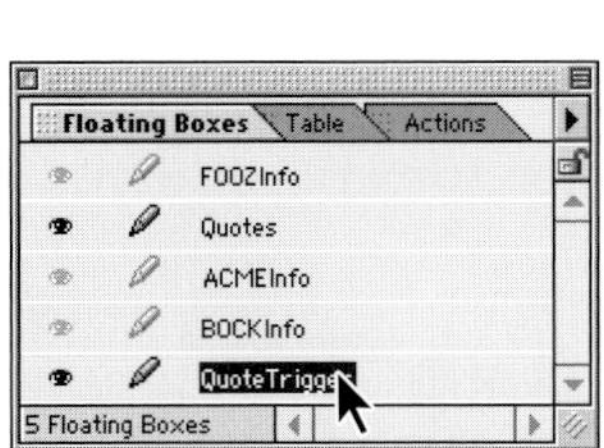

Selecting floating box

Repositioned floating box

20 Choose File > Save.

21 Choose Special > Show in Default Browser to preview the page, and try out the new retractable stock ticker.

Creating actions on call

You've already seen in the first section of this lesson how head actions can be created that automatically load when the viewer first opens the page. In this section, you'll create some more head actions that rely on an OnCall trigger; that is, the action happens only when it is explicitly called in response to a viewer clicking a button or doing something on the page. You'll add an image to existing floating boxes, create some "on call" head actions, and then assign the actions to the image in order to display a More Info box with information on the selected company.

Prepping images for actions

To the right of the main body of the page are two overlapping floating boxes (not currently visible) containing more information on two companies featured on the site. These More Info boxes appear when the viewer clicks a More Info button next to a company in the main table. You'll take a quick look at these boxes and then add an image to act as a trigger to display a More Info box when clicked.

1 Choose Window > Floating Boxes.

2 Click the eye icon next to ACMEInfo. The ACMEInfo floating box appears to the right of the main table. You may have to scroll to the right to see it. Click the eye icon again to make the box disappear. Now you'll create a trigger so that a visitor can see the appropriate More Info box when the trigger is clicked.

3 From the Basic tab of the Objects palette, drag an Image icon to the right-most cell of the table containing company information, in the row for Acme Industries.

Dragging Image icon to table cell

4 Click the Image icon that you just placed, and set its Source, using the Browse button in the Basic tab of the Image Inspector, to the image More.gif located in the Lesson09/09Start/Stockblock Folder/Stockblock/Images folder.

5 Select the More.gif image. In the Image Inspector, select the Border option and set it to 0 so that the image does not have a border.

6 Click the Link tab in the Image Inspector, and click the Link button.

7 Change the (Empty Reference!) to # just as you did with the Tab.gif file earlier.

Adding "on call" actions to images

Now that the image has been prepped, you can create the "on call" head actions that will make the More Info boxes work properly when the image is clicked. Since you want to display only one More Info box at a time, you'll create a group of head actions that will close all of the boxes in case any are showing when the visitor clicks a More Info button.

1 If the head section of the page isn't visible, click the triangle next to the page title at the top of the document window to open the head section of the page.

2 From the Smart tab of the Objects palette, drag the Head Action icon to the head section of the document window.

3 If the Inspector is not open, double-click the icon that you just placed in the head section of the page to bring up its attributes in the Action Inspector.

4 Choose OnCall from the Exec. pop-up menu.

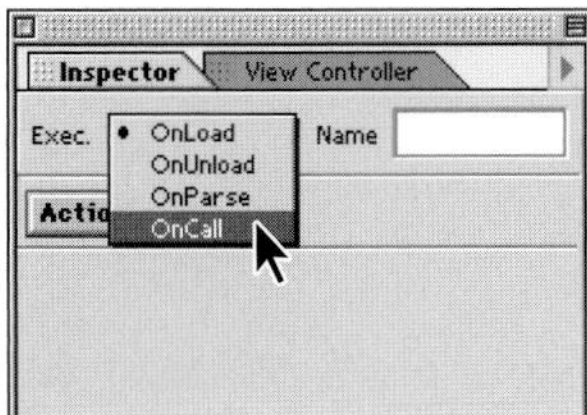

Choosing OnCall from Exec. pop-up menu

5 In the Name field, type **closeInfo**.

6 From the Action pop-up menu, choose Specials > Action Group. An action group can contain more than one action.

7 Click the New Action button (▣) to add an action to the group, and select the new action.

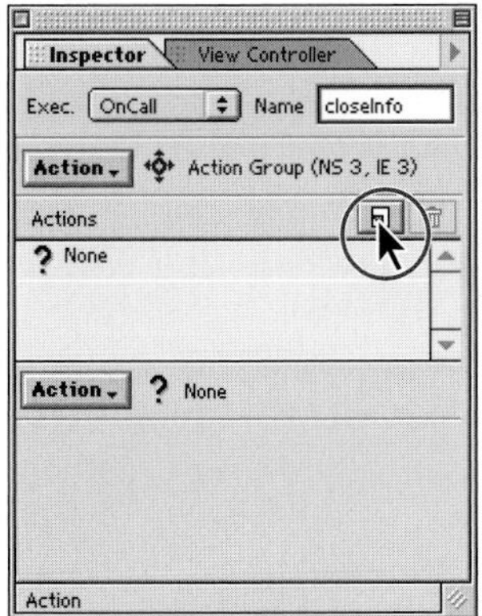

Clicking New Action button

8 Choose Multimedia > ShowHide from the lower Action pop-up menu.

9 Set the action's attributes using the Floating Box pop-up menu so that this ShowHide targets the ACMEInfo floating box, and set the mode to Hide using the Mode pop-up menu.

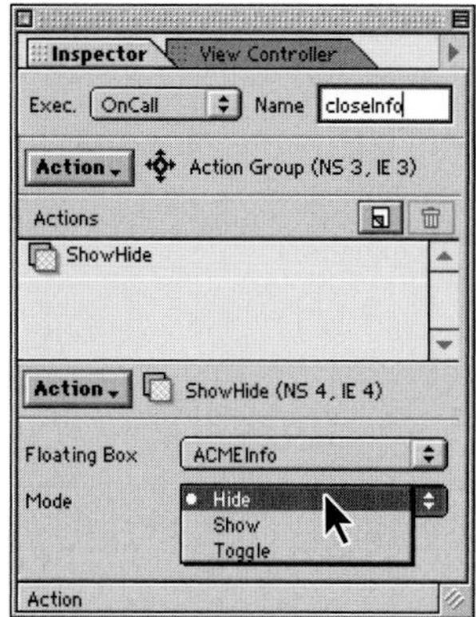

Choosing Hide from Mode pop-up menu

10 Click the New Action button ( ) again, and select the new action.

11 Again choose Multimedia > ShowHide from the lower Action pop-up menu, and set the target to the FOOZInfo floating box and the Mode to Hide, using the Floating Box and Mode pop-up menus.

12 Close the head section of the page.

Now that you have the necessary "on call" actions defined, you can assign the actions to the More Info image that you inserted earlier.

13 Select the More.gif image, and open the Actions palette by choosing Window > Actions, if necessary.

14 Select the Mouse Click event, and add three new actions by clicking the New Action button ( ) three times. Since the actions are not yet defined, each appears with the name None.

15 Select the first action, and choose Others > Scroll Right from the lower Action pop-up menu.

16 Set Scroll Pixels to 300 and Scroll Speed to 50.

17 Select the next action, and choose Specials > Call Action from the lower Action pop-up menu. This lets you call an action already defined—in this case, closeInfo.

18 Choose closeInfo from the Action pop-up menu.

Choosing CloseInfo

So far, the assigned actions scroll to the right and close any info boxes that might be open. Now it's time to define the final action, so that it opens the correct More Info floating box.

19 Select the final action, and choose Multimedia > ShowHide from the Action pop-up menu. Since the image is in the ACME row, set the floating box to be ACMEInfo and the Mode to Show.

20 Choose File > Save.

Copying graphics with actions attached

Instead of doing all these steps for each company, you can easily duplicate the More Info button that you just created for ACME for use elsewhere and change attributes as necessary. Here you'll copy the More Info button and modify it for the next company listed.

1 Begin dragging the More Info image, and press Ctrl (Windows) or Option (Mac OS) to drag a copy of the original to the last cell in the FOOZ row.

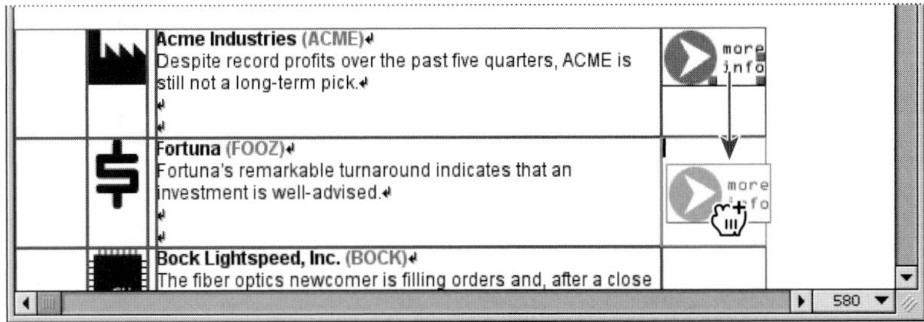

Dragging More Info image

2 Make sure that the copy is selected, and open the Actions palette. All the actions should remain the same, except the final ShowHide.

3 Select the ShowHide action.

4 Change the pop-up menu that reads ACMEInfo to FOOZInfo. Remember that ACMEInfo and FOOZInfo are the names of the two More Info floating boxes. This will now display the proper information for the row.

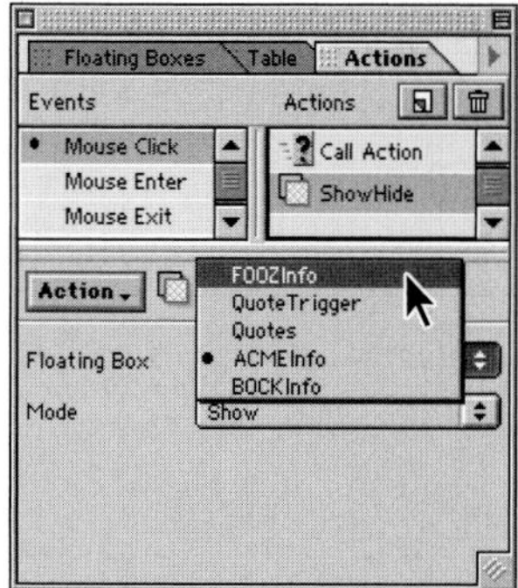

Choosing FOOZInfo from pop-up menu

5 Choose File > Save.

6 Choose Special > Show in Default Browser to preview the page, and experiment with the More Info buttons to see how they work.

Adding actions to text links

Notice that once a More Info box is opened, there is no way to close it. You can fix this by adding mouse events to the "close this" text link already set up in the two More Info floating boxes, ACMEInfo and FOOZInfo. If you look at the text link in the Inspector, you'll notice that it's set as a link to #—the same technique that you used earlier with images so that you could assign actions to them.

1 Show the ACMEInfo floating box, and make it editable by clicking the pencil icon in the Floating Boxes palette.

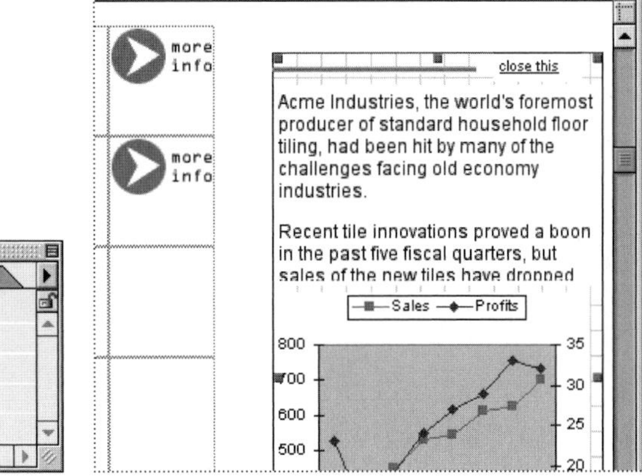

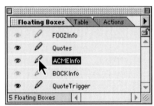

Clicking pencil icon *Selected floating box*

2 Select the "close this" text, and open the Actions palette (Window > Actions).

3 Select the Mouse Click event, and add two actions by clicking the Add Action button ( ) twice.

4 Select the first None action, and choose Others > Scroll Left from the Action pop-up menu, setting Scroll Pixels to 300 and Scroll Speed to 50.

5 Select the other None action, and choose Multimedia > ShowHide from the Action pop-up menu.

6 Set the target to be the ACMEInfo floating box and the Mode to Hide.

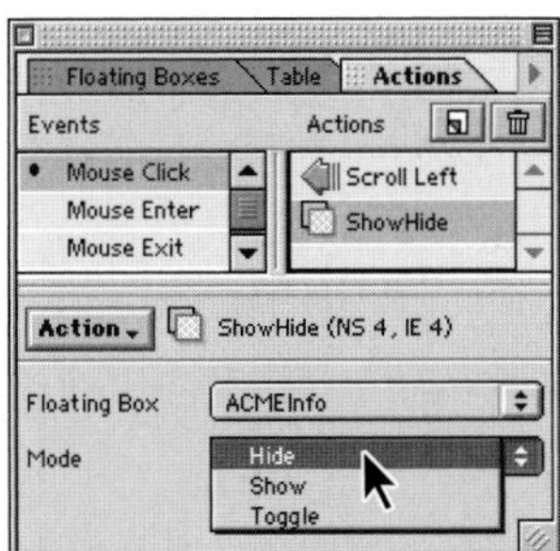

Choosing Hide from Mode pop-up menu

7 Hide the ACMEInfo floating box by clicking its eye icon in the Floating Boxes palette.

8 Repeat steps 1–7 for the FOOZInfo floating box.

9 Choose File > Save.

10 Choose Special > Show in Default Browser to preview the page, and see how the "close this" link functions.

Using JavaScript scripts

In this section, you'll see how to assign JavaScript scripts to various page elements. We've already inserted several scripts in the head section of the document. You could also write your own custom scripts and use them in your own projects. See the *Adobe GoLive 5.0 User Guide* for details on inserting scripts.

Assigning scripts to page elements

The included JavaScript scripts serve as functions that let viewers increase, decrease, or dump an amount of stock at the Web site, and then show an update in the lower part of the page for the current number of stocks in the visitor's portfolio. You'll first add some buttons that will call these scripts when triggered.

1 Drag the Image icon from the Basic tab of the Objects palette to the row immediately below the text about ACME Industries (to the left of the first return arrow) and add a space.

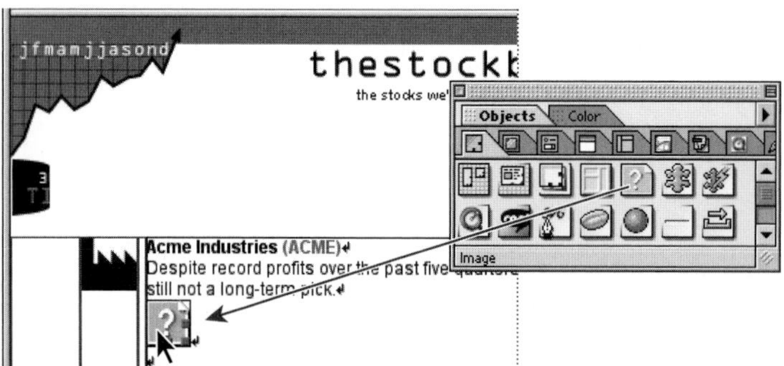

Dragging Image icon to row below text

2 Repeat step 1 twice so that you have three images, each separated from the previous one by a space.

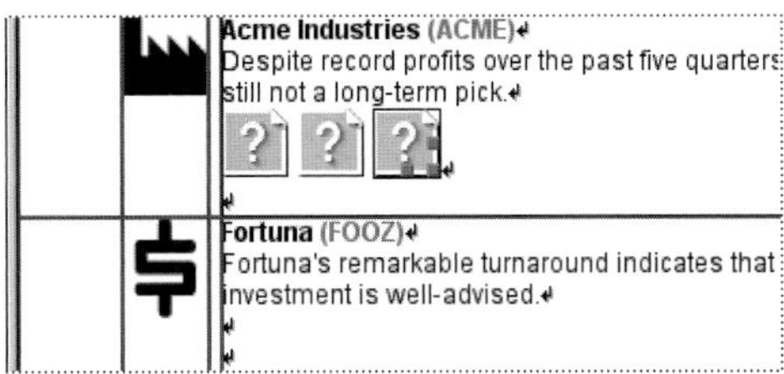

3 Using the Image Inspector's Basic tab, set the Source of the first image to Buy.gif, the second to Sell.gif, and the third to Dump.gif. All are located in the Lesson09/09Start/ Stockblock Folder/Stockblock/Images folder.

4 In the Image Inspector's Link tab, set each image as a link using the Link button, entering # as the link.

5 In the Image Inspector's Basic tab, select the Border option for each image and set the Border to 0, if necessary.

You'll want to let the visitor know that something has changed when a transaction has been made by notifying them in the browser's status bar.

6 Click the triangle next to the page title at the top of the document window to open the head section of the page.

7 Drag a Head Action icon from the Smart tab of the Objects palette into the head section of the document. Make sure that it's selected.

8 In the Inspector, set Exec. to OnCall and choose Message > Set Status from the Action pop-up menu.

9 Enter **Your portfolio has been updated. See below.** in the text box.

10 Enter **statusMessage** as the action name in the Name text box.

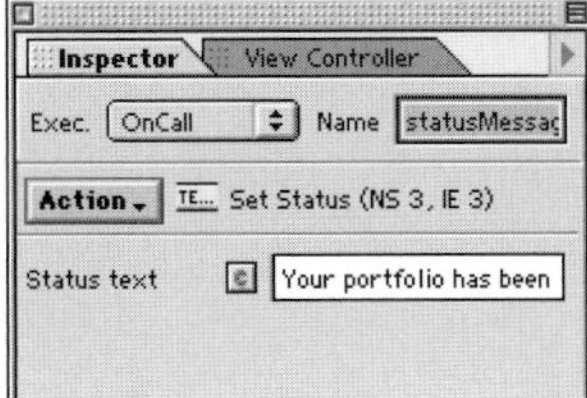

Now you'll assign actions and scripts to the Mouse Click event for the first graphic.

11 Select the Buy.gif image, select Mouse Click in the Actions palette, and add two actions to this event by clicking the New Action button ( ) twice.

12 Select the first None action, and choose Specials > Call Function from the Action pop-up menu. The Call Function action lets you access a ready-made JavaScript script.

13 Choose the increment function from the Function pop-up menu.

14 Enter **0** as the Argument. The Argument in this function simply identifies the company. ACME will be 0, FOOZ will be 1, and so on. Entering 0 tells the action to increment ACME's information.

15 Select the second None action, and choose Specials > Call Action from the Action pop-up menu.

16 Choose statusMessage from the Action pop-up menu.

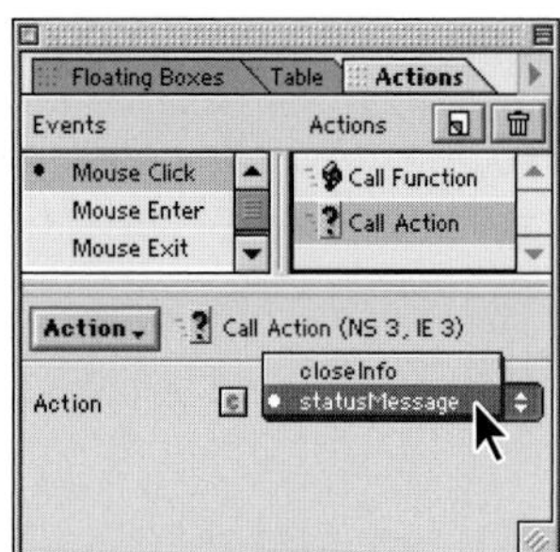

Choosing statusMessage

17 Choose File > Save.

18 Choose Special > Show in Default Browser to preview the page, and try out the Buy button. Clicking the Buy.gif image adds one of ACME's stocks to your portfolio and notifies you of the transaction in the browser status bar (bottom left of the browser window).

19 Repeat steps 11–16 for the Sell.gif and Dump.gif images, choosing the decrement function for Sell.gif and the dump function for Dump.gif, and leaving the Argument in each instance as 0, since all relate to ACME.

20 Select, and then copy and paste the three buttons into the appropriate cells for the remaining companies. Be sure to increment the Argument of each button for each subsequent company by 1, so that all FOOZ buttons are 1, BOCK buttons are 2, and so on.

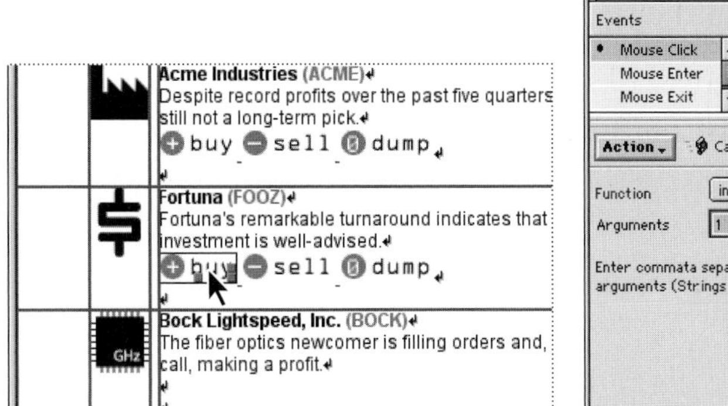

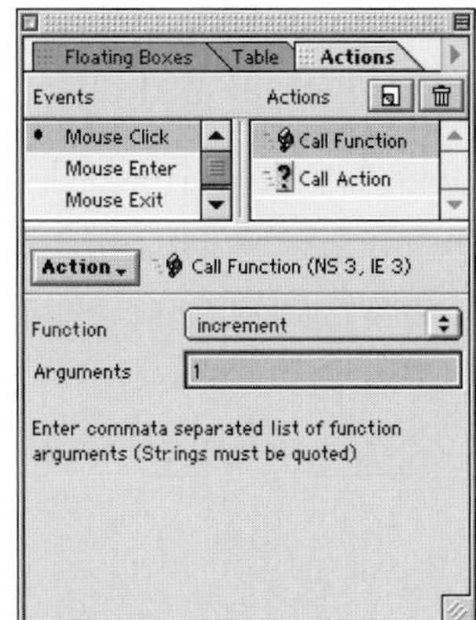

21 Choose File > Save.

22 Choose Special > Show in Default Browser to preview the page, and to see the final results.

Review questions

1 How do you create a head action?

2 Why is including a browser switch action a useful feature for a home page of a Web site?

3 How do you set an image as a link that allows you to assign an action to the image and lets the visitor to remain on the current page?

4 How do you assign an action to a link?

5 What is the difference between OnCall and OnLoad actions?

6 How is a JavaScript script differ from an action in the Actions palette?

Review answers

1 You create a head action by dragging a Head Action icon from the Smart tab of the Objects palette to the head section of a document.

2 Including a browser switch action on the home page of your Web site lets you direct visitors using older browsers to an alternate version of your site. This lets you use the latest Web technologies without worrying whether the site will appear as designed on older browsers that cannot display frames, or cope with JavaScript scripts or floating boxes.

3 You select the image, click the Link button in the Inspector, and set the link to #. Once you do this, you can assign actions to the image so that it can respond to mouse clicks or other events.

4 You select the desired link and assign actions to it using the Actions palette.

5 An OnCall action runs only when some event such as a mouse click by a viewer triggers the action. An OnLoad action automatically runs when a viewer first opens the page in a browser.

6 The actions available in the Action palette are premade actions that come with Adobe GoLive. A JavaScript script is a function called by the Call Function action. Writing your own scripts, if you're familiar with JavaScript, provides a way to augment the Adobe GoLive built-in actions with your own custom scripting code.

Lesson 10

```
<TITLE>We
<STYLE TYPE=

e{color:maroon;

</STYLE>
AD>
Y>
<!-- Begin main table -->
<TABLE BORDER="4" CELLPADDI
06">
    <TR>
        <TD><A
tp://www.adobe.com/">Adobe</A
        <TD>GoLive</TD>
        <TD><IMG BORDER="0" HEIGH
le.gif" ALT="Title"></TD>
    </TR>
    <TR>
        <TD><SPAN CLASS="headli
AN></TD>
    </TR>
    <TR>
        <TD><B>DHTML ani
    </TR>
</TABLE>
DY>

main table -->
DER="4" CELLPAD

D><A
dobe.com/">Adobe</A
D>GoLive</TD>
D><IMG BORDER="0" HEI
="Title"></TD>

D><SPAN CLASS="hea

D><B>DHTML a
```

10 Creating Forms

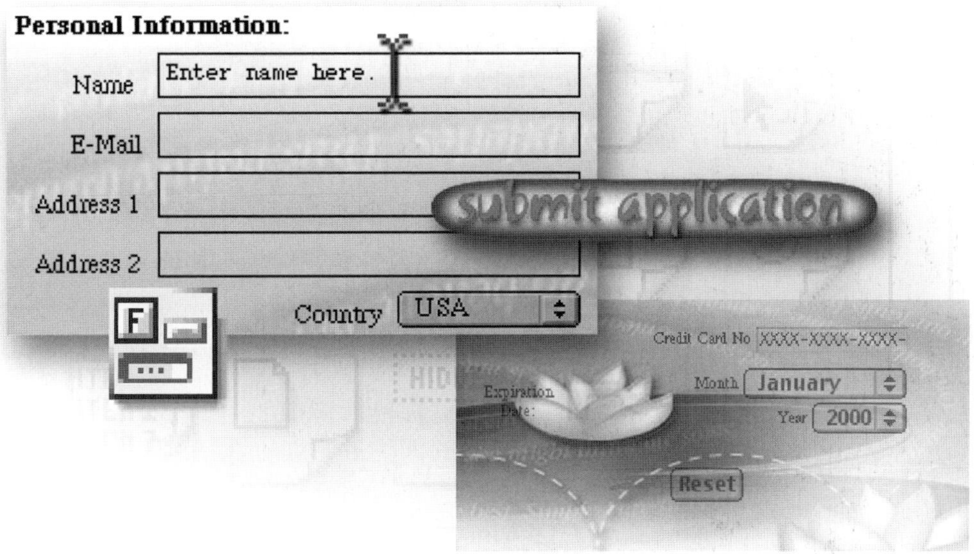

Forms are interactive elements that allow you to collect data from your visitors. They enable visitors to request information or products, and to submit personal information, such as their name, address, and credit card number.

About this lesson

In this lesson, you'll learn how to do the following:

- Use a table to place form fields precisely on a page.
- Add a variety of form fields to a table, including text fields and a pop-up menu.
- Store frequently used objects in the Site Extras tab of the Objects palette, and add the objects to a page.
- Add radio buttons, a clickable image, and a Reset button to a form.
- Modify a list box in a form.
- Specify the order in which form fields are selected when viewers press the Tab key repeatedly.

This lesson will take about 45 minutes to complete.

If needed, copy the Lesson10 folder onto your hard drive. As you work on this lesson, you'll overwrite the start files. If you need to restore the start files, copy them from the *Adobe GoLive 5.0 Classroom in a Book* CD.

Note: *Windows users need to unlock the lesson files before using them. For more information, see "Copying the Classroom in a Book files" on page 2.*

For information on setting up your work area, see "Setting up your work area" on page 9.

Getting started

In this lesson, you'll complete the design of a membership application form for a Web site called poetrypond.com. You'll create the section of the form that visitors will use to enter their personal information. You'll also add a variety of fields to existing sections of the form, including radio buttons, a clickable image, and a Reset button.

First you'll view the finished membership application form in your Web browser.

1 Start your browser.

2 Open the Index.html file to open the home page for the poetrypond.com Web site. The path to the file is Lesson10/10End/Forms Folder/Forms/Index.html.

3 Click the frog on the page to go to the membership application form.

The membership application form contains a variety of form fields, such as text fields for entering personal information, a list box for selecting poetry workshops, radio buttons for selecting a payment type, and a clickable image designed for submitting the application over the Web.

4 Try filling out the form by entering your personal information into the text fields and making selections from the list box, pop-up menus, and radio buttons.

The form has been designed for this lesson only. Therefore, you won't actually be able to submit your application over the Web.

5 When you have finished viewing the form, quit your browser.

To submit and collect information from a form over the Web, you must have a Common Gateway Interface (CGI) application on a Web server to collect and route the data to a database. The names of the form fields must also match those set in the CGI application. Keep in mind that CGI scripts must be built outside of Adobe GoLive and require some knowledge of computer programming. CGI applications are usually set up by a Web server administrator. In addition, your Internet Service Provider (ISP) may offer CGI scripts for use by customers with hosted sites. Be sure to check with your ISP about the availability of CGI scripts for handling forms.

About forms

The following illustration shows the finished layout of the membership application form in Adobe GoLive.

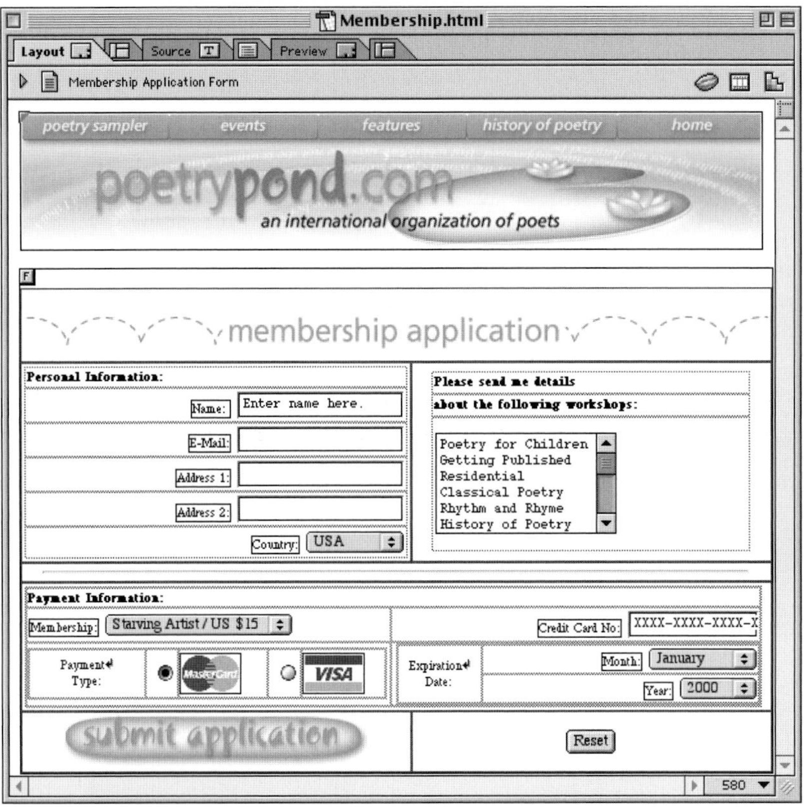

Membership application form in Layout view in Adobe GoLive

Notice that the form is laid out within a box enclosing the Form icon (F). When you add this icon to a page, you are actually adding a Form element to the HTML source code for the page. The Form element identifies a Web page or section of a Web page as a form, and instructs the browser where and how to return form information for processing. The presence of the Form icon is necessary for the form to display and function properly. Make sure that it precedes any form elements.

For information on how to add a Form icon to a page, see "Setting up the Form element" in Chapter 12 of the *Adobe GoLive 5.0 User Guide*.

Notice also that the form is actually laid out using a table with two columns and five rows, and some of the cells in the table contain nested tables. You can use tables to precisely place form fields on a page. For additional information on tables, see "Adding tables" on page 43.

The following describes the contents of each row in the main table:

- The first row of the main table contains the membership application image, which spans both columns.
- The second row contains two cells, each containing a nested table. The nested table in the first cell contains text fields for entering personal information. The nested table in the second cell contains text and a list box for selecting poetry workshops.
- The third row contains a line spanning both columns.
- The fourth row contains a nested table for entering payment information. This nested table actually contains two more nested tables, one for entering a membership type and payment type, and one for entering a credit card number and expiration date.
- The fifth row contains two cells, one with a clickable image designed for submitting the application over the Web and one with a Reset button.

Creating a section of a form

To get you started with the design of the membership application form, we've already created several sections of the form for you. You'll create the section of the form that visitors will use to enter their personal information. To do this, you'll use a new page. Later in this lesson, you'll add the contents of the page to the existing form.

1 Start Adobe GoLive. A new document named Untitled.html opens.

If you didn't start Adobe GoLive for the first time, a new document named Untitled.html may not be open on your desktop. If necessary, choose File > New to create a new page.

2 Choose File > Save As, rename the page **Name_form.html**, and save it in the Forms folder. The path to the folder is Lesson10/10Start/Forms Folder/Forms.

3 Select the page title, "Welcome to Adobe GoLive 5."

4 Type **Personal Information** as the new title, and press Enter of Return.

Adding a table for the form layout

Now you'll add a table to the page. You'll use the table to place form fields precisely on the page.

We recommend that you always lay out a form using one or more tables. As an alternative, you can place form fields on a layout grid on the page. However, we don't recommend this technique because the layout of a form created with a layout grid can vary depending on the visitor's browser and screen resolution.

1 If necessary, choose Window > Objects to display the Objects palette, and make sure that the Basic tab ( ) is selected.

2 If necessary, choose Window > Inspector to display the Inspector.

3 Drag a Table icon from the Objects palette to the page. The Inspector changes to the Table Inspector.

4 In the Table Inspector, enter **6** for Rows, enter **1** for Columns, choose Pixel from the Width pop-up menu, and enter **300** for Width.

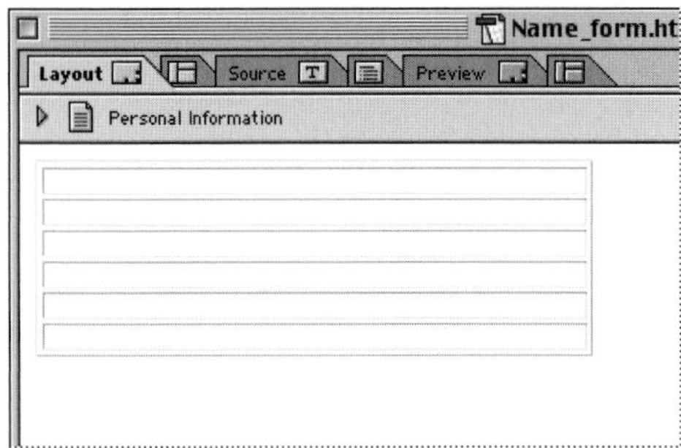

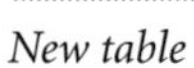

New table

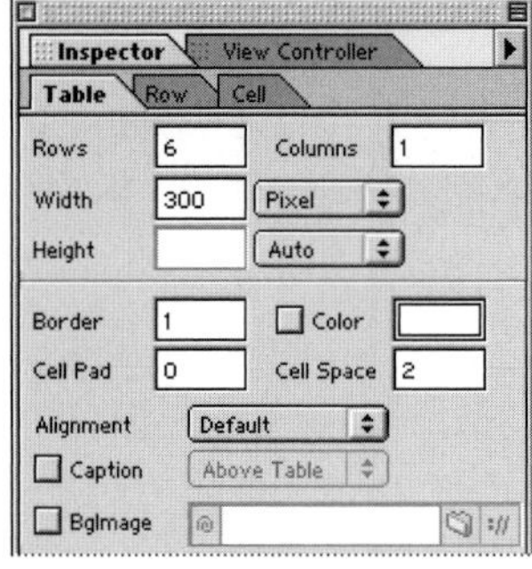

Setting table's properties in Table Inspector

Now you'll add a heading to the first cell of the table. This is the heading of the section of the form that you are creating.

5 In the document window, type **Personal Information:** in the first cell of the table.

6 Select the text that you just entered, and choose Type > Structure > Strong to make the text bold.

7 Choose 2 from the Font Size menu (None) on the toolbar. By choosing a smaller relative font size, you can prevent the text from wrapping in the table cell when viewed in most browsers.

Remember that text appears larger in browsers for Windows. If you are designing your forms in Mac OS, you should keep your text small and leave extra space in your table cells. As a general rule, you should check your forms in browsers for both Windows and Mac OS before uploading them to a Web server.

8 Choose File > Save to save the page.

Adding a name field

Now you'll add a text field to the table so viewers can add their names. When adding a text field, you'll also want to add a label. The label tells viewers what information should be entered into the field.

1 Click the Forms tab in the Objects palette. The Forms tab contains a variety of elements that you can add to a form, including the Form element icon itself.

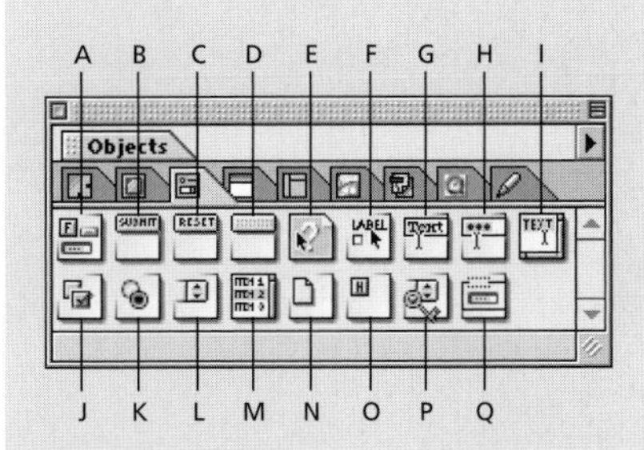

A. Form B. Submit Button C. Reset Button D. Button E. Form Input Image F. Label G. Text Field H. Password I. Text Area J. Check Box K. Radio Button L. Popup M. List Box N. File Browser O. Hidden P. Key Generator Q. Fieldset

2 Drag a Label icon from the Objects palette to the second cell of the table.

3 Select the word Label. Then type **Name** to change the label text.

To quickly select the label text, triple-click it.

4 Select the text that you just typed, and choose 2 from the Font Size menu (None) on the toolbar.

Now you'll add the text field for the visitor's name.

5 Click after the label to insert a cursor. (Be sure to click after the label, not the label text.) Then press the spacebar to add a space.

6 Drag a Text Field icon from the Objects palette to the cursor on the page.

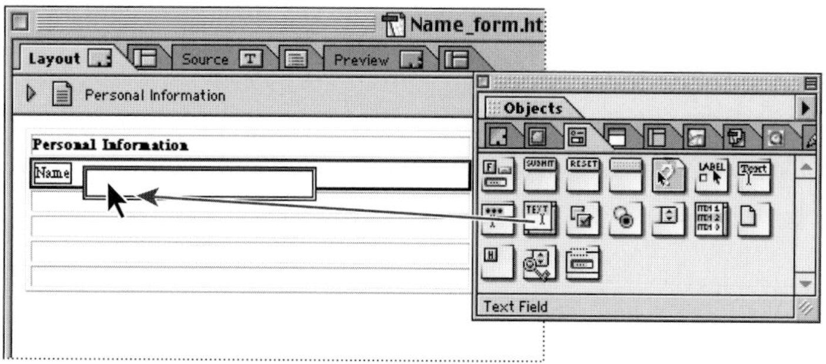

Dragging text field to table cell

The Inspector changes to the Form Text Field Inspector.

7 In the Form Text Field Inspector, enter **nameField** for Name. This names the text field.

8 For Content (Mac OS) or Value (Windows) type **Enter name here.**

The text that you just entered appears in the text field on the page. When filling out the text field, visitors can replace the text with their own information.

If you prefer to design your form without the use of labels, you can simply enter information for the text field in the Content (Mac OS) or Value (Windows) text box instead.

9 Enter **20** for Visible, and press Enter or Return. This is the number of characters that can be displayed in the field.

10 Enter **40** for Max, and press Enter or Return. This is the maximum number of characters that can be entered into the field.

Adding address fields

Now you'll add three text fields to the table that visitors will use to enter their e-mail address and postal information. To save time, you'll begin by copying and pasting the label and text field from the second cell of the table to the third, fourth, and fifth cells.

1 In the document window, select the contents of the second cell in the table. (The second cell contains the Name label and the text field that contains the text, "Enter name here.") An easy way to do this is to place the insertion point in the cell, and then choose Edit > Select All.

2 Ctrl-drag (Windows) or Option-drag (Mac OS) from the second cell down to the third cell. The contents of the second and third cell should now match.

3 Ctrl/Option-drag from the third cell down to the fourth cell. The contents of the third and fourth cells should now match.

4 Ctrl/Option-drag from the fourth cell down to the fifth cell. The contents of the fourth and fifth cells should now match.

5 Change the label text in the third cell to **E-Mail**, change the label text in the fourth cell to **Address 1**, and change the label text in the fifth cell to **Address 2**.

6 Select the text field in the third cell with the "E-Mail" label. (Be sure to select the text field, not the label.) In the Form Text Field Inspector, enter **emailField** for Name.

7 Delete the text in the Content (Mac OS) or Value (Windows) text box. Most viewers will understand what to enter in this field by following the example set by the name field. Alternatively, you could edit the Content (Mac OS) or Value (Windows) field by replacing the word "name" with "e-mail address."

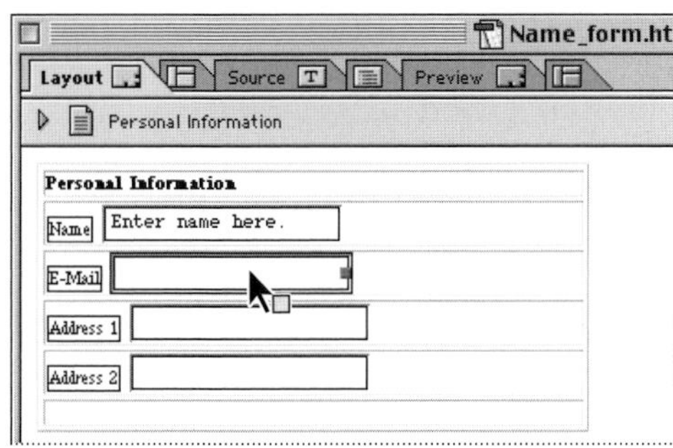

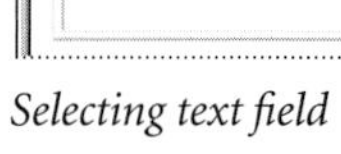

Selecting text field

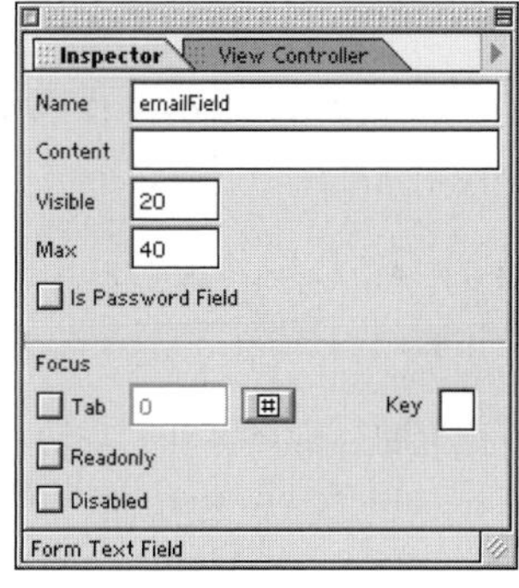

Specifying its properties

8 Select the text field in the fourth cell with the "Address 1" label. In the Form Text Field Inspector, enter **address1Field** for Name. Delete or change the text in the Content (Mac OS) or Value (Windows) text box.

9 Select the text field in the fifth cell with the "Address 2" label. In the Form Text Field Inspector, enter **address2Field** for Name. Delete or change the text in the Content (Mac OS) or Value (Windows) field.

Notice that every text field has an Is Password Field option in the Form Text Field Inspector. You select this option when you want a viewer to enter a password into the field.

Aligning table cells

Now you'll use the Table Inspector to align the contents of the table cells that contain text fields.

1 Move the pointer over the right or bottom edge of the second table cell until the pointer changes to an arrow. Click to select the cell.

The Inspector changes to the Table Inspector, with the Cell tab automatically selected.

2 Shift-click the third, fourth, and fifth table cells to add them to the selection. All table cells that contain text fields should now be selected.

3 In the Table Inspector, choose Middle from the Vertical Alignment menu. Choose Right from the Horizontal Alignment menu.

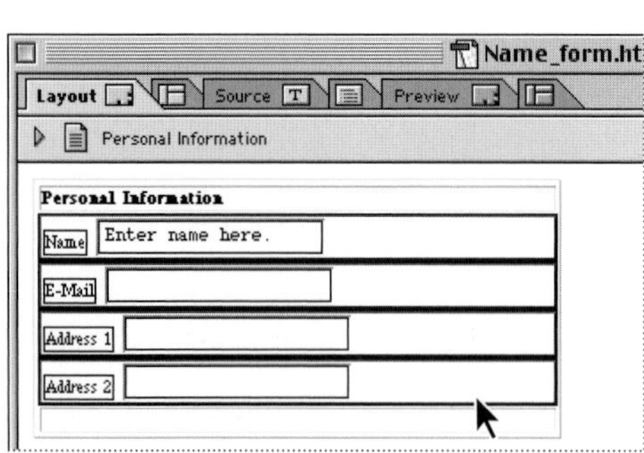

Selecting all cells that contain text fields

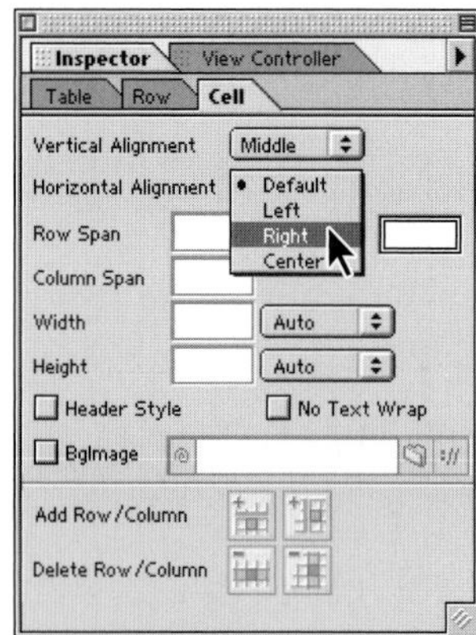

Choosing middle vertical and right horizontal alignment

4 Click in the blank space outside the table to deselect its table cells.

5 Choose File > Save to save the page.

Linking labels to text fields

Now you'll link each label to its corresponding text field on the page. By linking a label to a text field, viewers can activate the text field by clicking its label. For example, viewers can click the "Name" label to insert a cursor in the text box for entering their name.

First you'll link the "Name:" label to its corresponding text field.

1 Move the pointer to an edge of the "Name" label, so that the pointer turns into this ( ). Then click the label to select it. The Inspector changes to the Form Label Inspector.

2 In the Form Label Inspector, drag from the Point and Shoot button ( ) to the text field that corresponds to the "Name" label. The Reference text box in the Form Label Inspector displays a reference to the text field named nameField. The automatically generated number in the reference helps Adobe GoLive associate the label and field.

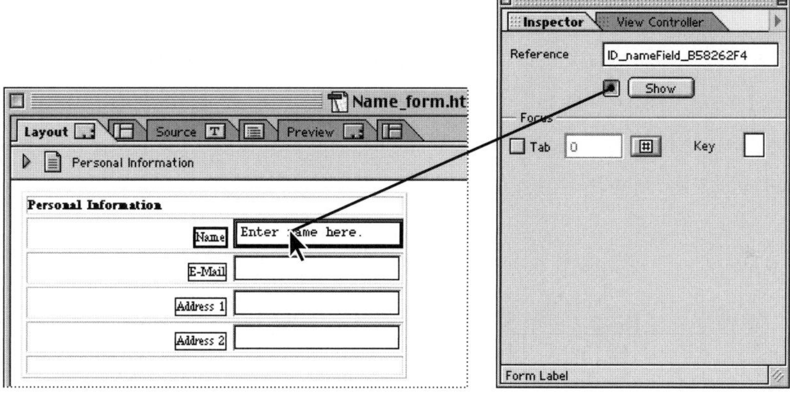

Linking label to text field

3 Select the "E-Mail" label, and link it to its corresponding text field using the Point and Shoot button in the Form Label Inspector.

4 Link the "Address 1" and "Address 2" labels to their corresponding text fields.

Note: *If you copy and paste a label that has been linked to a form field, you need to relink the new label to the correct field. Otherwise, both labels will refer to the same field.*

5 Choose File > Save to save the page.

Creating a pop-up menu

Pop-up menus provide viewers with multiple options from which they can choose. Now you'll add a pop-up menu that viewers will use to choose the country in which they live.

1 Drag a Label icon from the Objects palette to the sixth cell of the table.

2 Select the word Label. Then type **Country** to change the label text.

3 Select the text that you just typed, and choose 2 from the Font Size menu on the toolbar.

4 Click after the label to insert a cursor. (Be sure to click after the label, not the label text.) Then press the spacebar to add a space.

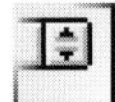

5 Drag a Popup icon from the Objects palette to the cursor on the page. A placeholder for the pop-up menu appears on the page.

6 Move the pointer over the right or bottom edge of the sixth table cell until the pointer changes to an arrow. Click to select the cell.

The Inspector changes to the Table Inspector, with the Cell tab automatically selected.

7 In the Table Inspector, choose Middle from the Vertical Alignment menu. Choose Right from the Horizontal Alignment.

8 Select the pop-up menu placeholder on the page. The Inspector changes to the Form Popup Inspector.

9 In the Form Popup Inspector, enter **countryPopup** for Name. This names the pop-up menu.

You'll leave the Rows option at 1. This means that one row (or item) will be visible in the pop-up menu.

Now you'll use the Form Popup Inspector to add items to the pop-up menu.

10 In the Focus list box, click the first item to select it. (The first item is currently labeled "First" with a value of "one.")

11 In the first text box at the bottom of the Form Popup Inspector, enter **Canada** to replace the word "First," and press Tab. In the second text box, enter **Country_Canada** to replace the word "one," and press Enter or Return.

The label “Canada” will appear as an item in the pop-up menu, and the value “Country_Canada” would be returned to the CGI script for the form when a visitor chooses this item.

12 Select the second item in the Focus list box. (The second item is currently labeled “Second” with a value of “two.”) Use the text boxes at the bottom of the Form Popup Inspector to enter **France** as its label and **Country_France** as its value.

13 Select the third item in the Focus list box, and enter **Germany** as its label and **Country_Germany** as its value.

Now you’ll add a fourth item to the pop-up menu.

14 To create a fourth item, click New. Then enter **USA** as its label and **Country_USA** as its value.

By default, the first item that you added to the pop-up menu (Canada) will display in the browser. However, because most potential viewers for this particular Web site will be from the United States, you’ll change the default to display the USA.

15 In the Form Popup Inspector, click the check box next to the text box that contains the text “USA.”

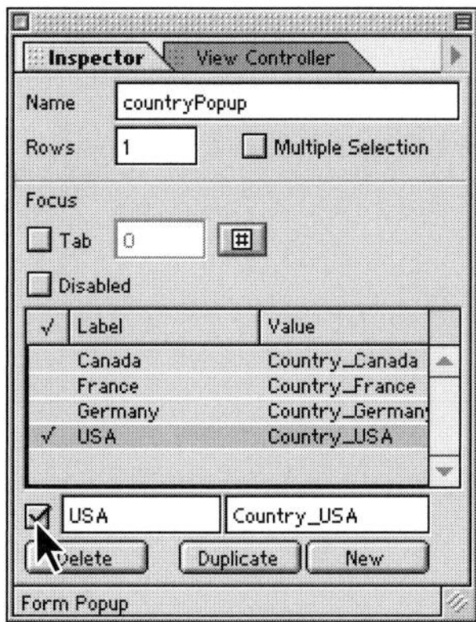

Specifying menu item display by default

The pop-up menu on the page now displays the text “USA.”

16 Choose File > Save to save the page.

Setting table properties

You have finished adding the form fields to the table. Now you'll remove the border from the table and set other table properties. If you plan on removing the table's border in your forms, we recommend that you do it. It's easier to select table cells when the border is set at its default value of 1.

1 Move the pointer over the left or top edge of the table, so that the pointer turns into this ( ). Then click the table to select it. The Inspector changes to the Table Inspector, with the Table tab automatically selected.

You can use the Inspector to determine whether you have selected the table or a form field.

2 In the Table Inspector, enter **0** for Border, **2** for Cell Pad, **0** for Cell Space, and press Enter or Return.

3 Choose File > Save to save the page.

Storing frequently used objects

With Adobe GoLive, it's easy to copy and paste objects from one page to another. You can store frequently used objects in the Site Extras tab of the Objects palette, and then quickly add the objects to your pages.

Now you'll store the table that you've just created in the Site Extras tab of the Objects palette, so that you can quickly add it to the membership application form.

1 Click the Site Extras tab ( ) in the Objects palette.

2 Click the left or top edge of the table on the page to select it.

3 Drag the selected table from the page to the Site Extras tab of the Objects palette. (Release the table when a thick black line appears around the tab panel.) An icon for the table appears in the Objects palette.

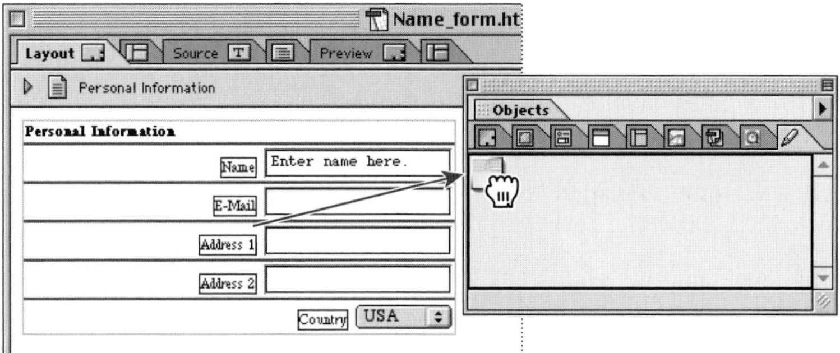

Dragging table to Site Extras tab of Objects palette

4 Double-click the table icon to display the Palette Item Editor. Then enter **Name and Address** for Item Name, and click OK. This names the table icon.

Objects in the Site Extras tab of the Objects palette are stored in your Adobe GoLive preferences. They can be added to pages in an existing site or a new site, and remain in the Objects palette until you clear or reinstall your preferences. You can delete an object from the Site Extras tab by selecting it, and choosing Edit > Clear or pressing Delete.

Now you'll use the Site Extras tab of the Objects palette to add the table to the membership application form.

5 Choose File > Close to close the Name_form.html file.

6 Choose File > Open, and open the Membership.html file. The path to the file is Lesson10/10Start/Forms Folder/Forms/Membership.html.

The membership application form opens.

7 Resize the Membership.html window to view as much of the form as possible.

Notice that the form is missing a few images and form fields.

8 Drag the Name and Address table icon from the Objects palette to the table cell in the form that is directly below the words "Membership Application."

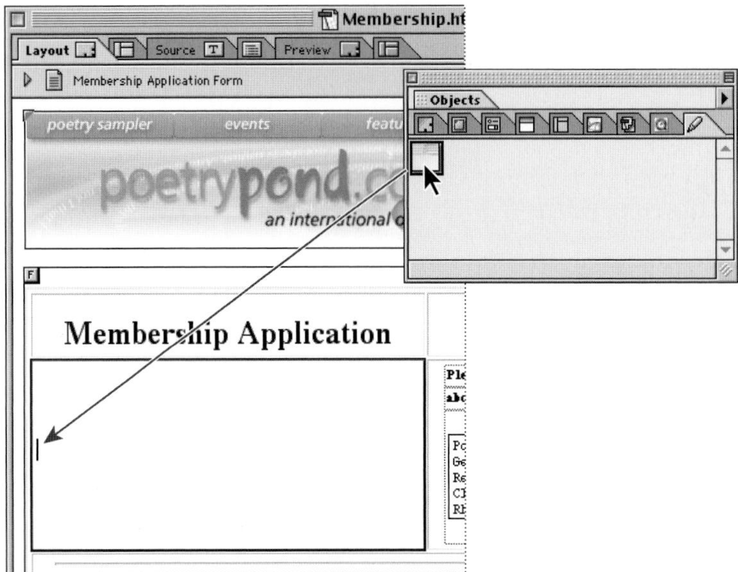

Dragging table icon from Objects palette to membership application form

The main table for the membership application form has been set up so that the Personal Information table fits properly in its designated table cell. Normally, you'll need to adjust the size of a cell in the main table, so that the nested table fits properly.

Before you begin creating a form, it's a good idea to carefully plan its layout. You should decide on the contents of the main table, paying special attention to whether or not you will add nested tables to it. Careful planning will save you from having to redesign your form's layout during the creation process.

9 Choose File > Save to save the page.

Adding an image that spans two columns

Now you'll replace the words "Membership Application" by adding an image to the page. First you'll adjust the table columns so that the words "Membership Application" span two columns.

1 Move your pointer over the cell that contains the words "Membership Application," so that the pointer changes to an arrow. Then click to select the cell.

The Inspector changes to the Table Inspector, with the Cell tab automatically selected.

2 In the Table Inspector, enter **2** for Column Span, and press Enter or Return.

Now you'll replace the text with an image.

3 Select the words "Membership Application," and press Delete.

You'll add the image to the form using a file in the site window.

4 Choose File > Open, and open the Forms.site file. The path to the file is Lesson10/10Start/Forms Folder/Forms.site.

The site window opens. It contains a Media folder, the Index.html file, and the Membership.html file. It also contains the Name_form.html file that you created earlier in this lesson; however, for this file to display in the site window, you need to update the contents of the window.

5 Click the Update button (✔) on the toolbar to update the contents of the site window.

6 In the site window, expand the Media folder. Then drag Form_header.jpg from the Media folder in the site window to the empty table cell that previously contained the words "Membership Application." The image is added to the cell.

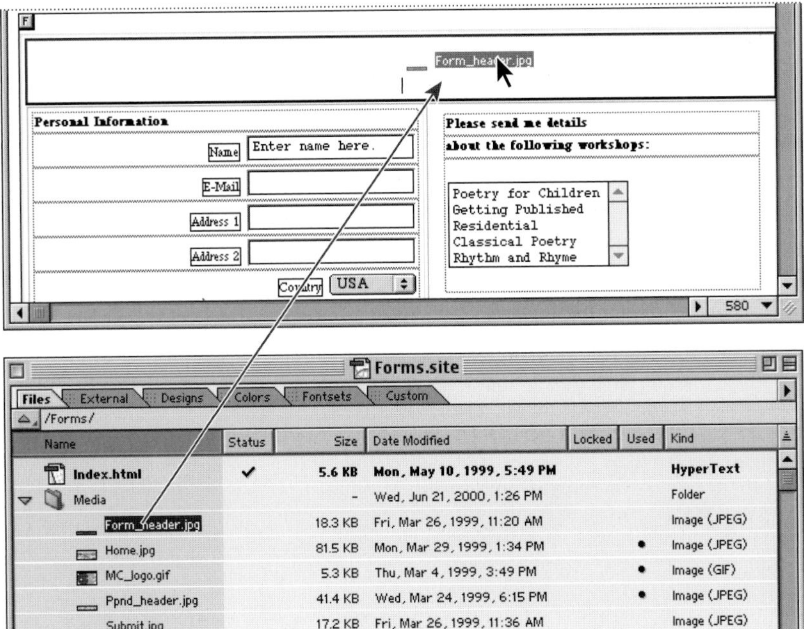

Dragging image file from site window to table cell

7 Choose File > Save to save the page.

Adding radio buttons

The Payment Information section in the lower right corner of the form already contains a nested table with one row and five columns that has been inserted into the main table. You'll add a group of radio buttons to this section so that viewers can select a payment type.

Payment Information section of form

If you created the Payment Type section from scratch, you would create it much in the same way as the Personal Information section. You would create a table with one row and five columns. Then, you would type the text "Payment Type" in the first cell and insert images of a MasterCard and VISA card into the third and fifth cells. You would then add radio buttons to the second and fourth cells, as you are about to do in this lesson.

1 Click the Forms tab (▤) of the Objects palette. Then drag the Radio Button icon from the palette to the empty table cell located to the left of the MasterCard image on the page.

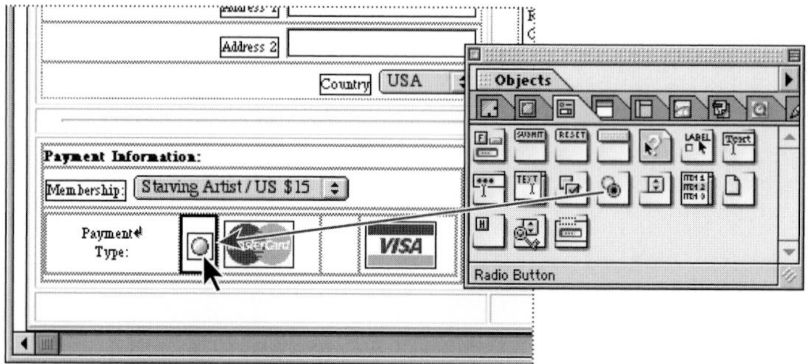

Dragging Radio Button icon from Objects palette to table cell

The Inspector changes to the Form Radio Button Inspector.

2 Drag another Radio Button icon from the Objects palette to the empty table cell located to the left of the VISA image on the page.

You can also copy the existing radio button on the page and paste it into the empty table cell. To do this, Ctrl-drag (Windows) or Option-drag (Mac OS) the radio button to the empty table cell.

3 Click the first radio button that you added to the page to select it.

4 In the Form Radio Button Inspector, enter **paymentType** for Group. This names the group of radio buttons.

You'll use the same group name for the second radio button on the page. Using the same group name for the two radio buttons ensures that visitors can only select one option from the group.

5 Enter **mastercard** for Value. This is the value that would be returned to the CGI script for the form when a viewer chooses this option.

6 Select the Selected option. This makes MasterCard the preselected option.

Note: *It's not required that you preselect any of the radio buttons.*

7 Select the second radio button that you added to the page.

8 In the Form Radio Button Inspector, choose paymentType from the Group pop-up menu next to the text box. Enter **visa** for Value.

9 Choose File > Save to save the page.

Now you'll preview the page in Adobe GoLive to test the form fields that you've added to the page so far.

10 Click the Layout Preview tab in the document window to preview the page in Adobe GoLive.

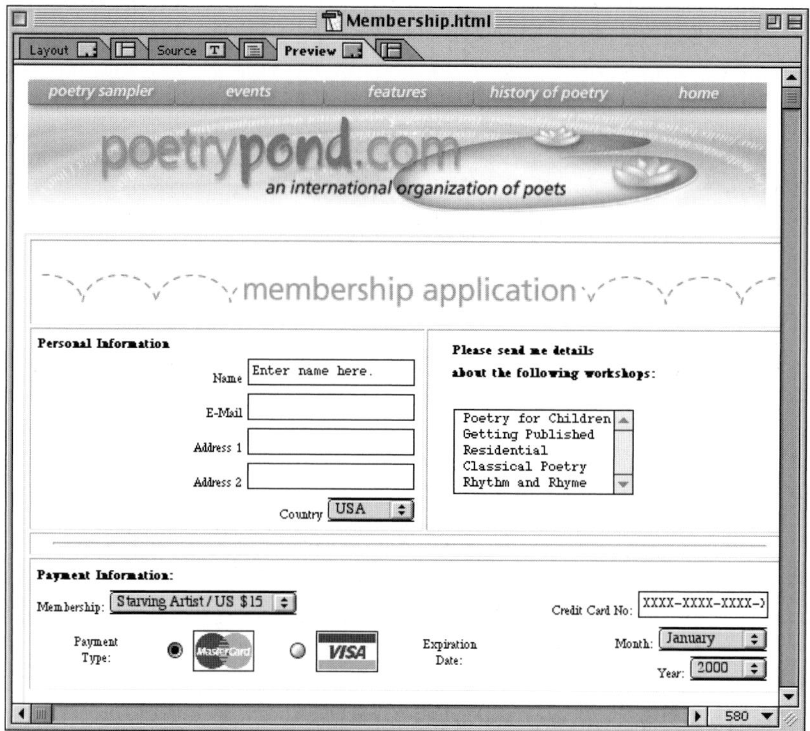

Previewing form fields that you've added to page

11 Test the form fields that you've created by entering your name and addresses, choosing a country, and selecting a payment type.

12 Click the Layout Editor tab in the document window to return to Layout view.

Modifying a list box

A list box in the upper right of the form provides viewers with a list of workshops from which they can choose. The list box was created much in the same way as the Country pop-up menu. You'll make several changes to the list box. First you'll specify that the list box display six items rather than five.

1 Click the list box to select it. The Inspector changes to the Form List Box Inspector.

In the Form List Box Inspector, notice how the items for the list box have been entered in the same way as the Country pop-up menu. Each item has a specified label and value.

2 Enter **6** for Rows, and press Enter or Return. This will increase the rows (or items) visible in the list box to six.

Now you'll make the list box into a multiselection form field, so that users can select more than one workshop.

3 Select the Multiple Selection option.

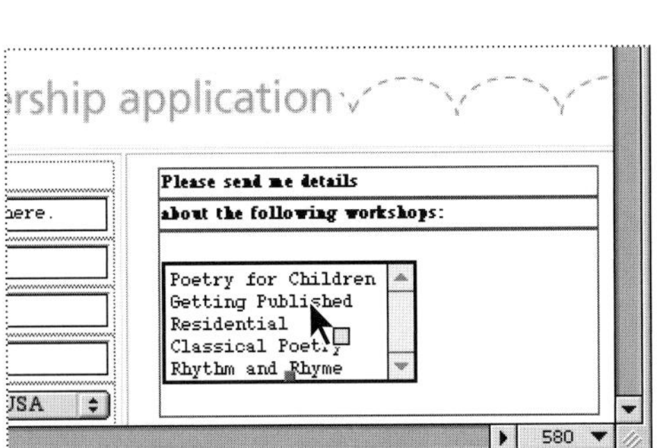

Selecting list box

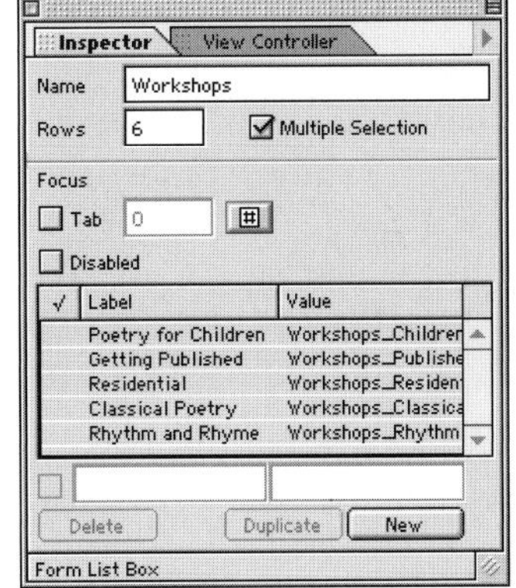

Setting options in Form List Box Inspector

Now you'll add three more items to the list box.

4 Click New to create a new item. In the first text box at the bottom of the Form List Box Inspector, enter **History of Poetry**, and press Tab. In the second text box, enter **Workshops_History**, and press Enter or Return.

5 If necessary, scroll down the Focus list box in the Form List Box Inspector to view the item you just added. (As an alternative, you can increase the size of the Inspector by dragging its lower right corner.)

6 Click New to create another new item, and enter **European Poetry** as its label and **Workshops_European** as its value.

7 Click New to create another new item, and enter **African Poetry** as its label and **Workshops_African** as its value.

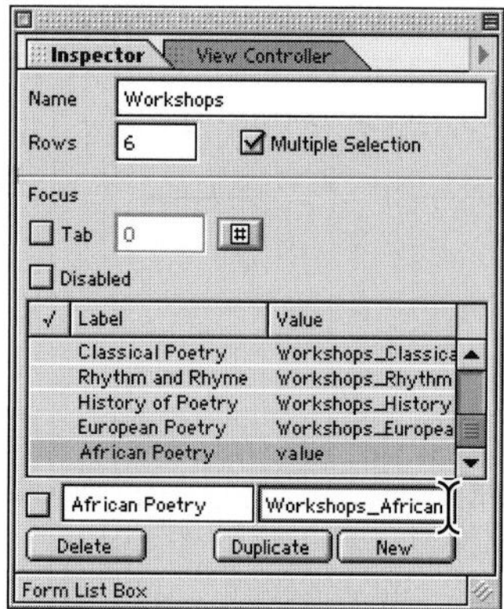

Creating additional labels and values in Focus list box

8 Choose File > Save to save the page.

Now you'll preview the page in Adobe GoLive to verify that the list box works as it should.

9 Click the Layout Preview tab in the document window. To select more than one item in the list box, click the first item and then Command-click (Mac OS) or Ctrl-click (Windows) to add additional items to your selection. You can also Shift-click to select a contiguous range of items in the list.

10 Click the Layout Editor tab in the document window to return to the Layout view.

Adding a clickable image

Next, you'll add a clickable image to the form for submitting the application over the Web. This feature is one of the ways you can enable viewers to submit a form. An alternative way is to add a Submit button, which is discussed in "Adding a Reset button" on page 296.

1 If necessary, scroll down the Membership.html window to display the bottom of the form. The main table used to lay out the form has two empty cells in its last row.

2 Click below the MasterCard image to insert a cursor in the empty table cell on the left.

3 Drag a Form Input Image icon from the Forms tab of the Objects palette to the cursor on the page. A Form Input Image placeholder is added to the table cell, and the Inspector changes to the Form Input Image Inspector.

4 If necessary, rearrange your desktop so that the Form Input Image placeholder is visible in the document window, and the Submit.jpg file is visible in the Media folder in the site window. Then click the Form Input Image placeholder on the page to reselect it.

5 Drag from the Point and Shoot button (◎) in the Form Input Image Inspector to Submit.jpg in the Media folder in the site window. The submit application image is added to the table cell.

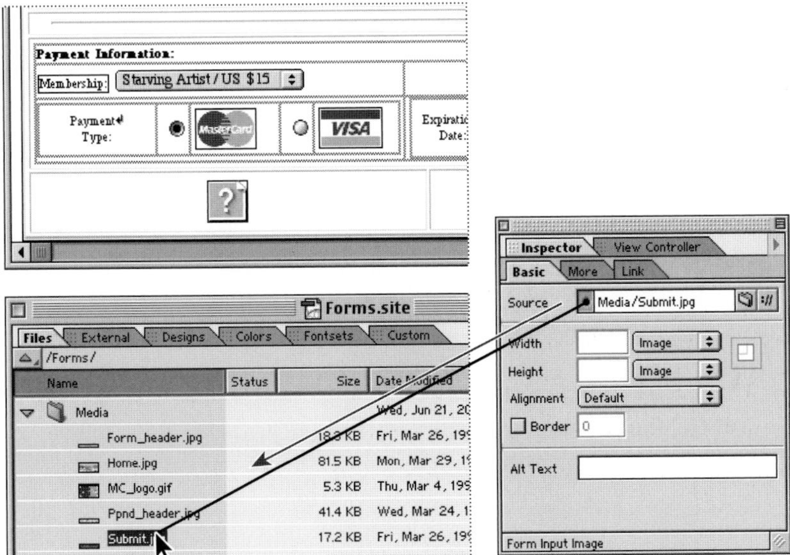

Connecting Form Input Image placeholder on page to image file in site window

6 In the Alt Text box, enter **Submit Image** as an alternative text message for the image, and press Enter or Return.

7 Click the More tab of the Form Input Image Inspector. Enter **submitImage** for Name next to the Is Form option, and press Enter or Return. This names the clickable image.

8 Click the Basic tab of the Form Input Image Inspector. Select the Border option so it's checked and enter a value of **0**, if necessary. This prevents a border from marring the appearance of the image.

9 Choose File > Save to save the page.

Adding a Reset button

You can add buttons to your form in at least two ways. The first method is to create an image of a button and link it to one or more actions. The second method is to use the Submit or Reset button in the Forms tab of the Objects palette. The following describes what happens when the viewer clicks one of these premade buttons:

- The Submit button sends a visitor's information to your database and closes the form.
- The Reset button deletes all of the visitor's information and returns the form to its default settings.

Now you'll add a Reset button to the form.

1 Drag a Reset Button icon from the Forms tab of the Objects palette to the empty table cell to the right of the submit application image. The Inspector changes to the Form Button Inspector.

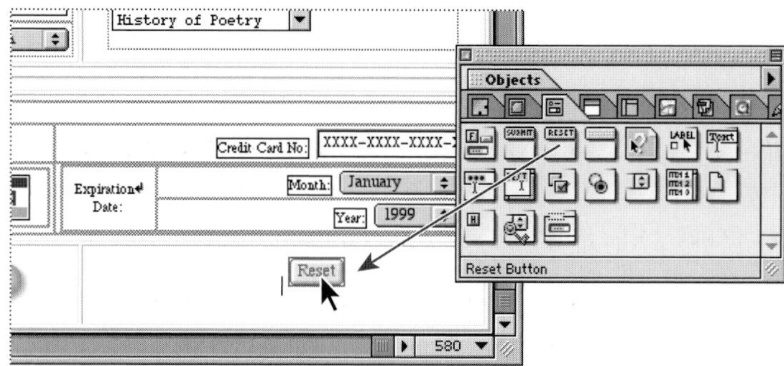

Dragging Reset Button icon from Objects palette to table cell

The necessary options for the Reset button are preset. You enter a name and label only if you want to create a Normal button.

For more information about creating a Normal button, see "Setting up buttons and check boxes" in Chapter 12 of the *Adobe GoLive 5.0 User Guide.*

2 Choose File > Save to save the page.

Changing the main table's border and cell spacing

Now that you have finished adding images and form fields to the form, you can remove the border of the main table and the cell space of its table cells. (Both the border and cell space are currently set at 2, which has made it easier for you to select the table and its cells while modifying the form.)

1 In the document window, click the left or top edge of the main table to select it. The Inspector changes to the Table Inspector, with the Table tab automatically selected.

2 In the Table Inspector, enter **0** for Border, **0** for Cell Space, and press Enter or Return.

3 Choose File > Save to save the page.

4 Click the Layout Preview tab in the document window, and check how the page appears in Preview.

5 Click the Layout Editor tab in the document window to return to Layout view.

Creating a tabbing chain

Now you'll add a navigational aid to your form—a tabbing chain that allows viewers to use the Tab key to move between form fields. To create a tabbing chain, you specify the order in which the form fields are selected by the Tab key. Adding a tabbing chain should be the last thing that you do to your form, after you are satisfied with its layout.

Note: *Some Web browsers will automatically allow users to use the Tab key to move between text fields. In addition, some browsers only allow users to use the Tab key to move between text fields and not other types of form fields. Also, be aware that the tabbing order that you create may or may not be recognized, depending on the browser and which version the visitor is using.*

You can start your tabbing chain with any form field. You'll start the tabbing chain for this form with the text field for entering a name.

1 Select the text field on the page that contains the text "Enter name here." The Inspector changes to the Form Text Field Inspector.

2 In the Form Text Field Inspector, select the Tab option. Enter **1** in the Tab text box. This specifies the text field as the first form field in the tabbing chain.

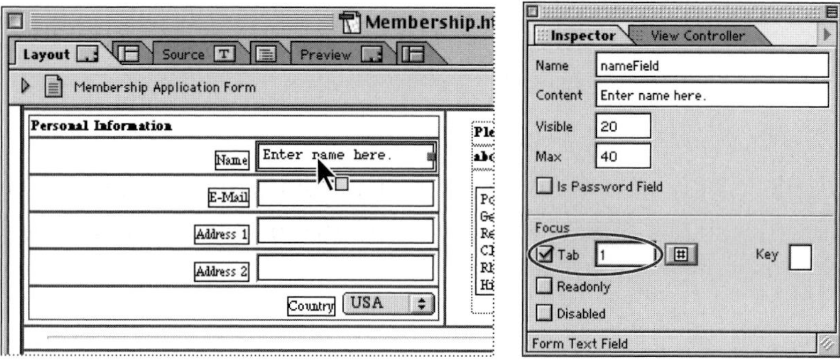

Selecting text field

Specifying text field as first in tabbing chain

3 Click the Start/Stop Indexing button (⊞). Yellow squares appear on each form field that can be part of the tabbing chain. (The yellow squares also appear on the form labels, although you can't add labels to your tabbing chain.)

The yellow square in the text field for entering a name already has a 1 in it, indicating that this field is the first in the tabbing chain.

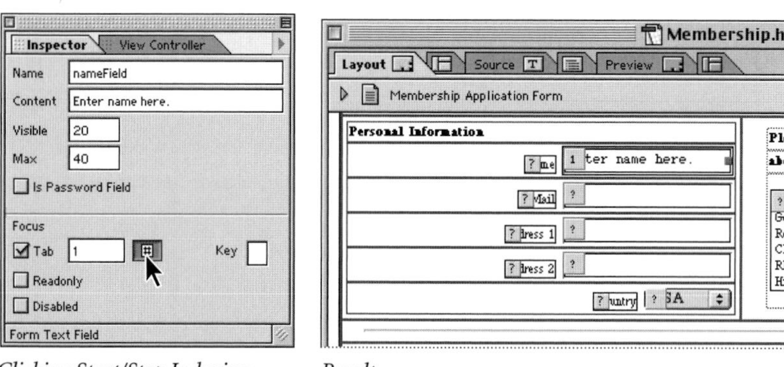

Clicking Start/Stop Indexing button

Result

4 Click the text field for entering an e-mail address. A 2 appears in its yellow square.

5 Continue to create the tabbing chain by clicking on the yellow squares for the remaining form fields. (Be sure to click on the yellow squares for the form fields, not the labels.)

6 When you have finished creating the tabbing chain, click the Start/Stop Indexing button in the Inspector. The tabbing chain has been created, and the yellow squares disappear.

If you want to change the order of your tabbing chain, you can select each form field and enter a new number for it in the Tab text box of the Inspector.

7 Choose File > Save to save the page.

8 Choose Special > Show in Default Browser. Place your cursor in the text field for entering a name, and press Tab repeatedly to check that the tabbing chain works as it should.

9 Close your browser.

10 Choose File > Close to close the Membership.html file.

In this lesson, you've learned how to lay out form fields using a table, and how to add a variety of form fields to a form. Other form fields and functions that you can add to your forms include the following: check boxes, a file browser, a key generator, read-only and disabled form fields, bounding boxes with legends to group form fields, and hidden form fields.

For complete information about creating forms in Adobe GoLive, see Chapter 12, "Creating Forms," of the *Adobe GoLive 5.0 User Guide*.

Review questions

1 What are form fields?

2 Why do you need to add the Form element icon to each form?

3 Why should you avoid creating forms using a layout grid?

4 How can you add a clickable image to a form?

5 How do you add an item to a list box?

6 How do you create a tabbing chain for your form?

Review answers

1 Form fields are elements that you can add to your forms, such as text fields, radio buttons, or list boxes. Viewers can interact with form fields by entering information, clicking items, or selecting items.

2 The Form element creates the container for a form, and allows the form to display and function properly in a browser.

3 A form created using a layout grid can vary according to a visitor's browser and screen resolution.

4 To add a clickable image to a form, you can do one of the following:

- Drag an Input Image icon from the Objects palette to the form, and use the Point and Shoot button in the Input Image Inspector to connect the placeholder to an image file.
- Drag an Input Image icon from the Objects palette to the form, and use the Browse button in the Input Image Inspector to browse for an image file.
- Drag an image file directly to the input image placeholder in the form.

You should also make sure that the Is Form option is selected in the Input Image Inspector.

5 In the Form List Box Inspector, click New to create a new item. Then enter a label and value for the item.

6 To create a tabbing chain, select any form field in your form, and click the Start/Stop Indexing button in the Inspector. Click the yellow squares for the form fields (not the labels) in the order in which you want viewers to be able to select the form fields using the Tab key. Click the Start/Stop Indexing button in the Inspector to turn off the tabbing chain.

Lesson 11

```
<TITLE>Wel
<STYLE TYPE=

e{color:maroon;font

</STYLE>
AD>
Y>
<!-- Begin main table -->
<TABLE BORDER="4" CELLPADDIN
06">
    <TR>
        <TD><A
tp://www.adobe.com/">Adobe</A>
        <TD>GoLive</TD>
        <TD><IMG BORDER="0" HEIGH
le.gif" ALT="Title"></TD>
    </TR>
    <TR>
        <TD><SPAN CLASS="headli
AN></TD>
    </TR>
    <TR>
        <TD><B>DHTML
    </TR>
</TABLE>
```

11 Using Cascading Style Sheets

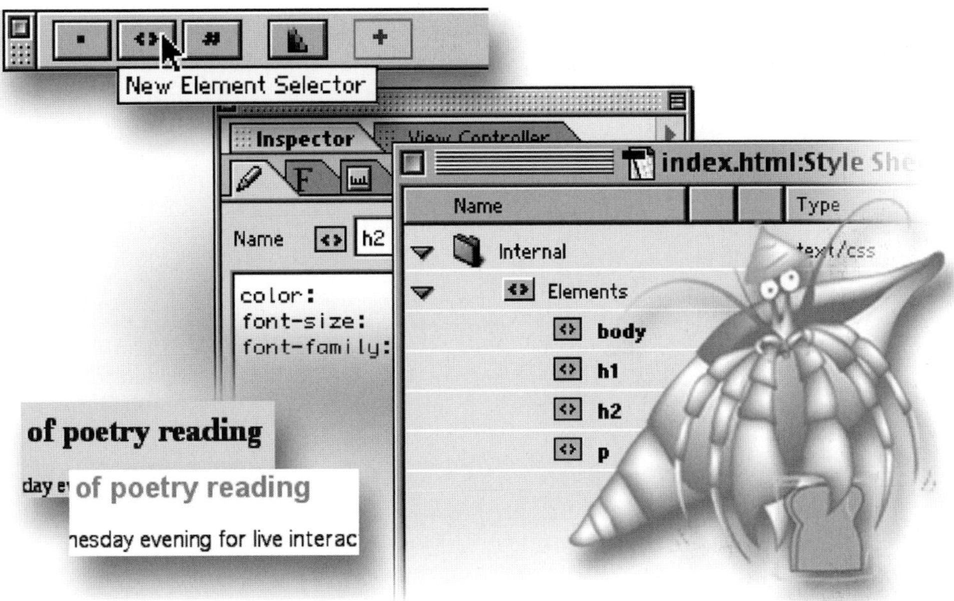

Using style sheets, you can easily update the style of large amounts of text and maintain consistency in typography and formatting throughout a Web site. Good, consistent design makes a site more inviting to visitors and easier to explore.

About this lesson

In this lesson, you'll learn how to:

• Identify styles applied to a document.

• Create styles that apply to HTML elements in a document, blocks of text, and only selected text.

• Update styles and apply style changes globally.

• Duplicate and modify existing styles.

• Change the page color and margins using styles.

• Differentiate between internal and external style sheets.

• Link external style sheets to a document, and use them to update a document's formatting.

This lesson takes approximately 1 hour to complete.

If needed, copy the Lesson11 folder onto your hard drive. As you work on this lesson, you'll overwrite the start files. If you need to restore the start files, copy them from the *Adobe GoLive 5.0 Classroom in a Book* CD.

If needed, copy the Lesson02 folder onto your hard drive. As you work on this lesson, you'll overwrite the start files. If you need to restore the start files, copy them from the *Adobe GoLive 5.0 Classroom in a Book* CD.

Note: *Windows users need to unlock the lesson files before using them. For more information, see "Copying the Classroom in a Book files" on page 2.*

For information on setting up your work area, see "Setting up your work area" on page 9.

Getting started

To see what you'll do in this lesson, first you'll view the final lesson file in your browser.

1 Start your browser.

2 Choose File > Open, and open the Index.html file. The path to the file is Lesson11/11End/PoetryPond.com folder/PoetryPond.com/Index.html.

3 Scroll through the page, and note its formatting.

4 Click the link "Benjamin Lucas." All the formatting, including the formatting of links, is controlled by a cascading style sheet.

5 When you have finished viewing the file, close your browser.

About style sheets

HTML is a simple language intended to control the structure of information, not its presentation. Style sheets let Web designers enhance HTML's basic formatting by using styles to position text precisely, control type, and format elements on the page.

Cascading style sheets (CSS for short) are a simple way to add style to HTML documents and enhance the basic formatting of HTML elements. A style sheet is a set of stylistic rules that describe how HTML documents should appear to viewers. In HTML code, a *rule* is a statement about a stylistic aspect of one or more elements, in which a *selector* specifies what elements a *declaration*—consisting of a property and its value—will affect. For example, the style rule h1 { color : red } makes all head level 1s in a document appear red.

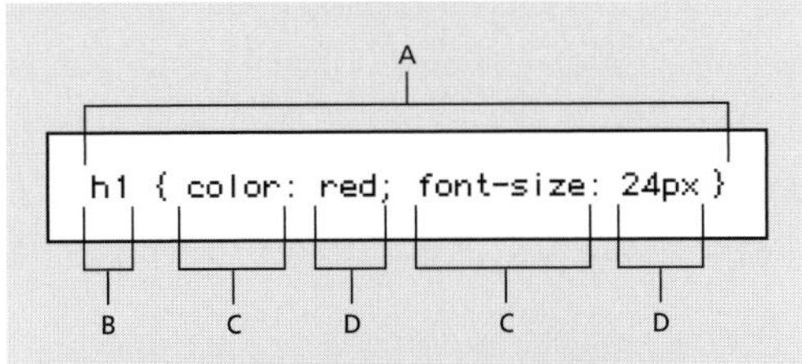

A. Rule B. Selector C. Property D. Value

In the past, designers had to understand these concepts in-depth so they could write cascading style sheet code by hand in HTML. Now Adobe GoLive writes this code for you as you apply simple formatting commands much like in familiar word-processing or page layout applications. In addition, styles are applied in a cascading fashion, from the most general to the most specific.

Adobe GoLive supports Level 1 Cascading Style Sheets (CSS1), which are part of the HTML 4.0 specification. Major Web browsers that support style sheets include Microsoft Internet Explorer 3, 4, and 5.0; Netscape Navigator 4.0; and Netscape Communicator 4.0. (Microsoft and Netscape browsers differ in which CSS features they support.) Browsers must support CSS1 tags to be able to recognize and properly interpret style sheets.

A few considerations are key to using style sheets successfully:

• Be familiar with what style sheet properties are supported by current browsers. The CSS specification is constantly evolving. Refer to http://www.w3.org/Style for the latest information.

• Experiment with applying different properties to different HTML elements. It's important always to preview the results in the current browsers to test your style sheet's effectiveness.

Exploring the style sheet tools

Three Adobe GoLive tools let you create and edit style sheets, and link to external style sheets: the Style Sheet window, the Style Sheet toolbar, and the CSS Selector Inspector. This illustration shows the relationship between these three tools.

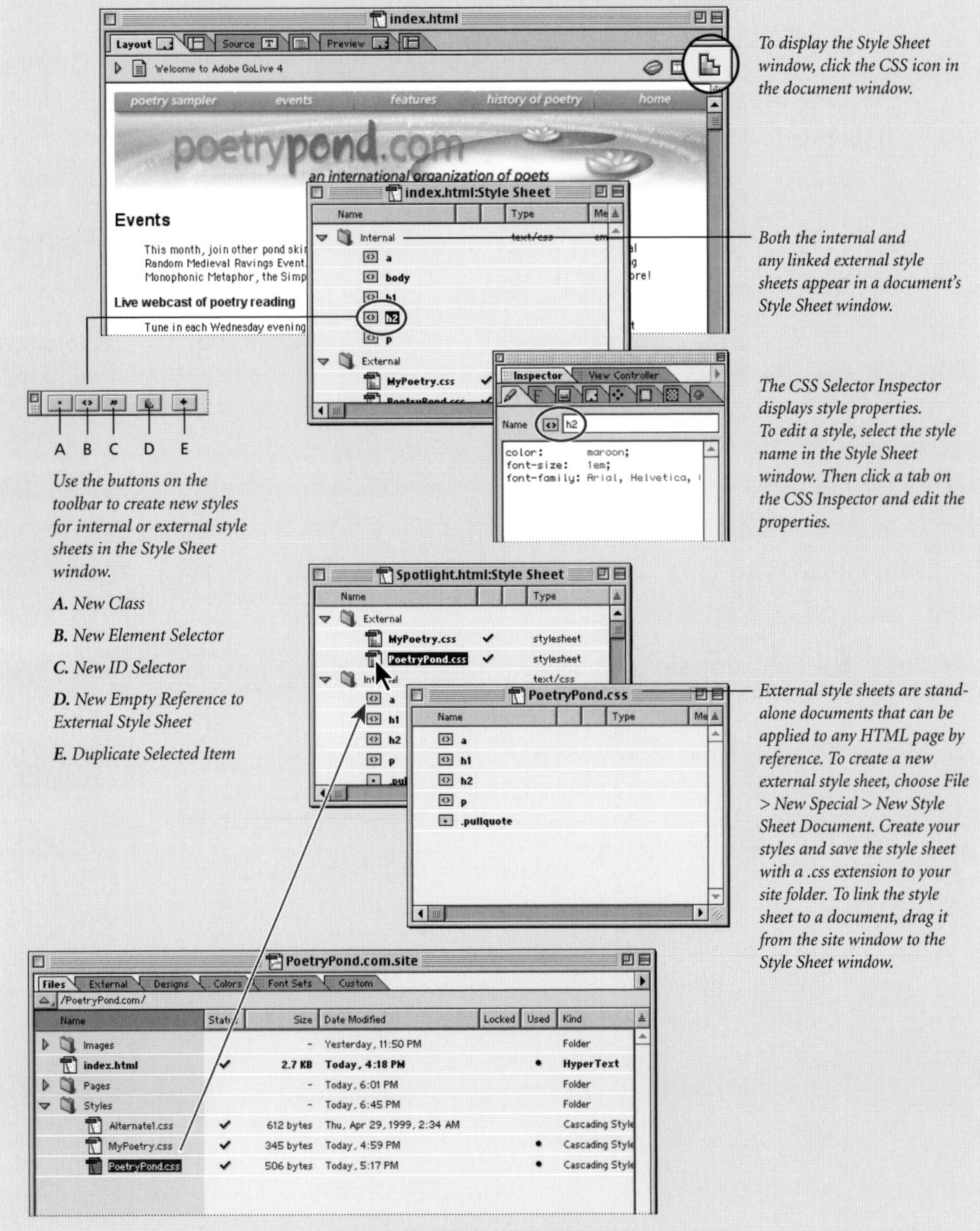

To display the Style Sheet window, click the CSS icon in the document window.

Both the internal and any linked external style sheets appear in a document's Style Sheet window.

The CSS Selector Inspector displays style properties. To edit a style, select the style name in the Style Sheet window. Then click a tab on the CSS Inspector and edit the properties.

Use the buttons on the toolbar to create new styles for internal or external style sheets in the Style Sheet window.

***A.** New Class*

***B.** New Element Selector*

***C.** New ID Selector*

***D.** New Empty Reference to External Style Sheet*

***E.** Duplicate Selected Item*

External style sheets are standalone documents that can be applied to any HTML page by reference. To create a new external style sheet, choose File > New Special > New Style Sheet Document. Create your styles and save the style sheet with a .css extension to your site folder. To link the style sheet to a document, drag it from the site window to the Style Sheet window.

Exploring style sheets

Adobe GoLive supports two different kinds of style sheets: internal and external. Internal and external style sheets differ in how they work with Web pages. Internal style sheets apply only to the document in which they were created, although their styles can be exported for use with other documents.

Far more flexible than internal style sheets, external style sheets can apply to a group of documents, or to an entire Web site. Rather than defining an internal style sheet for each and every page to which you want to apply some extra formatting, it's easier to create a stand-alone external style sheet document. You can then refer to this external style sheet from any page and make its style options available.

Exploring an internal style sheet

You'll start your work in the lesson by exploring a style sheet that was created with a document.

1 Start Adobe GoLive.

2 Choose File > Open, and open the PoetryPond.com.site file. The path to the file is Lesson11/11Start/PoetryPond.com folder/PoetryPond.com.site.

3 In the site window, double-click Index.html to open the home page of the PoetryPond.com Web site.

The basic structure and simple formatting of this document was achieved by applying the basic HTML elements such as <h1>, <h2>, and <p> to raw text. The finer styling such as the font size and color, margin widths, and even the white background of the document have been applied using a style sheet.

First, you'll view the document without the style sheet formatting.

4 Click the document window to make it active. In the View Controller, choose the Explorer 3 option for your platform (Windows or Mac OS) from the Root CSS pop-up menu.

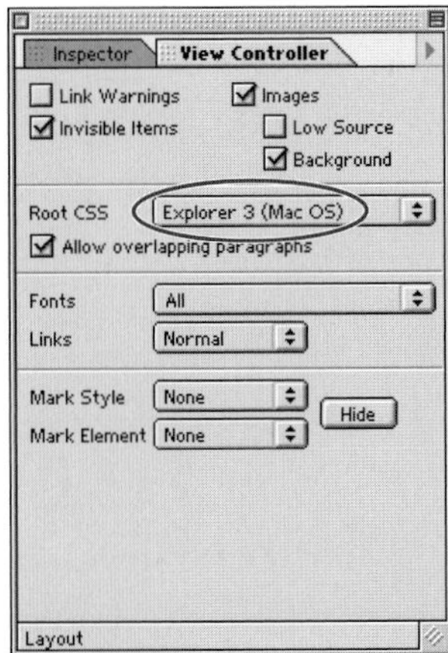

Choosing browser that does not support CSS in View Controller

Explorer 3 does not support CSS, so choosing it, in effect, turns off style sheets for the current document. In the document window, notice how the document display changes when the style sheet isn't used.

In this example, the headings lose their color properties, the fonts change to a larger serif face, and the background of the entire document reverts to the standard gray of a basic HTML page.

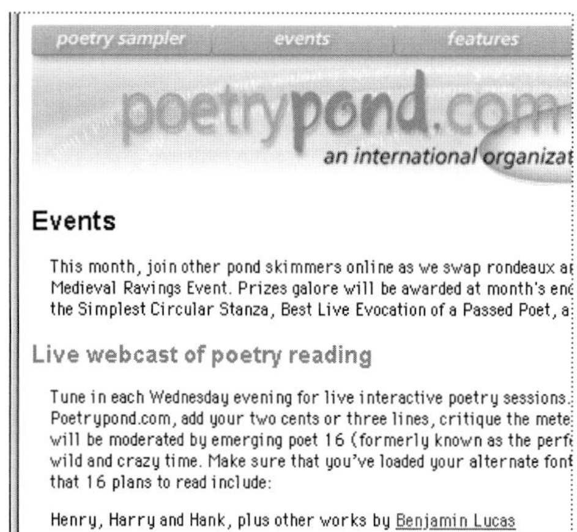

Style sheet active

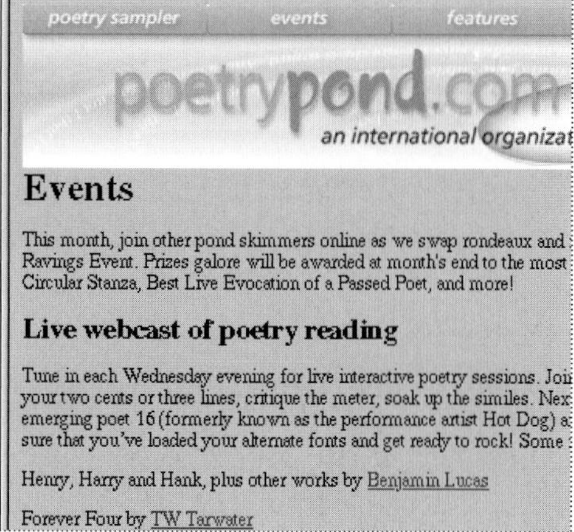

Style sheet turned off

You can see how the document got this basic HTML structure by checking the Format menu on the toolbar.

5 In the document window, insert the text cursor in the "Live webcast of poetry reading" heading, and then notice the Format menu on the toolbar.

The Format menu displays the text's current HTML formatting. Header 2 indicates that the text is tagged as an HTML <h2> element. Similarly the "Events" text is formatted as a Header 1, which translates to an HTML <h1> element; the body paragraphs are formatted as None, which translates to an HTML <p> element.

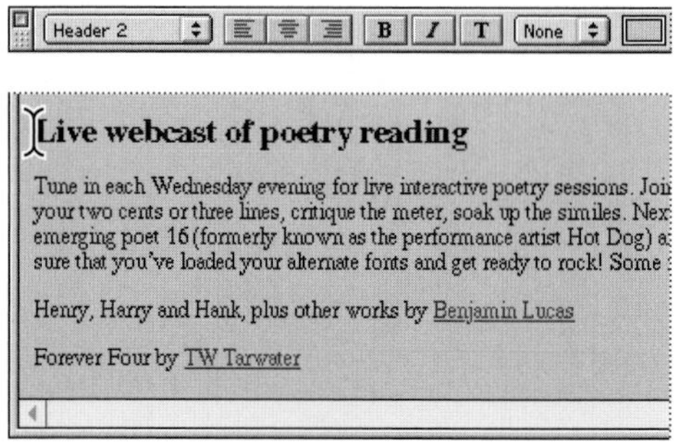

Header 2 format and corresponding text in document

6 If you're new to HTML, click the HTML Source Editor tab () in the document window to see how Adobe GoLive has written the HTML code and tagged the various chunks of text.

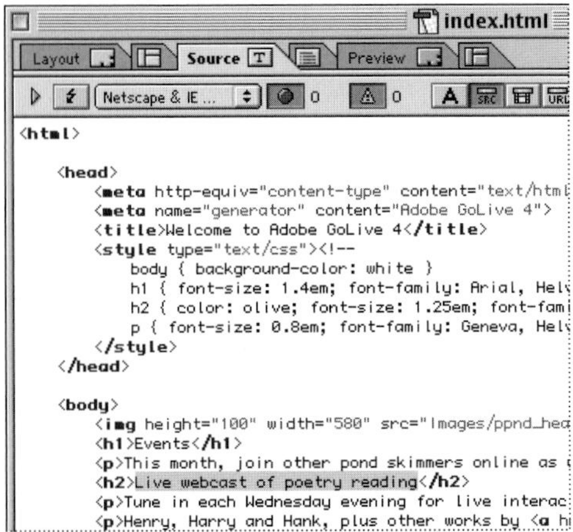

Source view

7 Click the Layout Editor tab () to return to the Layout view of the document.

Now you'll take a look at the formatting that the style sheet controls.

8 Choose Explorer 5 for your platform from the Root CSS pop-up menu in the View Controller. The document window now displays formatting with styles.

Using the Root CSS menu in the View Controller, you can choose any of the popular browsers and see how the visual presentation changes. However, previewing with the View Controller only simulates how the pages will appear in a browser, and is not a substitute for previewing pages in an actual browser.

9 To view the style sheet, click the CSS button ( ) in the upper right corner of the document window. This opens the Index.html Style Sheet window.

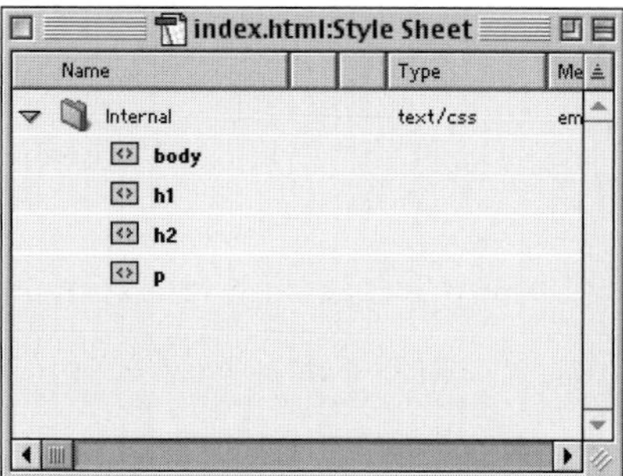

The Internal folder in the Style Sheet window displays the different style sheet selectors defined for this document already. You can see all the CSS selectors available in Adobe GoLive by choosing Edit > Web Settings, and then clicking the CSS tab.

Element selectors are perhaps the most flexible selectors: they let you reformat the visible part of an HTML document based on its structure. The designer can define a style for any HTML element, and it is applied automatically to all instances of the HTML element throughout a document. Element-based styles are fully compatible with browsers that can't read CSS1 information. So viewers with older browsers that don't support style sheets see the tag's plain HTML formatting, while viewers with newer browsers that support style sheets see the enhanced formatting. Element selectors are also useful for ensuring that your documents will be readable in alternative browsers or on nonstandard viewing devices, such as a handheld PDA.

Class selectors apply style formatting to specific instances of a text block, rather than all instances that share a common HTML element. Unlike element selectors, class selectors are independent of the document's structure; they are defined by the designer but must be manually applied. Classes are useful for creating distinctive formatting like warning notes or pull quotes that you want to stand out from the rest of your text, or for creating special effects such as varying font sizes or colors within a word. However, don't use classes to structure a document visually; the formatting won't stick if viewers have non-CSS-compatible browsers. Instead, use element selectors to achieve as much styling as you can, and reserve class selectors for special (but not imperative) styling, at least until browser support for cascading style sheets improves and you are sure that most of your viewers are using the latest browsers.

ID selectors let you embed a specific style for a unique paragraph or range of text in your document, and create unique type treatments. ID selectors also let you set properties for a floating box, and control its width, visibility, and absolute position. Applying an ID selector in Adobe GoLive requires that you edit HTML code.

10 Notice that the Internal folder in the Index.html Style Sheet already lists some common HTML elements.

11 If the Inspector is not already open, choose Window > Inspector to display it.

12 In the Index.html Style Sheet window, click an element selector to select it. The CSS Selector Inspector becomes active.

13 Make sure that the Basics tab () in the CSS Selector Inspector is selected.

14 In the Style Sheet window, click different elements. In the Basics tab in the CSS Selector Inspector, notice that the styles with their associated selectors, properties, and values appear.

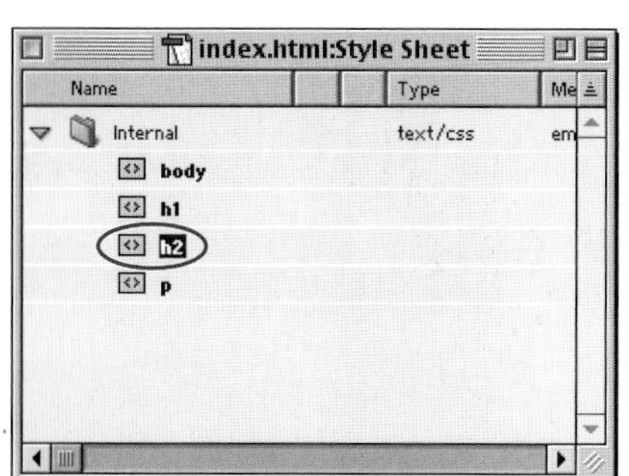

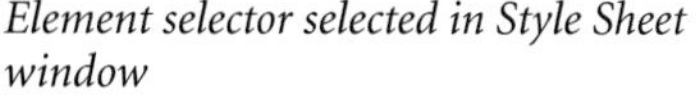

Element selector selected in Style Sheet window

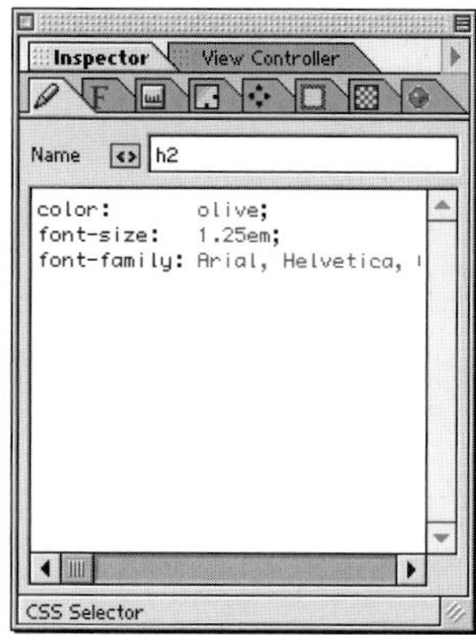

Style rules displayed in CSS Selector Inspector

Exporting an internal style sheet

You can easily export an internal style sheet for use with other documents or as a backup for the style sheet your using.

1 If Index.html is not still open, open it by double-clicking the file in the site window.

2 Right-click (Windows) or Control-click (Mac OS) anywhere in the Style Sheet window, and choose Export Internal CSS from the context menu.

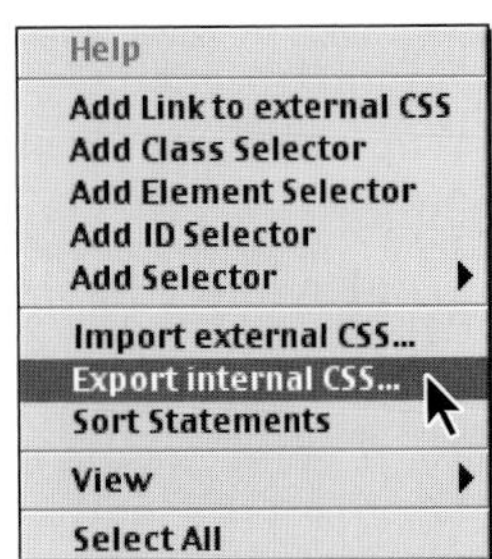

3 Navigate to the Styles folder in the PoetryPond.com folder, name the file Internal.css, and click Save.

Exploring an external style sheet

Style sheets can also be external to the current document. A link in the page to the external style sheet file will format the elements on the page. You'll be creating and linking an external style sheet to a page later in the lesson. Right now, let's simply see what an external style sheet looks like.

1 Choose File > Open, and open the file Alternate1.css that is located in the Styles folder in the PoetryPond.com folder. The style sheet opens in its own window named Alternate1.css.

2 Notice that the external style sheet lists some common HTML elements.

3 If the Inspector is not already open, choose Window > Inspector to display it.

4 In the Alternate1.css window, select an element selector. The CSS Selector Inspector becomes active.

5 Make sure that the Basics tab (✎) in the CSS Selector Inspector is selected, and click different elements.

6 In the Basics tab in the CSS Selector Inspector, notice that the styles with their associated selectors, properties, and values appear just as with the internal style sheet you examined earlier.

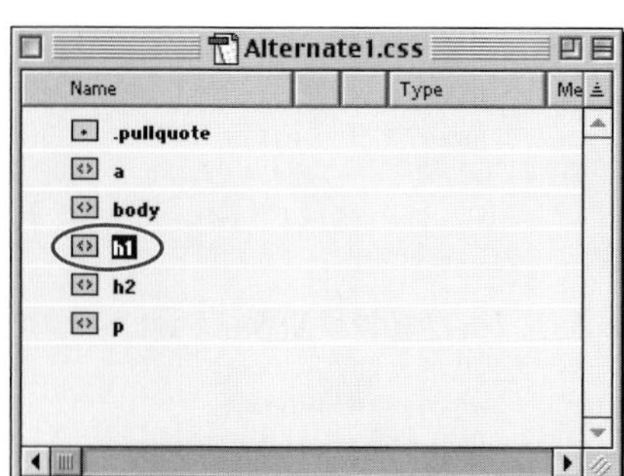

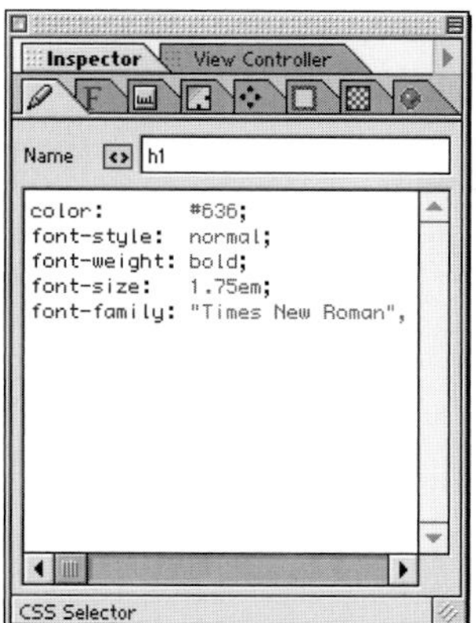

7 Close the Alternate.css style sheet window without saving it.

Working with styles

Adobe GoLive lets you work with style sheets and their styles in a variety of ways, including updating a style throughout a document, editing a style, and adding a style.

Updating a style throughout a document

Now you'll edit a style to see how your document is updated instantly.

1 If necessary, resize the document window so that you can see several different headings and body text.

2 In the Index.html Style Sheet window, select the h2 tag. Notice its attributes displayed in the Basics tab in the CSS Selector Inspector.

3 In the CSS Selector Inspector, click the Font tab (**F**). Choose a different color from the Color pop-up menu (we chose Maroon), and see how the change is immediately reflected in the document window.

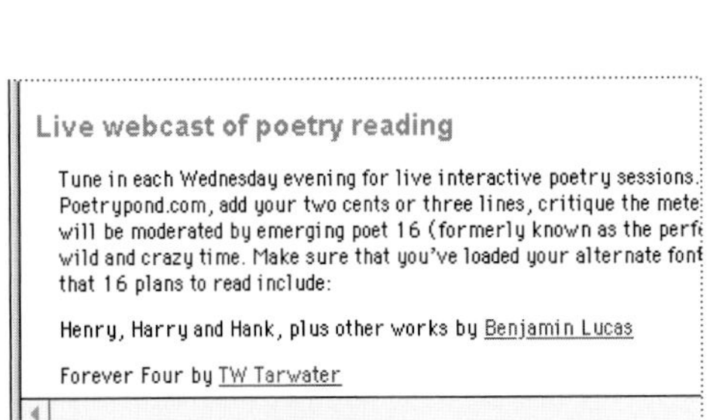

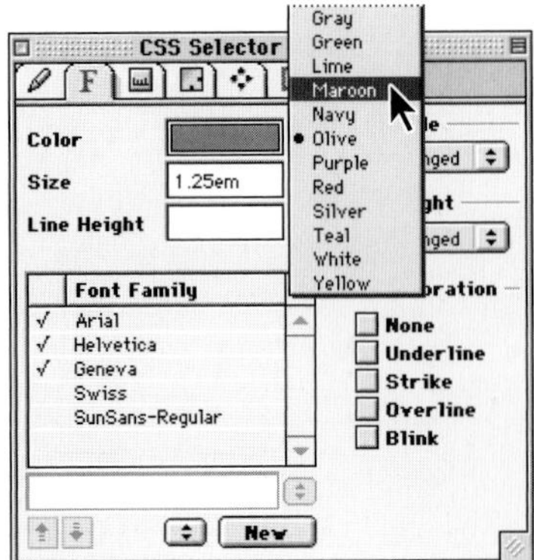

Different color applied to h2 tag

It's that easy to change a style that you've defined and apply it globally.

4 To make the font size a little smaller, enter **1** for Size and choose em from the pop-up menu. Then press Enter or Return.

About absolute versus relative font sizes

Note the different units of measure in the size pop-up menu. CSS support two types of measurements: absolute and relative. An absolute unit of measurement such as pixel is useful when you need precise control over the placement of text and graphics on a page. But type sized in pixels may not print well from some browsers, and it can limit accessibility to your site for visually impaired viewers since it forces them to view type at a fixed size. A relative unit of measurement, such as the em, sizes type in relation to the font size settings active in a visitor's browser, and is a better choice if you are concerned about accessibility issues, or if the exact placement of type and graphics on your pages is not essential.

When you create a style using the CSS Inspector, Adobe GoLive writes the HTML code for you. Now you'll take a look at that source code.

5 Click the Basics tab in the CSS Selector Inspector, and note the properties of the h2 element.

6 Now switch to HTML Source Editor view in the document window by clicking the Source tab above the window.

7 Notice the statement in the following illustration:

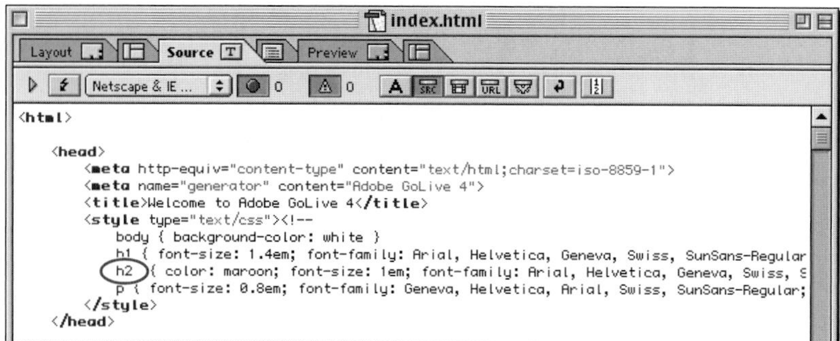

In the statement, h2 is the selector, and the information in brackets declares that the color property has a value of maroon, the font size property has a value of 1 em, and so on.

Remember that style rules are a statement consisting of a selector and a declaration on that element's property and value (that is, its specific appearance).

8 Click the Layout Editor tab in the document window to return to Layout view.

Editing a style in a style sheet

You'll continue the lesson by editing another style in the internal style sheet. This time, you'll edit the style of the <p> element to change the margins of the body text.

1 Click the CSS button ( ) in the upper right corner of the Index.html document window to make the Index.html Style Sheet window active.

2 In the Style Sheet window, select the <p> element under the Internal folder. Notice its attributes displayed in the Basics tab in the CSS Selector Inspector.

3 Click the Block tab ( ) in the CSS Selector Inspector. The right and left margins are currently set to 2%.

4 Enter **5** in the side margin text boxes, pressing Enter or Return after each entry, to indent the margins proportionally.

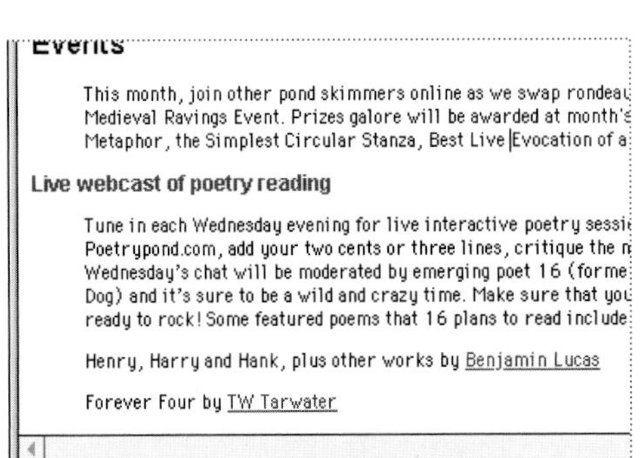

Side margins indented proportionally

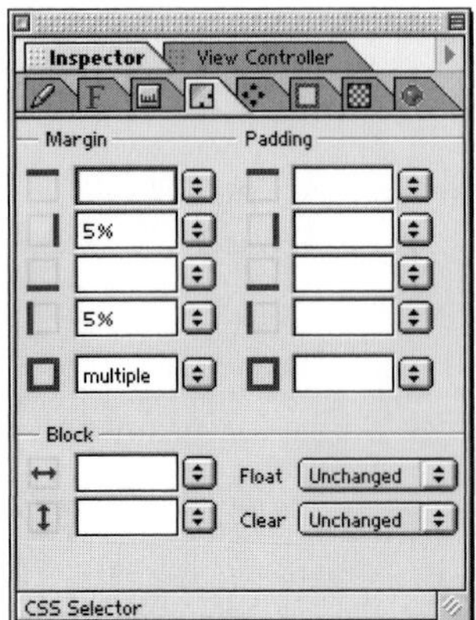

Block tab settings

Notice how the left and right margins around all body text adjusts in the document window.

As you can see, properties can control the font, text (including the indentation, spacing, and alignment), box or document boundaries, positioning, border, background, and list elements. Values specify measurements or colors.

Note: *Currently, all version 4.0 browsers display only a few style properties including basic and some font properties. But browsers continue to add support for style sheet properties. For best results, test the properties that you want to use in the latest versions of the most popular browsers. See "Previewing the results in current browsers" on page 332 for more information.*

Adding a style

Now you'll create a new element-based style to alter the way the hypertext links appear throughout this document, removing the standard HTML underline, changing the color, and applying a boldface font. The standard HTML element for formatting hypertext links is <a>. Whenever you create a hypertext link using the link command, Adobe GoLive automatically writes the source code for you, tagging the element as <a>.

1 To add a new style to the style sheet, click the New Element Selector button ( ) on the Style Sheet toolbar. A new item labeled “element” appears in the Style Sheet window under the Internal folder.

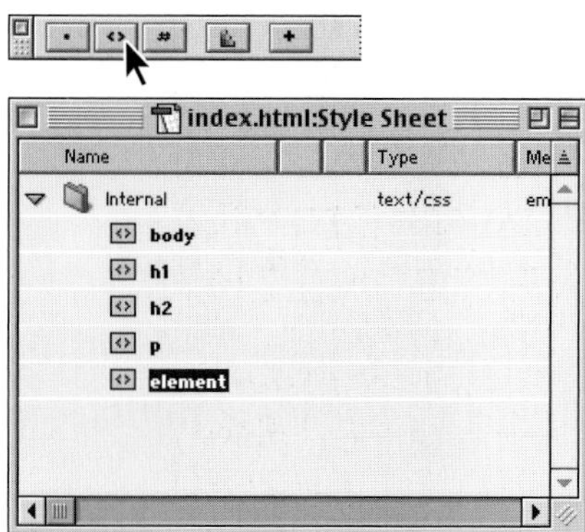

2 Click the Basics tab in the CSS Selector Inspector, and name the style **a** to match the HTML link element.

Whenever you create an element selector, the element names must match those of the HTML code. Style definitions don’t use brackets, so don’t include them as part of the name. The table “Common HTML elements” on page 320 lists common HTML tags and describes the Adobe GoLive commands used to apply them.

3 Press Enter or Return to create the element.

4 Click the Font tab (**F**) in the CSS Selector Inspector.

5 Beneath the Decoration options, select None to remove the underline beneath hypertext. Notice that the underlines are removed from the existing links in the document.

Now you’ll change the color of the hypertext font.

6 Choose a color from the Color menu and a weight from the Weight menu. (We chose Olive and a Bolder weight.)

Adobe GoLive features numerous ways to change the color of links. However, when you use an element-based style to change the appearance of hypertext, you can then update all links on your site globally simply by editing the style. Later in this lesson, you'll use a similar technique to update the page's background color.

Note: *In Windows, to delete an element or class selector from a style sheet, select the item in the Style Sheet window, and choose Edit > Clear.*

7 Make the Index.html document window active.

8 Choose File > Save to save the Index.html document. Saving this document also saves the internal style sheet.

9 Close the document.

Common HTML elements

Here are some common HTML elements that you can use when creating element-based styles in a cascading style sheet.

Element name	Abbreviation for	GoLive toolbar or menu command	Block or inline	Description
a	Link or anchor	New link	Inline	Highlighted
blockquote		Alignment commands	Block-level	Indented
body			Block-level	Inside canvas
br	Break	Shift+Return	Block-level	Breaks the line
em	Emphasis	Emphasis or Italic	Inline	Italic
h1, h2... h6	Heading levels	Header 1, Header 2, and so on	Block-level	Large fonts
i	Italic	Italic or Emphasis	Inline	Italic
img	Image		Inline	As an image
li	List item	Unnumbered list commands	Block-level	Bulleted list
ol	Ordered list	Numbered list commands	Block-level	Numbered list
p	Paragraph	Return	Inline	Regular text
strong		Strong or Boldface	Inline	Boldface

Creating a style sheet

Now that you've explored both internal and external style sheets, it's time to create your own from scratch. You'll create an external style sheet and link it to a document.

1 Double-click the Spotlight.html file in the Pages folder in the site window to open the file.

2 In the document window, click the CSS button ( ) to display the Spotlight.html Style Sheet window.

Notice that no styles appear under an Internal folder in the Style Sheet window. The document has only the basic formatting from HTML elements; no styles are associated yet with any elements.

3 To create a new external style sheet, choose File > New Special > Style Sheet Document to open an untitled .css window.

4 If the Inspector is not open, choose Window > Inspector to display it.

5 To add a new style to the style sheet, click the New Element Selector button in the Style Sheet toolbar. A new item named "element" appears in the untitled .css window.

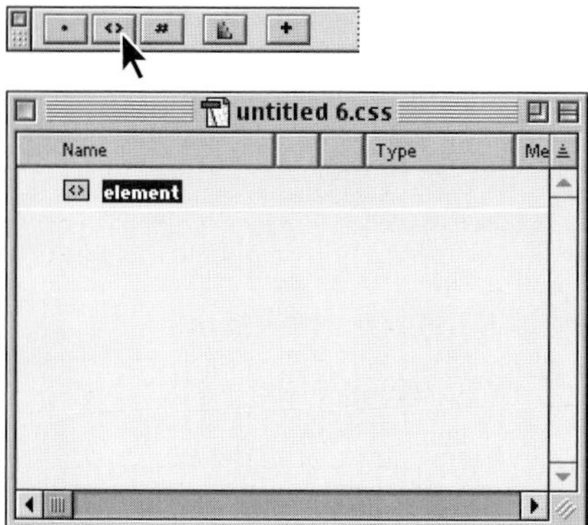

6 Click the Basics tab in the CSS Selector Inspector, and name the style **h2**. Press Enter or Return to create the element.

7 Click the Font tab (**F**) in the CSS Selector Inspector so that you can set font properties.

8 Click the New button in the Font tab of the CSS Selector Inspector, and use the pop-up menus to select a font color and font family. Choose a font size. (We chose Maroon, 1 em, and the Arial, Helvetica sans serif group for font family.) Choose a font family from the pop-up menu next to the New button.

You've created the style, but nothing has changed in the document. In contrast with internal style sheets that instantly update their associated document, external style sheets must first be saved and attached to a document for the styles to be applied.

Saving and linking a style sheet

Now you'll save and link the style sheet to your HTML document. Once you link a style sheet to your document, Adobe GoLive applies its styles automatically.

1 Make sure that the untitled.css window is active. Then choose File > Save, and name the untitled.css document **MyPoetry.css**, and save it in the Styles folder within the PoetryPond.com folder.

It's important to use the .css extension so that browsers recognize the document as a style sheet. Saving the style sheet in a Styles folder is not mandatory, but helps to keep your site organized and more manageable.

2 Click the CSS button (▙) in the upper right corner of the document window to display the Spotlight.html Style Sheet window if it's not visible. This window shows any internal and external style sheets that are associated with your HTML page.

3 Make sure that the MyPoetry.css file in your PoetryPond.com site window is visible. You may have to choose Site > Rescan to see the MyPoetry.css file.

4 Drag the MyPoetry.css file from the site window to the Spotlight.html Style Sheet window.

The second heading in your document (tagged h2) is reformatted automatically to reflect the style changes that you specified in the previous procedure, and the Style Sheet window is updated to reflect the linking of the MyPoetry.css document to your HTML page.

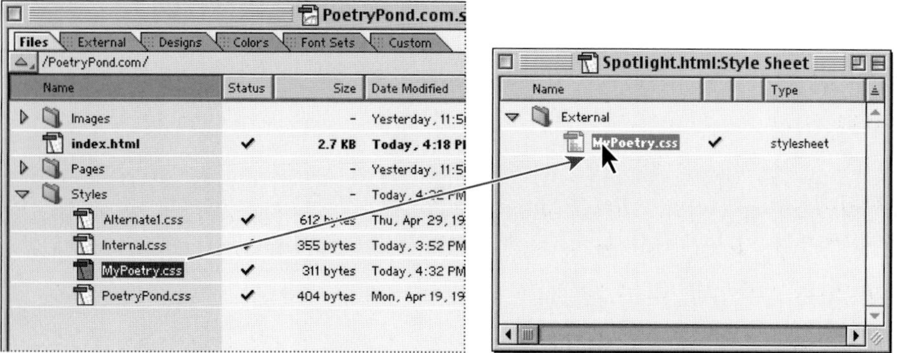

Style sheet applied (top); linking external style sheet by dragging it to Style Sheet window (bottom)

It's that simple to create an external style sheet and link it to a document. Now you'll continue to refine the formatting of the Spotlight.html document by linking an additional style sheet to it. This style sheet already contains several styles to give you a jump start. You'll edit those styles and add some new ones.

5 In the site window, select the PoetryPond.css file in the Styles folder within the PoetryPond.com folder. This time, drag the style sheet to the Page icon (▤) of the Spotlight.html document window.

This is another technique for linking external style sheets to a document.

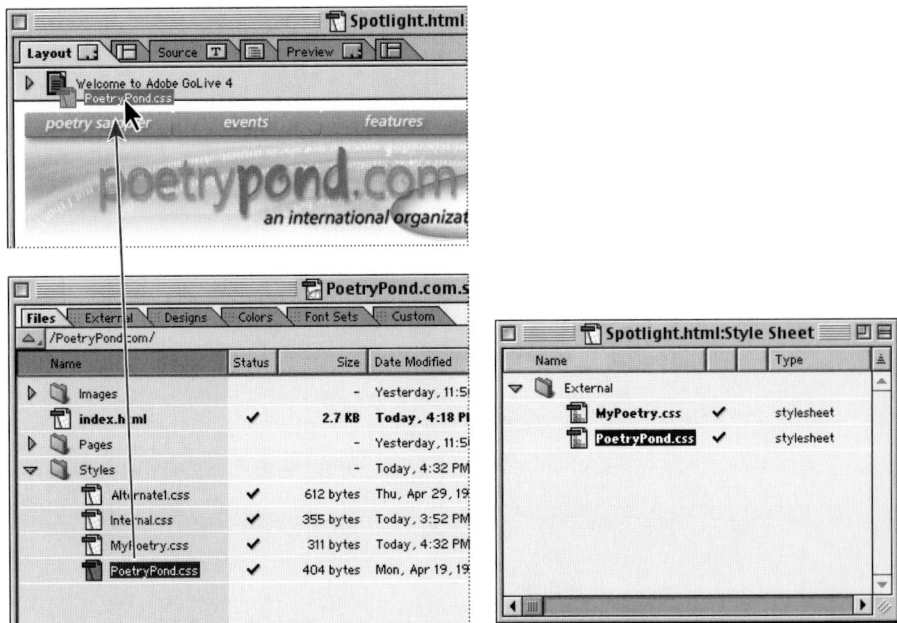

Linking to external style sheet by dragging to Page icon (left); updated Style Sheet window (right)

Once again, the second heading (tagged h2) is reformatted, to reflect the properties in the style sheet that you just attached. A feature of cascading style sheets is that you can attach more than one style sheet to a document and apply styles cumulatively or separately.

When a new style sheet uses the same style names as the previous one, the newer styles will take precedence and override the styles in the old style sheet. In this case, the h2 tag overrides that in the previous one (MyPoetry.css).

About cascading style sheets

A key feature of CSS is that they can cascade. That is, several different style sheets from different sources can be attached to a document, and all of them can influence the presentation of the document. For example, the default Web browser can attach a style sheet, a designer can have a style sheet to format a document, and viewers can add their own style sheets to address, for example, a larger font to compensate for poor eyesight or personal font preferences. In the case of conflicts, the CSS always chooses only one value, typically weighted first in favor of the designer, then the individual viewer, and then the default browser. (To override a designer's style rules, the viewer can turn off the designer's style sheet or mark certain style rules as "important.")

Linking and unlinking a style sheet to multiple pages

Adobe GoLive lets you easily apply an external style sheet to several pages all at once, doing away with the tedious task of linking it to each page in a site one page at a time.

1 Double-click the MyPoetry.css style sheet in the site window to open it.

2 Create a new element selector. Name it h1, set the color to Red, and the type size to 2 em.

3 Save and close MyPoetry.css.

4 In the Files tab of the site window, hold down Shift and select PoetryBuilder.html and Spotlight.html.

5 In the File Inspector, click the Styles tab.

6 Enter the URL of the external style sheet MyPoetry.css into the text box at the bottom of the Inspector. You can also use the Point and Shoot button to select the style sheet in the Files tab of the site window, or click the Browse button in the Styles tab and locate the MyPoetry.css style sheet in the Styles folder of the PoetryPond.com folder.

7 Click the Add button to link the selected style sheet to the pages selected in the Files tab. If prompted to close and save any open pages, click Close to proceed.

That's all there is to it! You can just as easily unlink the style sheet from multiple pages.

8 In the Files tab of the site window, select PoetryBuilder.html and Spotlight.html again.

9 In the File Inspector, click the Styles tab.

10 In the Styles tab, select the MyPoetry.css style sheet.

11 Click the Remove button.

Creating a class style

Class selectors apply style formatting to specific instances of a text block, rather than all instances that share a common HTML tag. Unlike tag selectors, which are applied automatically to the corresponding HTML tag, class selectors must be explicitly applied to a selection.

Now you'll create a new class selector and apply its style to text in the Poetry page's Spotlight.html file. The first class that you'll create will format a *pullquote*—some text or a quotation that is set off from the rest of the text for emphasis and for graphic impact.

1 Open Spotlight.html by double-clicking it in the site window.

2 Click the CSS button () in the upper right corner of the document window to display the Spotlight.html Style Sheet window.

3 In the Style Sheet window, double-click the PoetryPond.css to open it.

4 On the Style Sheet toolbar, click the New Class Selector button () to create a new class. The Inspector changes to the CSS Selector Inspector.

5 In the Basics tab () in the CSS Selector Inspector, name the class **.pullquote**, and press Enter or Return.

Note: *Class selector names must begin with a period or they will not be recognized as class selectors, and will not appear in the Style tab of the Text Inspector.*

6 Click the Font tab (F) in the CSS Selector Inspector, and use the menus and text boxes to set the pullquote's font properties. (We chose Olive, a font size of 0.75 em, and Italic style.)

7 Click the Block tab () in the CSS Selector Inspector, and set the left and right margins. (We used 15%.)

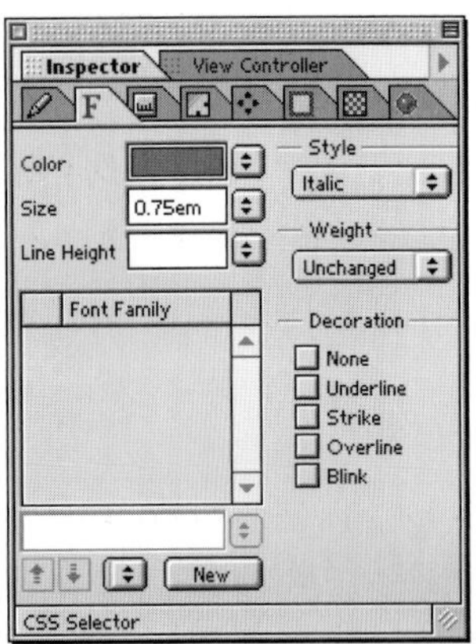

Font tab settings

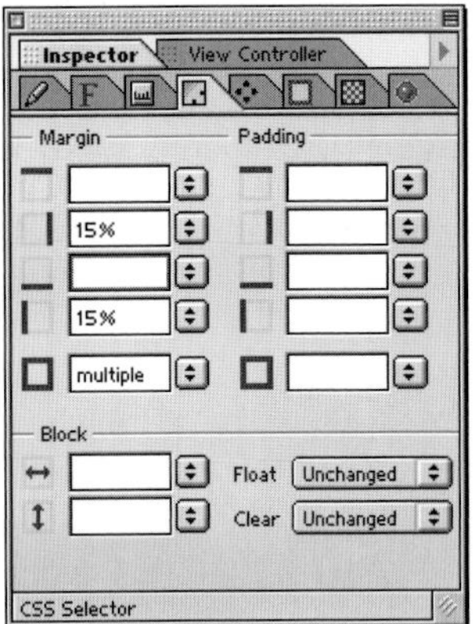

Block tab settings

Although you've created the class selector, it doesn't take effect until you apply it to a selection on the page.

8 Save the PoetryPond.css style sheet.

9 In the document window, insert the text cursor in Lucas' sample poem. The Inspector changes to the Text Inspector.

10 Click the Style tab in the Text Inspector.

11 Click the Par column next to the .pullquote class to apply that class to your selected text.

Text selection

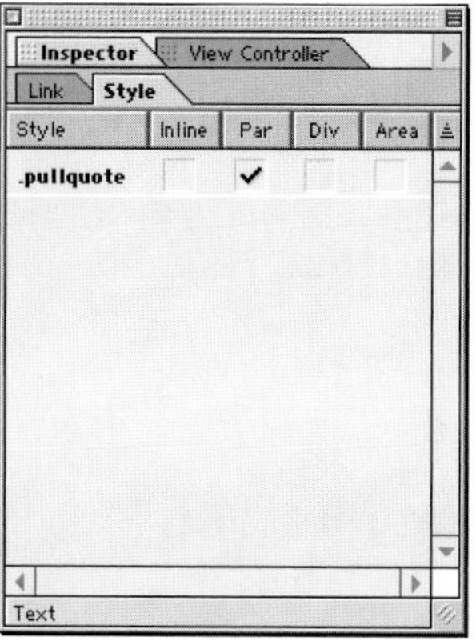

Class applied to Par (paragraph) element

The Par option applies a style to an entire paragraph (or HTML block element). In contrast, formatting an inline element applies the style only to the selection. See the table, "Common HTML elements" on page 320, for a list of block and inline HTML elements.

The Style tab also lists the Div element, which is a separate section of the HTML page, and the Area style, which applies a class to the entire body section of an HTML page. This lesson won't cover using these elements.

Importing an external style sheet

You can import the PoetryPond.css external style sheet, changing it to an internal style sheet.

1 Right-click (Windows) or Control-click (Mac OS) anywhere in the Style Sheet window, and choose Import External CSS from the context menu.

2 Select PoetryPond.css and click Open.

All the styles defined in the external style sheet now appear under the Internal folder in the Style Sheet window as part of the document's internal style sheet.

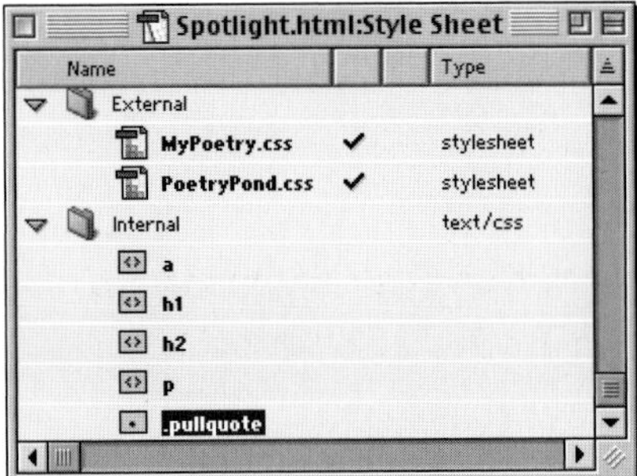

Duplicating a style

Now you'll create a new class for the author's attribution by copying the selector that you just created.

1 In the Spotlight.html Style Sheet window, select the .pullquote class that you created earlier. It's now part of the document's internal style sheet. You'll duplicate this class and then modify its font to create a new class.

2 Click the Duplicate button () on the Style Sheet toolbar to duplicate the class selector. A new item called .pullquote1 appears in both the Style Sheet window under the Internal folder and in the Basics tab of the CSS Selector Inspector.

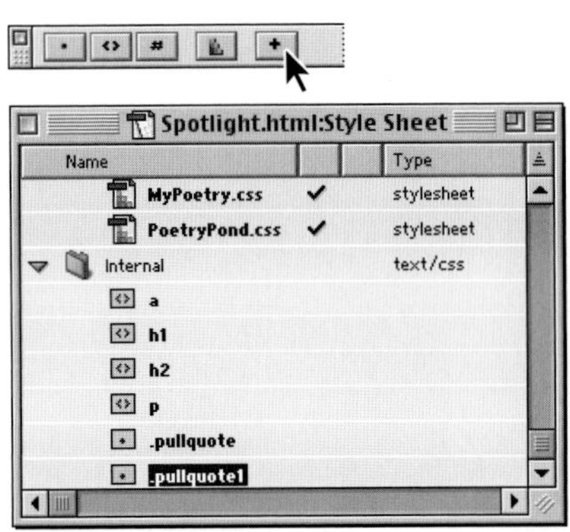

Duplicated class

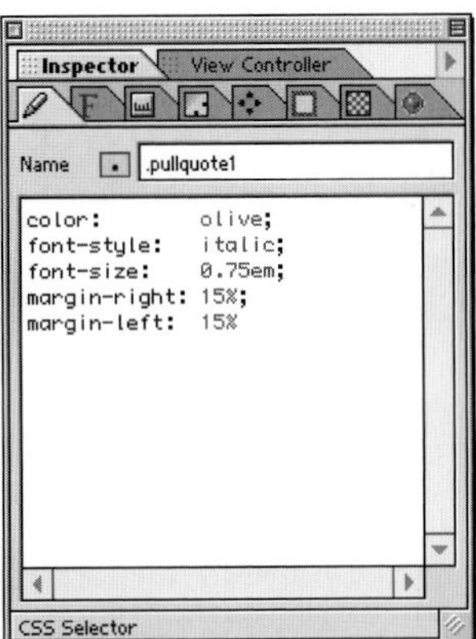

Duplicate class properties

Now you'll edit the properties of this duplicate class.

3 In the Basics tab of the CSS Selector Inspector, rename the class **.author.class,** and press Enter or Return.

4 Click the Font tab (F) in the CSS Selector Inspector. Notice that the attributes for the .pullquote class already appear. Change the font color to Black and the font style to Normal.

5 Click the Block tab of the CSS Selector Inspector, and enter a top margin of **–1%** to close up the space between it and the pullquote. Then press Enter or Return.

Now you'll apply this new class style to your page.

6 In your document window, select the text "Benjamin Lucas" immediately below the pullquote.

7 In the Style tab in the Text Inspector, next to the author selector, click the Par column. This updates your page with this new format.

8 Make the Spotlight.html document window active, and choose File > Save to save your changes.

Changing the background color

Now you'll change the page's background color by using a style sheet. Adobe GoLive features numerous ways to change a page's background color. Doing it by using a style sheet is handy because you can change the backgrounds of all pages that use the style sheet with a single procedure.

To apply a background color to your document using a style, you use an element selector for the HTML body element. The body element contains all the displayed content of your HTML page.

1 View the body element by clicking the HTML Source Editor tab ( ) in your document window. Look at what is contained between <body> and </body>.

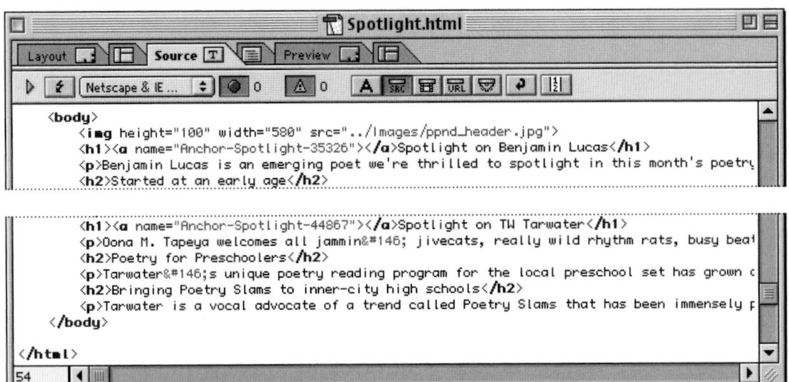

2 Click the Layout Editor tab to return to Layout view.

3 Click the CSS button ( ) in the upper right corner of the document window to display the Style Sheet window. Then click the New Element Selector button on the Style Sheet toolbar. A new item named "element" appears in the Style Sheet window under the Internal folder.

4 In the Basics tab of the CSS Selector Inspector, name the item **body**, and press Enter or Return.

5 Click the Background tab (▩) of the CSS Selector Inspector, and choose a color from the Color menu. (We chose Aqua.) The background of your document changes to the new color.

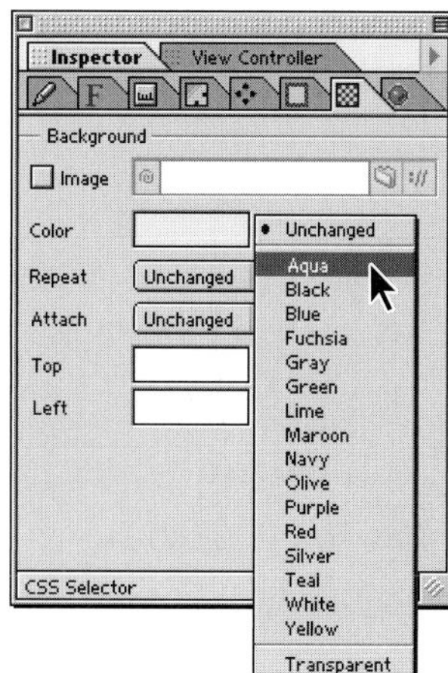

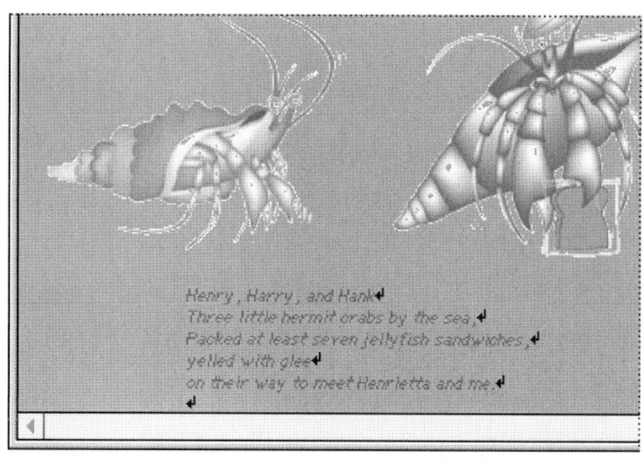

Choosing Aqua background color　*Result*

6 Choose White as the background color again.

You can also use the body element to change the color of the body text by selecting the body selector in the Style Sheet window, clicking the Fonts tab in the CSS Selector Inspector, and then choosing a color, and other properties.

If you like, try experimenting with other background colors. You can also try different color combinations for the background and text font.

7 Choose File > Save to save your changes.

As you saw with the h2 element selector applied to the heading level 2, cascading style sheets first apply formatting generally, and then more specifically. The body element controls the color of all text in the document, until another more specific style (for example, h1 or h2) specifies a different color for a more specific text selection.

Previewing the results in current browsers

It's a good idea to have the latest versions of both Netscape and Microsoft browsers installed on your computer system, so that you can preview how effectively and accurately your style sheets work in these different environments.

Web browsers must support CSS1 elements to recognize and properly interpret style sheets. Currently, all version 4.0 browsers display only a few style properties. Some properties work with a single browser only, some don't work at all but cause no harm, and others cause the browser to crash. For a list of browser-safe features, visit the Web Review's Style Sheets Reference Guide at http://www.webreview.com/pub/guides/style/style.html.

1 If you haven't specified a preferred browser, choose Edit > Preferences, and click the Browsers icon in the left pane of the Preferences dialog box. In the right pane, select a browser and then select the browser option next to the browser name (make sure that a check mark appears). Click OK.

If no browser is specified, you'll be prompted to select a browser to prevent the preview from displaying a blank page.

2 Click the Show in Browser button on the toolbar in the document window, or choose Special > Show in Default Browser to display the Spotlight.html document in your browser.

For additional information on previewing pages, see "Previewing in Adobe GoLive" on page 24, and "Previewing in a Web browser" on page 25.

Notice how the different element selectors (a, body, h2, and so on) and class selectors (pullquote and author) applied to the document appear in each browser.

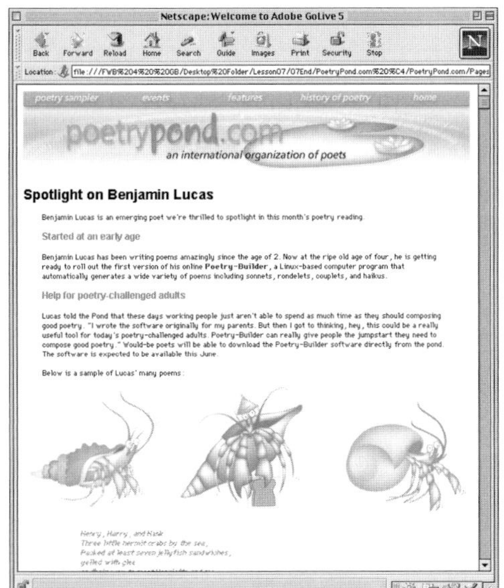

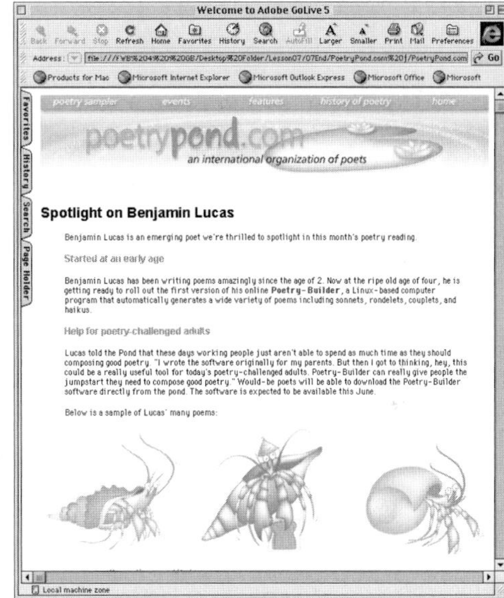

Netscape Communicator 4.0 style sheet preview *Internet Explorer 5 style sheet preview*

3 For greater accuracy, launch your browser and then open the Spotlight.html document in your browser to preview the formatting.

Adobe GoLive simulates how a browser will apply the style sheet, but may not replicate the latest implementations of the style sheet standards.

4 Close your browser(s).

5 Return to Adobe GoLive, and close the Spotlight.html document and its style sheets.

6 Close the PoetryPond.com site window.

This concludes the lesson. For additional practice using a style sheet, try the exercise in the next section, "Exploring on your own."

Exploring on your own

Cascading style sheets are easy to apply or remove from your document. For additional practice, try a style sheet that uses the same basic HTML elements, but has different style properties. When you apply the different style sheet to the same HTML document, you'll notice how easy it is to apply and change styles.

1 Start Adobe GoLive, if it is not still running.

2 Choose File > Open and open the PoetryPond.com site file. The path to the file is Lesson11/11Start/PoetryPond.com folder/PoetryPond.com.site.

3 In the site window, double-click Spotlight.html in the Pages folder to open the document. You'll add an external style sheet reference to this document.

4 Click the CSS button ( ) in the upper right corner of the document window to open the Style Sheet window.

5 Click the New Style Sheet File button ( ) on the Style Sheet toolbar. A new item appears as "(Empty Reference!)" in the Style Sheet window, and the Inspector changes to the External Style Sheet Inspector.

6 From the External Style Sheet Inspector, link the Alternate1.css file to the Spotlight.html document using one of these techniques:

- Drag the Alternate1.css file from the site window to the Style Sheet window.
- Drag from the Point and Shoot button to the Alternate1.css file in the Styles folder in the site window.

• Click Browse, use the directory and folder controls to locate the Alternate1.css file in the PoetryPond.com/Styles folder, and click Open.

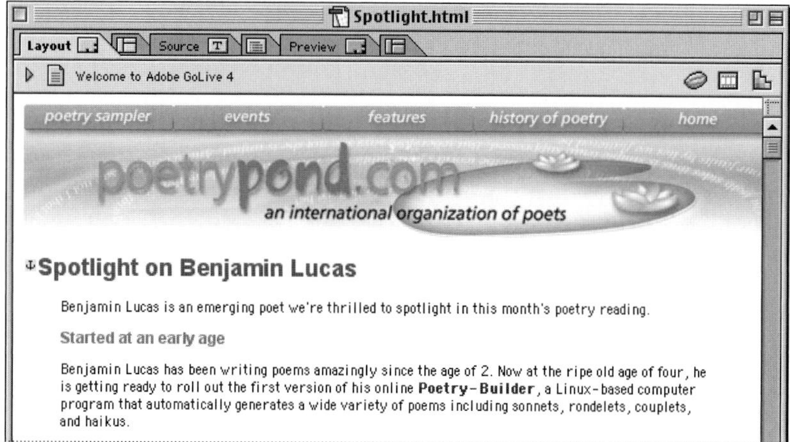

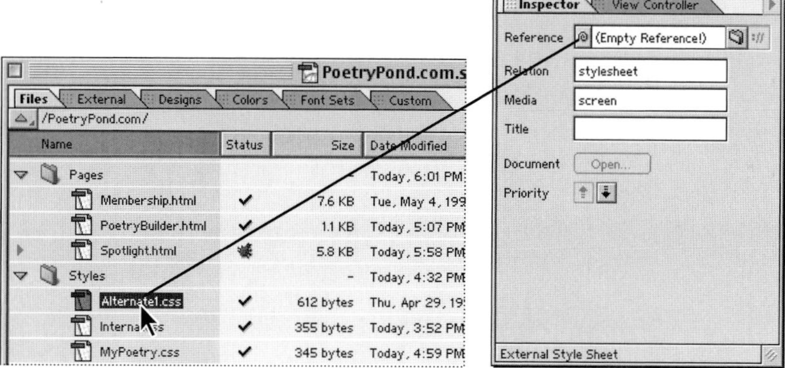

Alternate1.css style sheet applied (top); linking external style sheet from Point and Shoot button (bottom)

7 Notice how this style sheet reformats the document.

8 Try deleting any other external style sheets, except Alternate1.css, already linked to the page. Simply select the style sheet(s) in the Style Sheet window and press Delete.

9 Notice how the page is reformatted as you delete style sheets.

10 Close the PoetryPond.com site window.

11 Close the Spotlight.html document without saving your changes.

Review questions

1 How do styles differ from basic HTML formatting?

2 What does "cascading" mean when used to describe style sheets?

3 Why would a browser not display styles applied to a document?

4 How can you ensure that your style sheets work on the widest range of browsers?

5 What tools do you use in Adobe GoLive to create a style sheet?

6 What is the difference between an internal and external style sheet?

7 What is the difference between a class and element selector?

8 What's the advantage of using an external style sheet to set the color of hypertext or the page background?

Review answers

1 HTML controls the structure of information (for example, different relative headings), but not its presentation. Style sheets let Web designers enhance HTML's formatting with precise positioning of text, control over type, and formatting of other elements on the page. For example, style sheets can be used to apply font size and color, margin widths, and even the background color to a document.

2 One or more cascading style sheets (CSS) can be attached to a document to influence the document's presentation. For example, a browser, then a designer, and then the individual viewer can all attach style sheets to a document. The influence of several style sheets "cascades" so that only one value is applied, typically that from the designer's style sheet. Styles within a style sheet also cascade, and apply progressively to a document. In addition, if a document uses multiple style sheets, the latest style sheet can override previously applied style sheets if they share the same tags; or it can enhance previously applied style sheets.

3 A Web browser must support CSS1 selector elements to recognize and properly interpret style sheets. Currently, all version 4.0 browsers display only a few style properties, and the browsers vary in which properties they support.

4 To use style sheets successfully, it's important to stay current with what style sheet properties are supported by current browsers; to experiment with applying different properties to different HTML elements; and always to preview the results in the current browsers to test your style sheet's effectiveness.

5 Three Adobe GoLive tools let you create and edit style sheets and link to external style sheets: the Style Sheet window, the Style Sheet toolbar, and the CSS Selector Inspector.

6 Internal style sheets are part of a document and are saved with it. They must be defined individually for each page to which their formatting will apply. External style sheets can apply to a group of documents or to an entire site. You can then refer to this external style sheet from any page to make its style options available.

7 Element selectors are applied automatically by Adobe GoLive to their corresponding HTML elements and are fully compatible with browsers that can't read CSS1 information. Perhaps the most flexible selectors, element selectors let you reformat the visible part of an HTML document based on its structure.

Class selectors apply style formatting to specific instances of a text block, rather than all instances that share a common HTML element. Unlike element selectors, class selectors are independent of the document's structure; they are defined by the designer but must be manually applied.

8 When you set the color or attributes of hypertext or the page background using an external style sheet, you can then change the hypertext or backgrounds of all pages that use that style sheet with a single procedure.

Lesson 12

```
<TITLE>We
<STYLE TYPE=

{color:maroon;

</STYLE>
AD>
/>
<!-- Begin main table -->
<TABLE BORDER="4" CELLPADD
06">
    <TR>
        <TD><A
tp://www.adobe.com/">Adobe
        <TD>GoLive</TD>
        <TD><IMG BORDER="0" HEI
le.gif" ALT="Title"></TD>
    </TR>
    <TR>
        <TD><SPAN CLASS="headli
AN></TD>
    </TR>
    <TR>
        <TD><B>DHTML an
    </TR>
</TABLE>
DY>

    P-EQUIV="content-typ
    ml;charset=iso-8859
    come to Adobe GoLive
    

main table -->
ER="4" CELLPADD

D><A
dobe.com/">Adobe</
D>GoLive</TD>
D><IMG BORDER="0" HE
="Title"></TD>

D><SPAN CLASS="hea

D><B>DHTML an
```

12 Combining Adobe LiveMotion Animations with QuickTime Movies

In this lesson, you'll use Adobe LiveMotion to create a composition that includes placeholders for QuickTime movies, and export the composition to an SWF file. Then you'll use Adobe GoLive to integrate the SWF file with QuickTime movies into a final QuickTime movie for your Web page. You'll also use Adobe GoLive to edit the final movie by adding sound and special effects, including tinting, pictures, and transitions between movies.

About this lesson

In this lesson, you'll learn how to do the following:

- Use Adobe LiveMotion to create a composition that includes placeholders for QuickTime movies.
- Use LiveMotion to export a composition to an SWF file.
- Use Adobe GoLive to integrate an SWF file with QuickTime movies into a final QuickTime movie.
- Use Adobe GoLive to add sound to QuickTime movies.
- Use Adobe GoLive to add special effects to QuickTime movies, including tinting, pictures, and transitions between movies.

Note: *If you don't have LiveMotion installed on your system, you can skip the beginning section in this lesson on using LiveMotion and proceed directly to the section on using Adobe GoLive. We've provided you with the required start file for you to begin your work in Adobe GoLive.*

This lesson takes approximately 1 hour to complete.

If needed, copy the Lesson12 folder onto your hard drive. As you work on this lesson, you'll overwrite the start files. If you need to restore the start files, copy them from the *Adobe GoLive 5.0 Classroom in a Book* CD.

Note: *Windows users need to unlock the lesson files before using them. For information, see "Copying the Classroom in a Book files" on page 2.*

For information on setting up your work area, see "Setting up your work area" on page 9.

Getting started

You'll begin this lesson by viewing the final movie file, which contains the finished Adobe LiveMotion composition combined with three QuickTime movies in Adobe GoLive.

1 Start Adobe GoLive or a QuickTime movie player.

2 Choose File > Open, select the 12End.mov file, and click Open. The path to the file is Lesson12/12End/12End.mov.

3 Click the play button (▶) at the bottom of the window to play the movie.

4 Move the mouse pointer over the orbiting stars as they come into view.

Notice that the pointer changes to a hand, indicating that the stars are actually rollover buttons. Each rollover button is linked to a different QuickTime movie.

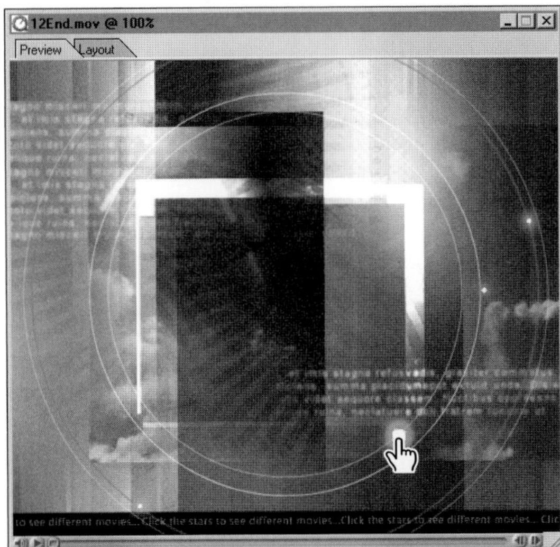

Moving mouse pointer over orbiting star (rollover button)

5 Click one of the orbiting stars to play a movie.

To create this file, we set up a timeline in LiveMotion, including placeholders for three QuickTime movies. We used LiveMotion to create the line of text scrolling at the bottom of the movie by changing the X coordinate of a text object over time. Then we used Adobe GoLive to integrate the final LiveMotion composition with the QuickTime movies. Finally, we used Adobe GoLive to add sound and special effects to the movies.

6 Click another orbiting star to see another movie.

7 When you're done previewing the movie, choose File > Close to close the file. Then choose File > Quit to quit Adobe GoLive or the QuickTime movie player.

Opening the composition

To get you started with this lesson, we've already created a composition in Adobe LiveMotion. The composition contains a background image created in Adobe Photoshop, and an opening animation of circles, orbiting stars, and scrolling text all created in LiveMotion.

Now you'll open the composition in LiveMotion. If you don't have LiveMotion installed on your system, skip this section and proceed directly to "Integrating the composition with QuickTime movies" on page 350.

1 Start LiveMotion.

2 Choose File > Open, select the 12Start.liv file, and click Open. The path to the file is Lesson12/12Start/12Start.liv.

You can open the 12End.liv file any time during this lesson to check your progress against the finished LiveMotion version of the file.

3 Choose Window > Reset To Defaults to set all the palettes to their original default settings.

4 Choose Window > Timeline to open the Timeline window.

The Opening Animation is a time-independent group, which contains ten objects. Six of the objects are time-independent groups, three of the objects are non-animated circles, and one object is a black rectangle that serves as the movie's background.

5 Double-click Opening Animation to open its timeline and expand Group of 10 objects to see what's in the composition.

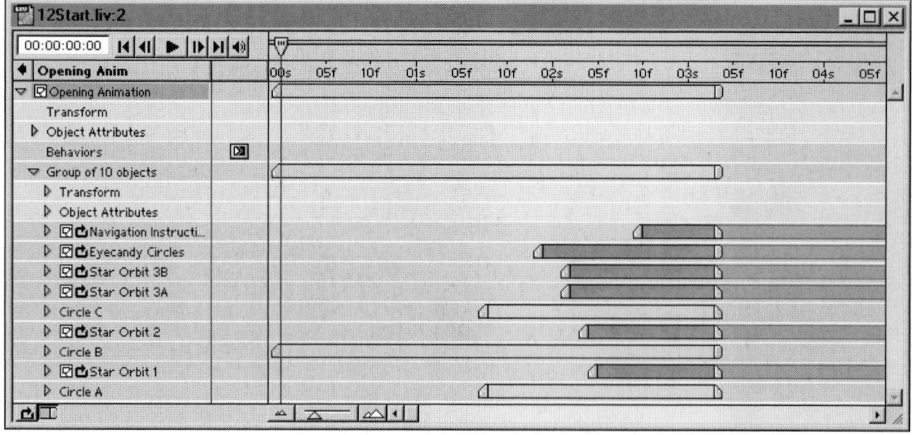

Setting up labels for behaviors

Adobe LiveMotion lets you create behavior labels in a timeline to mark specific positions in time. You can then refer to the labels when you're creating other behaviors. You'll set up behavior labels for three QuickTime movies. Later, you'll add a Play behavior to each rollover button in the opening animation that refers back to these movie labels. You'll use the same timeline positions when you integrate the composition with the actual movies in Adobe GoLive.

Note: *When you set up the LiveMotion timeline for QuickTime movies, you need to know the length of the movies in advance.*

Setting up the Main label

You'll set up a Main label to mark the beginning of the composition's timeline. Then you'll add a Stop behavior, so that when other behaviors refer back to the Main label, all movies will halt and wait for a rollover trigger by the user. (The Opening Animation will be unaffected by this Stop behavior because it has its own independent timeline.)

1 In the Timeline window, click the left arrow (◆) to go back to the Composition timeline and make sure that the current-time marker is at 00:00.

2 Click the Behaviors button ( ).

3 In the Edit Behaviors dialog box, enter **Main** in the Label text box, choose Stop from the Add Behavior menu, choose Composition from the Target menu, and click OK.

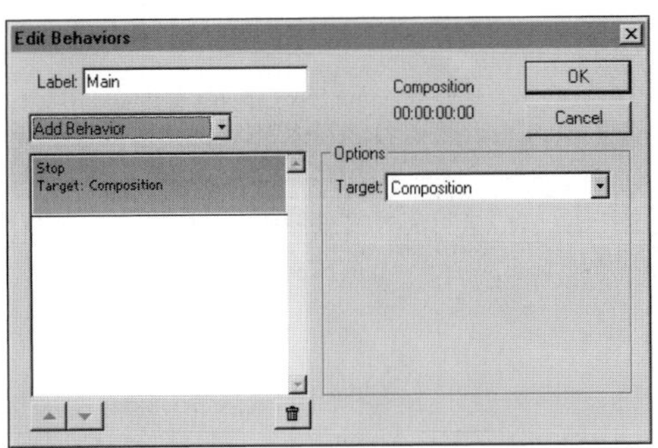

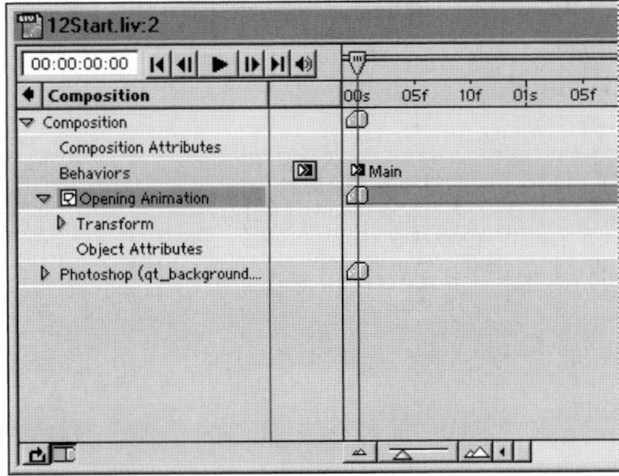

Setting up movie labels

You'll set up start and end labels for three QuickTime movies, and add behaviors for returning to the Main label when each movie is finished playing. Each movie in this lesson is 20 seconds long.

1 In the Timeline window, click the zoom out control ( ) several times, or drag the slider to the left so that only seconds are displayed in the timeline.

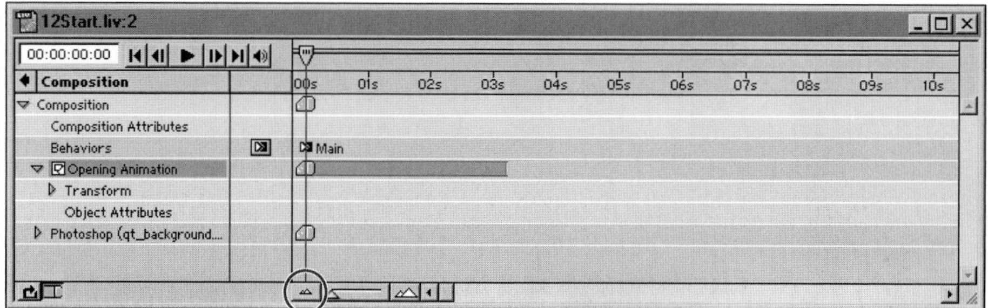

2 For the start time of the first movie, move the current-time marker to 01:00 (1 second), and click the Behaviors button ( ).

3 In the Edit Behaviors dialog box, enter **Movie A** in the Label text box, and click OK.

Notice that you don't add a Play behavior to the Movie A label. This is because you don't want the movie to start playing until the user clicks the orbiting star. (Later, you'll add the Play behavior to the orbiting star rollover button and a GoToLabel behavior that refers back to this Movie A label.)

4 For the end time of the first movie (which is 20 seconds long), move the current-time marker to 21:00, and click the Behaviors button ( ).

5 In the Edit Behaviors dialog box, enter **GoToMain** in the Label text box, and choose Go to Label from the Add Behavior menu. Choose Composition from the Target menu, choose Main from the Label menu, and click OK.

After 20 seconds when the movie has finished playing, the current-time marker jumps back to the Main label and the animation stops.

6 Repeat steps 2 through 5 to create the start and end labels for Movie B and Movie C, setting time markers as indicated in the following table and spacing the movies one second apart on the timeline.

Labels	Start time	End time
Movie A, GoToMain	01:00	21:00
Movie B, GoToMain	22:00	42:00
Movie C, GoToMain	43:00	63:00

Note: *The settings in this table are based on the actual times of the QuickTime movies that we've provided for this lesson.*

7 Choose File > Save to save the 12Start.liv file.

Adding behaviors to play movies

Each orbiting star in the opening animation is a rollover button with an Over state and a Down state. You'll add a GoToLabel behavior and a Play behavior to each button's Down state for playing one of the movies.

1 In the Timeline window, double-click Opening Animation to open its own timeline.

2 Expand Group of 10 Objects, and move the current-time marker to the end of the duration bars of the Star Orbit objects.

This ensures that you'll be able to select the objects when you open an independent timeline.

3 Double-click Star Orbit 1 to open its own timeline. Then select the Star Button 1 object.

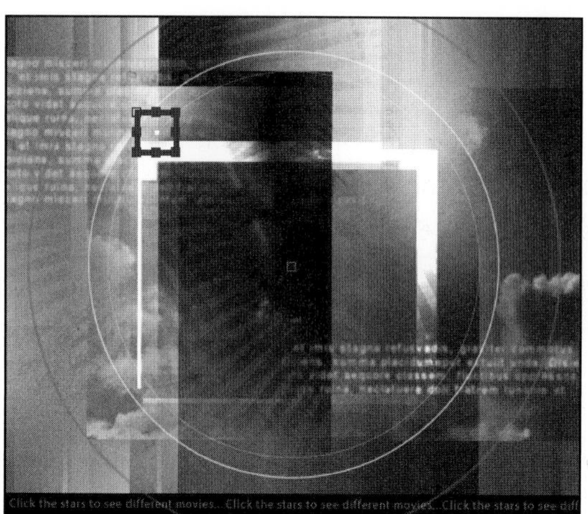

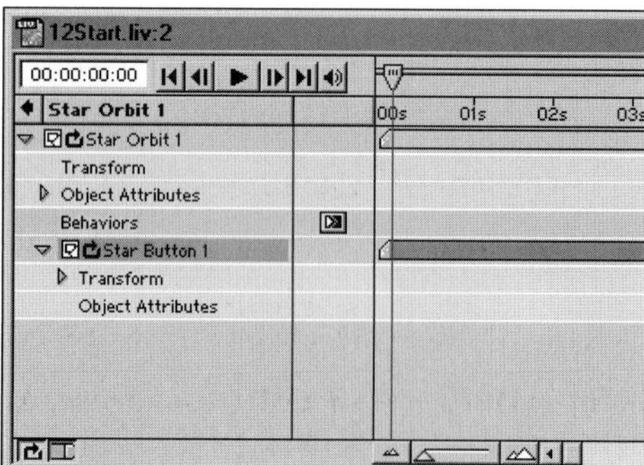

4 Choose Window > Rollovers, or click the palette's tab to display the Rollovers palette. Select the Down state for Star Button 1, and click the Edit Behaviors button ( ) at the bottom of the palette.

5 In the Edit Behaviors dialog box, choose Go To Label from the Add Behavior menu, choose Composition from the Target menu, and choose Movie A from the Label menu. Then choose Play from the Add Behavior menu, choose Composition from the Target menu, and click OK.

***Note:** The Go To Label behavior must be assigned before the Play behavior.*

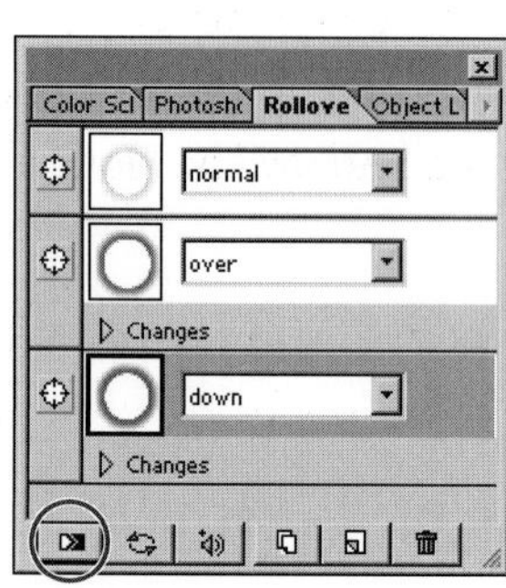

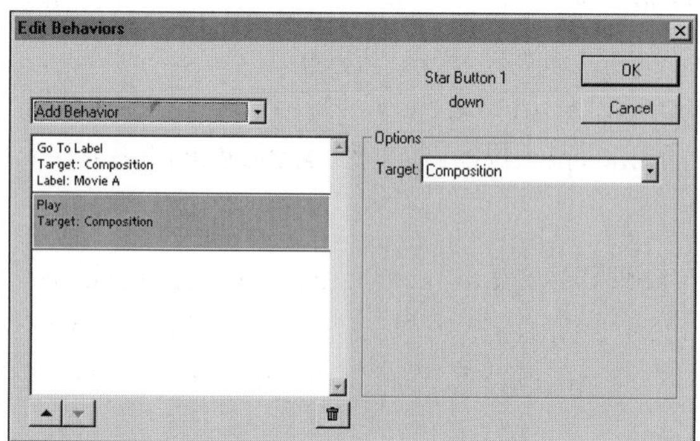

6 Click the left arrow (◆) in the upper left corner of the Timeline window to go back to the Opening Animation timeline.

7 Assign movies to the other orbiting star buttons, as you did for Star Button 1. For each orbiting star button, double-click the star orbit group object to open its independent timeline, select the star button object in the Timeline window, select its Down state in the Rollovers palette, click the Edit Behaviors button at the bottom of the palette, and assign behaviors to the Down state as described in the following table.

Note: *If you can't select the Down rollover state of an object, make sure the current-time marker is over the object's duration bar in the Timeline window.*

Double-click this object	Select this object	Add these behaviors to its Down state
Star Orbit 1	Star Button 1	GoToLabel, Target = Composition, Label = Movie A Play, Target = Composition
Star Orbit 2	Star Button 2	GoToLabel, Target = Composition, Label = Movie B Play, Target = Composition
Star Orbit 3A	Star Button 3A	GoToLabel, Target = Composition, Label = Movie C Play, Target = Composition
Star Orbit 3B	Star Button 3B	GoToLabel, Target = Composition, Label = Movie C Play, Target = Composition

8 Choose File > Save.

Exporting the composition

As the final preparation step, you'll export the composition to an SWF file. For the final movie to play smoothly, the frame rate must be the same for the SWF file as it is for the QuickTime movies. The movies that we've provided for this lesson all have frame rates of fifteen frames per second, which is the default frame rate for an Adobe LiveMotion composition.

1 Choose Edit > Composition Settings and verify these settings for the composition: 500 for Width, 420 for Height, 15 for Frame Rate, Entire Composition for Export, and the Make HTML checkbox is deselected. Then click OK.

2 Choose Window > Export to display the Export palette. Choose SWF and JPEG from the pop-up menus, enter **50** for Quality, **6** for Opacity Resolution, choose Auto Data Rate (Windows) or Auto Bit Rate (Mac OS) for MP3, and choose Document Rate for Frame Rate.

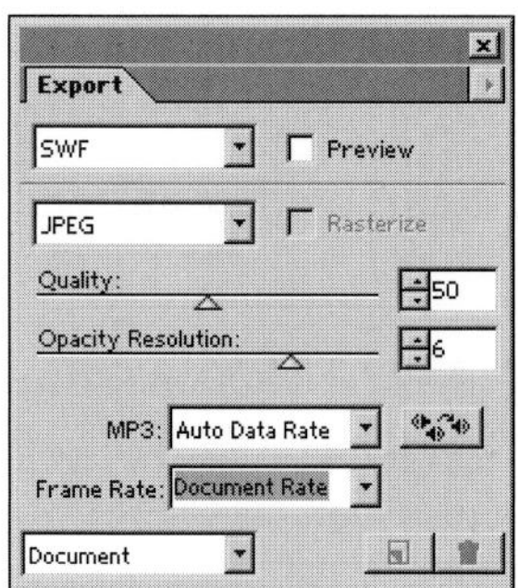

3 Choose File > Export As, name the file with the .swf extension, and click Save to save it in the Lesson12/12Start folder.

4 Choose File > Quit to quit Adobe LiveMotion.

Integrating the composition with QuickTime movies

Using the QuickTime editing tools in Adobe GoLive, it's a matter of a few simple steps to integrate your final Adobe LiveMotion composition with the actual QuickTime movies. You'll insert the SWF file into a new QuickTime movie, add video tracks for three QuickTime movies, link the video tracks to three movies that we've provided for this lesson, and add sound tracks for each of the movies.

Creating a new QuickTime movie

Adobe GoLive lets you create QuickTime movies from scratch. You'll create a movie to contain the Adobe LiveMotion composition and three provided QuickTime movies.

1 Start Adobe GoLive.

2 Choose File > New Special > QuickTime Movie.

3 In the New QuickTime Movie dialog box, enter a name for the movie. Under Movie Size, enter **500** for Width and **420** for Height. Then click OK.

Inserting the composition

You'll insert an SWF track into the movie's timeline and link it to the SWF file that you created. If you didn't create an SWF file using Adobe LiveMotion, you can link it to an SWF file that we've provided for this lesson.

1 Choose Movie > Show TimeLine to open the TimeLine window.

2 Choose Window > Objects to display the Objects palette. Then click the QuickTime tab ( ) of the Objects palette.

3 Drag the SWF Track icon from the Objects palette to the bottom of the track list in the TimeLine window. In the dialog box that appears, navigate to the Lesson12/12Start folder, select the SWF file that you created or the provided 12Start.swf file, and click Open.

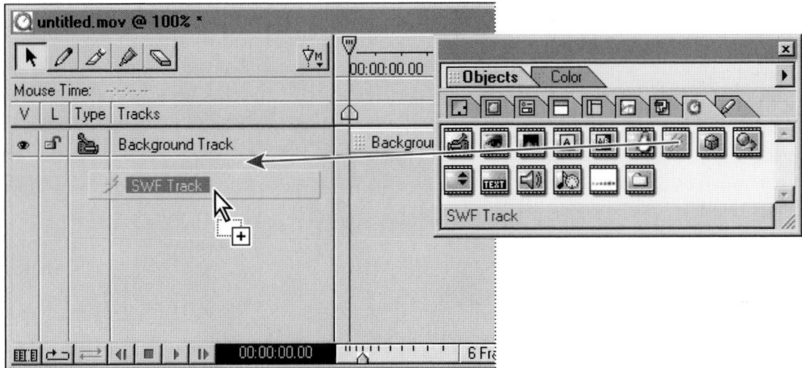

Dragging SWF Track icon from Objects palette to track list

The first frame of the animation appears in the movie window, which is black.

Note: *It's important that you don't stretch the SWF track's duration bar in the TimeLine window because it can cause the movie playback to jump to the wrong frame.*

Now you'll use the Save command to save the movie. The first time that you save a movie, the Save As Movie dialog box appears and the movie will be flattened. Flattening a movie resolves all track references and optimizes the movie, so that your movie is ready to be placed on the Web.

4 Choose File > Save, name the file with the .mov extension, navigate to the Lesson12/12Start folder, and click Save.

Inserting video tracks for each movie

You'll insert three video tracks, link them to three provided QuickTime movies, and set the movie properties in the Video Track Inspector. We designed the movies using Adobe Premiere®, where we added a title page and applied special effects to the original footage, including color correction, tinting, transitions between views, and audio fade in and fade out.

First you'll adjust the time resolution of the movie using the Time Slider scale, so that you can better examine the timing relationships between the multiple video tracks that you'll add. The Time Slider scale extends from one frame (maximum resolution) to one minute (minimum resolution).

1 In the TimeLine window, drag the Time Slider scale to the right to decrease the time resolution to 4 seconds.

2 Drag the Video Track icon from the Objects palette to the bottom of the track list in the TimeLine window. In the dialog box that appears, select Mov1.mov, and click Open. The path to the file is Lesson12/12Start/Media/Mov1.mov.

3 In the TimeLine window, select the new video track in the track list. Then click the Layout tab in the movie window to go to Layout view.

Notice that the movie appears selected in the upper left corner of the movie window. Layout view lets you reposition elements in your movie document. You'll place each movie in the same position by entering precise horizontal and vertical coordinates in the Video Track Inspector. (You can also reposition a movie by dragging.)

4 Choose Window > Inspector to display the Inspector.

The Inspector changes to the Video Track Inspector. (As a reminder, the phrase "Video Track" appears at the bottom of the Inspector to indicate that it has changed to the Video Track Inspector.)

5 In the Video Track Inspector, enter **170** in the left text box and **155** in the right text box for Position.

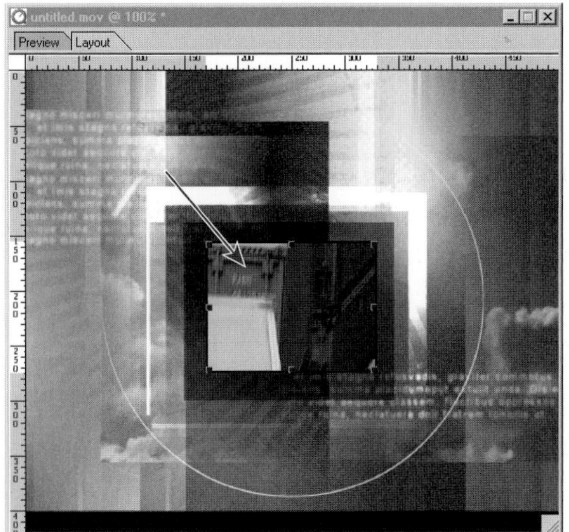

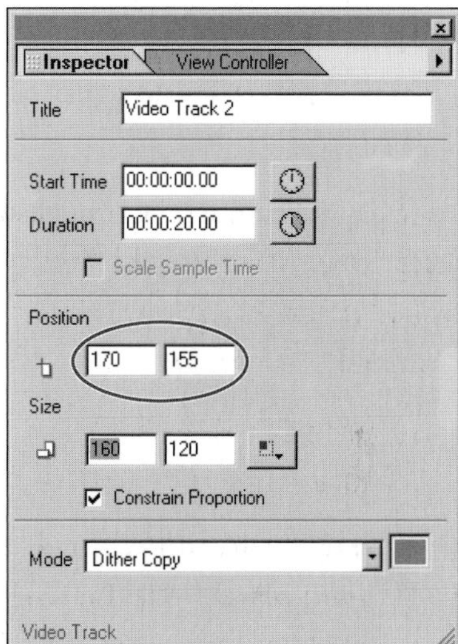

Now you'll name the movie track and position it in the timeline.

6 In the Video Track Inspector, enter **Movie A** in the Title text box and **00:00:01.00** in the Start Time text box.

Notice that this is the same start time that you set up in the LiveMotion composition timeline for Movie A. Also notice that the movie has disappeared from view in the movie window at the current time.

7 Repeat steps 2 through 6 to insert video tracks for Movie B and Movie C, and enter the settings from this table in the Video Track Inspector.

Insert this track	Select this file	Title	Start Time	Position
Video Track	Mov1.mov	Movie A	00:00:01.00	170 and 155
Video Track	Mov2.mov	Movie B	00:00:22.00	170 and 155
Video Track	Mov3.mov	Movie C	00:00:43.00	170 and 155

8 Choose File > Save to save the movie.

Adding sound to QuickTime movies

Adobe GoLive lets you add sound to your movie in several formats, including AIFF, WAV, and MP3. For each movie track that you inserted, you'll add a sound track and link it to a sound file for the movie. The sound files that we've provided for this lesson are approximately the same length as the QuickTime movies, about 20 seconds each.

Note: *When you export an Adobe LiveMotion composition that already contains sound to an SWF file, LiveMotion compresses the sound into MP3 audio format, which works with the Flash 4 player plug-in. Because QuickTime 4.0 only supports Flash 3, you lose the compressed sound when you insert the SWF file into a QuickTime movie in Adobe GoLive.*

1 Drag the Sound Track icon from the Objects palette to the track list in the TimeLine window, and place it in between Movie A and Movie B. In the dialog box that appears, select the Mov1_audio.aif file, and click Open. The path to the file is Lesson12/12Start/Media/Mov1_audio.aif.

2 In the TimeLine window, select the new sound track in the track list.

The Inspector changes to the Sound Track Inspector.

3 In the Sound Track Inspector, enter **Sound for Movie A** in the Title text box, and enter **00:00:01.00** in the Start Time text box.

4 Repeat steps 1 through 3 to add sounds to Movie B and Movie C, and enter the settings from the following table in the Sound Track Inspector. Place the sound track for Movie B in between Movie B and Movie C, and place the sound track for Movie C at the bottom of the track list.

Insert this track	Select this file	Title	Start Time
Sound Track	Mov1_audio.aif	Sound for Movie A	00:00:01.00
Sound Track	Mov2_audio.aif	Sound for Movie B	00:00:22.00
Sound Track	Mov3_audio.aif	Sound for Movie C	00:00:43.00

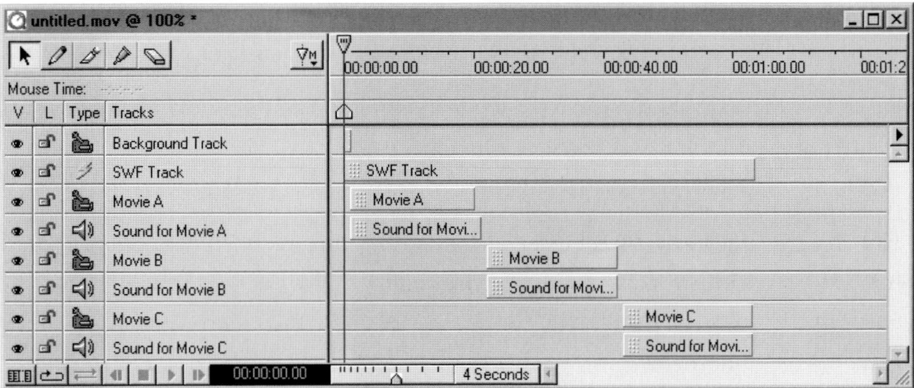

TimeLine window with added sound tracks

5 ChooseFile > Save.

How to separate sounds from movies in Adobe Premiere 5.0

The three QuickTime movies provided for this lesson include sound tracks within the movie files. You can use Adobe Premiere 5.0 to separate the sounds from the movies and save them as individual AIFF files.

1. *Start Adobe Premiere 5.0.*

2. *Choose File > Open, and open the movie file.*

3. *Choose File > Export > Audio.*

4. *Click Settings.*

5. *Under General Settings, choose AIFF Sound for the File Type. Then choose Audio Settings from the pop-up menu, choose 11 kHz for the Rate, choose 8-Bit Mono for Format, and click OK.*

(For better quality and a larger file size, choose 22 or 44 kHz for the Rate and 16-Bit Stereo for the Format.)

6. *Name the file with the .aif extension, and click OK.*

Adding special effects to QuickTime movies

You can use filter tracks to add special effects to your QuickTime movies. Adobe GoLive includes one-source and two-source filter tracks. You can use one-source filter tracks to change the visual presentation of a single video track and two-source filter tracks to apply transitions between two tracks, such as a picture track and a video track.

Adding a one-source filter track

Now you'll add a one-source filter track to apply a tint to Movie B.

1 Drag the One Source Filter Track icon from the Objects palette to the track list in the TimeLine window, and place it in between Movie B and Sound for Movie B.

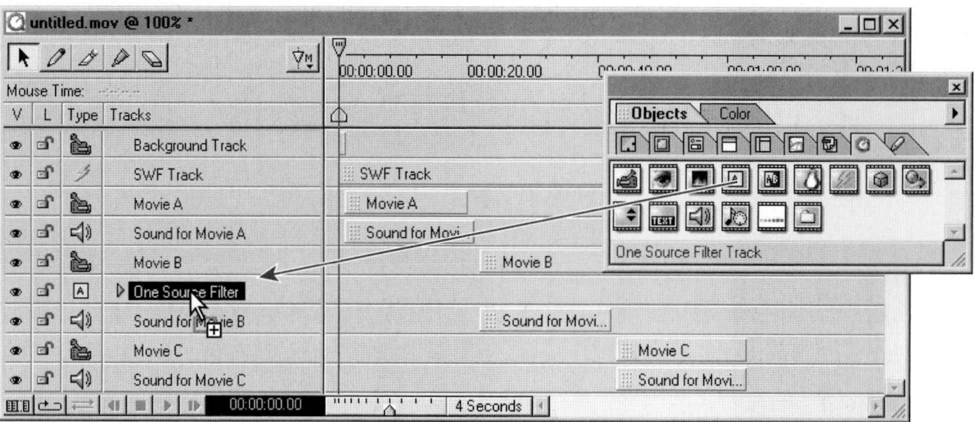

Dragging One Source Filter Track icon from Objects palette to track list

You use the filter track to specify properties of the track such as its title, start time, duration, and position. However, before you can specify these properties, you need to create a sample for the filter track, which you use to specify the effect that you want to apply. Now you'll add a sample for the one-source filter track that you've added to the track list.

2 Click the triangle next to the One Source Filter Track to expand the track and display the samples.

3 In the TimeLine window, click the Create Sample tool (✎) on the toolbar to select it. Then drag in the sample content area of the TimeLine window to create a sample content bar.

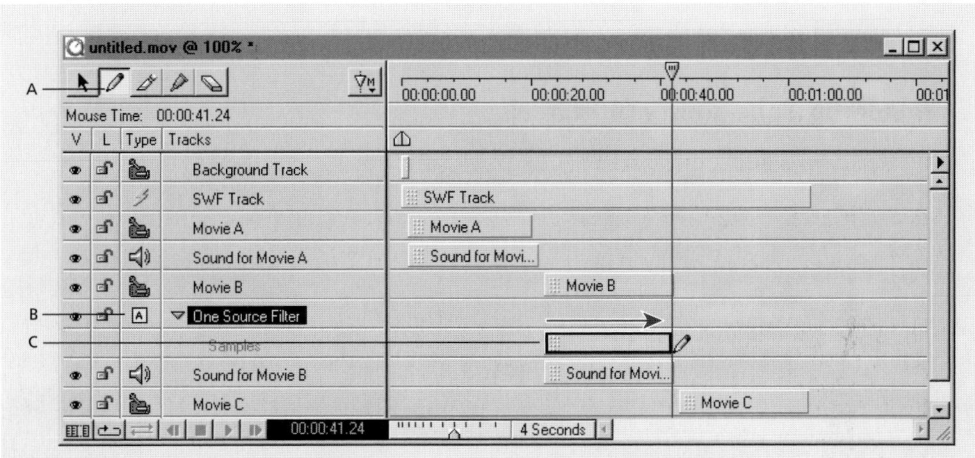

***A.** Create Sample tool* ***B.** One-source filter track* ***C.** Sample content bar created by dragging*

Now you'll set properties for the one-source filter track.

4 In the TimeLine window, select the new one-source filter track in the track list.

The Inspector changes to the One Source Filter Track Inspector.

5 In the One Source Filter Track Inspector, enter **Tint for Movie B** in the Title text box.

You'll enter the same start time, duration, position, and size for the one-source filter track as Movie B.

6 Enter **00:00:22.00** in the Start Time text box, and enter **00:00:20.00** in the Duration text box. Enter **170** in the left text box and **155** in the right text box for Position. Deselect the Constrain Proportion option, and then enter **160** in the left text box and **120** in the right text box for Size.

7 Choose Movie B from the Source pop-up menu to specify Movie B as the source for the filter track.

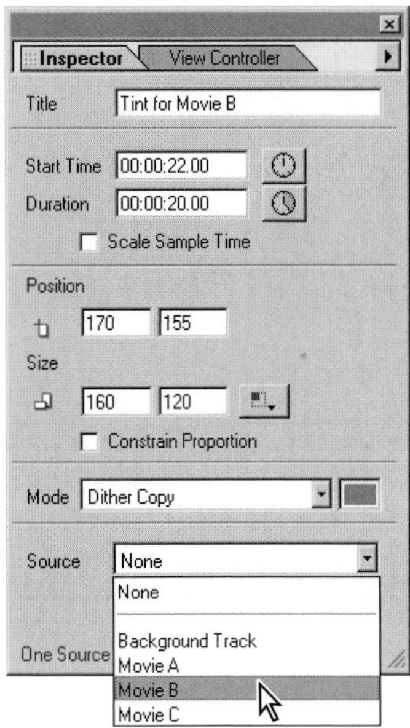

Choosing Movie B from Source pop-up menu

Now you'll set properties for the sample to apply a tint to Movie B.

8 Select the sample content bar in the TimeLine window.

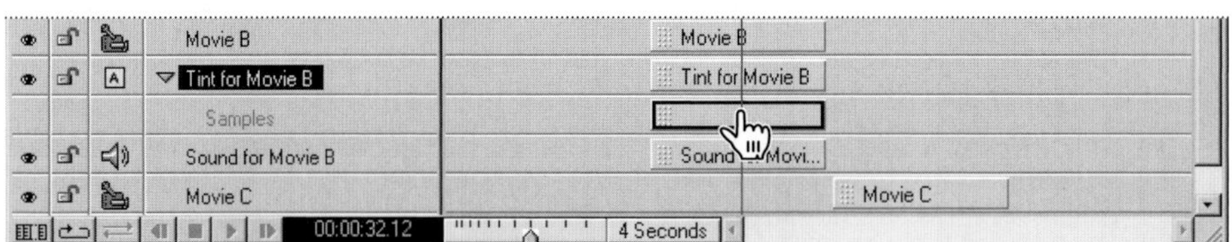

Selecting sample content bar

The Inspector changes to the One Source Filter Sample Inspector.

9 In the One Source Filter Sample Inspector, click Select. In the Select Effect dialog box, select Color Tint from the list box in the upper left corner, choose Other for Tint Type, and click to select the Light Color option.

10 In the Color Picker, choose a color, and click OK. (We used green.)

11 In the Select Effect dialog box, click OK.

Notice that a tint is added to the movie in the movie window.

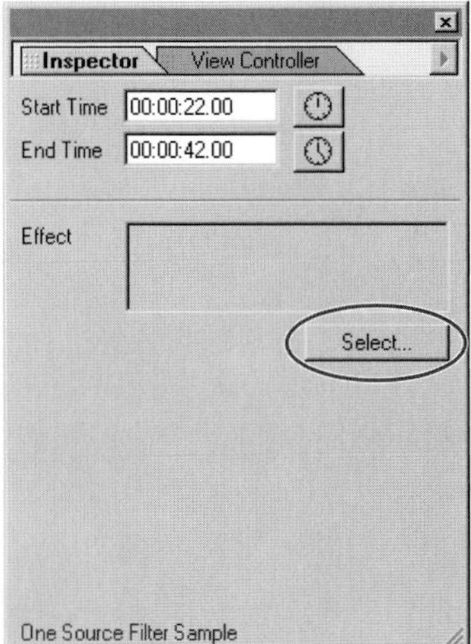

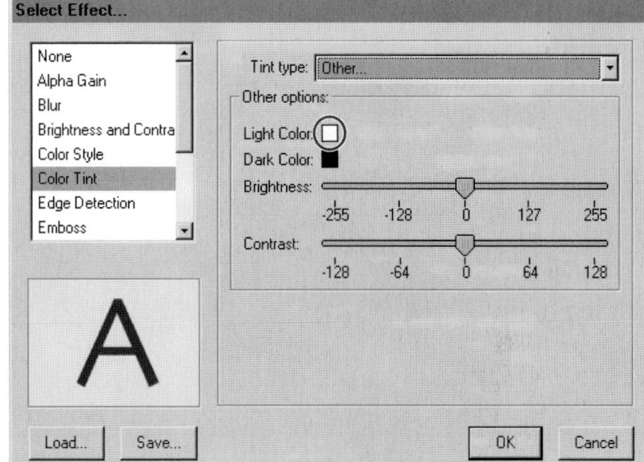

12 Choose File > Save.

Adding a two-source filter track

Now you'll add a title page to Movie A by adding a picture track to the track list in the TimeLine window. The title page is an image created in Adobe Photoshop. Then you'll add a two-source filter track to apply a transition between the title page and Movie A. Besides using picture tracks to add title pages to QuickTime movies, you can also use picture tracks to present slide shows.

1 Drag the Picture Track icon from the Objects palette to the track list in the TimeLine window, and place it in between Movie A and Sound for Movie A.

2 In the TimeLine window, select the new picture track in the track list.

The Inspector changes to the Picture Track Inspector.

Now you'll specify the image file for the title page that you want to add to the QuickTime movie.

3 In the Picture Track Inspector, click the Images tab to select it. Then deselect Images Constrain Proportion, and click Import. In the dialog box that appears, navigate to the Lesson12/12Start/Media folder, select TitlePage.psd, and click Add and then click Done.

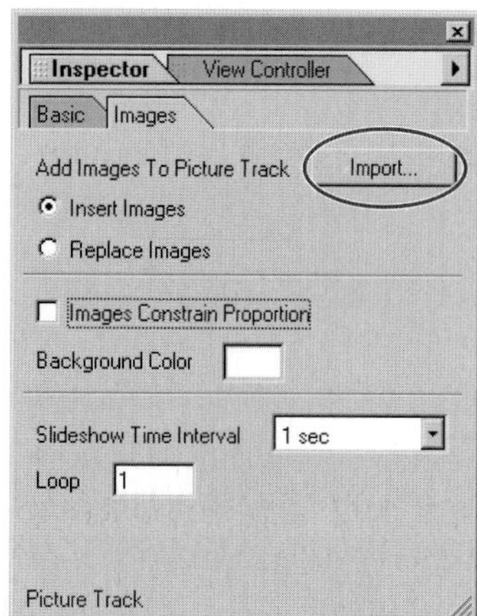

4 In the dialog box that appears, click OK to accept the default compression settings for the image file.

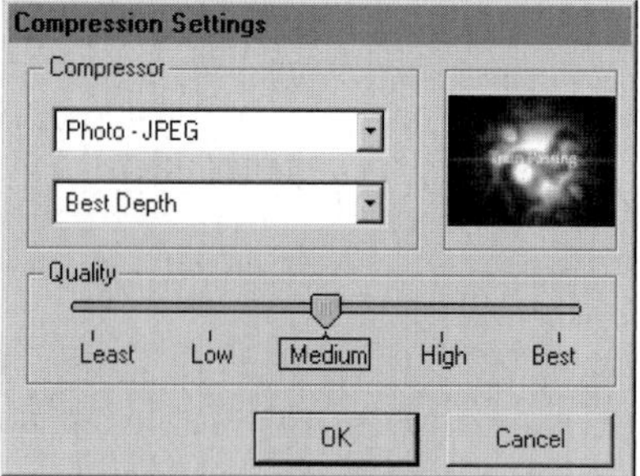

Now you'll set properties for the title page, including specifying for it to be displayed after 1 second and for a duration of five seconds.

5 In the Picture Track Inspector, click the Basic tab to select it. Then enter **Movie A Title Page** in the Title text box. Enter **00:00:01.00** in the Start Time text box, and enter **00:00:05.00** in the Duration text box. Enter **170** in the left text box and **155** in the right text box for Position. Make sure that the Constrain Proportion option is deselected, and then enter **160** in the left text box and **120** in the right text box for Size.

Now you'll add a two-source filter track to the track list to create the transition between the title page and Movie A.

6 Drag the Two Source Filter Track icon from the Objects palette to the track list in the TimeLine window, and place it in between Movie A and Movie A Title Page.

Now you'll add a sample for the two-source filter track.

7 Click the triangle next to the Two Source Filter Track to expand the track and display the samples.

8 In the TimeLine window, click the Create Sample tool (✎) on the toolbar to select it. Then drag in the sample content area in the TimeLine window to create a sample content bar.

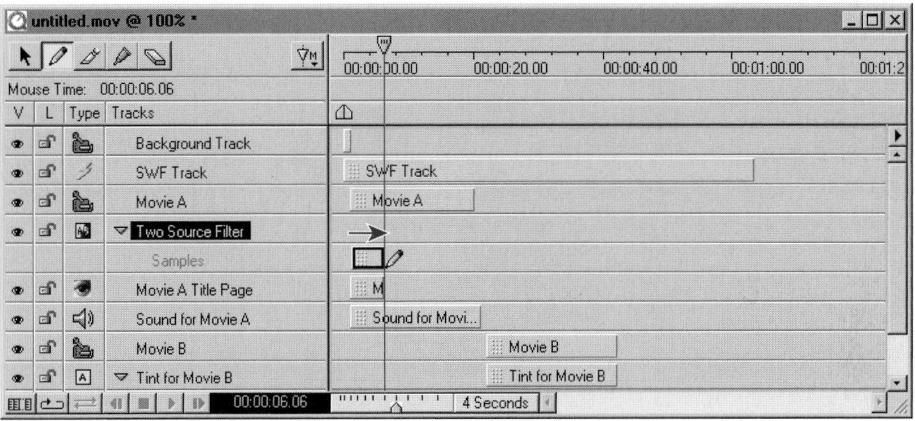

Dragging to create sample content bar for two-source filter track

Now you'll set properties for the two-source filter track.

9 In the TimeLine window, select the new two-source filter track in the track list.

The Inspector changes to the Two Source Filter Track Inspector.

10 In the Two Source Filter Track Inspector, enter **Transition** in the Title text box.

You'll enter the same position and size for the two-source filter track as Movie A.

11 Enter **00:00:03.00** in the Start Time text box, and enter **00:00:03.00** in the Duration text box. Enter **170** in the left text box and **155** in the right text box for Position. Deselect the Constrain Proportion option, and then enter **160** in the left text box and **120** in the right text box for Size.

12 Choose Movie A Title Page from the Source A pop-up menu, and choose Movie A from the Source B pop-up menu. Notice that the area where you are applying a transition in the movie window turns white. It remains white until you choose the transition effect that you want to apply.

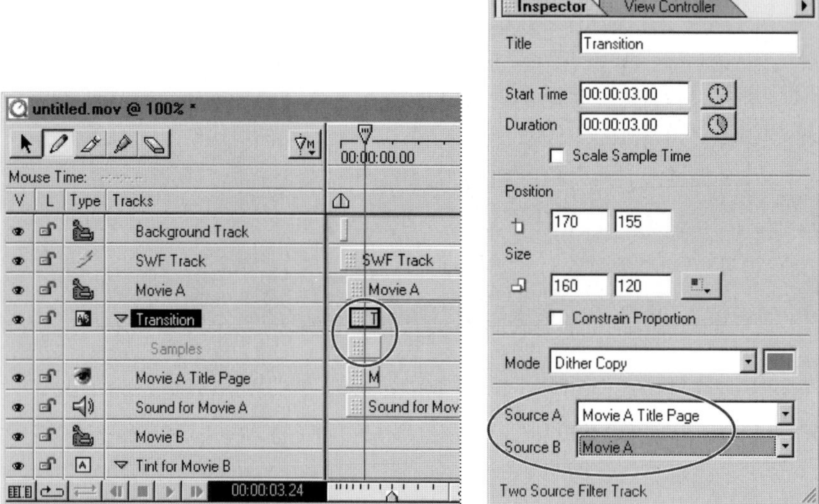

Now you'll set properties for the sample to apply a Cross Fade effect between the title page and Movie A. The Cross Fade effect provides a smooth transition that fades out the picture track and fades in the video track.

13 Select the sample content bar in the TimeLine window.

The Inspector changes to the Two Source Filter Sample Inspector.

14 In the Two Source Filter Sample Inspector, enter **00:00:03.00** in the Start Time text box, and enter **00:00:06.00** in the End Time text box. Make sure that the Transition from Source A to B option is selected, and click Select. In the dialog box that appears, select Cross Fade from the list box in the upper left corner, and click OK.

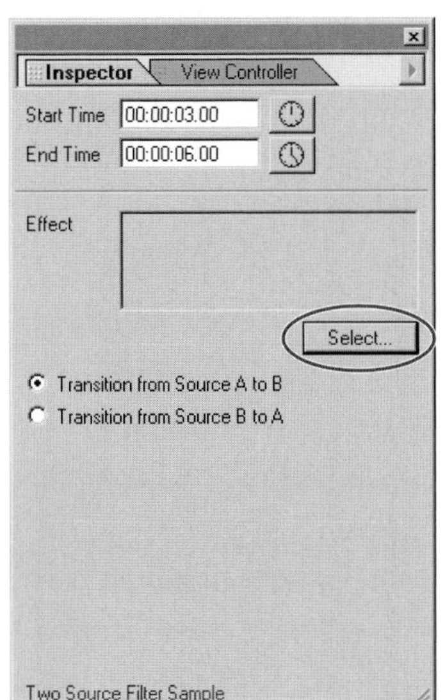

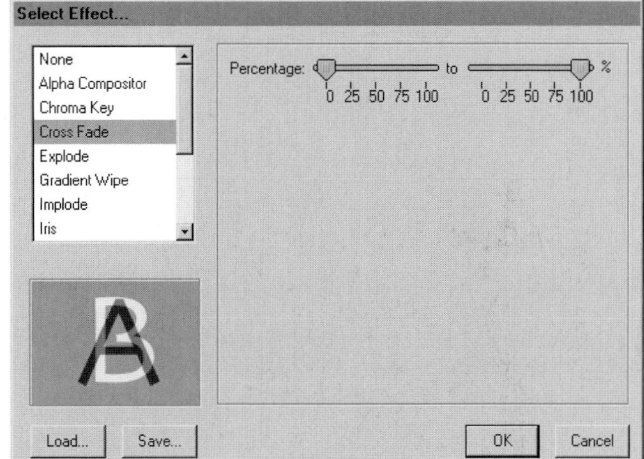

Now you'll both flatten and save the movie using the Flatten Movie command. Flattening a movie resolves all track references and optimizes the movie, so that your movie is ready to be placed on the Web.

15 Choose Movie > Flatten Movie, name the file with the .mov extension, navigate to the Lesson12/12Start folder, and click Save.

Now that you've finished editing your QuickTime movie using Adobe GoLive, you'll preview it.

16 Click the Preview tab in the movie window. Then click the play button ( ) at the bottom of the movie window.

Review questions

1 How do you add a placeholder for a QuickTime movie to an existing composition in Adobe LiveMotion?

2 How do you export a composition from LiveMotion to an SWF file?

3 How do you create a new QuickTime movie in Adobe GoLive?

4 Why would you add an SWF track to a QuickTime movie in Adobe GoLive?

5 What does it mean to flatten a movie? And how do you do it?

6 How do you integrate QuickTime movies and sound in a final QuickTime movie in Adobe GoLive?

7 What can you use to add special effects, such as tinting and transitions, to QuickTime movies in Adobe GoLive?

Review answers

1 To add a placeholder for a QuickTime movie to a composition, set up a start and an end label for the movie using Adobe LiveMotion.

2 To export a composition from LiveMotion to an SWF file, choose Window > Export to display the Export palette, and set options in the Export palette. Then choose File > Export As, name the file with the .swf extension, and click Save.

3 To create a new QuickTime movie in Adobe GoLive, choose File > Special > QuickTime Movie. In the dialog box that appears, enter a name for the movie, size for the movie, and click OK.

4 You would add an SWF track to a QuickTime movie in Adobe GoLive if you want to add an SWF file to the movie.

5 Flattening a movie resolves all track references and optimizes the movie, so that your movie is ready to be placed on the Web. To both flatten and save a movie, choose Movie > Flatten Movie.

6 To integrate movies and sound in a final QuickTime movie in Adobe GoLive, you need to add video tracks for the movies and sound tracks for the sound to the track list in the TimeLine window.

7 To add special effects to QuickTime movies, you can use filter tracks. One-source filter tracks let you change the visual presentation of a single video track. Two-source filter tracks let you apply transitions between two tracks, such as a picture track and a video track.

Lesson 13

```
<TITLE>Wel
<STYLE TYPE=

e{color:maroon;

</STYLE>
AD>
Y>
<!-- Begin main table -->
<TABLE BORDER="4" CELLPADDI
06">
    <TR>
        <TD><A
tp://www.adobe.com/">Adobe</A>
        <TD>GoLive</TD>
        <TD><IMG BORDER="0" HEIG
le.gif" ALT="Title"></TD>
    </TR>
    <TR>
        <TD><SPAN CLASS="head
AN></TD>
    </TR>
    <TR>
        <TD><B>DHTML an
    </TR>
</TABLE>
DY>

EQUIV="content-type
charset=iso-8859-
ome to Adobe GoLive

main table -->
DER="4" CELLPADD

D><A
dobe.com/">Adobe</
D>GoLive</TD>
D><IMG BORDER="0" HEI
="Title"></TD>

D><SPAN CLASS="hea

D><B>DHTML an
```

13 Managing Web Sites

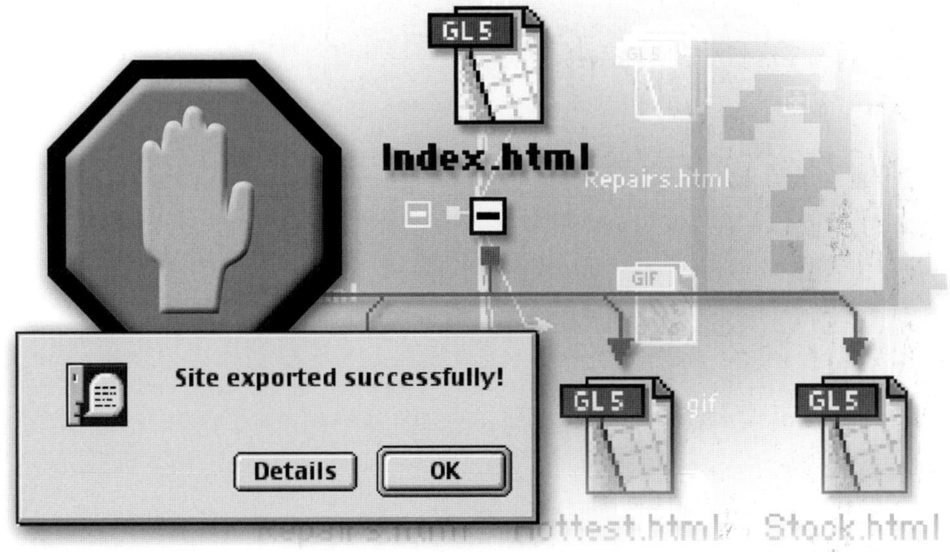

You can use the powerful Web site management tools in Adobe GoLive to create and manage your site. These tools include the site window, which shows all the objects in your site, and the Navigation view, which is a hierarchical viewer and designer. Other management tools allow you to manage folders, files, and links; import sites into Adobe GoLive; and, upload your site to a Web server.

About this lesson

In this lesson, you'll learn how to do the following:

- Look at a well-managed Web site.
- Import an existing site created in an application other that Adobe GoLive into Adobe GoLive.
- Explore the site window.
- Correct errors in a site.
- Manage folders in a site.
- Add new pages to a site.
- Manage and design your site using the Navigation view.
- Change links and file references.
- Import resources and remove unused resources.

This lesson takes approximately 90 minutes to complete.

If needed, copy the Lesson13 folder onto your hard drive. As you work on this lesson, you'll overwrite the start files. If you need to restore the start files, copy them from the *Adobe GoLive 5.0 Classroom in a Book* CD.

Note: *Windows users need to unlock the lesson files before using them. For more information, see "Copying the Classroom in a Book files" on page 2.*

For information on setting up your work area, see "Setting up your work area" on page 9.

About Adobe GoLive Web site management

An Adobe GoLive Web site contains a site file, which it uses to manage and store data about the site. It is important that you do all your work, especially adding, removing, or renaming files, within the Adobe GoLive site file and not on the desktop. If you do add a file from the desktop, you will need to update your site window when you next open Adobe GoLive.

Another reason to work exclusively in Adobe GoLive is that it creates additional files and folders to contain the tools it uses to manage a site. For example, it creates a .data folder to hold components, stationeries, and site trash.

Getting started

In this lesson, you'll learn how to manage an existing Web site using Adobe GoLive.

1 Start Adobe GoLive.

2 Choose File > Open and open the Gage.site file.

The path to the file is Lesson13/13End/Gage.site.

This site contains a number of HTML pages and two folders, Animations and Images, that contain image files. When you have completed this lesson, your site will look like this.

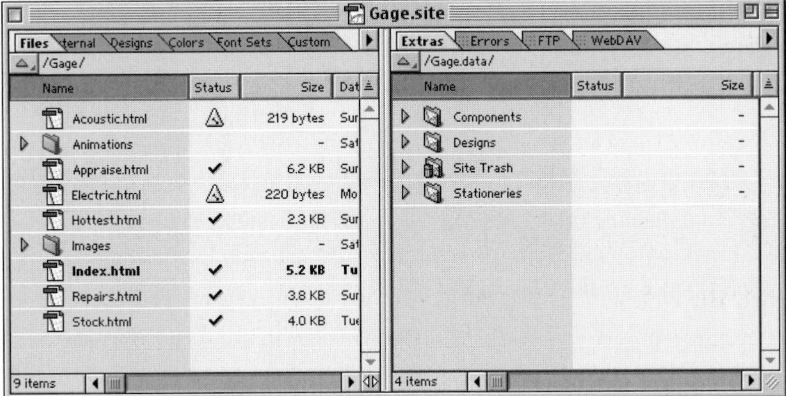

Gage site window, showing files and folder structure and the pane containing Extras, Errors, and FTP tabs

The right pane of the site window usually contains three tabs: Extras, Errors, and FTP (and WebDAV, if you have that module active). The finished site contains no errors and has not been uploaded to an FTP site, so those tabs are empty.

3 Close the Gage.site window. This closes the Web site.

Importing an existing site into Adobe GoLive

You will now work with the files in the Start folder, which contains a site called Gage, which was created in another application. Your first task is to import the site into Adobe GoLive.

1 Choose File > New Site > Import from Folder. Click the top Browse button and navigate to the 13Start folder. Select the Gage folder. This is the Web site that you will import into Adobe GoLive.

2 Click OK (Windows) or Choose "Gage" (Mac OS). The path to the folder is entered into the top text box of the Import Site Folder dialog box.

Because the site already has an Index.html page, Adobe GoLive recognizes this as the home page and automatically enters it into the bottom text box. If the Index.html page was missing, you would need to browse for the site's home page.

Note: *If a site folder is visible on your desktop, you can drag it straight to the top text box of the Import Site Folder dialog box.*

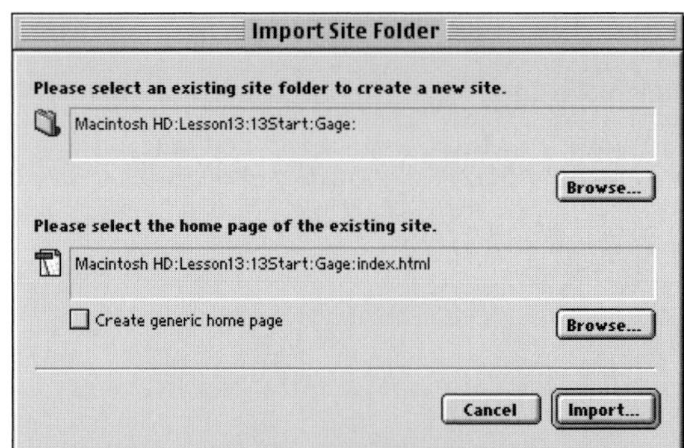

Importing site using Import Site Folder

3 Click Import.

The Web site is imported into Adobe GoLive, showing all its folders, files, and other site objects.

4 Name the file Gage.site when prompted, and save it in the 13Start folder. (Be careful not to save it in the 13End folder.)

For information on creating a Web site from scratch in Adobe GoLive, see "Creating a new Web site" on page 69.

Exploring the site in the site window

In the site window, the Files tab shows all the objects in your site. You can use it to create, rename, move, and delete folders, files, and other site objects. The site has an Animations folder, some image files, and several HTML pages. Notice that some files have check marks in the Status column, indicating that their links are OK. Other files have little green bugs (🐞) beside them, indicating that they have broken links. These broken links show up in the Errors tab of the site window, which you will look at later in this lesson.

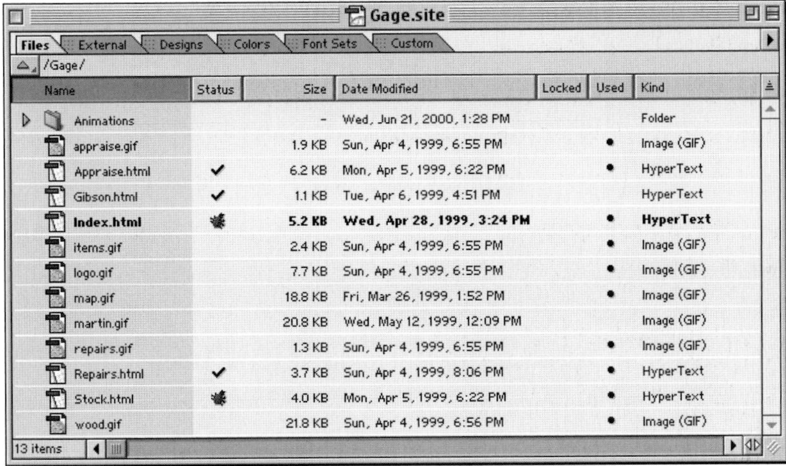

Displaying site in Files tab of site window

1 In the site window, select the Index.html file.

The Inspector changes to the File Inspector. The File Inspector lets you rename files, manage their properties, see their contents, and change your home page. You can use it to manage a number of different file types, such as page, image, and media files.

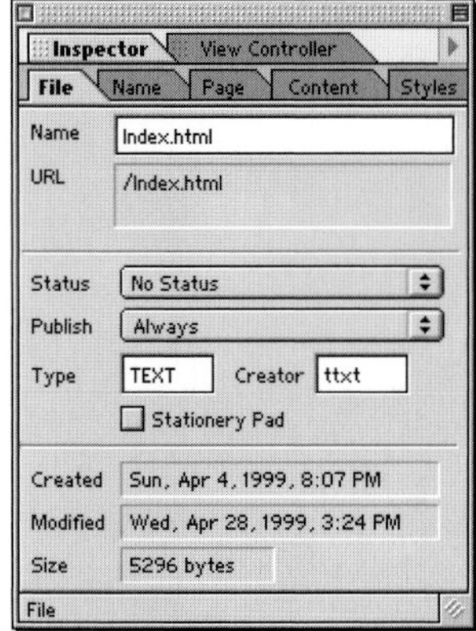

File Inspector

2 Click the Page tab of the File Inspector and notice that the Home Page option is selected, making this your home page. However, the option is inactive. The only way to designate another file as the home page is to open it and select its Home Page option.

3 In the site window, select Logo.gif. The File Inspector's tabs now reflect image properties.

4 Click the Content tab of the File Inspector to see the image. Select a second image, and then a third image.

You can use the Content tab of the Image Inspector to scroll through your images and search for the one that you want.

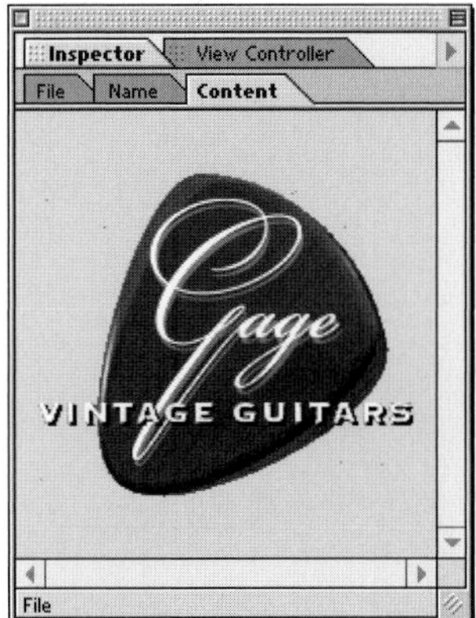

5 Choose Window > In & Out Links. This opens the In & Out Links palette.

The In & Out Links palette shows links to the image from the HTML pages in which it appears. (Again, select several other images to see how the In & Out Links palette changes.) The In & Out Links palette is a very useful tool that enables you to see, manage, and correct links. Its Point and Shoot button (@) lets you easily create and change links, or correct broken links.

6 Click the Index.html page icon in the In & Out Links palette. The palette changes to show all links to and from that page. (If necessary, resize the palette so that you can see all the links.)

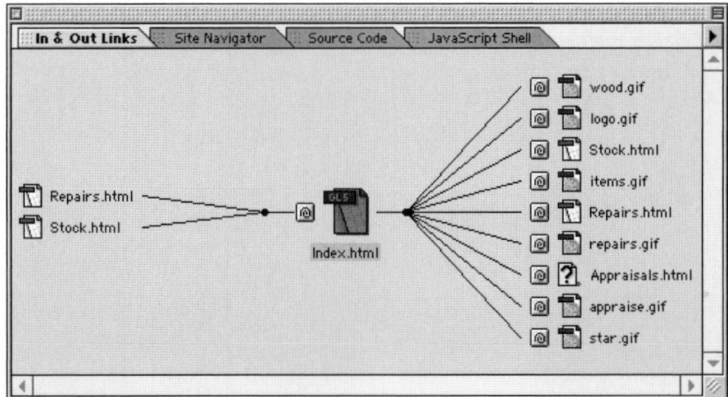

In & Out Links palette

If you click one of the links from Index.html, the focus of the In & Out Links palette changes again. In this way, you can use the palette to check all the links in your site. In addition, you can use the various Inspector windows to update and edit information about your site objects and their links.

7 Close the In & Out Links palette.

Exploring the expanded site window

You will now take a look at the features of the expanded site window.

1 If necessary, expand the site window by clicking the double-arrow icon ( ) in the bottom right corner of the site window.

You can drag the vertical tab bar between the two panes to resize them, if you wish. You may also want to move the site window to the bottom of your screen. This will help you keep it in view when you open site files.

Note: *To collapse the expanded pane, click the double-arrow icon at the bottom of the scroll bar for the left pane.*

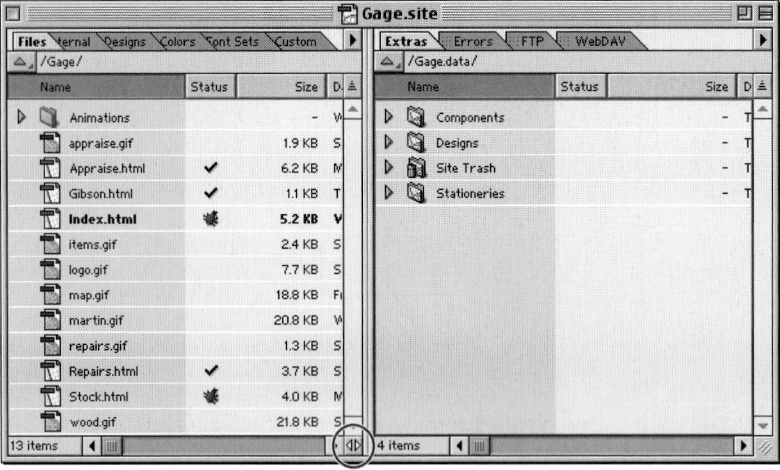

The expanded pane of the site window contains three tabs: Extras, Errors, and FTP (and WebDAV, if that module is active).

2 Click the Extras tab, if it is not already selected.

This tab contains four folders: Components, Designs, Site Trash, and Stationeries. These folders were created by Adobe GoLive and put into the Gage.data folder when you imported the site.

• The Components folder stores HTML pages that you can embed inside others. You can make a single component, and use it again and again. Examples include a navigation bar set up with its own images and links, a copyright pane, or formatted text.

• The Designs folder stores prototype designs that you have created for your current site. You can move a prototype design to your site once you have finished it.

• The Site Trash folder stores any site objects that you have removed from your site, but not your hard drive. From here, you can either drag them into the desktop Recycle Bin (Windows) or Trash (Mac OS), or drag them back to your site.

About the Site Trash folder

Moving a file in the site window to the Adobe GoLive Site Trash folder is not the same as moving a file to the Recycle Bin (Windows) or Trash (Mac OS). A file or site object in the Site Trash folder remains on your hard drive, but is no longer included in your site. You can drag the file to the system trash and discard it permanently, or drag it back into your site structure.

You can change what Adobe GoLive does when you move items to the Site Trash folder by changing preferences. By default, items are not permanently thrown away, and you are warned before they are moved. To permanently discard site items:

1. *Choose Edit > Preferences to open the Preferences dialog box.*

2. *Select Site, and then choose Move Them To The System Trash (Windows) or Move Them To The Finder Trash (Mac OS).*

This option sends all selected items straight to the system Recycle Bin or Trash, and not the Site Trash folder in Adobe GoLive.

3. *Click OK.*

• The Stationeries folder stores page templates that may contain framesets, images, style sheets, and so on, for repeated use.

At this point all four folders are empty.

3 Click the FTP tab to select it.

This tab is also empty. When connected to your FTP server, it lists all files and folders that you have uploaded to the server, along with the date they were last revised.

4 Click the Errors tab to open it.

This tab lists any errors in your site. Notice that several types of errors appear in it: an orphan file, an unspecified link (or empty reference), and some missing hypertext links.

5 Click the triangle to the left of the Orphan Files folder to expand it, if it is not already expanded. The one orphan file, Star.gif is displayed.

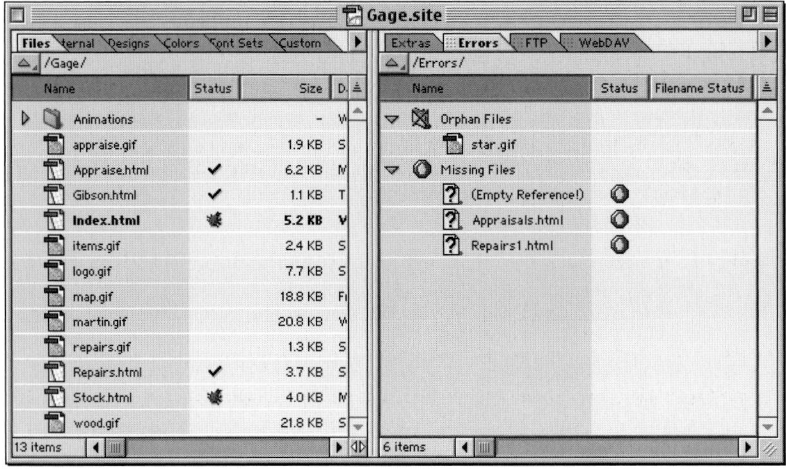

Displaying errors in Errors tab of site window

Correcting errors

You will now correct the errors displayed in the Errors tab. First, you'll solve the problem of the orphan file.

Resolving orphan files

An orphan file is one that is referenced in your site, but either can't be found in the site file, or is in the Site Trash folder. Copying the file to the Files tab of the site window will fix the problem.

1 In the Errors tab, select the Star.gif file. Notice that the Inspector changes to the File Inspector. The Content tab displays the image, which is an animation that flashes on and off. This confirms that you are working with the correct file.

2 Drag the file from the Errors tab to the Animations folder in the Files tab of the site window.

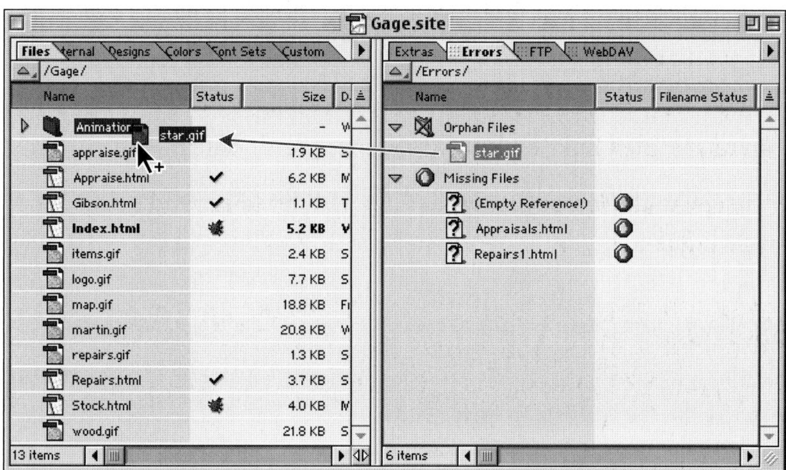

Dragging file from the Errors tab back into Files tab of site window

3 Click OK in the Copy Files dialog box. This confirms that you want to copy the file into your site and update its links.

If you are too slow dropping the file on the Animations folder, you may end up inside it. You can return to the root folder by clicking the Navigation button (▲) near the Files tab.

Why was Star.gif an orphaned file? Remember that when you first created this site, you imported the Gage folder. The Star.gif image was not in that folder, but in the Other Files folder, and was therefore never imported into the Gage.site file. Since it was referenced by Index.html, Adobe GoLive marked it as orphaned.

Note: *When you copy a file to your site window, your desktop also makes a copy. So a copy of Star.gif now exists both in the site window and inside the Animations folder in the Gage folder on your desktop.*

Correcting missing file and hypertext link errors

Now, you'll fix the missing file errors that appear in the Errors tab of the site window. Use the In & Out Links palette to find out which files contain the broken references or links. You can resolve missing file errors in at least three ways:

- By removing all references to the file.
- By changing all references to point to a new file.
- By browsing for the file from the Error Inspector and copying it to your site.

1 In the Errors tab of the site window, select the missing file that says (Empty Reference!). Notice how the Inspector changes to the Error Inspector, and (Empty Reference!) appears in the URL text box.

2 Choose Window > In & Out Links. The In & Out Links palette shows the empty reference, and the file containing it, Stock.html.

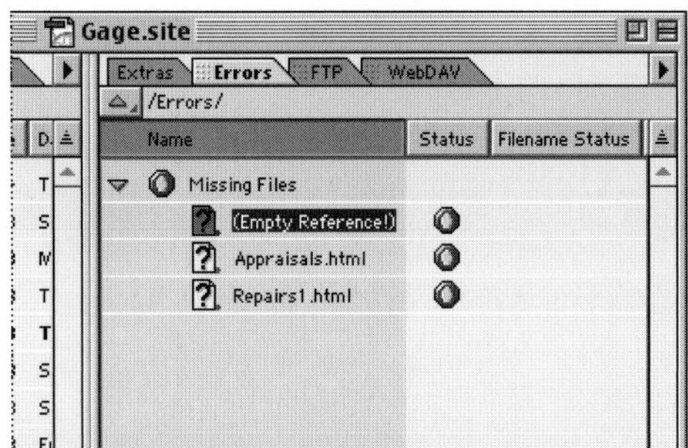

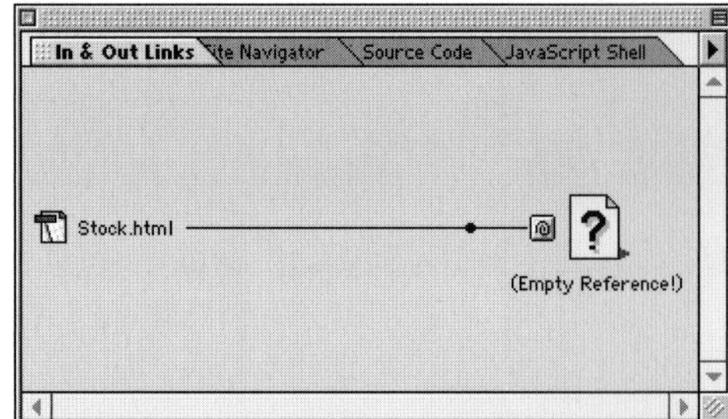

Viewing empty reference in In & Out Links palette

3 Double-click on the Stock.html file in the Files tab of the site window. An image is missing from the top-left corner of the page. In its place is an empty image placeholder. If necessary, resize or move the Stock.html file so that you can clearly see the Files tab of the site window.

4 Select the image placeholder in Stock.html.

5 Hold down Alt (Windows) or Command (Mac OS), and drag from the image placeholder to the Logo.gif file in the Files tab of the site window. The black Gage logo appears on the page.

Adobe GoLive has removed the Empty Reference error warning from the site window.

***Note:** If the Files tab is partially hidden, just hold the pointer over the part of it that you can see, until the tab comes to the front.*

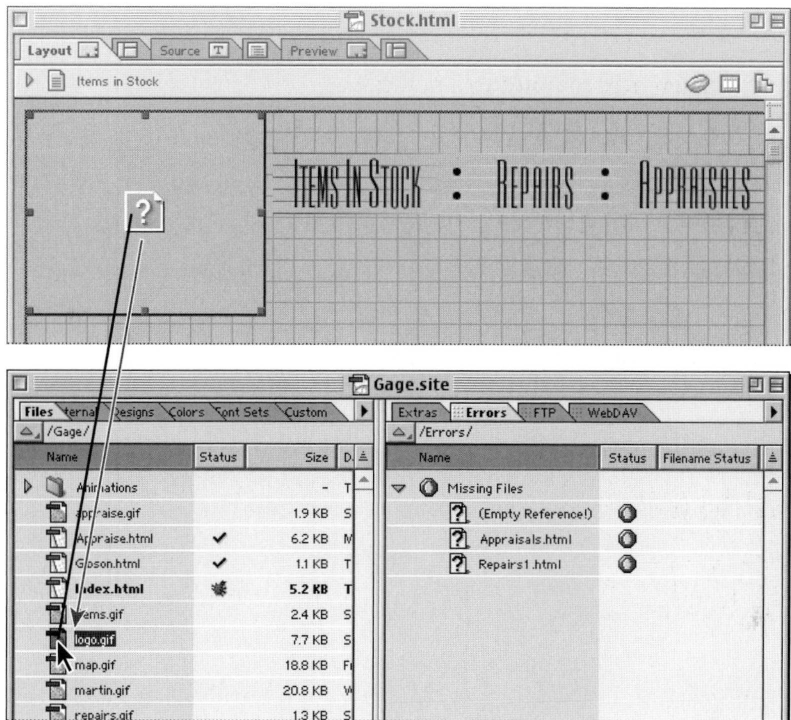

Linking image to HTML page by dragging from image placeholder to file in site window

There is also a broken hypertext link on this page, but this error is more difficult to find.

6 If necessary, resize or move the Stock.html file, so that you can see all its contents.

7 Click the Link Warnings button ( ) on the toolbar. The bad link is highlighted in red. (You may have to scroll down the page a little to see it.)

8 Double-click the highlighted text (the word "Repairs") to select the link. The Inspector changes to the Text Inspector, and the bad URL is highlighted in pink in the URL field.

9 In the Text Inspector, drag from the Point and Shoot button to the Repairs.html file in the Files tab. If the Files tab is partially hidden, hold your pointer over it until the tab comes to the front. If you can't see the Repairs.html file in the tab, you can scroll down the list of files if you hold your pointer down over the lowest visible file in the pane.

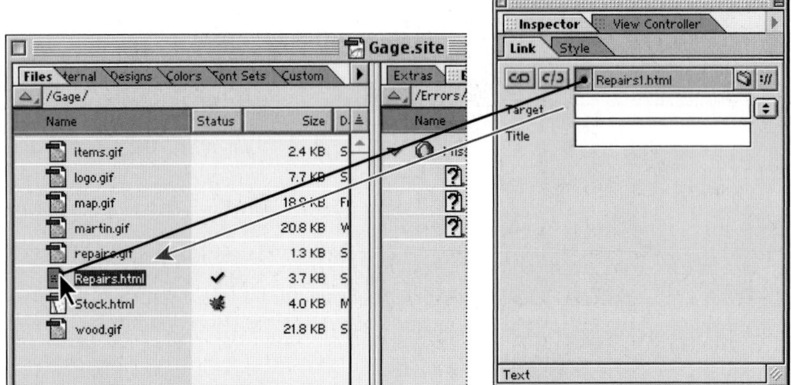

Using Point and Shoot button in the Text Inspector to fix broken link

The pink highlight disappears from the URL field of the Text Inspector and from the word "Repairs." Notice that the Repairs1.html hypertext link warning has been removed.

10 Choose File > Save to save your work. Close the Stock.html file.

Only one missing file error remains to be fixed. You will next use the In & Out Links palette to repair the connection to Appraisals.html.

11 Select Appraisals.html in the Errors tab of the site window. The In & Out Links palette shows that Index.html is the only page that contains a link to the missing file.

The link from Index.html refers to a file called Appraisals.html, but the Files tab contains a file called Appraise.html. At some point, the file was renamed without updating all the links to it.

You will use the Point and Shoot button in the In & Out Links palette to fix this error. Be sure that you can see both the site window and the Appraisals.html file in the In & Out Links palette.

12 Drag from the Point and Shoot button next to the Appraisals.html file to the Appraise.html file in the Files tab of the site window.

Note: *The Point and Shoot button (◉) in the In & Out Links palette, Error Inspector, Text Inspector, the file itself, and the Errors Tab operates in the same way.*

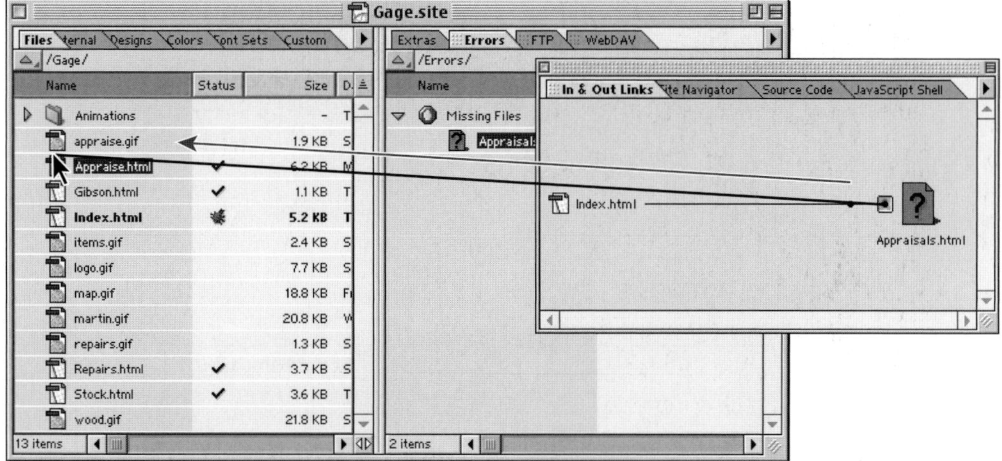

Fixing file references with In & Out Links palette

13 Click OK in the Change Reference dialog box to confirm that you want to change all references to the file.

14 Close the In & Out Links palette.

All the errors and bugs should now be gone and checkmarks should appear next to all your HTML pages in the Files tab, indicating that all their links are OK.

15 In the Files tab, click the Kind column header (scroll to the right, if necessary, to see it) to sort all your files by type. This groups all your HTML files and can help you verify their links.

16 In the Files tab, click the Name column header to return to viewing files by name.

Managing folders

You will now improve the organization of the Web site by rearranging its folders and files. Because Adobe GoLive dynamically updates all your links as you go, you don't have to worry about redoing them each time that you change the files or folders.

Creating a folder and adding files to it

As your site grows, you will need to create folders to hold and organize all the files. You'll begin by creating a new folder for images and move files into it.

1 Click anywhere in the Files tab of the site window to make it active.

2 Click the New Folder button on the Site toolbar ( ).

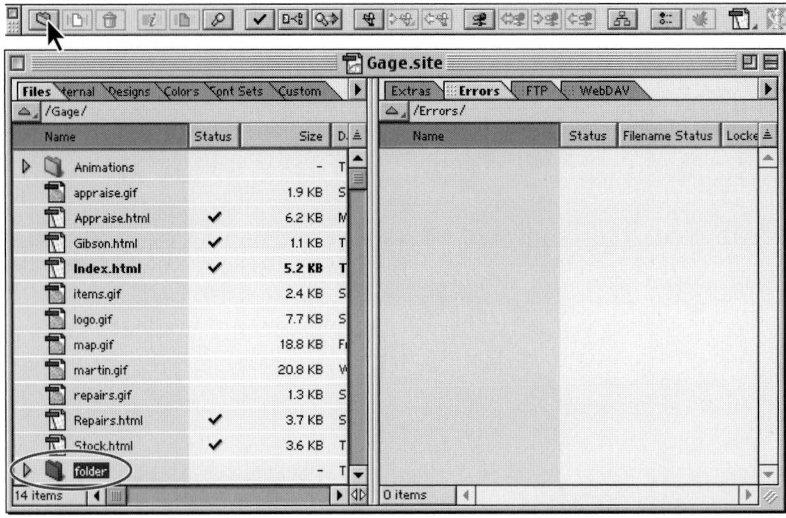

3 In Mac OS, click the Inspector, so that it changes to the Folder Inspector.

4 In the Name text box in the Folder Inspector, enter **Pix**. Then press Enter or Return. The name of the folder changes.

You can change the name of any folder or file either by selecting it in the Files tab, and typing a new name directly over the old one, or by entering the new name in the Inspector.

5 In the Files tab, deselect the Pix folder. Ctrl-click (Windows) or Shift-click (Mac OS) to select all the image files (any files with a .gif extension) and the Animations folder.

In Windows, once you have selected all the items, release the Ctrl key or you will copy rather than move them.

6 Drag the selected items to the Pix folder.

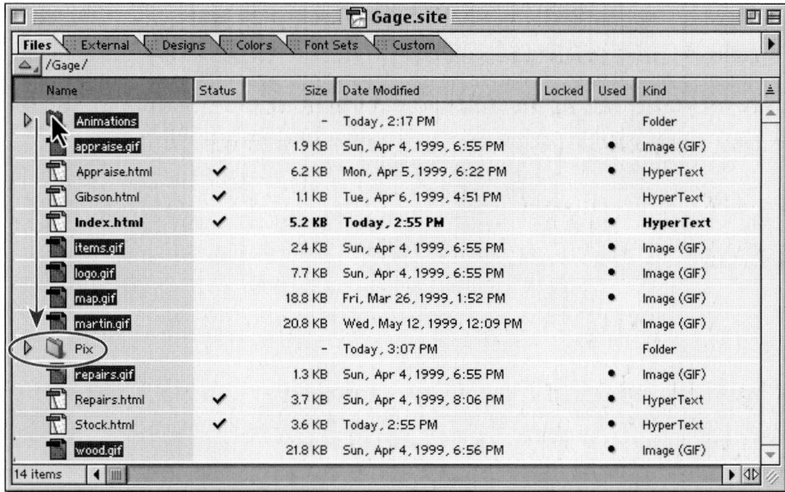

Dragging items to Pix folder

7 Click OK in the Move Files dialog box. Adobe GoLive dynamically updates all the links.

8 Choose File > Save to save the changes to your site.

Moving a folder

Next you'll move the Animations folder from the Pix folder back into the Gage folder, and update all its links.

1 Click the triangle to the left of the Pix folder in the site window, to expand it if necessary.

2 Select the Animations folder, and move it to the root of the Gage site by dragging it to the Name title bar.

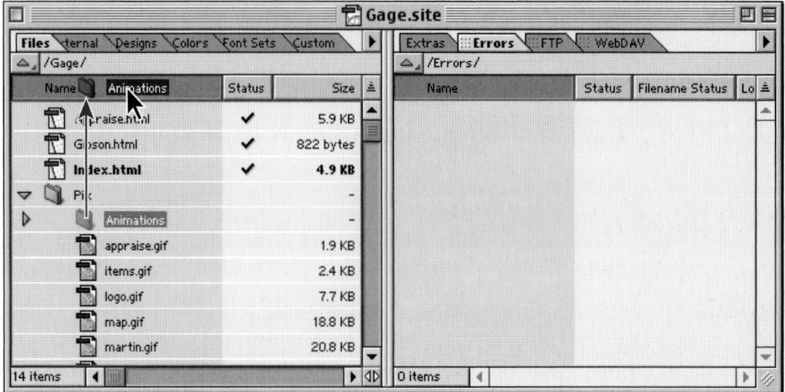

3 Click OK in the Move Files dialog box. The Animations folder appears in the root of the site, and all the links are updated.

Renaming a folder

Now, you'll rename the Pix folder, and see how changes made inside Adobe GoLive automatically update your desktop.

1 In Windows, resize the Adobe GoLive application window to half of your screen size. Keep the site window in view.

2 Open the Pix folder through your operating system, and reposition the window so you can see its contents.

3 In the site window, do one of the following:

• In Windows, select the Pix folder and click the Reveal Explorer button ( ) on the toolbar. (You can also right-click the Pix folder and choose Reveal in Explorer.) Resize the Explorer window and drag it next to the Adobe GoLive application window.

• In Mac OS, select the Pix folder and click the Reveal in Finder button ( ) on the toolbar. (You can also Command-click the Pix folder in the Files tab and choose Reveal in Finder.) If necessary, resize the window and drag it next to the site window.

You should have both the Adobe GoLive and Explorer (Windows) or Finder (Mac OS) windows visible side-by-side.

4 In the Files tab of the site window, change the name of the Pix folder to **Images**. Press Enter or Return.

5 Click OK in the Rename Folder dialog box to confirm that you want to update the files.

Notice how the folder name has also changed on your desktop. Adobe GoLive works with your operating system to ensure reliability of the links within your site.

6 Close the Explorer (Windows) or other windows on your desktop.

Adding new pages to your site

You are now going to add two new pages to your site using two different techniques. Each method automatically copies the file and places it in your site folder, without moving the original file.

You'll first add a file using the Add Files command.

1 Make sure that the site window is active and that nothing is selected.

2 Choose Site > Explorer > Add Files (Windows) or Site > Finder > Add Files (Mac OS) and navigate to the Other Files folder inside your 13Start folder. Open it and select the Hottest.html file.

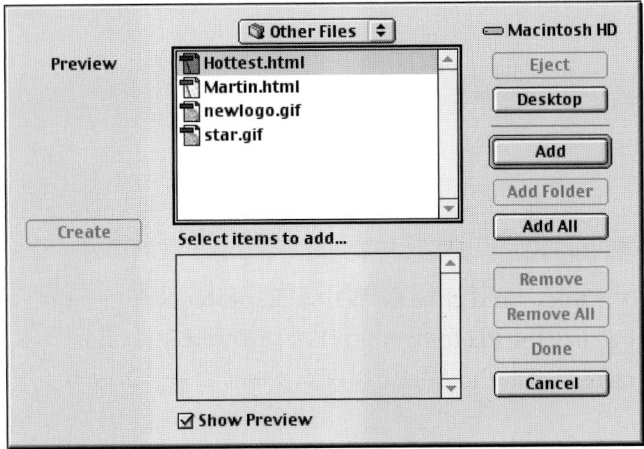

Using Add Files command to add file to your site

3 Click Add and then click Done. You should see Hottest.html in the Files tab of the site window.

The second method of adding a file is to drag it from the Explorer (Windows) or the desktop (Mac OS) to your site.

4 In the Explorer (Windows) or on the desktop (Mac OS), open the Other Files folder located inside the 13Start/Gage folder. If necessary, resize the windows.

5 Drag the Martin.html file from the Other Files folder to the Gage folder in the Files tab in the site window.

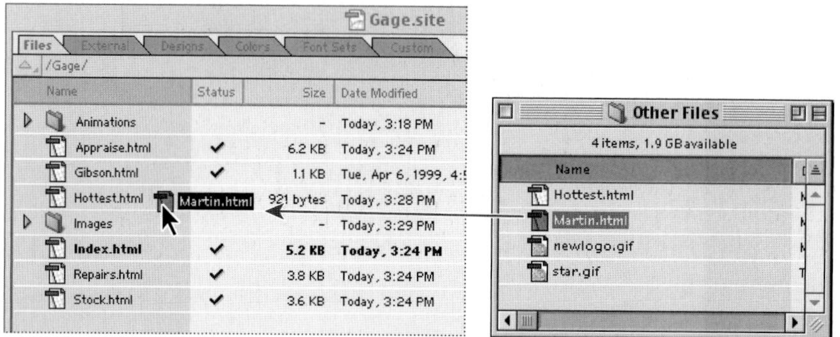

Dragging file from Explorer (Windows) or desktop (Mac OS or Windows) to Files tab of site window

If you open the Gage folder in the Explorer or Finder, you'll notice how the two newly added files appear there.

6 Close the Explorer (Windows) or any desktop windows (Mac OS).

Note: *If you remove or add files from within folders in the Explorer (Windows only) or on the desktop without copying them into Adobe GoLive, you must use the Update button ( ) on the Site toolbar to include or remove the files in your site.*

Managing a site with the Navigation and Links views

The Navigation and Links views are powerful tools for controlling your site and are accessed from the same palette group. You can view your site in a graphical or outline mode, see how pages and other site objects relate to each other, and manage links and pages. The Navigation view lets you see the overall structure of your site. The Links view lets you see all site objects, including media files and how they are linked to various pages. Here, you will use these views to check the links in your site, add pages, and create links to them.

1 Choose Design > Navigation View to open the Navigation view.

2 If necessary, choose Window > View Controller to open the Site View Controller, and choose Window > In & Out Links to open the In & Out Links palette.

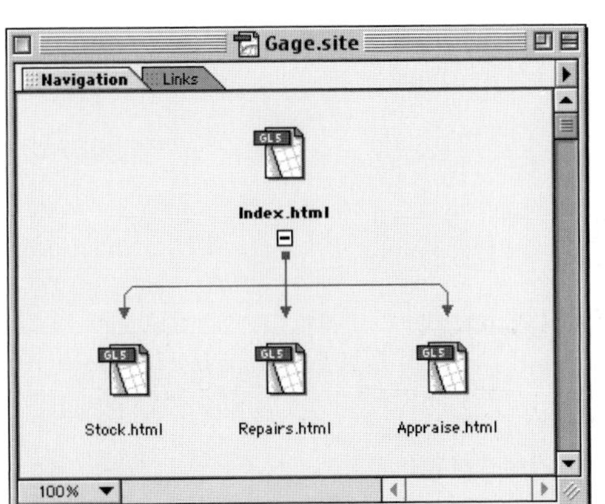

Navigation view

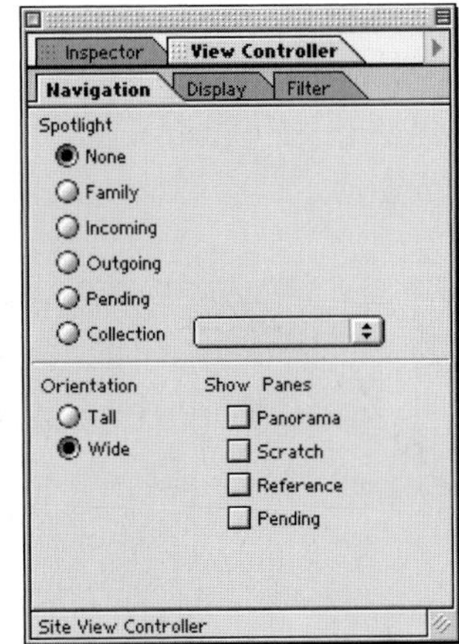

Site View Controller

3 In the Navigation view, click the plus sign (⊞) below Index.html to see more of the site.

The Navigation view shows the Index.html page at the top of the site hierarchy and three other pages on the level below. There are link indicators into (—•) and out of (•—) pages, which show links to and from pages that are located in other parts of the site hierarchy.

4 Click on the Appraise.html page. The In & Out Links palette now shows all the links to and from that page.

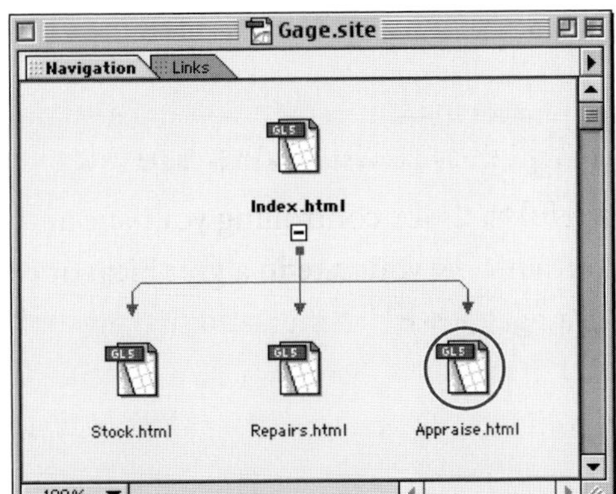

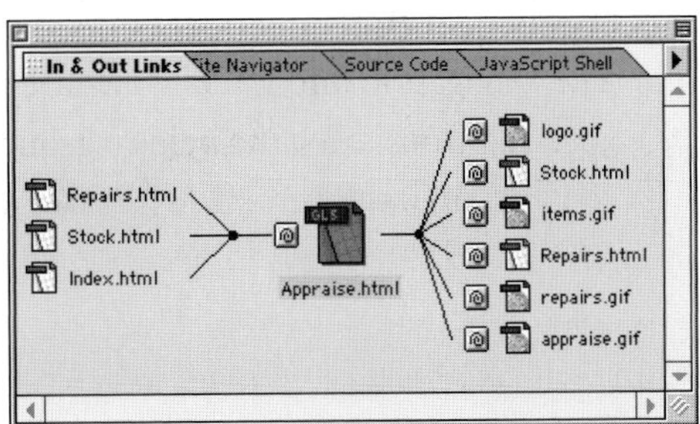

Selecting page to view its links in In & Out Links palette

5 Select another page in the Navigation view. The In & Out Links palette changes to display that page.

6 Close the In & Out Links palette when you have finished.

You can also collapse and expand parts of your site hierarchy. This is especially useful if you have a large site.

7 Click the minus sign (⊟) below the Index.html page icon. The site collapses into the Index.html page icon.

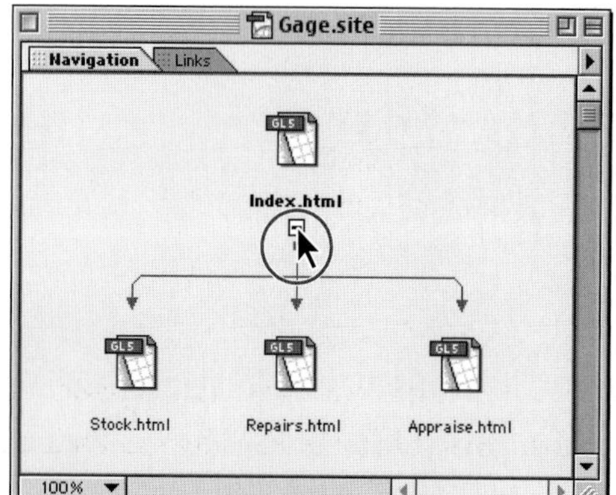

Collapsing site hierarchy into Index.html page icon

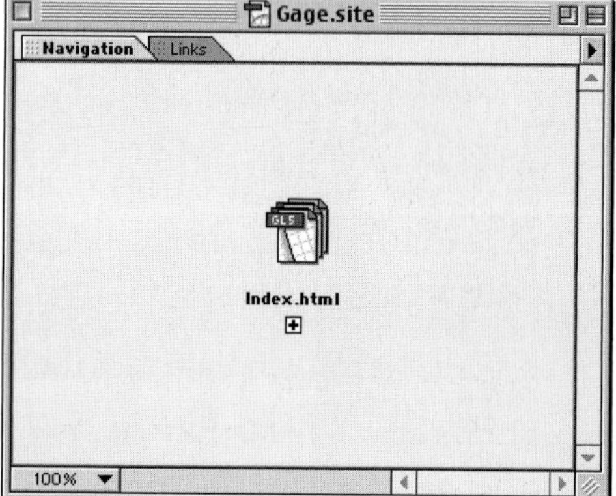

Result

8 Expand the site again by clicking the plus sign (⊞) below the Index.html page icon. The site expands to show all the other pages directly linked to Index.html.

You can also change the way the Navigation view displays your site.

9 Click anywhere in the Navigation view window to deselect the Index.html page, if it's still selected.

10 In the Display tab of the Site View Controller, the Graphical option is currently selected. You would normally use this mode to arrange and navigate across the objects in your site.

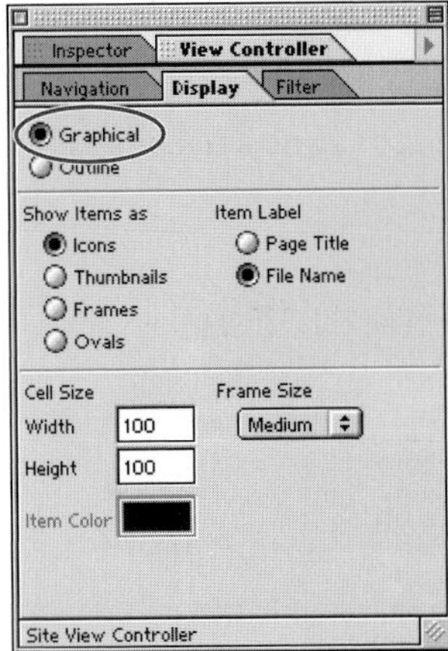

The Site View Controller has three tabs that let you set the Navigation, Display, and Filter properties of the Navigation and Links views. Take a look at the tabs and their options before continuing.

11 Click the Links tab next to the Navigation tab to switch from the Navigation to the Links view (the two views are grouped together in a palette). Then click the right plus sign next to Index.html.

12 Click the Filter tab of the Site View Controller, and click the Toggle Media button.

The Filter tab lets you choose which site objects that you see in the Links view. Notice how the content of the Links view has changed (you may have to scroll to see the changes). All the media files in your site are shown or not shown alongside the HTML pages when you click the Toggle Media button.

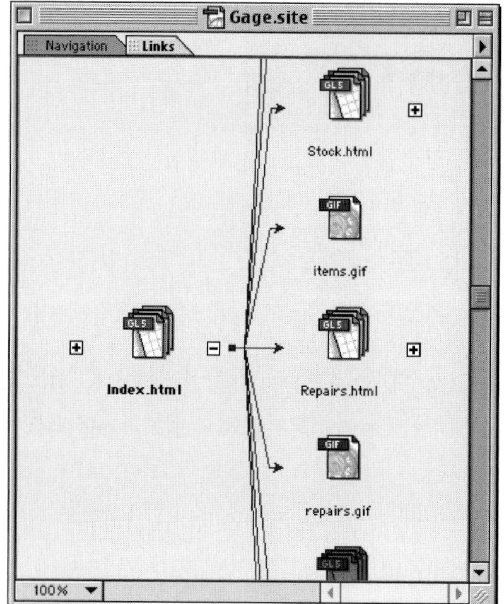

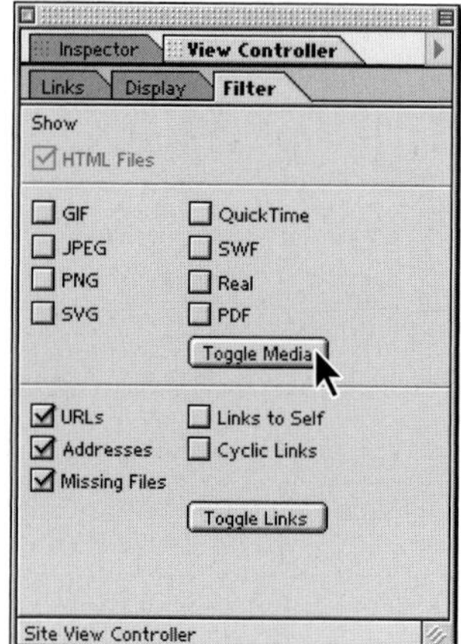

13 Drag the horizontal scrollbar of the Links view to the right to see all the added media files, if necessary.

14 Switch back to the Navigation view by clicking its tab.

15 Choose Scratch Pane from the Navigation view's pop-up menu. The Scratch pane lets you see pages that have been added to your site, but which remain unlinked.

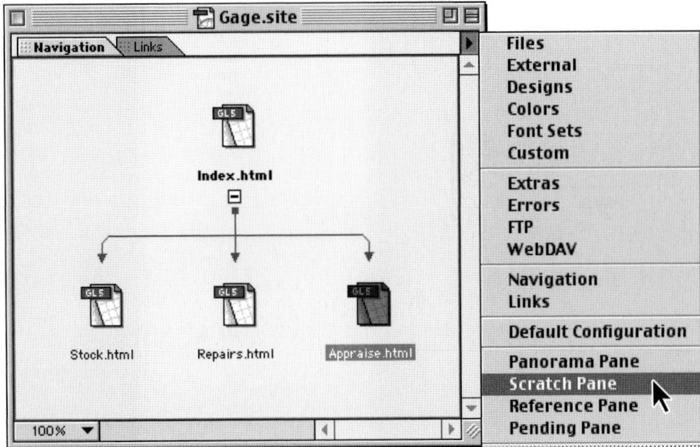

16 The pages that you recently added to your site, Martin.html and Hottest.html, as well as an unreachable image file, Martin.gif, and an unused HTML page, Gibson.html, are displayed. If necessary, scroll to see the files.

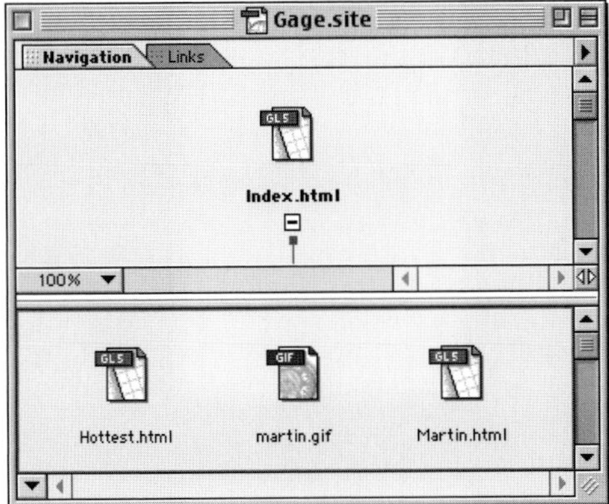

Adobe GoLive also provides an Outline view of the site hierarchy.

17 Click the Display tab of the Site View Controller. At the top of the Display tab, select Outline.

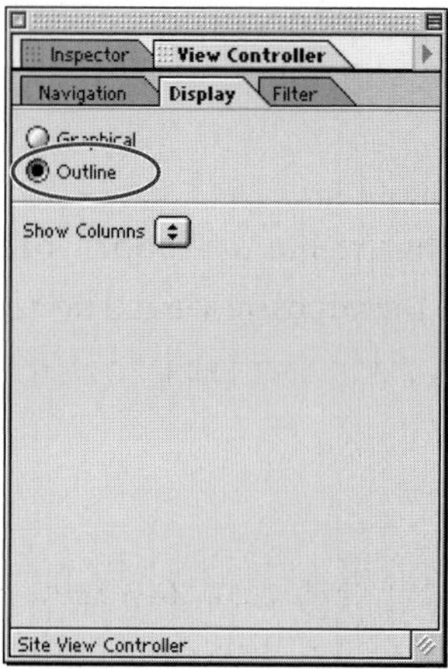

The Outline mode displays a tabular view of your site. It also provides information about each object's status, type, and URL.

18 In the Outline mode, click the symbol next to the Index.html page to expand the tree view, if necessary. In this mode, you can expand and collapse the view, as well as move site objects. Outline mode provides a more compact view that resembles the site window's Files tab.

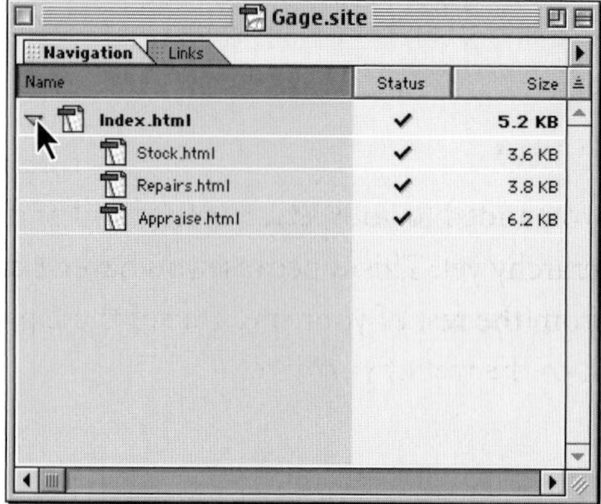

Expanding Outline mode of Navigation view

19 In the Display tab of the Site View Controller, select Graphical to return to a graphical view of your site.

20 In the Display tab, try some of the other view options. When you have finished, select Icons and File Name, and set the Cell Size Width value to **55** and the Height value to **140**.

Using the Site Navigator

Your monitor may not be large enough to display your entire site, so Adobe GoLive has a Site Navigator to help you move throughout the entire hierarchical view. The Site Navigator is a separate window that displays your whole site, and has a marquee that highlights the part of your site currently visible in the Navigation view.

1 Choose Window > Site Navigator.

2 Place the pointer within the marquee in the Site Navigator, and use the hand to drag the marquee back and forth across the site. Notice how the Navigation view changes as you move the marquee.

3 Close the Site Navigator window when you have finished viewing your site.

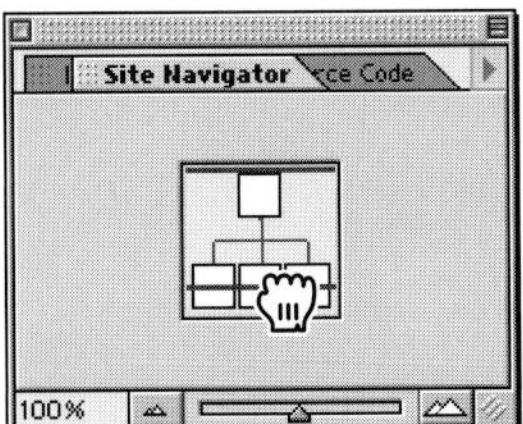

Moving Site Navigator marquee

Inserting pages into your site hierarchy

As you can see, the two new pages that you added to your site, Hottest.html and Martin.html, aren't part of the main hierarchy yet. This is because you haven't created links to them, so they are unreachable from the rest of your site. One of these pages is ready for public viewing, so you'll link it to the rest of your site.

1 Drag the Hottest.html page from the Scratch Pane below the Index.html page in the Navigation view, and drop it when a solid horizontal line appears below Index.html.

The Hottest.html page moves under the Index.html page, to the right of the other pages.

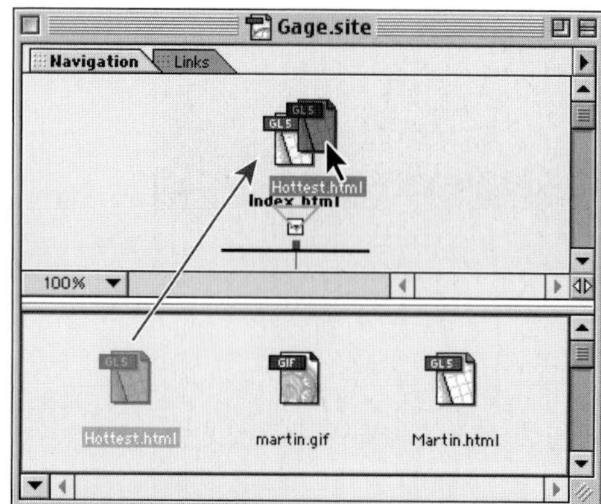

Inserting an unreachable file in site hierarchy

When you drag pages over other pages in the hierarchy, solid lines can appear above, below, or on the same hierarchical level as an existing file, allowing you to drop pages wherever you want in the tree.

2 Leave the Martin.html file where it is. It's still under construction.

Creating links between pages using the Navigation view

Now you'll create the link from the Index.html page to the Hottest.html page.

1 In the Navigation view, double-click the Index.html page to open it.

2 If necessary, resize or move the Index.html page so that you can see both the Navigation view and the "Check Out This Week's Hottest Buy" text.

3 Select the text "Check Out This Week's Hottest Buy".

4 Hold down Alt (Windows) or Command (Mac OS), and drag from the selected text to the Hottest.html page in the Navigation view. (This page may be partially hidden by the Index.html page, but hold the pointer over the window until the Navigation view is brought to the front.)

The Text Inspector shows the new link to the Hottest.html page in the URL field.

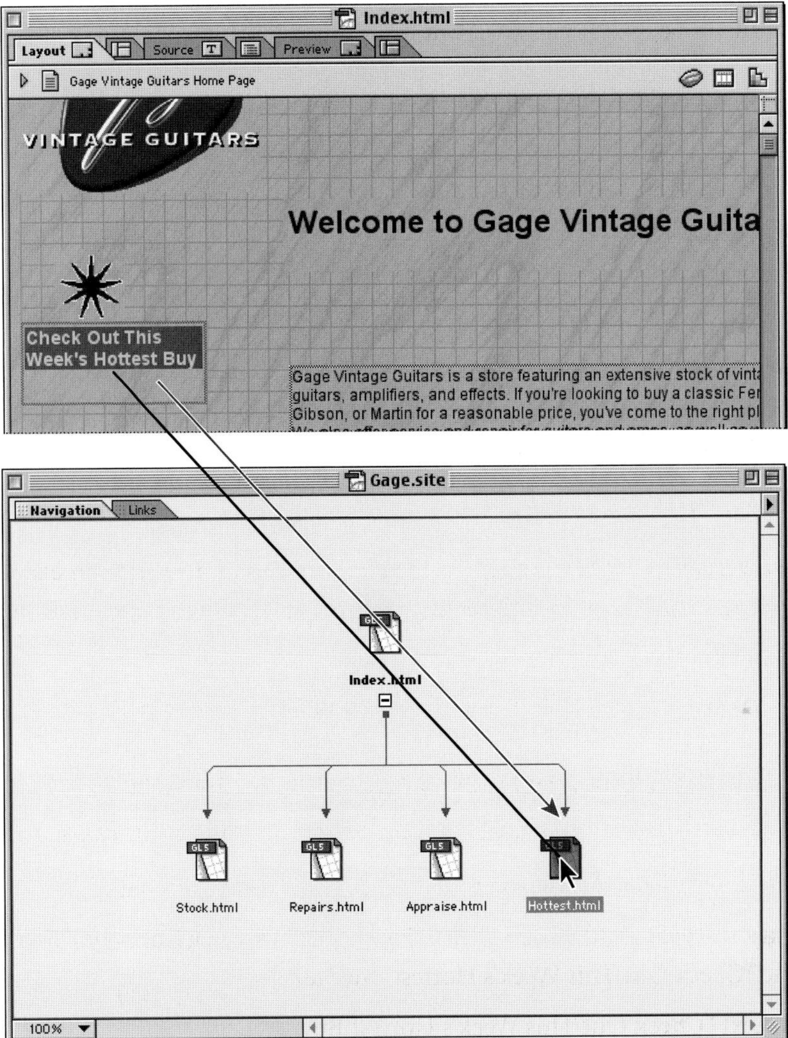

Dragging Point and Shoot line to create link

5 Save and close the Index.html page.

Creating new pages in the Navigation view

Your site needs two new pages featuring your latest items. You can do this directly from the Navigation view.

1 In the Navigation view, select the Stock.html page icon.

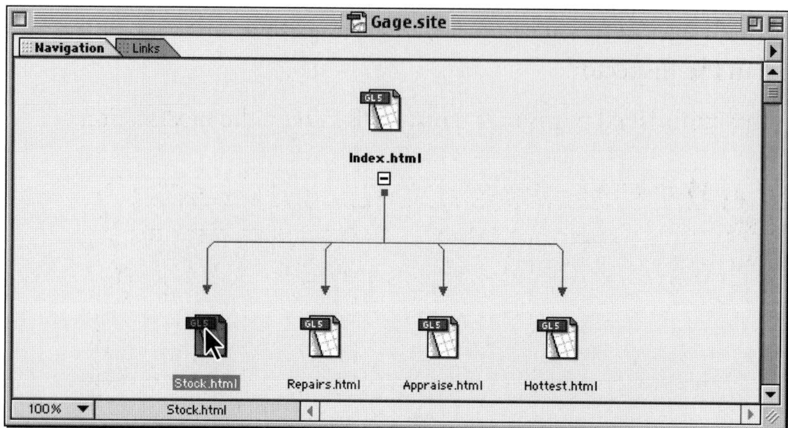

2 Click the New Child Page button ( ) in the Site toolbar. A new, untitled page appears below the Stock.html page. If necessary, use the Site Navigator marquee or the vertical scrollbar to see this new page.

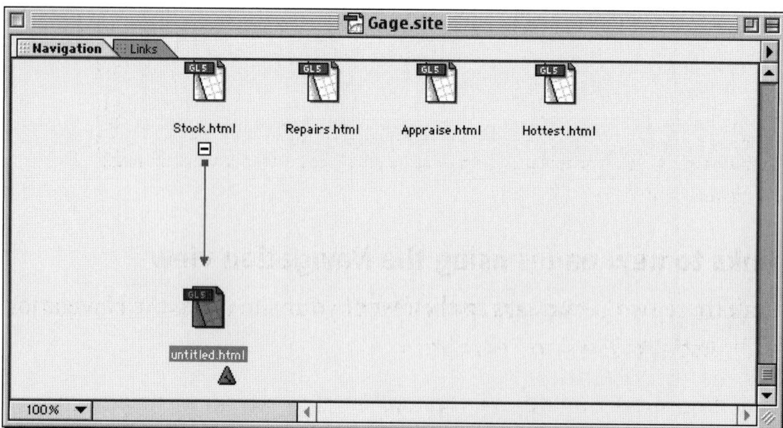

3 Select Stock.html again and repeat Step 2 to create another untitled page. Notice that both new pages appear on the same level of the hierarchy.

Note: *If you add a page where you don't want it, select the page and click the Delete Selected Item button (▣) on the Site toolbar. Then confirm that you want to move the page to the Site Trash folder.*

4 Select the new pages in the site window, and change their names to Acoustic.html and Electric.html in the Inspector.

You'll link these unfinished pages to the rest of the site in the next section.

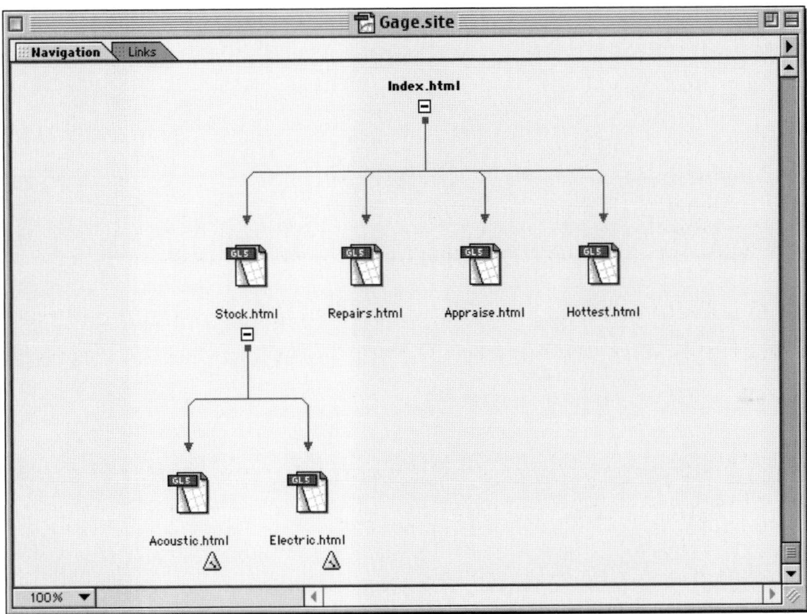

New pages in Navigation view

Creating links to new pages using the Navigation view

Now you'll link these two new pages to the rest of your site using the Navigation view. First, you'll link Acoustic.html to Stock.html.

1 In the Navigation view, double-click the Stock.html page icon to open the page.

2 Select "Acoustic Guitars" at the bottom of the page.

3 Hold down Alt (Windows) or Command (Mac OS), and drag from the selected text to the Acoustic.html page icon in the Navigation view. This links the text to the page.

4 Select "Electric Guitars" at the bottom of the page.

5 Repeat Step 3, this time linking the text to the Electric.html page icon in the Navigation view.

6 Save and close the Stock.html page.

7 Refresh the screen by selecting another icon.

You have just created two new pages, remapped your site hierarchy, and linked them to other pages.

Moving newly created files into the root folder

Whenever you create new pages in the Navigation view, Adobe GoLive creates a NewFiles folder in the Files tab of the site window to hold them. This is a useful place to keep files that are under construction, but now you'll move the files into another folder.

1 Click the Files tab in the site window to view it. Then open the NewFiles folder to display the new Acoustic.html and Electric.html pages.

There are two yellow construction icons (⚠) next to these pages, which indicate that they are under construction. The icons will disappear once you start adding content.

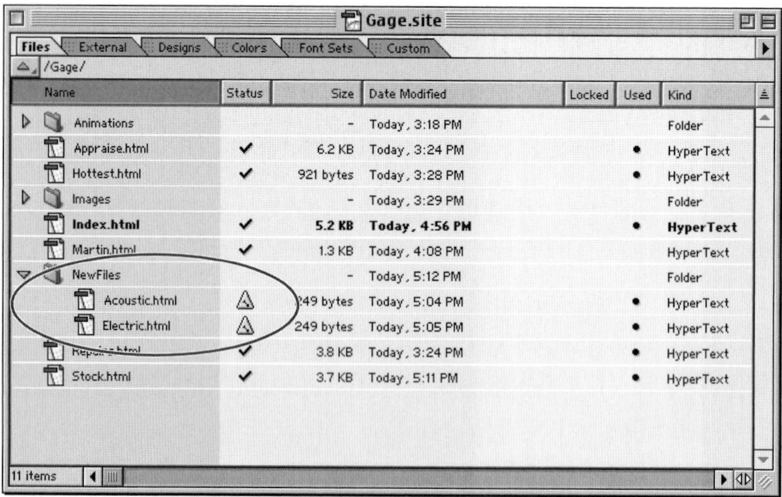

Under Construction icons appearing next to the two new files

2 Shift-click to select the two pages, move them to the root level of the Gage site by dragging them to the Name title bar, and update the links.

Changing all links and file references

When you remove a page and replace it with another, at the same time you can dynamically transfer all the links to the page. This also applies to changing an image that occurs throughout your site. The Change References option is a simple way to do this.

You'll try this feature by changing the logo image that appears on most pages of the Gage site from Logo.gif to Newlogo.gif.

1 Double-click the Index.html file in the Files tab of the site window. You'll find the Gage Vintage Guitars logo in the top-left corner of the page. This is the image that you are going to change.

2 If necessary, resize Index.html so that you can clearly see both the site window and the logo.

3 Select the Logo.gif file in the Images folder in the Files tab of the site window.

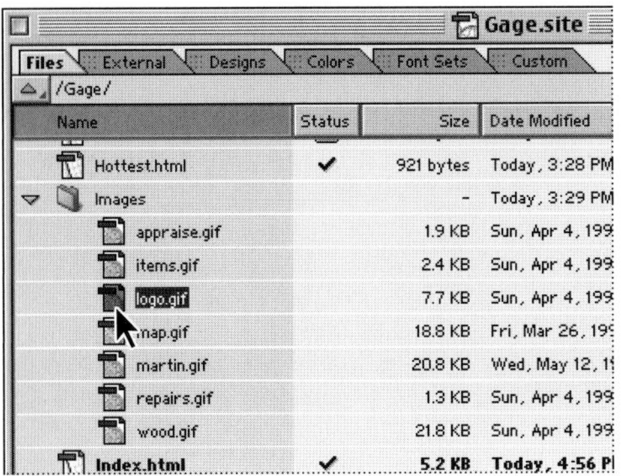

4 Choose Site > Change References. Click the Browse button ( ) and navigate to the 13Start/Other Files folder, and open newlogo.gif. The new file path appears in the Change References dialog box.

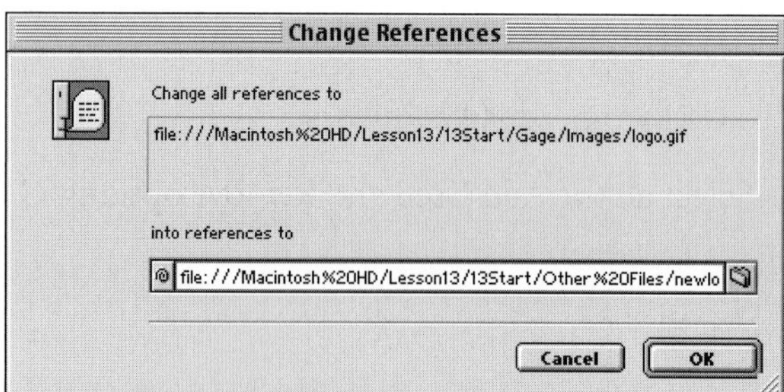

Browsing for Newlogo.gif file

5 Click OK, and then confirm that you want to change all references to the image.

All references to the old file are changed, and the new logo appears in the Index.html page.

New logo displayed in Index.html page

6 Save and close the Index.html page.

If you want to check that the logos on other pages have been updated, open those pages.

Cleaning up a site

Your site now has a file that you don't want (Logo.gif), and a file referenced by your site that is not in the site folder (Newlogo.gif). The latter is an orphan file; it appears in the Errors tab in the site window. You'll import the Newlogo.gif file into your site using the Clean Up Site dialog box. At the same time, you'll remove Logo.gif and any other unused files and non-file objects, such as URLs and e-mail addresses.

1 Choose Site > Clean Up Site. Select all the Add Used and Remove options. Click OK.

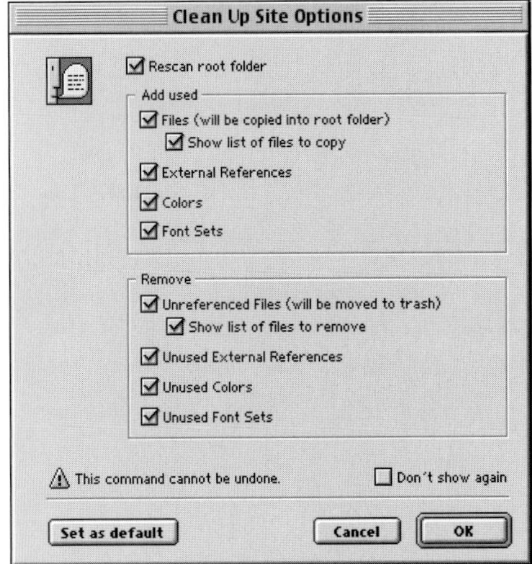

Note: *Cleaning up the site rescans the whole site and updates it; it also updates the files on your desktop.*

The Clean Up Site dialog box shows that the Newlogo.gif file is referenced in the site, but is not included in the site folder.

2 Click OK to copy the Newlogo.gif file into the site folder.

A list of all the files that need to be updated appears in the Copy Files dialog box.

3 Click OK to update them.

A list appears of unreferenced files that will be sent to the Site Trash folder. They are Gibson.html, Logo.gif, Martin.gif, and Martin.html.

4 Click OK to remove these objects from your site.

Note: *You can prevent any file from going to the Site Trash folder by deselecting the option next to it. However, it will remain unlinked and unused.*

In the Errors tab of the site window, notice that the orphan file error has been resolved. Adobe GoLive has moved the orphan file (Newlogo.gif) into the NewFiles folder in the Files tab of the site window.

5 Select Newlogo.gif and move it from the NewFiles folder into the Images folder, and update the links to it.

6 Remove the empty NewFiles folder by selecting it and clicking the Delete Selected Item button.

7 Click Move to confirm the action.

8 Save your site.

Congratulations! You have completed the Adobe GoLive 5.0 Classroom in a Book. You have learned the essential concepts and skills necessary to master the application. You created Web pages with images; worked with text, animations, forms, and cascading stylesheets; and, prepared your site for presentation.

The last step is to upload your site to a Web server, so the world can enjoy your work. Because this requires certain hardware and software not included with the Adobe GoLive 5.0 package, you can try this on your own.

Exploring on your own

Before visitors can view your Web site, you must copy it to an FTP site on a Web server. Your Internet service provider can help you with the details of uploading and maintaining your site. For details on uploading a site to a server using Adobe GoLive's FTP features, see "Uploading and downloading sites" in Chapter 19 of the *Adobe GoLive 5.0 User Guide*.

Review questions

1 What is an orphan file and how do you fix it?

2 How do you create a new folder and move files into it? What happens once you move the files?

3 How do you change between a graphical and an outline layout in the Navigation view?

4 What are the two ways to add a file to your Web site from a folder outside your site?

5 How do you create a new page icon in the Navigation view below an existing page icon?

6 How do you create a link from some text in a parent page to a child page using the Navigation view?

Review answers

1 An orphan file is one that is referenced in your Web site, but either is in a location not included in the site file, or has been removed to the Site Trash folder. You fix it either by moving it into the site file, by changing references to it, or by dragging the file from the Site Trash folder back to your site.

2 You use the New Folder button to create a new folder. You can add files to it either by dragging them to the folder (if they are already in your site) or by using the Add Files command (if they are not in your site). Once you move files that are already in your site into the new folder, Adobe GoLive dynamically updates the links to these files.

3 Choose Window > View Controller, and select either Graphical or Outline in the Display tab of the View Controller.

4 You can add a file to your site from an outside folder either by using the Add Files command or by dragging from the outside folder to the Files tab in the site window.

5 You select the existing page icon and click the New Child Page button on the Site toolbar.

6 Open the parent page, select the text, hold down Alt (Windows) or Command (Mac OS), and then drag from the text to the child page icon in the Navigation view.

Index